British Islam and English Law

British Islam and English Law presents a novel argument about the nature and place of groups in society. The encounter with Islam has led English law to tread a line between two theoretical models, liberal individualism and multiculturalism, competing for dominance over the law of organised religion. This philosophical rivalry has generated a set of seemingly intractable conflicts between individual and community, religion and state, nation and culture. This book resurrects the long-buried theory of classical pluralism to address and resolve these tensions. Applying this to five understudied institutions that give structure and form to British Islam – banks, charities, schools, elections, clans – it outlines and justifies reforms that would optimise the relationship between law and religion. Unflinching and unorthodox, this book places law and theory in context, employs innovative methods such as nudge theory and applied history, and provides detailed answers to hard questions about British Islam.

Patrick S. Nash is a research fellow at the Woolf Institute and a postdoctoral research associate at St Edmund's College, Cambridge. He taught jurisprudence, public law, criminal law, tort law and family law at the Universities of Bristol and Newcastle before moving to Cambridge. He was called to the Bar of England and Wales in 2019 (Lincoln's Inn).

The Law in Context Series

Since 1970, the Law in Context series has been at the forefront of a movement to broaden the study of law. The series is a vehicle for the publication of innovative monographs and texts that treat law and legal phenomena critically in their cultural, social, political, technological, environmental and economic contexts. A contextual approach involves treating legal subjects broadly, using materials from other humanities and social sciences, and from any other discipline that helps to explain the operation in practice of the particular legal field or legal phenomena under investigation. It is intended that this orientation is at once more stimulating and more revealing than the bare exposition of legal rules. The series includes original research monographs, coursebooks and textbooks that foreground contextual approaches and methods. The series includes and welcomes books on the study of law in all its contexts, including domestic legal systems, European and international law, transnational and global legal processes, and comparative law.

Books in the Series

Acosta: *The National versus the Foreigner in South America: 200 Years of Migration and Citizenship Law*
Ali: *Modern Challenges to Islamic Law*
Alyagon Darr: *Plausible Crime Stories: The Legal History of Sexual Offences in Mandate Palestine*
Anderson, Schum & Twining: *Analysis of Evidence*, 2nd Edition
Ashworth: *Sentencing and Criminal Justice*, 6th Edition
Barton & Douglas: *Law and Parenthood*
Baxi, McCrudden & Paliwala: *Law's Ethical, Global and Theoretical Contexts: Essays in Honour of William Twining*
Beecher-Monas: *Evaluating Scientific Evidence: An Interdisciplinary Framework for Intellectual Due Process*
Bell: *French Legal Cultures*

Bercusson: *European Labour Law*, 2nd Edition
Birkinshaw: *European Public Law*
Birkinshaw: *Freedom of Information: The Law, the Practice and the Ideal*, 4th Edition
Blick: *Electrified Democracy*
Broderick & Ferri: *International and European Disability Law and Policy: Text, Cases and Materials*
Brownsword & Goodwin: *Law and the Technologies of the Twenty-First Century: Text and Materials*
Cane & Goudkamp: *Atiyah's Accidents, Compensation and the Law*, 9th Edition
Clarke: *Principles of Property Law*
Clarke & Kohler: *Property Law: Commentary and Materials*
Collins: *The Law of Contract*, 4th Edition
Collins, Ewing & McColgan: *Labour Law*, 2nd Edition
Cowan: *Housing Law and Policy*
Cranston: *Commercial Law from the Nineteenth Century: Law as Backcloth*
Cranston: *Legal Foundations of the Welfare State*
Darian-Smith: *Laws and Societies in Global Contexts: Contemporary Approaches*
Dauvergne: *Making People Illegal: What Globalisation Means for Immigration and Law*
David: *Kinship, Law and Politics: An Anatomy of Belonging*
Davies: *Perspectives on Labour Law*, 2nd Edition
Dembour: *Who Believes in Human Rights? Reflections on the European Convention*
de Sousa Santos: *Toward a New Legal Common Sense: Law, Globalization, and Emancipation*
Diduck: *Law's Families*
Dupret: *Positive Law from the Muslim World*
Estella: *Legal Foundations of EU Economic Governance*
Fortin: *Children's Rights and the Developing Law*, 3rd Edition
Garnsey: *The Justice of Visual Art: Creative State-Building in Times of Political Transition*
Garton, Probert & Bean: *Moffat's Trusts Law: Text and Materials*, 7th Edition
Ghai & Woodman: *Practising Self-Government: A Comparative Study of Autonomous Regions*
Glover-Thomas: *Reconstructing Mental Health Law and Policy*
Gobert & Punch: *Rethinking Corporate Crime*
Goldman: *Globalisation and the Western Legal Tradition: Recurring Patterns of Law and Authority*
Haack: *Evidence Matters: Science, Proof, and Truth in the Law*
Harlow & Rawlings: *Law and Administration*, 4th Edition
Harris: *An Introduction to Law*, 8th Edition
Harris, Campbell & Halson: *Remedies in Contract and Tort*, 2nd Edition
Harvey: *Seeking Asylum in the UK: Problems and Prospects*
Herring: *Law and the Relational Self*
Hervey & McHale: *European Union Health Law: Themes and Implications*
Hervey & McHale: *Health Law and the European Union*
Holder & Lee: *Environmental Protection, Law and Policy: Text and Materials*, 2nd Edition

Jackson & Summers: *The Internationalisation of Criminal Evidence: Beyond the Common Law and Civil Law Traditions*
Kostakopoulou: *The Future Governance of Citizenship*
Kreiczer-Levy: *Destabilized Property: Property Law in the Sharing Economy*
Kubal: *Immigration and Refugee Law in Russia: Socio-Legal Perspectives*
Lewis: *Choice and the Legal Order: Rising above Politics*
Likosky: *Law, Infrastructure and Human Rights*
Likosky: *Transnational Legal Processes: Globalisation and Power Disparities*
Lixinski: *Legalized Identities*
Loughnan: *Self, Others and the State: Relations of Criminal Responsibility*
Lunney: *A History of Australian Tort Law 1901–1945: England's Obedient Servant?*
Maughan & Webb: *Lawyering Skills and the Legal Process*, 2nd Edition
McGlynn: *Families and the European Union: Law, Politics and Pluralism*
Mertens: *A Philosophical Introduction to Human Rights*
Moffat: *Trusts Law: Text and Materials*
Monti: *EC Competition Law*
Morgan: *Contract Law Minimalism: A Formalist Restatement of Commercial Contract Law*
Morgan & Yeung: *An Introduction to Law and Regulation: Text and Materials*
Nicola & Davies: *EU Law Stories: Contextual and Critical Histories of European Jurisprudence*
Norrie: *Crime, Reason and History: A Critical Introduction to Criminal Law*, 3rd Edition
O'Dair: *Legal Ethics: Text and Materials*
Oliver: *Common Values and the Public–Private Divide*
Oliver & Drewry: *The Law and Parliament*
Palmer & Roberts: *Dispute Processes: ADR and the Primary Forms of Decision-Making*, 1st Edition
Palmer & Roberts: *Dispute Processes: ADR and the Primary Forms of Decision-Making*, 3rd Edition
Picciotto: *International Business Taxation*
Probert: *The Changing Legal Regulation of Cohabitation: From Fornicators to Family, 1600–2010*
Radi: *Rules and Practices of International Investment Law and Arbitration*
Reed: *Internet Law: Text and Materials*
Richardson: *Law, Process and Custody*
Roberts & Palmer: *Dispute Processes: ADR and the Primary Forms of Decision-Making*, 2nd Edition
Rowbottom: *Democracy Distorted: Wealth, Influence and Democratic Politics*
Sauter: *Public Services in EU Law*
Scott & Black: *Cranston's Consumers and the Law*
Seneviratne: *Ombudsmen: Public Services and Administrative Justice*
Seppänen: *Ideological Conflict and the Rule of Law in Contemporary China: Useful Paradoxes*
Siems: *Comparative Law*, 2nd Edition
Stapleton: *Product Liability*
Stewart: *Gender, Law and Justice in a Global Market*
Tamanaha: *Law as a Means to an End: Threat to the Rule of Law*

Tuori: *Properties of Law*
Turpin & Tomkins: *British Government and the Constitution: Text and Materials*, 7th Edition
Twining: *General Jurisprudence: Understanding Law from a Global Perspective*
Twining: *Globalisation and Legal Theory*
Twining: *Human Rights, Southern Voices: Francis Deng, Abdullahi An-Na'im, Yash Ghai and Upendra Baxi*
Twining: *Jurist in Context: A Memoir*
Twining: *Karl Llewellyn and the Realist Movement*, 2nd Edition
Twining: *Rethinking Evidence: Exploratory Essays*, 2nd Edition
Twining & Miers: *How to Do Things with Rules*, 5th Edition
Wan: *Film and Constitutional Controversy*
Ward: *A Critical Introduction to European Law*, 3rd Edition
Ward: *Law, Text, Terror*
Ward: *Shakespeare and Legal Imagination*
Wells & Quick: *Lacey, Wells and Quick: Reconstructing Criminal Law: Text and Materials*, 4th Edition
Zander: *Cases and Materials on the English Legal System*, 10th Edition
Zander: *The Law-Making Process*, 6th Edition

International Journal of Law in Context: A Global Forum for Interdisciplinary Legal Studies

The *International Journal of Law in Context* is the companion journal to the Law in Context book series and provides a forum for interdisciplinary legal studies, which offers intellectual space for groundbreaking critical research. It publishes contextual work about law and its relationship with other disciplines including, but not limited to, science, literature, humanities, philosophy, sociology, psychology, ethics, history and geography. More information about the journal and how to submit an article can be found at http://journals.cambridge.org/ijc

British Islam and English Law

A Classical Pluralist Perspective

PATRICK S. NASH
University of Cambridge

CAMBRIDGE
UNIVERSITY PRESS

CAMBRIDGE
UNIVERSITY PRESS

University Printing House, Cambridge CB2 8BS, United Kingdom

One Liberty Plaza, 20th Floor, New York, NY 10006, USA

477 Williamstown Road, Port Melbourne, VIC 3207, Australia

314–321, 3rd Floor, Plot 3, Splendor Forum, Jasola District Centre, New Delhi - 110025, India

103 Penang Road, #05–06/07, Visioncrest Commercial, Singapore 238467

Cambridge University Press is part of the University of Cambridge.

It furthers the University's mission by disseminating knowledge in the pursuit of education, learning, and research at the highest international levels of excellence.

www.cambridge.org
Information on this title: www.cambridge.org/9781108493918
DOI: 10.1017/9781108636964

First published 2022

A catalogue record for this publication is available from the British Library.

Library of Congress Cataloging-in-Publication Data
Names: Nash, Patrick (Law teacher) author.
Title: British Islam and English law : a classical pluralist perspective / Patrick S. Nash, University of Cambridge.
Description: Cambridge, United Kingdom ; New York : Cambridge University Press, 2022. | Series: Law in context | Based on author's thesis (doctoral - University of Bristol, 2017) issued under title: How should English law relate to Islam? | Includes bibliographical references and index.
Identifiers: LCCN 2021034443 (print) | LCCN 2021034444 (ebook) | ISBN 9781108493918 (hardback) | ISBN 9781108636964 (ebook)
Subjects: LCSH: Muslims – Legal status, laws, etc. – England. | Legal polycentricity – England – Philosohy.
Classification: LCC KD4102.M86 N37 2022 (print) | LCC KD4102.M86 (ebook) | DDC 342.4208/5297–dc23
LC record available at https://lccn.loc.gov/2021034443
LC ebook record available at https://lccn.loc.gov/2021034444

ISBN 978-1-108-49391-8 Hardback
ISBN 978-1-108-71360-3 Paperback

For Larry

L'espérance réalisée
– from the seal of Admiral George Brydges Rodney (1718–92)

Contents

Acknowledgements

Academia is a catty, desperate, miserly, paranoid, odious world at the best of times, and these times are not the best. Still, working on this book has been great fun. Those who made it so are acknowledged here in vague thematic order.

Thanks to Policy Exchange and the Woolf Institute for making this happen in good time, and for leaving me to get on with it.

Thanks to Miriam Wagner and Ed Kessler for being such understanding bosses and for allowing me to commandeer the Weston Room.

Thanks to Lord and Lady Woolf for their generosity and warm encouragement.

Thanks to everyone in or around the Woolf Institute including Chris, Rodrigo, Simon, Efe, Sebastian, Sam, Kitty, Emma, Tara, Dunya, Alissa, Mohammed, Helen, John, Amy, Claire, Tina and David for all sorts.

Thanks a million to Jessica Tearney-Pearce for everything and for saving me from my own disastrous attempts at indexing. Thanks to Lori Heaford and Clare Ranson for copy-editing.

Thanks to Finola O'Sullivan, Marianne Nield, Tom Randall and Gemma Smith at Cambridge University Press for their patience and good-humoured support.

Thanks to Russell Sandberg, Pat Capps, William Twining, Richard Mullender, Philip Wood, Guglielmo Verdirame QC, Richard Mawrey QC, Peter Edge, Kenneth Dibble, Pauline Ridge, Mary Synge, Caroline Morris, Neville Harris, Martyn Frampton, Richard Ekins and Jack Cottrell for reading drafts and saving me from many mistakes. Thanks also to Deniz Guzel for informing me about lawfare. Any remaining errors are mine alone.

Thanks to Eirik Bjorge, Basil Salman, Jonathan Burnside, Julia Mizen, David and Eleanor Harte, Ann Sinclair, Thom Brooks, Mary Anne Case, Lindsey Bell, Steven Greer, Gwen Seabourne, Dave Cowan, Bronwen Morgan, Lois Bibbings, Gemma Short, Chris Wilmore, Antonia Layard, Michael Naughton, Kathryn Hollingsworth, Rebecca Probert, Rajnaara Akhtar, Vishal Vora, Julian Hargreaves, Katharine Charsley, Alison Young, David Feldman QC and the Mallinckrodts for their advice and kindness.

Thanks to Tom Holland, Adrian Goldsworthy and Robert Tombs for indulging my historical dilettantism.

Thanks to Catherine Arnold, Philip McCosker and Alban McCoy for the late-night revels at St Edmund's. May they never end.

Thanks to James, Helen, Godfrey and Honor for being such great hosts and friends.

The Bristol years would have been beige without Andy, Jonno, Jo, Mat, Perran, Rachel, Seb, Steve, Tom, Ellen, Adam, Nick, Rich, Barnes, Tom, Michael, Pablo, Maria, Ben, David, Ravan, Jonathan, my former law students and the *Cat and Wheel.* Thank you all. *Semper Bristoliensis.*

Thanks for all sorts to Tom, Tom, Tom, Alex, Robbie, Kyle, Stu, James, Gray, Seb, Elliot, Rupert, Hannah, Melissa, Plamena, Wiktoria, Jeff, Rex, Oscar, Amy, Josh, Marco, Matt, Matt, Sakshi, Lois, Adam, Yaz, Patrick, Rhys, Ed, Nathan, Vincent, Rob, Steve, Noah, Alexa, Pyth and the York boys Joel, Jack, James and Conor.

Special thanks to Sir Larry Siedentop for the conversation, guidance and friendship.

Above all, however, I owe my biggest debt of gratitude to Julian Rivers. Anyone who counts him as a mentor, colleague and friend is privileged indeed. Once again and one last time, thank you.

For better or worse, this is probably the first law book to have come out of Consett. Let it not be the last.

General Introduction

A great many things keep happening, some of them good, some of them bad.[1]

How should English law relate to British Islam? That is the question this book addresses. Yet it is not another survey of British Muslims, or another handbook on law and religion, or another rehearsal of dull material on done-to-death areas such as Muslim marriages and sharia councils. Those are legion. The point of this study is to do something different and more ambitious with a neglected philosophy and understudied institutions. Its aspirations are therefore threefold. The first is to act as a primer on the vocabulary of human groups, recovering for English jurisprudence a lost language ideally suited to deciphering and differentiating among group entities. The second is to use this idiom to pose an 'outside context problem' (OCP) by asking questions hitherto inconceivable because the right concepts and the means to express them have been lacking.[2] Whenever Islam or Muslims come up for discussion, one tendency is to pick a 'side', start 'motive mongering', and come away thoroughly dissatisfied and disillusioned.[3] Another is to debate the broadest questions of civilisational conflict and compatibility, a valid and stimulating exercise but one which leaves unanswered many of the less glamorous questions upon which everyday coexistence and cooperation depend.[4] The worst response of all is to go looking for plots behind every real or imagined difficulty.[5] Against this, the OCP strategy promises to redirect scholarship away from tired conversations over Islam and free speech, religious dress, anti-terror laws and opinion polls towards less compacted fields

1 Gregory of Tours, *The History of the Franks*, Lewis Thorpe (transl.) (London: Penguin Classics, 1974), p. 63.

2 This notion was first articulated by Iain M. Banks in *Excession* (London: Orbit, 1996).

3 See C. Wright Mills, 'Situated Actions and Vocabularies of Motive' (1940) 5(6) *American Sociological Review* 904–13.

4 Classics of the genre include Samuel P. Huntington, *The Clash of Civilizations and the Remaking of World Order* (London: Simon & Schuster, 1997); Christopher Caldwell, *Reflections on the Revolution in Europe: Immigration, Islam and the West* (London: Penguin, 2010); Douglas Murray, *The Strange Death of Europe: Immigration, Identity, Islam* (London: Bloomsbury, updated ed., 2018).

5 Renaud Camus, *Le Grand Replacement: Introduction au remplacisme global* (France: Chez l'auteur, 2017).

where breakthroughs are still possible. Finally, equipped with the proper words and questions, the book will attempt to answer its central research question by solving a set of the most pressing institutional challenges generated by religious diversity in the UK. Although British Islam is used as both a case study and a test case, the ultimate aim is to devise a principled blueprint for the better regulation of organised religion in general. These are the tasks of this book and pursuing them requires a process. Accordingly, the remainder of this introduction is devoted to making the author's definitions, techniques and working assumptions explicit, followed by a chapter summary setting out the overarching arguments and signposting themes while serving as a navigational aid to the rest of the book.

It is self-evident that if the law is to use a term then lawyers must first work out what it means for the purposes at hand.[6] A viable relationship between English law and religion is therefore dependent upon the former providing a clear definition of the latter. Done well, this delineates what is encouraged, what is tolerated, what is forbidden and all under what conditions; done poorly, compliance becomes impracticable and application haphazard. This is remarkably difficult to get right as the law must fashion a legal definition somewhere between the partisan approach of political actors and descriptive sociology. Before outlining how this is best achieved, it is worth considering why either a purely political or a purely sociological approach cannot form the basis of a workable legal one that can get things done.

0.1 Political Religion

Political definitions of religion are typically motivated by worldly, personal and often short-term considerations. These can include everything from a desire to sound inclusive and inoffensive through to conscious efforts to shock and provoke. As such, they are characterised by crass, politicised evaluations about religion in general or a particular religion: religion is a force for good/evil, X is a religion of peace and love, Y is a religion of violence and hate. Examples abound in the media, political activism and academia. To pick just one well-intentioned and commonly recurring instance, at the height of the war against Islamic State (IS or ISIS or ISIL), former US president Barack Obama declared with full confidence that 'ISIL is not "Islamic". No religion condones the killing of innocents.'[7] Similar sentiments have been expressed by other eminent politicians including John Kerry and Theresa May.[8] Regardless of origin or intention, each statement of this kind is little more than 'a reassuring assertion,

[6] Julian Rivers, *The Law of Organized Religion: Between Establishment and Secularism* (Oxford: Oxford University Press, 2010), p. vii.

[7] President Barack Obama, 'Statement by the President on ISIL' (The White House, 10 September 2014).

[8] Douglas Murray, 'Why Is Theresa May Pretending That "Islam Is a Religion of Peace"?' (*The Spectator*, 30 September 2014).

and one that almost everyone, including the vast majority of Muslims, would desperately like to believe – but wishful thinking, all the same'.[9] Indeed, the leaders of Muslim terrorist groups can often be better versed than their opponents, secular or religious, in the Islamic canon.[10] As Michael Rubin further explains:

> To argue that the Islamic State is not Islamic is about as productive as arguing that the world is flat. Islam, as with Christianity, Judaism and, indeed, any religion, exists on a spectrum of beliefs and religious interpretation. Those who lead and embrace the Islamic State are very much Muslim, albeit those who embrace a militant and often literal interpretation of Islam . . . which no amount of defensiveness or politically correct dribble will negate.[11]

The more general problem is as follows. Political definitions entail a normative manipulation of religion to exclude anything from the concept that undermines a given political project or point. Relying upon them for any scholarly purpose, to say nothing of designing legal policy around them, is by turns disingenuous and unconscionable. Again, there are two reasons for this. First, there is a constitutional imperative not to politicise the definition of religion. The secular state has no legitimacy or competency in theological matters, meaning that it cannot pronounce upon, intervene in or take sides during internal religious controversies (such as when a majority accuses a minority of not being true believers, etc.). This spares the good, the bad and the ugly alike, and may seem frustrating and cold, but it maintains the jurisdictional boundary upon which religious diversity and, ultimately, civil peace depend. Second, political definitions beget concept drift and mission creep. The clearest indication of this is that policy-makers have settled into a vain war with abstract nouns like 'extremism', 'hate', 'Islamism', 'racism' and 'terror'. English law has been no more successful than NATO (the North Atlantic Treaty Organization) at wiping out these evils directly. This is unsurprising given the practical difficulties involved. For example, up to 80 per cent of everyday human expression would be considered outrageous if encountered out of context.[12] Moreover, as the late Python Terry Jones pointed out:

> How do you wage war on an abstract noun? It's rather like bombing 'murder' . . . How will they know when they've won it? With most wars you can say you've won when the other side is either all dead or surrenders. But how is 'terrorism'

[9] Tom Holland, 'How Do We Prevent Radicalisation?' (*Theos*, 28 September 2014) and 'The West Can Never Hope to Understand Islamic State' (*New Statesman*, 21 January 2017).

[10] See generally Michael Cook, *Ancient Religions, Modern Politics: The Islamic Case in Comparative Perspective* (Princeton, NJ: Princeton University Press, 2014); Graeme Wood, *The Way of the Strangers: Encounters with the Islamic State* (London: Allen Lane, 2017).

[11] Michael Rubin, 'On Obama, Islam, and Misdirected Political Correctness' (American Enterprise Institute, 24 September 2014), www.aei.org/foreign-and-defense-policy/middle-east/on-obama-islam-and-misdirected-political-correctness/.

[12] Whitney Phillips and Ryan M. Miller, *The Ambivalent Internet: Mischief, Oddity, and Antagonism Online* (Cambridge: Polity, 2017), p. 26.

going to surrender? [. . .] It's very hard for abstract nouns to do anything at all of their own volition . . . It's difficult to find their hideouts, useless to try and [*sic*] cut off their supplies or intercept their paths of communication, and it's downright impossible to try and [*sic*] make them give in. Abstract nouns simply aren't like that. I'm afraid the bitter semantic truth is, you can't win against these sorts of words.[13]

0.2 Sociological Religion

By contrast, the point of any sociological definition is to describe religion in as scientific a manner as possible. Ideally, this generates a formulation capable of encompassing, for the purpose of further study, all the potential facets of this complex social phenomenon. Heather Selma Gregg provides an example of good practice with her apolitical purposive definition: 'religions are systems of beliefs organised around the concept of salvation or redeeming humanity and the earth from a fallen state, either in this world or the hereafter . . . The path to salvation can require any number of actions, including . . . acts of violence.'[14] From this comes a comprehensive and practical definition of a religious group: 'an organisation recognised as holy – relating to the divine or supernatural – consisting of beliefs, texts, leaders, community, resources, and group identity'. This in turn allows her to make general observations about organised religion, such as that while Christianity or Islam may be identifiable theoretical phenomena, in practice they do not each constitute an immutable 'singular unit'; rather, they display 'much diversity . . . across time and space'.[15] Framing religions in this way – in terms of their salvific objective as well as their human, material, intellectual, cultural and symbolic aspects – is useful for achieving a workable degree of objectivity and sidestepping theological debates about what is or is not truly Islamic, Christian, Judaic, etc. and whether religious law is compatible with English law and society.[16] For practical purposes, this means that each religion can be taken as interpreted by self-declared contemporary believers, not as 'politicians or ivory tower academics claim it to be'.[17] It also avoids one of the worst hangovers from Marxism: the tendency, still prevalent in the humanities and social sciences, to think about collective issues in crude class terms (Muslims, brown people, the poor, etc.).[18]

13 Terry Jones, *Terry Jones's War on the War on Terror: Observations and Denunciations by a Founding Member of Monty Python* (New York: Nation Books, 2005), pp. 1–2.

14 Gregg, *Path to Salvation*, p. 3. 15 Ibid., 14–15.

16 For a valiant attempt at this, see Salim Farrar and Ghena Krayem, *Accommodating Muslims under Common Law: A Comparative Analysis* (London: Routledge, 2018).

17 Rubin, 'On Obama, Islam, and Misdirected Political Correctness'.

18 Jasper Griffin, 'The Social Function of Attic Tragedy' (1998) 48(1) *Classical Quarterly* 39–61, 40: 'A spectre, we might perhaps say, is haunting the academic literature of the West: the spectre of Marxism, which lingers on, after its death in the world of practical affairs, among the critics and the scholiasts.'

Yet, for two reasons, descriptive sociology cannot be transposed into law. First, there is no realistic possibility of any legal definition being able to capture and process the unending complexity of human religiosity; some sect or practice or dispute or exception will always defy the pretentions of a purely factual general rule. This is a recipe for paralysis, the mere fact of intricacy being used to defeat decisive action. Second, just because something can be properly described as religious does not entail legal consequence. Suicide murder and pederasty are just as capable of being institutionalised as religious as are almsgiving and peacemaking – there is always a value commitment to be made beyond that to the bare facts.

0.3 Legal Religion

The legal definition of religion must overcome the shortcomings of the sociological and political approaches. In the abstruse language of autopoietic theory, legal systems remain 'normatively closed but cognitively open'.[19] In plain English, this means that they must combine observation with evaluation. This requires engagement with the sociological reality of religion while attaching normative consequences to descriptive propositions about it so as to condition religion on the law's own terms (with reference, for example, to key legalistic values including certainty, stability and fairness). Thus, the law sets a nuanced normative agenda by establishing formal criteria through which things must pass in order to earn the rewards of legal recognition. For example, Article 9(2) of the European Convention on Human Rights (ECHR) subjects the freedom to manifest (via organised religion or otherwise) thought, conscience and religion to 'such limitations as are prescribed by law and are necessary in a democratic society in the interests of public safety, for the protection of public order, health or morals, or for the protection of the rights and freedoms of others'. In this way, only those religions which clear the regulatory hurdles imposed by particular domestic legal systems will benefit from being recognised by, and included within, the legal definition of religion. This is all indicative of the law's great potential to indirectly shape and subtly influence religion via the formal structuring of group phenomena and social movements. In English law, functionality triumphs over neatness: there is no single authoritative definition of religion. Still, across a range of legal contexts, there is an obvious need for some kind of working definition so the courts tend to take a pragmatic approach and 'work by analogy from what they regard as being "clearly religious"'.[20] In the law of charities, for example, the common law has long recognised that 'two of the essentials of religion are faith and worship; faith in a god and worship of that god'.[21] This clearly encompasses monotheistic religions and has been supplemented by the acceptance of

[19] Niklas Luhmann, 'The Unity of the Legal System' in Gunther Teubner (ed.), *Autopoietic Law: A New Approach to Law and Society* (Berlin: Walter de Gruyter, 1988), pp. 12–35, p. 20.

[20] Peter W. Edge, *Legal Responses to Religious Difference* (The Hague: Kluwer Law, 2002), pp. 7, 9.

[21] *Re South Place Ethical Society* [1980] 1 WLR 1565 at 1572.

polytheistic and non-theistic religions.[22] In human rights law, the standard point of reference is Article 9 of the ECHR which protects the right to freedom of thought, conscience, belief and religion as well as the freedom to manifest these. In discrimination law, the courts use section 10 of the Equality Act 2010, which holds that (1) religion means any religion and a reference to religion includes a reference to a lack of religion; and (2) belief means any religious or philosophical belief and a reference to belief includes a reference to a lack of belief. The basic point here is that these are all very broad, partial and similar definitions that exist to 'help the court by pointing out some key characteristics that a religion may have, but they do not provide a list of protected religions'.[23]

Problems remain. Contemporary English law – as much as the jurisprudence underpinning it[24] –

> has tendencies to be blind to the social form of religious bodies . . . [in that] it is possible for a religion to have an organisational structure to which the law is completely blind. The structure still exists as a matter of social reality dependent for its continued viability on the beliefs and practices of individuals and groups, but without any validation or support from the law.[25]

At first glance, this may seem overstated. After all, non-established religious organisations can choose from a smorgasbord of legal forms ranging from full incorporation through charitable trusts and unincorporated associations to loose networks of differently structured institutions.[26] Generally speaking, the rules and structures of organised religions bind assenting members as well as the organisations themselves: they are perfectly entitled to 'adopt rules for enforcing discipline within their body' within the law, but must adhere to these internal regulations when seeking to enforce discipline or impose sanctions upon members.[27] As such, religious organisations are largely self-regulated and enjoy legal recognition of the binding effects of their own systems of rules, excepting criminal jurisdiction of any sort.[28] The underlying rationale behind the law of organised religions is to balance 'the need to protect the autonomy of the religious groups against the need to ensure that those religious groups still operate within the law of the state'.[29] Such is the legal apparatus from which religions are constituted in the modern state. The necessarily thin definitions of religion utilised by English law hold the centre against the competing demands of a highly politicised definition, on one hand, and a very capacious sociological definition, on the other. Consequently, any non-corporate

[22] Charities Act 2011, s.3(2)(a).
[23] Russell Sandberg, *Law and Religion* (Cambridge: Cambridge University Press, 2011), pp. 57–8.
[24] Nicholas Aroney, 'Individual, Community and State: Thoughts on Jane Norton, *Freedom of Religious Organizations*' (2017) 42(1) *Australian Journal of Legal Philosophy* 270–9.
[25] Rivers, *Law of Organized Religion*, pp. viii, 72.
[26] Sandberg, *Law and Religion*, pp. 72–3.
[27] *Long* v. *Bishop of Cape Town* (1863) 1 Moore NS Cases 461; *Davies* v. *Presbyterian Church of Wales* [1986] 1 WLR 323.
[28] Sandberg, *Law and Religion*, p. 74; Rivers, *Law of Organized Religion*, p. 103.
[29] Sandberg, ibid., p. 77.

manifestations of Islam will be ignored and must adjust themselves to the preferred English forms. For the most part, this kind of transformation does not cause many difficulties and, for practical purposes at least, is to be affirmed.[30] In any event, 'analogical expansion from historically dominant forms seems inevitable'.[31] Nevertheless, choosing not to see something does not negate its existence or significance, and, in certain cases, the law's wilful blindness comes at great and unnecessary cost. Averting this requires a bigger picture than black-letter law alone can provide.

Law in context is a disposition rather than a doctrine or discipline. It requires no ideological commitments and eschews political partisanship. Activism masquerading as scholarship is considered a breach of professional and ethical standards. It is not tied to any particular conception of what law is or should be. It draws omnivorously from empirical, theoretical, quantitative and qualitative studies from any relevant discipline to evidence claims and justify conclusions.[32] It ranges further and plumbs deeper than purely doctrinal jurisprudence, socio-legal studies with its funding committee airs, or any of the 'Law and X (society, religion, economics, literature, history, etc.)' movements.[33] It questions orthodoxy in ways that probe and provoke.[34] There is no ignoring, downplaying or excusing any relevant factor in any social ill to spare anyone or any group any embarrassment. Uncomfortable findings – and there are many in this book – are to be acknowledged and explained rather than brushed or fumed over.[35] This entails a general disregard for where one's work is perceived to fall on the political spectrum and whether the discoveries might be useful to any given faction. Stylistically, it lends itself to plain speaking, mercilessness towards pretention, and black humour. It holds that mastery of detail, perspective and craftsmanship are prerequisites for innovation. This entails empathy, not sympathy, with differing standpoints held by those from other times, places and traditions. There is an appreciation that contexts can be 'properly transcended and governed by more universal standards and broader ideals' – the point is not to abandon principle but to 'realize relevant ideals in the context at hand'.[36] In all

30 Julian Rivers, 'Islamic Courts in the English Legal System' in Steve Bell and Colin Chapman (eds.), *Between Naivety & Hostility: Uncovering the Best Christian Reponses to Islam in Britain* (Milton Keynes: Authentic Media, 2011), p. 184.

31 Rivers, *Law of Organized Religion*, p. 159.

32 William Twining, *Jurist in Context: A Memoir* (Cambridge: Cambridge University Press, 2019), pp. 161–4.

33 'Jurist in Context: William Twining in Conversation with David Sugarman' (2020) 47(2) *Journal of Law and Society* 195–220, p. 210.

34 'Editorial Introduction' (2005) 1(1) *International Journal of Law in Context* 3–4, p. 3.

35 For a good discussion of this tendency, see either Tom Shippey, *Laughing Shall I Die: Lives and Deaths of the Great Vikings* (London: Reaktion, 2018), pp. 13–22; or Bryan Ward-Perkins, 'Why Did Rome Fall?' in *The Folio Book of Historical Mysteries* (London: Folio Society, 2008), pp. 53–67.

36 Philip Selznick, 'Law in Context Revisited' (2003) 30(2) *Journal of Law and Society* 177–86, p. 184.

things, there is an emphasis on realism and what will fly or fall in practice.[37] All this makes it especially suited to the study of institutions in society and throughout history.[38] Civil society groups feature prominently in law in context scholarship, which acknowledges their role as key to 'resisting the debasement of culture, especially in journalism, education, and the arts'.[39] It is, in short, an unconventional but humane approach to law. Still, any disposition this promiscuous risks obscuring the lawyerly precision that it was intended to enhance. Something more is required to maintain discipline and focus.

Juridification yields a 'promising style of capturing, revealing, and ultimately taking a stand' on seemingly intractable controversies.[40] Put simply, it means translating amorphous, big-picture issues into a series of technical legal problems; cultural conflicts are rearticulated for 'the specificity and constraint of technical form'.[41] Law is thereby treated as a way of coding for human behaviour, and, like all programmes, it functions best when the inputs and expected outputs are eloquent. Out go the usual squabbles over identity, diversity and the character of Islam; in come solvable questions to do with property, regulatory powers and the structure of organisations.[42] This technique can be further enhanced when combined with the Tacitean insights of nudge theory.[43] Stifling bureaucracy and its attendant 'bullshit jobs' are now a cross-partisan concern, and this subdiscipline of behavioural economics shows that minor changes to the social environment can induce major behavioural shifts.[44] Successful examples include the installation in road vehicles of irritating dashboard noises to encourage seatbelt usage and etching houseflies onto urinals to promote better aim.[45] Such is its potential that the UK government even created a 'nudge unit', the Behavioural Insights Team, to

[37] Twining, *Jurist in Context*, pp. 163–9. [38] Selznick, 'Law in Context Revisited', p. 177.

[39] Ibid., p. 180.

[40] Karen Knop, Ralf Michaels and Annelise Riles, 'From Multiculturalism to Technique: Feminism, Culture, and the Conflict of Laws Style' (2012) 64 *Stanford Law Review* 589–656, p. 590.

[41] Ibid.

[42] Heather Selma Gregg, *The Path to Salvation: Religious Violence from the Crusades to Jihad* (Nebraska: Potomac Books, 2014), pp. 12–15.

[43] Cornelius Tacitus, *The Histories, Books IV–V, The Annals, Books I–III* (transl. John Jackson), Loeb Classical Library 249 (Cambridge, MA: Harvard University Press, 1931), *Annals* Book III, ch. 27, p. 567: '*Corruptissima re publica plurimae leges* [When the state was most corrupt, laws were most abundant]'.

[44] Claire L. Adida, David D. Laitin and Marie-Anne Valfort, *Why Muslim Integration Fails in Christian-Heritage Societies* (Cambridge, MA: Harvard University Press, 2016), p. 150; Niall Ferguson, *The Great Degeneration: How Institutions Decay and Economies Die* (London: Penguin, 2014); David Graeber, *The Utopia of Rules: On Technology, Stupidity, and the Secret Joys of Bureaucracy* (London: Melville House, 2015) and *Bullshit Jobs: A Theory* (London: Penguin, 2019).

[45] Department for Transport and Stephen Hammond MP, 'Thirty Years of Seatbelt Safety' (HMG, 31 January 2013); Steven D. Levitt and Stephen J. Dubner, *Superfreakonomics* (London: Penguin, 2015), pp. 146–50; Richard H. Thaler and Cass R. Sunstein, *Nudge: Improving Decisions about Health, Wealth and Happiness* (London: Penguin, 2008), p. 4.

improve governance.[46] Nudge theory is not about more regulation or deregulation but better regulation: the aim is to avoid a kludge – defined by the *Oxford English Dictionary* as 'an ill-assorted collection of poorlymatching parts forming a distressing whole' – by designing intuitive laws requiring minimal interpretation and enforcement. In this, it dovetails with law in context: 'the more integrated law is with other institutions, and with what people can accept as sensible, the easier it is to make the system work, and to deliver justice as well as law'.[47] None of this is to say that the solutions will be easy, in any sense of that word. However, juridification infused with nudge theory allows the jurist to bypass the culture wars, make a ruthless diagnosis and fix the underlying problems with general rules.

Definitional clarity, law in context, juridification – these are the techniques that inform the structure, style and substance of this book. It has been written with scholars, practitioners, policy-makers and – perhaps ambitiously – an interested public in mind. The arguments advanced are these. Conventional Anglo-American jurisprudence has failed to develop an adequate vocabulary for group entities. This has made it difficult to articulate collective problems generated by the growth of Islam in the UK. It has also precluded a coherent vision for an attractive settlement between English law and religion. These will remain unresolved until such a lexicon is introduced to mainstream policy-making. The necessary concepts already exist and, once recovered from obscurity, will allow for accurate diagnoses and precise solutions. These need not rely upon sweeping generalisations about nebulous concepts like ethnicity, culture or religion; they depend instead upon refinements to regulations governing autonomous institutions. This is part demolition job requiring the eradication of dangerous informal entities and part reconstruction effort as beneficial ones are strengthened by appropriate reforms. Non-state groups must be taken seriously on their own terms as they are key to the future of British Islam, which is not a meaningful entity in and of itself. This being accomplished, a great deal of anxiety and friction will dissipate. Social harmony, much like personal happiness, is best pursued indirectly through incremental improvements to seemingly mundane things within our control. In some areas, a great deal has been achieved already; in others, there is a lot left to do; in all of them, however, a lot more can be achieved than the incessant bickering over culture war talking points would suggest.

The study is divided into two consecutive parts: theory and practice. Each half is introduced separately and both are self-contained. This will enable the policy readership to skip straight to the diagnosis and recommendations without having to grapple with too much philosophy. Thus, while the book will be more persuasive when read in its entirety, each chapter should be

[46] David Halpern, *Inside the Nudge Unit: How Small Changes Can Make a Big Difference* (London: Penguin, 2016).

[47] Selznick, 'Law in Context Revisited', p. 178.

comprehensible enough in its own right to benefit those interested specifically in the titular topic. Part I serves as a comparative analysis of three different theoretical models for the regulation of religious groups. Chapter 1 is on liberal individualism as enunciated by Ronald Dworkin; it highlights the ways in which this dominant model is largely uninterested in the nature and significance of non-state groups. Chapter 2 considers the multiculturalism of Bhikhu Parekh and Tariq Modood; it highlights their erroneous and undue reliance on class/cultural agency as well as their unsystematic approach to the relationship among group, individual and state. Chapter 3 concerns classical pluralism, the neglected philosophical legacy of Otto von Gierke, a jurist who remains obscure despite the rigour of his method and the richness of his thinking around groups, law and society. These thinkers have been selected because they are all totems of their respective traditions.[48] The present author has endeavoured to read everything each has ever published so that restatements of their positions and criticisms of their arguments are accurate, representative and fair.

The standard format for the first two chapters is thus. The theory and its leading exponent(s) are introduced in historical context to convey a sense of the milieu and priorities at the time they were created. A concise philosophical exposition follows to give an accessible overview of their thought, leading into a discussion of their influence over English law. There is no general theoretical critique as this book is concerned chiefly with practical matters; the reader will doubtless be able to infer what the problematic tenets are from the attempts to implement them. Chapter 3 on classical pluralism is structured differently on account of the subject's relative obscurity and because it is the regulatory model advanced by the author. It introduces Gierke himself, outlines his philosophy and typology of groups, discusses his reception into English jurisprudence and traces his legacy down to the present. Two things should stand out from Chapter 3: (1) that our lexicon of group entities is extremely primitive and in dire need of enrichment; and (2) that placing modern problems in historical context is a fructifying mode of legal scholarship, not least because it holds up a distant mirror on today and reassures us that our forebears had many of the same complaints and even some of the answers.[49] It is by far the best antidote to moral panics and their obverse, the very academic tendency to believe that concerns over real problems are also moral panics. By the end of the theoretical part, the reader should be familiar with the dominant theory underpinning the English law of religion (liberal individualism), its most successful competitor (multiculturalism) and the most appealing alternative to both (classical pluralism). These establish the comparative and analytical framework for the remaining practical discussions.

[48] On selecting for a canon, see Harold Bloom, *The Western Canon* (London: Papermac, 1995), p. 2.

[49] Barbara Tuchman, *A Distant Mirror: The Calamitous 14th Century* (London: Penguin, 2017), pp. xix–xx.

The second half of the book contains five chapters, each covering a different type of institution relevant to the structure and functioning of British Islam. It aims to elucidate the issues, place them in historical context and resolve them with reference to the appropriate theory. The standard layout of each chapter is as follows. A short introduction will set the agenda and signpost the presenting legal issues; a brief history of the relevant institution and regulatory framework will, in keeping with the classical pluralist method, highlight the governing principles of that branch of law as well as the existence of comparable issues in the past and how previous generations dealt with them; the evidence concerning the contemporary problem in that sector will be examined to determine its nature and scale; the presenting issues will then be interpreted using the two conventional theoretical models; and, finally, a detailed pluralist response will be outlined to illuminate the real problems and best solutions. These policy recommendations are restated in brief in the book's Conclusion. This format will demonstrate that liberal individualism and multiculturalism are, for different reasons, consistently unable to articulate and address the underlying problems. Using the tenets and vocabulary of classical pluralism, seemingly intractable difficulties are rearticulated and suitable reforms suggested. This will have applications far beyond law, religion and the UK.

The emerging theme is that there is no singular relationship between English law and British Islam because the latter is not a meaningful entity. The relationships that matter, and the ones on which religion–state relations ultimately depend, are those between English law and tangible groups. Properly regulated institutions – banks, charities, schools, political organisations, families – are key to this. However, they have been largely neglected alongside the threat posed by groups to which the law turns a blind eye: subversive revolutionaries exploiting the system and transnational clans spreading corruption. These are universal sociological phenomena and are not confined to Muslim societies or populations. In the UK, however, they have presented most prominently in South Asian diasporas which happen to be predominantly Muslim. The connections between British Islam and English law are most obvious and direct in the case of banks, charities and schools. The problems highlighted in these chapters are all to do with hurdles to the establishment of these institutions and threats to their proper functioning according to their legitimate purposes. The reader will notice that the later chapters on elections and clans have a broader focus than the preceding ones, and that Islam enters the discussion at a later stage in each. This is because religious, cultural and non-state group norms are inextricably intertwined around the problems discussed.[50] Thus, while Islam is an identifiable and relevant factor in much of the election fraud case law and other recorded

[50] This point was stressed in relation to family matters and personal law in Mona Siddiqui et al., 'The Independent Review into the Application of Sharia Law in England and Wales' (HMG, February 2018), p. 3.

manifestations of clannish corruption, it is not necessarily the sole or even the central driver of such behaviour. Trying to isolate the 'religion factor' and measure its exact causal weight would be a futile and distracting endeavour. What is more, any issue that transcends a particular religion, culture or ethnic group can be addressed only with generally applicable rules. Getting those right without expecting too much of the law is as daunting a task as any, but there are many instances where this has already been done to a high standard. Making Islam as boring to the general public as every other major religion in the UK is the great prize here, and by the end of the book the reader should have many grounds for optimism in this regard. Writing it will have been worthwhile if: (i) scholars and practitioners obtain the terminology needed to argue better about religious groups; and (ii) policy-makers grasp the importance of making unglamorous changes to unexciting laws and then get on with doing just that.

Part I
Theory

Introduction to Part I

The primary purpose of this part is to familiarise the reader with three different theoretical approaches to law and religion. Chapters 1 and 2 introduce, respectively, liberal individualism and multiculturalism, which have been vying for influence over the law of religion for many decades. Chapter 3 introduces classical pluralism, which comes not to split the difference between the two but to bury them both. Otto von Gierke dominates this chapter, as he does the entire book, for good reason. His jurisprudence has been resurrected not because it is some hokey 'third way' or 'basically-just-X-with-a-few-concessions-to-Y kludge', but because it represents a genuine paradigm shift and opens up entirely new lines of inquiry. Every part, chapter and section of this book is implicitly structured according to Gierkean ideals of historicism and the symmetrical interrelationship between the whole and each partial whole. Read on its own, this part amounts to a self-contained thesis in favour of substituting classical pluralism for liberal individualism and multiculturalism in all matters concerning law and society; read on their own, each chapter is designed to ensure that the reader understands: where and how each theory arose, the nature of its core tenets and how they fit together, the degree of influence it has exerted over Anglo-American jurisprudence and English law, its current trajectory, and whether or not it convinces for the purposes of this book. They appear in descending order of influence and familiarity: liberal individualism is by far the best known and most successful, multiculturalism less so on both counts, while classical pluralism has barely registered at all. If, by the end of the part, the reader finds this order of precedence regrettable, it will have been a success. The success of Part I is prerequisite to the success of the book as a whole. While Part II can be read without any reference back to it, the persistence of the social problems discussed in its constituent chapters is owing in large part to an inability to articulate them. The most striking finding of Part I is just how threadbare the jurisprudence of groups – religious or otherwise – is within the Anglo-American tradition. Thus, while liberal individualism cannot distinguish collective entities from aggregations of individuals, multiculturalism cannot distinguish identities and classes from real group actors with genuine agency. That a German historian writing during the Second Reich has more to offer us today than anyone writing on social relations on either side of the twenty-first century is an indictment of the modern academy. It cannot even be claimed that our leading lights are failing better over time, for multiculturalism is patently inferior in every respect to liberal individualism, which predates and will probably outlast it. Regardless, the reader should come away from Part I confident that, when it comes to ordering the relationship between British Islam and English law, we need fail no more. This newfound optimism, combined with a new vocabulary of groups and the new questions it makes possible to ask and answer, is precisely what the reader needs to get the utmost out of Part II.

1

Liberal Individualism

The collective loses, the individual gains. Some will call it decadence, others liberation. Why not both?[1]

1.1 An Introduction to Ronald Dworkin

The history of liberalism is long, multinational and chequered. Long because it is a Christian idea whose growth was bound up with the successes and failures of that faith.[2] Multinational because it was developed in France, improved in Germany and spread by England.[3] Chequered because there have been as many slavers and snobs among its adherents as democrats, dons and do-gooders.[4] For all that, liberalism has contributed more to human freedom than any other idea in intellectual history.[5] Crudely put, its own history divides into two distinct phases: classical and modern. Classical liberalism, which reached its zenith in the Victorian era with the advent of the Industrial Revolution, laissez-faire capitalism and mass democracy, is now remembered for its emphasis on personal and property rights.[6] Yet many of its original exponents were moralists before they were economists or jurists. Their chief concerns were not free trade and personal rights but the transformative power of religion, the common good, the sanctity of family and the reciprocal obligations of social life.[7] Associations were regarded as vital to the health of society, although their value was understood in instrumental terms in that they

[1] Regis Debray, *Civilization: How We All Became American*, David Fernbach (transl.) (London: Verso, 2019), p. 175.

[2] Tom Holland, *Dominion: The Making of the Western Mind* (London: Abacus, 2020).

[3] Helena Rosenblatt, *The Lost History of Liberalism* (Princeton, NJ: Princeton University Press, 2018); Quentin Skinner, *Liberty before Liberalism* (Cambridge: Cambridge University Press, Canto Classics, 2012).

[4] Domenico Losurdo, *Liberalism: A Counter-History* (London: Verso, 2014).

[5] Larry Siedentop, *Inventing the Individual: The Origins of Western Liberalism* (London: Penguin, 2015).

[6] Edmund Fawcett, *Liberalism: The Life of an Idea* (2nd ed., Princeton, NJ: Princeton University Press, 2018).

[7] Rosenblatt, *The Lost History of Liberalism*, pp. 243–4; George H. Smith, *The System of Liberty: Themes in the History of Classical Liberalism* (Cambridge: Cambridge University Press, 2013), pp. 173–96.

enabled the individual to better participate in public life.[8] Whatever its attractions, classical liberalism did not long endure into the twentieth century. Though it was increasingly seen as decadent and hypocritical, the experience of totalitarianism and two world wars buried it and put liberals everywhere on the back foot. As *Pax Britannica* gave way to the American Century, so the seat of liberal thought shifted to the East Coast campus. Here, over the course of three decades, liberalism was reimagined for the modern age as anti-totalitarianism. For its post-war exponents, this meant stripping out all traces of communalism and a turn to rights. Liberalism therefore 'lost much of its moral core and its centuries-long dedication to the public good', not to mention any ambitions for moral or social transformation.[9] Thus, what began as a defensive reaction against collectivism and relativism became an all-conquering creed predicated on the singular importance of the individual.

The midwife and high priest of this new liberal individualism was John Rawls (1921–2002). One of the most formidable scholars ever to have lived, Rawls eschewed activism and the public eye his entire life.[10] His early thought was coloured by religion and war. In line with his Protestant upbringing, as a young man he adopted ethics that were theological and placed great emphasis on community and religious association: 'man is a being made to live in and to live for community. His gifts are a means to this end.'[11] First-hand combat experience during World War II changed all this. Having enlisted in 1943, he was deployed to the Pacific Theatre and there robbed of his faith by the brutality of the fighting.[12] Upon his return, he became deeply suspicious of religion and began to develop a political philosophy designed to protect the most vulnerable in society while avoiding 'false appeals to the common good'.[13] He became situated squarely within the deontological tradition derived from Kant and concerned chiefly with equality, universal rights and social welfare.[14] The culmination of this process, *A Theory of Justice* (1971), set out his conception of justice as fairness and remains his most highly regarded work, with his subsequent books – which are for the most part revisions, restatements or extensions of that seminal thesis – falling within its shade.[15]

8 Emile Lester, 'Two Types of Pluralism and the Catholic Church Scandal' (2005) 47(2) *Journal of Church & State* 309–34, pp. 311–14.

9 Rosenblatt, *The Lost History of Liberalism*, p. 271.

10 William A. Edmundson, *John Rawls: Reticent Socialist* (Cambridge: Cambridge University Press, 2017), pp. 1–2.

11 John Rawls, *A Brief Inquiry into the Meaning of Sin and Faith*, Thomas Nagel (ed.) (Cambridge, MA: Harvard University Press, 2010), p. 193.

12 Ibid., pp. 261–3.

13 Fawcett, *Liberalism*, p. 314; Andrius Galisanka, *John Rawls: The Path to a Theory of Justice* (Cambridge, MA: Harvard University Press, 2019).

14 Paul Kelly, *Liberalism* (Cambridge: Polity Press, 2005), p. 7; Michael J. Sandel, *Liberalism and the Limits of Justice* (*LLJ*) (2nd ed., Cambridge: Cambridge University Press, 1998), p. 1.

15 Thomas Pogge, *John Rawls: His Life and Theory of Justice* (Oxford: Oxford University Press, 2007), pp. 28, 178–95; David Gordon, 'Going off the Rawls' (*American Conservative*, 2008).

Needless to say, his *oeuvre* spawned a colossal amount of secondary literature and was subjected to intense critical scrutiny from many quarters.[16] Even so, it is difficult to overstate the magnitude of Rawls's achievement. More or less single-handedly, he put liberalism back on the offensive and captured the terms of political debate for the next half-century. After *A Theory of Justice*, the whole political spectrum – left, right, centre – had to operate within or around Rawlsian philosophy.[17] It became the new common sense, almost civilisational. The leaders of the free world drew from it.[18] It made socialism, in however light a form, conceivable in America.[19] Conservatism as an intellectual force was swept aside and its own advocates made to look like 'small men on the wrong side of history'.[20] Liberal individualism had been imbued with that peculiar magic of Americanisation whereby something foreign and mundane somehow becomes glamorous and natural the world over. Like the hot dog or the blow job, it became a signature US export and a runaway global success.[21] Most important of all, however, Rawls attracted a calibre of talent comparable to his own to the cause.

Ronald Dworkin (1931–2013) was in every respect the ultimate American lawyer. A Harvard philosophy major and Rhodes Scholar, he clerked for Judge Learned Hand and practised at Sullivan & Cromwell in New York before reaching his final form as a law professor.[22] He regarded biographical detail as 'odd and trivial' and cherished robust argument his entire life.[23] Hailed during his lifetime as 'the greatest living theorist of law in the English-speaking world',[24] he is still regarded as 'arguably the pivotal jurist of the last 40 years'[25] and 'probably the most influential English-language legal theorist of his generation'.[26] His jurisprudence has universal relevance and has been lauded worldwide.[27]

Dworkin came to Rawls early and regarded him with the reverence due a prophet: 'Each of us has his or her own Immanuel Kant, and from now on we will struggle, each of us, for the benediction of John Rawls. And with very good

16 Pogge, *John Rawls*, pp. 197–214. 17 Rosenblatt, *The Lost History of Liberalism*, p. 271.

18 Galisanka, *John* Rawls, p. 1 note 1. 19 Edmundson, *John Rawls.*

20 Ed West, *Small Men on the Wrong Side of History: The Decline, Fall and Unlikely Return of Conservatism* (London: Constable, 2020).

21 Christopher Hitchens, 'As American as Apple Pie' (*Vanity Fair*, 10 October 2006); Debray, *Civilization.*

22 Stephen Guest, *Ronald Dworkin* (3rd ed., Stanford, CA: Stanford University Press, 2013), p. 12.

23 Arthur Ripstein, *Ronald Dworkin* (Cambridge: Cambridge University Press, 2007), p. 2; James Fleming, 'Ronald Dworkin: A Eulogy' (2014) 94 *Boston University Law Review* 1201–5, pp. 1201–3.

24 Niall Ferguson, *The Great Degeneration: How Institutions Decay and Economies Die* (London: Penguin, 2014), p. 83.

25 Michael Freeman, *Lloyd's Introduction to Jurisprudence* (9th ed., London: Sweet & Maxwell, 2014), p. 593.

26 Brian H. Bix, *Jurisprudence: Theory and Context* (7th ed., London: Sweet & Maxwell, 2015), p. 93.

27 Salman Khurshid, Lokendra Malik and Veronica Rodriguez-Blanco (eds.), *Dignity in the Legal and Political Philosophy of Ronald Dworkin* (Oxford: Oxford University Press, 2018).

reason.'[28] Perhaps modestly, he went so far as to say that 'no theorist has made a greater contribution to legal philosophy in modern times'.[29] Dworkin's own work was congruous with Rawls's and succeeded it within the tradition of 'American welfare-state liberalism'.[30] Dworkinian liberalism is all about 'radical individualism', which breaks from classical liberalism by putting the value of equality on par with, instead of beneath, the value of liberty.[31] The priority of the right over the good, innate human dignity, the unencumbered self, moral consensus and egalitarianism all feature prominently. Even so, Dworkin was no mere disciple and sought to distinguish himself from Rawls in several important respects.[32] Although he certainly took up Rawls's deontological liberalism, it is in fact Dworkin 'who can be said most clearly to ground justice in rights'[33] and who 'provides the most sustained intervention of radical liberalism within jurisprudence'.[34] Further, he 'reacts against Rawls' in so far as he denies the possibility of compartmentalising questions and arguments on good living into distinct realms of public reason and private personal ethics; indeed, 'no line can be drawn between those parts of moral argument that are acceptable parts of public discourse and those that are not'.[35] This crucial difference gets to the heart of what Dworkin was trying to achieve and reveals the animating force behind his own life's work: the pressing need for 'a defense against hedgehogs gone mad and the need for a different liberalism of hope against lazy and selfish foxes'.[36]

Put simply, Dworkin aspired to avoid rigidly abstract, totalising thought by engaging with particular debates on practical issues while 'resisting the quietism and resignation that comes from an excessive focus on the particular'.[37] This concern is reflected in his methodology for, while Rawls maintained a fairly tight focus on the abstract, Dworkin 'writes as an applied philosopher'.[38] His corpus includes works which are predominantly theoretical, but also covers a greater span of worldly issues such as US electoral law, abortion and euthanasia, affirmative action and genetic engineering, as well as the relationship between pornography and the American Constitution.[39] As

28 Ronald Dworkin, *Justice in Robes* (Cambridge, MA: Harvard University Press, 2008), p. 261.
29 Ibid., p. 34.
30 Ibid.; Alan Ryan, *The Making of Modern Liberalism* (Princeton, NJ: Princeton University Press, 2012), p. 506.
31 Alan Hunt (ed.), *Reading Dworkin Critically* (New York: Berg Press, 1992), p. 1.
32 Dworkin, *Justice in Robes*, ch. 9. 33 Freeman, *Lloyd's Introduction to Jurisprudence*, p. 500.
34 Hunt, *Reading Dworkin Critically*, p. 1. 35 Ripstein, *Ronald Dworkin*, pp. 4–5.
36 Dworkin quoted in Ripstein, *Ronald Dworkin*, p. 19. 37 Ibid.
38 A. C. Grayling, 'The Birth of a Classic' (*New York Review*, 28 April 2011), p. 3.
39 See, respectively, Ronald Dworkin, *Law's Empire* (Oxford: Hart-Bloomsbury, 1998, reprint of Fontana Press original, 1986); *Justice for Hedgehogs* (Cambridge, MA: Harvard University Press, 2011); *A Badly Flawed Election: Debating Bush v. Gore, The Supreme Court and American Democracy* (ed.) (New York: New Free Press, 2002); *Life's Dominion: An Argument about Abortion, Euthanasia and Individual Freedom* (New York: Vintage Books, 1994); *Sovereign Virtue: The Theory and Practice of Equality* (Cambridge, MA: Harvard University Press, 2000); *Freedom's Law: The Moral Reading of the American Constitution* (Oxford: Oxford University Press, 1996); *Is Democracy Possible Here? Principles for a New Political Debate* (Princeton, NJ: Princeton University Press, 2006).

a consequence, Dworkin's philosophy must be synthesised from across this range and it is best to start with his organising ideas before working through the details of how they apply to matters of religion.

1.1.1 Integrity and Interpretation

Coherence is the single word that best sums up Dworkinian philosophy. That is to say the coherence of *absolutely everything*. Truth, art, good living, morality, ethics, ideals, politics, rights, law, adjudication, justice – these and all else besides are necessarily linked under one unifying system of value.[40] Built up across decades and numerous publications, Dworkin's grand vision is laid out explicitly in his superlative penultimate book, *Justice for Hedgehogs*: 'The truth about living well and being good and what is wonderful is not only coherent but mutually supporting: what we think about any one of these must stand up, eventually, to any argument we find compelling about the rest.'[41] In this he was no relativist: 'there are objective truths about value . . . [and] some institutions really are unjust and some acts really are wrong no matter how many people believe that they are not . . . We cannot defend a theory of justice without also defending, as part of the same enterprise, a theory of moral objectivity.'[42]

The key to this system of thought was consistent interpretation. Arthur Ripstein observes that Dworkin's 'account of interpretation is itself interpretative' as well as being 'anti-Archimedean'.[43] Starting with the latter, Dworkin defined Archimedean philosophy – exemplified by H. L. A. Hart and Isaiah Berlin – as 'some form of conceptual analysis that does not involve normative judgement, assumptions, or reasoning'.[44] In other words, Archimedean scholars judge the success of any interpretation based on whether it reflects the original author's mind and intentions.[45] Dworkin rejected this 'conversational' approach and instead set out a 'constructive' model for interpretative success.[46] He argued that the relevance of what an author intended is itself a matter of interpretation, and in order to address it one must engage with questions of value and whether or where the text fits within the wider canon.[47] In order to ensure the integrity of the tradition as a whole, one has to construct an interpretation of the text in question that is 'the best possible example of the form or genre to which it is taken to belong'.[48] As the tradition builds and further significant texts are added as points of reference, then, like a chain novel, the constraints placed upon each successive interpreter (or judge) multiply accordingly while the range of objectively justifiable interpretations, or potential best answers to pertinent questions, is correspondingly reduced.[49] The law is best seen as a 'seamless

[40] Dworkin, *Justice for Hedgehogs*, pp. 1–2. [41] Ibid., p. 1. [42] Ibid., pp. 7–8.
[43] Ripstein, *Ronald Dworkin*, pp. 5, 10. [44] Dworkin, *Justice in Robes*, p. 146.
[45] Ripstein, *Ronald Dworkin*, p. 14. [46] Dworkin, *Law's Empire*, pp. 51–2.
[47] Ripstein, *Ronald Dworkin*, pp. 14–15. [48] Dworkin, *Law's Empire*, p. 52.
[49] Ibid., pp. 228–32.

web' of rules, rights, principles and policies with the doctrine of precedent ensuring that each of these is given the appropriate 'gravitational force' in any difficult case at hand.[50] Judges, therefore, are not legislators in these cases contra Hart's 'conventionalism'.[51] This is because the law as such exists a priori and is thus being discovered rather than made – a view that led Roger Scruton to suggest that Dworkin made many traditionally conservative, as opposed to radically egalitarian, assumptions about something that is akin to a priori natural law.[52] As long as the presiding judge is a committed internal participant within his legal system (i.e. he is 'wide-ranging and imaginative in his search for coherence with fundamental principle')[53] then whatever decision he arrives at will be the correct one because it is preserving the integrity of law.[54] Again, Dworkin claimed that this simply reflected actual legal practice because lawyers and judges talk and act as though there is a correct answer to be found in the case at hand. Lawyers are compelled to give the advice they understand to be valid just as judges are compelled to reach an answer and accept that one answer will be better than another.[55] The entire process of legal practice is like plotting a line of best fit through points on a scatter graph.[56]

1.1.2 Responsibility and Good Living

Grappling with any kind of moral, ethical or legal dilemma requires the deliberate exercise of our free will as responsible moral actors. Interpretation is therefore a genuinely creative practice set within the real world as we experience it as part of the 'unfolding drama of self-conscious life'.[57] Dworkin called this the 'capacity principle' which

> locates responsibility within the brackets of an ordinary life lived from a personal perspective. It makes an assumption of ethical independence: that our conscious decisions are, in principle, crucially and independently important in their own right and that their importance is in no way contingent on any remote causal explanation . . . our decisions are genuine facts and whether we live well depends on how good those decisions are.[58]

This is to be distinguished from the deterministic 'causal principle' which contradicts the former and holds that we lack responsibility for our actions

[50] Ibid., pp. 110–15. [51] Ibid., ch. 4.

[52] Roger Scruton, *Fools, Frauds & Firebrands: Thinkers of the New Left* (London: Bloomsbury, 2015), pp. 52–3, 65–8.

[53] Dworkin, *Law's Empire*, p. 220.

[54] Ibid., ch. 11; Freeman, *Lloyd's Introduction to Jurisprudence*, pp. 593–609.

[55] Raymond Wacks, *Understanding Jurisprudence* (4th ed., Oxford: Oxford University Press, 2015), p. 142; Bix, *Jurisprudence*, pp. 100–1.

[56] Bix, *Jurisprudence*, p. 96.

[57] Dworkin, *Justice for Hedgehogs*, p. 242; A. C. Grayling, *The Challenge of Things* (London: Bloomsbury, 2015), pp. 233–5.

[58] Dworkin, ibid., p. 229.

unless we are the uncaused cause of them in their entirety.[59] Although true in a scientific sense, the issue with this is that it offers us no guidance whatsoever in terms of charting a path forward through our lives as we 'cannot change the way we actually live'; it is an 'interpretive orphan: we can find or construct no good reason why it should be part of our ethics'.[60] Neither does it reflect our concrete, everyday experience of the 'way it feels deliberately to act . . . [in] the moment when the decision to act merges with the action decided on'.[61] Thus, by making responsibility an ethical rather than a scientific matter, Dworkin was able to say that we can indeed be responsible for things we have not chosen if we can nevertheless do something about them, such as our character and traits (cruel, lazy, selfish, kind, etc.): 'I cannot excuse my indolence, or you your impatience, because neither of us chose to have these qualities.'[62] Coercion by others, handicaps and accidents are obviously to be treated differently because they are entirely beyond our control.[63] Only if we own our decisions, take an active interest in and responsibility for the direction of our lives, eschew moral ambivalence, hypocrisy, arbitrariness and manipulative behaviour – then, and only then – can we truly be said to be living as responsible human beings.[64] G. A. Cohen looked admiringly upon Dworkin's attempt to deal with matters of individual responsibility in the face of unchosen endowments and circumstances: '[he] has, in effect, performed for egalitarianism the considerable service of incorporating within it the most powerful idea in the arsenal of the anti-egalitarian right: the idea of choice and responsibility'.[65]

From this, a rather agreeable conception of the good life as a 'dense glitter of alternatives' – 'the philanthropic solution, the alcoholic solution, the mask of eccentricity, the search for salvation in perfect taste' – emerges from *Justice for Hedgehogs*.[66] Dworkin's idea of what it means to live well and wonderfully is essentially one of self-creation or artistry:

> [W]e each have a sovereign ethical responsibility to make something of value of our own lives, as a painter makes something valuable of his canvas . . . We must treat the making of our lives as a challenge, one we can perform well or badly. We must recognise, as cardinal among our private interests, an ambition to make our lives good lives: authentic and worthy rather than mean or degrading . . . We must find the value of living – the meaning of life – in living well, just as we find value in loving or painting or writing or singing or diving well.[67]

Further, individual style counts, as 'doing it your way is creative'.[68] Crucial to this are the 'indispensable conditions' of dignity and self-respect whereby

[59] Ibid. [60] Ibid., pp. 227–9. [61] Ibid., p. 226. [62] Ibid., pp. 237, 242–3.
[63] Ibid., pp. 226, 243.
[64] Ibid., ch. 10; Stuart Jeffries, 'Ronald Dworkin: We Have a Responsibility to Live Well' (*The Guardian*, 31 March 2011).
[65] Dworkin quoted in Ripstein, *Ronald Dworkin*, p. 94.
[66] Edward St Aubyn, *The Patrick Melrose Novels: At Last* (London: Picador Classics, 2016), p. 716.
[67] Dworkin, *Justice for Hedgehogs*, pp. 1, 13. [68] Ibid., p. 420.

people wish to 'hold their heads high as they struggle for all the other things they want'.[69] Thus, it is important that people take their own lives seriously, meaning that they accept that how they live is objectively important and insist upon taking ethical responsibility for their decisions.[70] The bearer of a life lives well when he 'pursues a good life for himself and does so with dignity: with respect for the importance of other people's lives and for their ethical responsibility as well as his own'.[71] In order for us to 'make our lives tiny diamonds in the cosmic sands', it is once again essential that any government upholds the principles of justice by treating 'those under its dominion with equal concern and respect', principles which ultimately make it 'easier and more likely for each of us to live a good life well'.[72] In short, the more we reflect upon our lives in general and our position on any particular controversy, the more we must consult our views on related topics and values and thus the more interdependent our arguments become. The outcome is an altogether more considered, responsible and consistent worldview from which we – individually and collectively – may progress to solve the most pressing questions of our age.

1.1.3 Equality and Self

The consequence of Dworkin's philosophy is that, contra Berlin's theory of value pluralism or Joseph Raz's argument for the incommensurability of values, there can be no such thing as a conflict between values.[73] This enables him to 'be read as a fully developed response to the libertarian and egalitarian challenges to Rawls' as he seeks to move beyond what Ripstein calls the 'egalitarian plateau'.[74] This is dominated by arguments from left-wing and right-wing scholars claiming, respectively, that Rawls placed either too little or too much emphasis on the value of equality vis-à-vis liberty. As far as Dworkin was concerned, these 'must be interpreted together. When that is done, no conflict remains.'[75]

Equality requires that any legitimate government must adhere to 'two reigning principles' that bound the acceptable limits of distributive justice.[76] These are, first, that equal concern is shown for all within its dominion and, second, that it respect each person's right to take responsibility for making something valuable out of their lives. This is integrated with the idea of liberty which itself cannot be determined without considering 'what distribution of property and opportunity shows equal concern for all'.[77] Liberty is made up of all the various aspects of freedom that government cannot rightfully constrain. This means that our rights to liberty rest on different bases and not upon some

[69] Ibid., pp. 13–14. [70] Ibid., p. 14. [71] Ibid., p. 419. [72] Ibid., pp. 422–3.

[73] John Gray, *Isaiah Berlin: An Interpretation of His Thought* (Princeton, NJ: Princeton University Press, 2013), ch. 2; Joseph Raz, *The Morality of Freedom* (Oxford: Oxford University Press, 1988).

[74] Ripstein, *Ronald Dworkin*, pp. 83–5. [75] Ibid., p. 84.

[76] Dworkin, *Justice for Hedgehogs*, p. 2. [77] Ibid., pp. 2–4.

general right to freedom. Free speech, for example, is one part of a more general right to govern ourselves, which is in turn one aspect of personal responsibility. Due process and property rights flow from the more general right to equal concern. As such, his theory of liberty forms part of, and draws from, a much more general political morality.[78] Equality and liberty are in turn linked to Dworkin's 'partnership conception' of democracy whereby all citizens participate as equal partners with an equal voice with an equal stake. This in turn requires the protection of his principles of equality and rights to liberty. Law is itself a 'branch of morality' which emphasises 'procedural justice, the morality of fair governance as well as just outcome'.[79] The importance of equality in the overall interpretive scheme of things – he has called it 'the nerve of liberalism'[80] – is made perfectly clear by the title of *Sovereign Virtue*. In it, he attempted to ground his model of equality – 'the sovereign virtue of political community' – within a particular (and contentious) account of the good life.[81] The book is itself premised upon 'ethical individualism', which holds that it is of equal importance that each human life is successful and in the control of its responsible bearer.[82] Dworkin preferred the 'challenge model' of the good life over the 'impact model'.[83] In brief, he rejected the idea that the value of a life should be measured primarily by its objective impact on the world (what it produces: i.e. tangibly reducing misery or performing great deeds) in favour of the view that it must be critically assessed in Aristotelian terms of skilful performance, much like a work of art.[84] This model is bounded by the Platonic idea that living well is inextricably linked to living justly as well as the need for ethical integrity, or the notion that individuals are responsible for contemplating and leading their own lives well.[85]

Nevertheless, Dworkin's grounding of the right in a good constituted of rational choice led him to argue that his liberal egalitarianism does not inflict 'any collective judgement about the comparative importance of people or the comparative worth of projects or personal moralities'.[86] Individuals are to be relieved of responsibility for their bad luck as opposed to their personal choices, meaning that it would be unfair to allow someone to 'retain the benefits of superior talent' because a just society should 'compensate' (via progressive tax and welfare policies) the talentless for their misfortune.[87] The notion of the liberal self envisaged here is one stripped of its unchosen features and whose natural talents are to be treated as common assets.[88] Michael Sandel notes that the only sort of community to which it could belong is

[78] Ibid., p. 4. [79] Ibid., pp. 4–6.

[80] Ronald Dworkin, 'Liberalism' in Stuart Hampshire, T. M. Scanlon, Bernard Williams, Thomas Nagel and Ronald Dworkin (eds.), *Public & Private Morality* (Cambridge: Cambridge University Press, 1987), p. 115.

[81] Dworkin, *Sovereign Virtue*, p. 1. [82] Ibid., p. 5. [83] Ibid., pp. 251–4. [84] Ibid., p. 258.

[85] Ibid., pp. 242–76. [86] Ibid., p. 154. [87] Ibid., pp. 90, 287.

[88] Michael J. Sandel, 'Liberalism and the Claims of Community: The Case of Affirmative Action' in Marshall Cohen (ed.), *Ronald Dworkin & Contemporary Jurisprudence* (London: Duckworth, 1984), p. 227.

a cooperative, as opposed to a constitutive, one.[89] Dworkin's liberalism, he suggests, assumes that once the rights of individuals are disposed of, there is no need for a richly textured account of society with its myriad communities and our allegiances to them. Further, by treating an individual's talents (which form an inseparable part of the constitution of each person) as common property, Dworkin was in fact 'failing to take seriously the distinction between persons'.[90] Robert Nozick made a similar point (in relation to Rawls's difference principle) when he criticised the idea that natural talents can be a collective asset. He argued that this negates the inviolability and distinctness of persons which is supposed to lie at the heart of liberal individualism. Indeed, it can be done 'only if one presses *very* hard on the distinction between men and their talents, assets, abilities, and special traits. Whether any coherent conception of a person remains when the distinction is so pressed is an open question.'[91] Dworkin's reply was to say that 'the idea of ownership ... has no useful role to play in the abstract levels of political theory, because it is parasitic on rather than generative of basic principles of political and personal morality'.[92] In other words, we can talk productively only about how to regulate the rewards of people's talents – a question of political morality rather than metaphysics.[93]

This position is backed up by Dworkin's conception of rights. He stated that liberalism requires a scheme of civil rights that function as trump cards held by the individual to protect them from the majoritarian state. They are justified by reference to the more general right to equal concern and respect.[94] This foundational right is again a postulate of political morality which prevents the government from constraining someone's liberty on the ground that one group's conception of the good life is superior to another's. All citizens are to be treated as ethically responsible human beings capable of deciding what is good for themselves.[95] In *Taking Rights Seriously*, he clarified: 'Individual rights are political trumps held by individuals. Individuals have rights when, for some reason, a collective goal is not a sufficient justification for denying them what they wish, as individuals to have or to do, or not a sufficient justification for imposing some loss or injury upon them.'[96] Dworkin's essential and consistent point is restated succinctly by Ripstein: 'a government that treats its citizens with equal concern and respect must take responsibility for providing them with adequate liberties and opportunities, including protection against outcomes that are disastrous for their ability to take up their own responsibility for their own lives'.[97]

89 Ibid., p. 228. 90 Ibid., p. 236.

91 Robert Nozick, *Anarchy, State & Utopia* (New York: Basic Books, 1974), p. 228.

92 Ronald Dworkin, 'A Reply' in Cohen, *Ronald Dworkin & Contemporary Jurisprudence*, p. 292.

93 Cohen, *Ronald Dworkin & Contemporary Jurisprudence*, p. xii.

94 Ronald Dworkin, *Taking Rights Seriously* (London: Duckworth, 1977), pp. 134–6, 142.

95 Ibid., pp. 272–3. 96 Ibid., p. xi. 97 Ripstein, *Ronald Dworkin*, p. 104.

1.1.4 Community and Obligation

In *Sovereign Virtue*, Dworkin elucidates the nature of a liberal community and its relationship with liberal tolerance, 'which insists that it is wrong of government to use its coercive power to enforce ethical homogeneity'.[98] The central thrust of the argument is that it is essentially wrong to attempt to personify – or anthropomorphise – communities by saying that they have a life of their own.[99] He begins by rejecting (on the basis of this ground) majoritarianism (the idea that the majority sets the ethical standards), paternalism (where upstanding citizens have a duty to reform reprobates and deviants), communitarianism (which emphasises the need people have for community in their self-development, etc.) and integration (whereby the individual's life is a function and reflection of his community's life, which is itself independent of, and prior to, the individual).[100] Although he accepts that people should identify their interests with those of their political community, he takes a 'meagre view' of that community's life which is composed purely of its collective acts, meaning those 'acts treated as collective by the practices and attitudes that create the community as a collective agent'.[101] In other words, the community is simply

> its official political acts: legislation, adjudication, enforcement, and other executive functions of government. An integrated citizen will count his community's success or failure in these formal political acts as resonating in his own life, as improving or diminishing it. On the liberal view, nothing more should be added. These formal political acts of the community as a whole should be taken to exhaust the communal life of a political body, so that citizens are understood to act together, as a collective, only in that structured way.[102]

Dworkin accepts the need for integration of the private and the public identities in the limited sense (which he calls 'liberal civic republicanism') that a truly liberal citizen accepts that the value of his own life ultimately depends on his community treating all with equal concern. So long as it does so, and is seen to do so, it will remain stable and legitimate in its members' eyes despite considerable disagreement about what justice is. Success in this regard means that politics will be considered a joint venture in which everyone has a personal stake in justice for themselves and others.[103]

Stephen Perry has developed an important commentary on Dworkin's account of associative obligations. Dworkin accepted that fraternal obligations within 'true communities' are not universal but 'special and individualized'. This means that they are limited to persons within a particular association who must accept them as special to themselves as members of that group; personal in that they link members to each other as individuals; based on a general concern for the well-being of all other members; and that they create an

[98] Dworkin, *Sovereign Virtue*, p. 211. [99] Ibid., pp. 212, 223. [100] Ibid., pp. 211–12.
[101] Ibid., pp. 212, 227, 232. [102] Ibid., pp. 231–2. [103] Ibid., p. 233.

egalitarian concern for all members as equals.[104] The basic theme here is a kind of reciprocity among individuals.[105] Yet, for Perry, genuine associative obligations arise from, and are justified by, practices with intrinsic value, such as family and friendship groups, regardless of the levels of inequality in the associative relationship.[106] Likewise, if the state is to be a genuine political community, it must also be shown to have intrinsic value for its members.[107] He suggests that 'properly understood, this is ... precisely Dworkin's argument'.[108] Thus, obligations are typically thought to be owed to the community or state rather than each individual citizen one by one. If that is true, and the obligation is owed to the community itself, then that community must be considered to have agency 'in some appropriate sense'.[109]

Dworkin, however, was quick to refute this interpretation. A duty of obedience, arising from the four proper normative conditions he describes, is owed to the individuals as members and not to the collective entity to which they belong. The state enforces this duty as an agent of its citizens who are acting through it.[110] Indeed, Dworkin was implacably hostile to the notion of group personality throughout his career. In *Law's Empire*, he ridicules the 'difficult ontology' behind the idea of 'some spooky, all-embracing mind that is more real than flesh-and-blood people ... [and we should not] treat the state or community as a real person with a distinct interest or point of view or welfare of its own', even though we casually personify groups in everyday language.[111] He further reinforces this highly individualistic position in both *Freedom's Law*, where he seems to suggest that the state alone creates corporate personality,[112] and *Justice for Hedgehogs*, where he states that 'political communities are only collections of individuals' and 'only individuals have political rights'.[113] Yet, at the same time, there is something odd in Dworkin's objection to 'the anthropomorphic conception of communal life'.[114] He claims, for example, that 'a political community has a life' but not a 'national sex life' because 'our conventions recognise no distinctly collective national sexual activity ... nor do we have conventions or practices that provide structures for cooperative sexual activity on a national scale'.[115] There is at once here a reliance upon something very close to anthropomorphic description as well as an obvious overlooking of marriage as an ancient and near-universal social institution which sets out just such conventions and practices. In light of all this, it is hard not to agree with Allan Hutchinson's conclusion that Dworkin's apparent concession to the communitarian critique – 'a society devoted [to

[104] Dworkin, *Law's Empire*, pp. 199–201.

[105] Stephen Perry, 'Associative Obligations & the Obligation to Obey the Law' in Scott Hershovitz (ed.), *Exploring Law's Empire: The Jurisprudence of Ronald Dworkin* (Oxford: Oxford University Press, 2006), p. 192.

[106] Perry, ibid., pp. 189, 192. [107] Ibid., p. 189. [108] Ibid. [109] Ibid., p. 191.

[110] Ronald Dworkin, 'A Response' in Hershovitz, *Exploring Law's Empire*, p. 305.

[111] Dworkin, *Law's Empire*, pp. 64 footnote 15, 168. [112] Dworkin, *Freedom's Law*, p. 88.

[113] Dworkin, *Justice for Hedgehogs*, pp. 327, 473–4 footnote 1.

[114] Dworkin, *Sovereign Virtue*, p. 232. [115] Ibid., pp. 229, 231.

Dworkinian liberalism] may pay a price . . . in the communitarian spirit'[116] – via his increased focus on community and associational obligations in *Law's Empire* and later works, is largely cosmetic given that the highly individualistic foundations of his thought remain essentially unchanged.[117]

1.1.5 Religion and Neutrality

Regarding religious freedom and liberal neutrality, Dworkin wrote that 'ethical independence means that government must never restrict freedom just because it assumes that one way for people to live their lives – one idea about what lives are most worth living just in themselves – is intrinsically better than another, not because its consequences are better than another['s] but because people who live that way are better people'.[118] Andrew Koppelman terms this 'neutralitarianism', which basically means that if the state sides with one ethical view over another it is failing to show equal concern to all its citizens.[119] For Dworkin, religious freedom was a general rather than a special right. This means that it does not attach to religion in general or to any particular religion. If it were a special right, it would attach, like civil rights, to the subject (religion) and require that the government not interfere with or constrain religious exercise in any way absent an extraordinary emergency. It is instead an aspect of the even more general right to ethical independence which fixes citizen–state relations by limiting the reasons government can rely upon to constrain the exercise of that broader right. Belief in God is therefore simply one more manifestation of the claim that 'value is objective, independent of mind, and immanent in the world'.[120] Theistic religion is itself an 'interpretive concept' alongside any non-theistic worldview such as atheistic humanism, which is equally deserving of protection.[121] The definition of religion need go no further than including 'all ethical views about how to live life well'.[122] It is beyond the scope of liberal government to decide between these sincere convictions and afford any one of them privileged status.[123] The practical implication is that religious freedom does not then require a 'high hurdle of protection and therefore its compelling need for strict limits and careful definition'.[124] In sum, a commitment to equality and ethical independence gives rise to a demand for liberal neutrality.[125] As Jeremy Waldron notes, this is all just another reflection of his lifelong project to

[116] Ronald Dworkin quoted by Allan C. Hutchinson in Hunt, *Reading Dworkin Critically*, p. 59.
[117] Ibid., pp. 59–60.
[118] Ronald Dworkin, *Religion Without God* (Cambridge, MA: Harvard University Press, 2013), p. 130.
[119] Andrew Koppelman, 'Ronald Dworkin, Religion & Neutrality' (2014) 94 *Boston University Law Review* 1241–54, p. 1241; Cecile Laborde, 'Dworkin's Freedom of Religion Without God' (2014) 94 *Boston University Law Review* 1255–72, p. 1258.
[120] Dworkin, *Religion Without God*, pp. 117, blurb. [121] Ibid., p. 7.
[122] Laborde, 'Dworkin's Freedom of Religion Without God', p. 1256.
[123] Dworkin, *Religion Without God*, p. 123. [124] Ibid., pp. 132–3.
[125] Laborde, 'Dworkin's Freedom of Religion Without God', p. 1258.

defend the interconnectedness, objectivity and unity of value.[126] Cécile Laborde helpfully categorises Dworkin as a typical example of 'egalitarian theories of religious freedom' which make three connected claims: that the traditional idea of religion is merely one branch of a broader category of morally respectable beliefs and practices; that religious people (traditionally understood) have no special right to be exempted from general law; and that the equal status of all citizens must be guaranteed by the state.[127]

Dworkin's egalitarian liberal tolerance is not, however, neutral or passive towards ethical ideals which threaten its own integrity.[128] In the context of American education, he wrote that 'a tolerant secular society would not allow its institutions to be used for practising, as opposed to studying, religion'.[129] He does not make particularly clear what all this means for dangerous religious fanaticism, only that liberals must deny themselves 'only one weapon: they must not use the law, even when they are in the majority, to forbid anyone to lead the life he wants, or punish him for doing so, just on the ground that his ethical convictions are, as they believe, profoundly wrong'.[130] On this point, Laborde seems to suggest that Dworkin's theory struggles with Islam, which lacks any clear internal private–public / secular–religious structure, and is therefore very difficult to legislate for when trying to target only its dangerous political manifestations.[131] Still, Dworkin believed it right that the government is 'unambiguously prohibited from penalising membership in any conventional religion . . . or . . . permit[ting] legal constraints of any sort that assume that one religion is preferable to others'.[132] In other words, while the government may prohibit what a religion demands (e.g. killing infidels) because it violates the rights of others, it cannot disapprove of or prohibit the religion from which that demand emanates without violating the right to free exercise.[133] It follows that any attempt to 'instil a sense of a shared secular identity of citizens' through law (e.g. a ban on headscarves) will violate the principle of ethical independence by preferring one method of identification over another.[134] The application of equality and non-discrimination laws to religions is also made inescapably clear: 'If we deny a special right to free exercise of religious practice, and rely only on the general right to ethical independence, then religions may be forced to restrict their practices so as to obey rational, non-discriminatory laws that do not display less than equal concern for them. Do you find that shocking?'[135] It is therefore difficult to see a secure place for third-sector religious charities (especially those providing some sort of public service) under this worldview as it presupposes a clear

[126] Jeremy Waldron, 'Religion Without God by Ronald Dworkin – Review' (2014) 94 *Boston University Law Review* 1207–12, pp. 1209–12.

[127] Laborde, 'Dworkin's Freedom of Religion Without God', pp. 1256–7.

[128] Dworkin, *Sovereign Virtue*, p. 283. [129] Dworkin, *Is Democracy Possible Here?*, p. 60.

[130] Dworkin, *Sovereign Virtue*, p. 283.

[131] Laborde, 'Dworkin's Freedom of Religion Without God', pp. 1268–9.

[132] Dworkin, *Religion Without God*, p. 106. [133] Ibid., p. 113. [134] Ibid., pp. 139–40.

[135] Ibid., pp. 135–6.

public–private boundary and seems to represent something of a drive towards collectivisation in the sense that the free choice of individuals to associate on their own terms is cut back in favour of a homogenising application of anti-discrimination law.

1.2 Liberal Individualism in the English Law of Religion

The English law of religion has been tending towards liberal individualist principles for the last century or so. This can be seen in three related trends. The first is the ongoing expansion of what does or should constitute protectable religious belief. This is increasingly being lumped in with protectable biologically grounded features such as race and sex. The Equality Act 2010, which replaced the previous but similar Employment Equality (Religion or Belief) Regulations 2003 and the Equality Act 2006, recognises religious belief as a protected characteristic alongside unchosen biological characteristics such race, sex, gender, sexual orientation, age and disability.[136] Section 10(2) holds: 'Belief means any religious or philosophical belief and a reference to belief includes a reference to a lack of belief.' Early Employment Tribunal (ET) decisions under the 2003 Regulations 'took a broad conception of "religion" and a narrow conception of "belief"'.[137] Thus, 'attendance at home for bereavement purposes' was accepted as religious,[138] whereas claims involving loyalty to a national flag or one's country[139] and political beliefs (specifically, membership of the BNP (British National Party)) were denied the status of protectable beliefs.[140] Yet, ET jurisprudence began to expand the category of protectable beliefs following *Grainger Plc* v. *Nicholson*, which concerned one Mr Nicholson who believed very strongly in man-made climate change and claimed that he had been made redundant as a result, and that this belief deserved Article 9 protection.[141] Mr Justice Burton ruled that it did: 'if a person can establish that he holds a *philosophical belief* which is based on science, as opposed, for example, to religion, then there is no reason to disqualify it from protection'.[142] Further, it was suggested that political beliefs may now also qualify for protection[143] and, since then, all manner of beliefs have been granted protection: humanism,[144] beliefs in spiritualism and psychic powers,[145] anti-fox-hunting beliefs,[146] beliefs in the value of public

[136] Section 4. Section 2(1) specifies that '"religion or belief" means any religion, religious belief, or similar philosophical belief'. The Equality Act 2006, ss. 44, 77 removed from this definition the 'similar' requirement and included a lack of religion or belief.

[137] Mark Hill, Russell Sandberg and Norman Doe, *Religion and Law in the UK* (2nd ed., Alphen aan den Rijn: Kluwer Law International, 2014), p. 142.

[138] *Hussain* v. *Bhuller Bros*, ET, Case Number: 1806638/2004.

[139] *Williams* v. *South Central Ltd*, ET, Case Number: 2306989/2003.

[140] *Baggs* v. *Fudge*, ET, Case Number: 1400114/2005.

[141] (2009) UKEAT 0219/09/ZT.

[142] Para. 30.

[143] Para. 28.

[144] *Streatfield* v. *London Philharmonic Orchestra Ltd* [2012] 2390772/2011.

[145] *Greater Manchester Police Authority* v. *Power* [2009] EAT 0434/09/DA.

[146] *Hashman* v. *Milton Park (Dorset) Ltd* [2011] ET 3105555/2009.

service broadcasting,[147] and even 'ethical veganism'.[148] However, 9/11 conspiracy theories,[149] the Marxist/Trotskyite beliefs of trade union members,[150] a belief that poppies should be worn a week prior to Remembrance Sunday,[151] and transgender-critical feminism[152] have not achieved protected status.[153] While it follows Dworkinian logic, there is neither an obvious endpoint to this expansion nor a clear principle to dictate why the lines are drawn where they are. The law has come to encompass all manner of things – from atheism through political ideology to contestable scientific worldviews – which do not really correspond with a common-sense understanding of what religion actually involves. The point here is made clear enough by Ben Emerson QC: 'Atheism is a religion in the same way as "off" is a television station.' Atheism as a movement, if it is indeed such a thing, is fractious at best and simply 'is not a creed'.[154] It denotes little more than non-belief: '"atheist" is a term that we do not need, in the same way that we don't need a word for someone who rejects astrology'.[155]

The second trend is the privatisation of faith as the judiciary retreats from adjudicating upon matters internal to religions. The courts have repeatedly stated that religion 'is something to be encouraged',[156] that they assume that 'it is good for man to have and to practise a religion',[157] and that 'any religion is at least as likely to be better than none'[158] because it will take a person 'outside his own petty cares and lead him to think of others'.[159] However, they have long sought to adhere to what has variously been called the 'principle of non-interference', the 'doctrine of non-justiciability' and the 'doctrine of judicial abstention'.[160] This doctrine simply means that the courts

> will not attempt to rule upon doctrinal issues or intervene in the regulation or governance of religious groups. That is partly because the courts are secular and stand back from religious issues while according respect to the rights of those who are adherents or worshippers in any such grouping. It is also partly because such disputes as arise between the followers of any given religious faith are often likely to involve doctrines or beliefs which do not

[147] *Maistry* v. *BBC* [2011] ET 1213142/2010.

[148] *Casamitjana* v. *The League Against Cruel Sports* [2020] UKET 3331129/2018.

[149] *Farrell* v. *South Yorkshire Police Authority* [2011] ET 2803805/2010.

[150] *Kelly* v. *Unison* [2009] ET 2203854/08.

[151] *Lisk* v. *Shield Guardian Co Ltd & Others* [2011] ET 3300873/2011.

[152] *Forstater* v. *CGD Europe and others* 2200909/2019.

[153] See generally Hill et al., *Religion and Law*, pp. 143–4.

[154] Christopher Hitchens, 'Christopher Hitchens Quotes: The Writer's Most Memorable bons mots' (*The Guardian*, 16 December 2011).

[155] Sam Harris, 'The Problem with Atheism' (author's blog, 2 October 2007) https://samharris.org/the-problem-with-atheism/.

[156] *R* v. *Disciplinary Committee of the Jockey Club, ex parte Aga Khan* [1993] 1 WLR 909 at 932.

[157] *Gilmour* v. *Coats [1949] AC 426* at 458–9. [158] *Neville Estates* v. *Madden* [1962] Ch 832.

[159] *Holmes* v. *AG* (1981) unreported; Hill et al., *Religion and Law*, pp. 76–7.

[160] Sandberg, *Law and Religion*, p. 74; Rivers, *Law of Organized Religions*, p. 73; *HH Sant Baba Jeet Singh Maharaj* v. *Eastern Media Group Ltd* [2010] EWHC (QB) 1294 per Eady J at para. 6.

> readily lend themselves to the sort of resolution which is the normal function of a judicial tribunal. They may involve questions of faith or doctrinal opinion which cannot be finally determined by the method regularly brought to bear on conflicts of factual and expert evidence. Thus it can be seen to be partly a matter of a self-denying ordinance, applied as a matter of public policy, and partly a question of simply recognising the natural and inevitable limitations upon the judicial function.[161]

This principle adheres to a long line of well-established authority. In *Gilmour* v. *Coats*, Lord Reid ruled: 'No temporal court of law can determine the truth of any religious belief: it is not competent to investigate any such matter and it ought not to attempt to do so.'[162] Another example can be seen in *Re Watson*: 'the court does not prefer one religion to another and it does not prefer one sect to another' unless 'the doctrines inculcated are "adverse to the very foundations of all religion, and ... subversive of all morality"'.[163] Yet another is in *R* v. *Chief Rabbi, ex Parte Wachmann* where Mr Justice Brown held that 'the court is hardly in a position to regulate what is essentially a religious function – the determination [of] whether someone is morally and religiously fit to carry out the spiritual and pastoral duties of his office. The court must inevitably be wary of entering so self-evidently sensitive an area, straying across the well-recognised divide between church and state.'[164] The courts' attitude was summed up by Lord Hoffmann in *R* v. *Disciplinary Committee of the Jockey Club, ex parte Aga Khan*: 'The attitude of the English legislator to racing is much more akin to his attitude to religion: it is something to be encouraged but not the business of government.'[165] Recent cases have added to the gravitational force of non-justiciability. In *Varsani* v. *Jesani*, Mr Justice Patten held that 'where the assets of a religious charity fall to be divided following a rift on theological grounds[,] the court has no choice but to assume an agnostic role'.[166] Likewise, in *Blake* v. *Associated Newspapers*, Mr Justice Gray declared his reluctance to enter 'the forbidden territory of non-justiciability'.[167] In *Amicus* v. *Secretary of State for Trade and Industry*, the court refused to adjudicate on the matter of whether there was a 'coherent theological basis for the interveners' views on sexual morality' as Mr Justice Richards held: 'It is not the court's function to judge whether those beliefs are fairly based on the passages said to support them.'[168] In short, the courts will not rule on the theological correctness of religious beliefs. From these dicta, it

[161] Para. 5. See also *R (on the application of Hodkin and another) (Appellants)* v. *Registrar General of Births, Deaths and Marriages (Respondent)* [2013] UKSC 77 per Toulson LJ at para. 63 – 'fine theological or liturgical niceties ... more appropriate for theologians'.
[162] (1949) AC 426 at 455.
[163] (1973) 1 WLR 1472 at 1482–3, quoting Romilly MR in *Thornton* v. *Howe* (1862) 31 Beav. 14 at 20.
[164] (1992) 1 WLR 1036 at 1042–3. [165] (1993) 1 WLR 909 at 932.
[166] (2002) 1 P & CR DG11 at para. 11. [167] (2003) EWHC 1960 at para. 33.
[168] (2004) EWHC 860 (Admin) at paras. 36–7, quoting Arden LJ in (*R (Williamson)* v. *Secretary of State for Education and Employment* [2003] QB 1300 at para. 252.

is clear that the courts tend strongly and generally towards (i) non-interference with internal affairs of religions, (ii) neutrality among religions and (iii) a view of religion as a matter for the individual conscience alone. All this is very much in line with Dworkinian jurisprudence.

The third trend is a tendency for collective liberty to be reworked as a matter of individual rights. This is largely the triumphal story of equality and human rights law. In 1985, for example, the philosopher Alan Ryan concluded a discussion on Rawls by stating: 'British politics is unaccustomed to a strenuous insistence on people's rights.'[169] By 2015, however, the celebrated activist lawyer Shami Chakrabarti (as she then was) could safely declare that 'human rights are the only truly universal language other than war'.[170] Elevated by Dworkin from the fringes of legal practice, rights became the new 'moral lingua franca' and acquired an ideological, even religious, status at the heart of public discourse.[171] This has been interpreted in the academy '[as] a sign [not] of a movement going off-track, but rather of its continuing relevance and attraction'.[172] The courts have accordingly adopted the view that the collective dimension to religious liberty is merely a derivative interest, that is, 'that collective rights are an important aspect of individual rights, but … they derive their value from individual interests. Full enjoyment of the individual interest in freedom of religion entails a measure of protection for the collective expression of that freedom, but collective rights gain their validity and value from the individuals who make up the collective.'[173] The law seems to reflect this position: 'When a church body lodges an application under the Convention[,] it does so, in reality, on behalf of its members. It should, therefore, be accepted that a church body is capable of possessing and exercising the rights contained in Article 9(1) in its own capacity as a representative of its members.'[174] This is all part of a broader pattern.

Whenever a common culture breaks down and a diversifying population loses its shared reference points, law rushes in to fill the void. For example, the doctrine of binding precedent arose in this way as judicial appeals to literature, history and scripture became increasingly impractical.[175] Similarly, the British

[169] Alan Ryan, 'John Rawls' in Quentin Skinner (ed.), *The Return of Grand Theory in the Human Sciences* (Cambridge: Cambridge University Press, 1985), p. 118.

[170] Shami Chakrabarti, 'On Liberty, Reading and Dissent' (The Reading Agency, 30 November 2015).

[171] Lorenzo Zucca, 'Exit Hercules: Ronald Dworkin and the Crisis of the Age of Rights' in Salman Khurshid, Lokendra Malik and Veronica Rodriguez-Blanco (eds.), *Dignity in the Legal and Political Philosophy of Ronald Dworkin* (Oxford: Oxford University Press, 2018), pp. 326, 332; Nick Spencer, 'The Religion of Christianity and the Religion of Human Rights' (Theos, 2018); Roger Scruton, 'The Religion of Rights' (BBC Radio 4, 3 September 2017).

[172] David Petrasek, 'Human Rights "Inflation" – What's the Problem?' (OpenGlobalRights, 19 February 2020).

[173] Lucy Vickers, *Religious Freedom, Religious Discrimination & The Workplace* (Oxford: Hart, 2008), p. 42.

[174] *X & The Church of Scientology* v. *Sweden*, No. 7805/77 16 DR 68 (1979) at 70.

[175] A. W. B. Simpson, 'The Ratio Decidendi of a Case and the Doctrine of Binding Precedent' in A. G. Guest (ed.), *Oxford Essays in Jurisprudence* (Oxford: Oxford University Press, 1961), pp. 148–75.

constitution has become less political and more legalistic over the past century, especially now that it is jealously guarded by a Supreme Court.[176] Senior judges have acquired celebrity status; one is even the subject of a saccharine hagiography aimed at young children and self-describes as 'world famous'.[177] Another has been quite open about the rightfulness of unaccountable judicial activism: 'Judges have a legitimate law-making function . . . The common law is judge-made law.'[178] The British public has become more litigious in general and has a greater propensity to sue than it did in 1970.[179] In the early 2000s, new barristers' chambers were set up to capitalise on the human rights legislation then coming into force.[180] Modern tort law is perceived as a deterrent against heroism and other socially beneficial activities.[181] Claims that once would never have been entertained are now being heard.[182] This in turn has attracted strong judicial condemnation: 'after every mishap, every tragedy, the cupped palms are outstretched for the solace of monetary compensation'.[183] There is a growing sense that 'the pursuit of an unrestrained culture of blame and compensation has many evil consequences and one is certainly . . . interference with the liberty of the citizen'.[184] Most recently, activists have weaponised public law and established that strategic litigation can serve their ends better than the political process.[185] The list goes on. The upshot is that the radius of social trust narrows as the general population finds it harder to relate to one another on any basis other than as wronged individuals and in any terms other than law.[186] The practical outcome is that British

[176] Adam Tomkins, *Public Law* (Oxford: Clarendon Law Series, Oxford University Press, 2003); Sir Stephen Laws, 'There Are Substantial and Unacceptable Risks in Moving to a Legal Constitution from Our Current Political One' (LSE Blog, 15 September 2014).

[177] Afua Hirsch and Henny Beaumont, *Equal to Everything: Judge Brenda and the Supreme Court* (London: Legal Action Group, 2019); Joshua Rozenberg, 'An Insider's Account of the Brenda Agenda' (*Law Society Gazette*, 3 February 2020).

[178] *Re Spectrum Plus Ltd* [2005] UKHL 41 per Nicholls LJ at para. 32.

[179] My thanks go to Professor Richard Mullender for sharing his superb lecture series on 'Tort Law and Blame Culture' at Newcastle Law School. See Annette Morris, 'Spiralling or Stabilising? The Compensation Culture and Our Propensity to Claim Damages for Personal Injury' (2007) 70(3) *Modern Law Review* 349–78. See, however, Kevin Williams, 'State of Fear: Britain's "Compensation Culture" Reviewed' (2005) 25(3) *Legal Studies* 499–514.

[180] Matrix Chambers, 'About Us' (accessed 15 February 2021): www.matrixlaw.co.uk/about-us/; Linda Tsang, 'A Change of Order at the Bar' (*The Independent*, 16 August 2013).

[181] Compensation Act 2006 and Social Action, Responsibility and Heroism Act 2015.

[182] Jane Stapleton, 'In Restraint of Tort' in Peter Birks (ed.), *The Frontiers of Liability* (Oxford: Oxford University Press, 1994), pp. 83–4.

[183] *John Munroe (Acrylics) Ltd* v. *London Fire and Civil Defence Authority and others* [1996] 4 All ER 318 at 322.

[184] *Tomlinson* v. *Congleton Borough Council* [2003] UKHL 47 at para. 81. See also Patrick S. Attiyah, *The Damages Lottery* (Oxford: Hart, 1997).

[185] See, for example, *R (Miller)* v. *Secretary of State for Exiting the European Union* [2017] UKSC 5; *R (on the application of Miller)* v. *The Prime Minister, Cherry and others* v. *Advocate General for Scotland* [2019] UKSC 41; *R (on the application of Friends of the Earth Ltd and others) (Respondents)* v. *Heathrow Airport Ltd (Appellant)* [2020] UKSC 52.

[186] Richard Mullender, 'Truth, Bullshit, and Blame Culture' (2015) 11(2) *Legal Ethics* (2015) 273–84.

society is more dependent on law and lawyers than ever before. This is despite persistent concerns over judicial representativeness and the tendency of the legal profession to disregard any limits of the law by treating politics and policy as litigable.[187]

1.3 Counter-Trends and Declining Influence

Liberal individualism explains a great deal behind these trends and is, for the most part, the interpretive logic behind the law. Even so, it is a problematic reading of what is going on in the English law of religion, both in terms of its explanatory power – there are notable counter-trends – and in terms of its desirability as a comprehensive programme for reform. To draw upon Dworkin's method of interpretative integrity, liberal individualism is far from ideal as a model theory because its prescriptions do not 'fit' the whole picture and it cannot cast the best possible light upon the English legal system so as to present it at its most balanced, coherent and illustrious.

First, the general retreat of political and legal establishment from the religious sphere is counteracted in significant ways. Although the law attempts to operate under a neutral framework and the courts generally refrain from oversight, they will intervene 'when the parties to the dispute have deliberately left the sphere of matter spiritual over which the religious body has exclusive jurisdiction and engaged in matters that are regulated by the civil courts'.[188] Where a person's civil rights have been infringed, such as in a case of discrimination, '[h]owever distasteful or offensive this may appear to be to some, it is an issue in an area regulated by a statute that must be faced up to. It must be resolved by applying the law laid down by Parliament according to the principles that have been developed by the civil courts.'[189] This principle was laid down in *Forbes* v. *Eden* where it was held that '[a] Court of Law will not interfere with the rules of a voluntary association, unless to protect some civil right or interest which is said to be infringed by their operation'.[190] The recent case of *Shergill* v. *Khaira* gives a clear statement of the current law.[191] It held that there are two categories of case which are non-justiciable. The first is 'where the issue in question is beyond the constitutional competence assigned to the courts under our conception of the separation of powers', such as transactions between states or proceedings in Parliament.[192] The court cannot

[187] Owen Bowcott, 'White and Male UK Judiciary "from Another Planet", Says Lady Hale' (*The Guardian*, 1 January 2019); N. W. Barber, Richard Ekins and Paul Yowell (eds.), *Lord Sumption and the Limits of the Law* (Oxford: Hart, 2016); Jonathan Sumption, *Trials of the State: Law and the Decline of Politics* (London: Profile Books, 2019). For the related problem of judicial deference to unelected administrators, see Adrian Vermeule, *Law's Abnegation: From Law's Empire to the Administrative State* (Cambridge, MA: Harvard University Press, 2016).

[188] *R (on the application of E)* v. *JFS Governing Body* [2009] UKSC 15 at para. 158.

[189] Para. 160. [190] (1867) LR 1 Sc & Div 568 at 568. [191] (2014) UKSC 33.

[192] *Buttes Gas and Oil Co.* v. *Hammer (No 3)* (1982) AC 888; *Prebble* v. *Television New Zealand Ltd* (1995) 1 AC 321.

adjudicate upon such areas even if another justiciable issue depends upon its resolution.[193] The second category covers cases involving neither private legal rights/obligations nor reviewable matters of public law and where the court is asked to decide things such as domestic disputes or international law purely in the abstract. It may resolve such a matter if some other justiciable issue turns upon it.[194] Thus, 'disputes about doctrine or liturgy are non-justiciable if they do not as a consequences engage civil rights or reviewable questions of public law'.[195] Where a voluntary religious association is divided on doctrine, the court will not simply follow the majority of adherents but 'will go to the part of the body that adheres to its fundamental religious principles, as identified in its contract of association'.[196] This means that 'the governing bodies of a religious voluntary association obtain their powers over its members by contract. They must act within the powers conferred by the association's contractual constitution.'[197] In sum: 'The jurisdiction of the court is not excluded because [there] is a dispute about theology or ecclesiology. The civil court does not resolve the religious dispute . . . Its role is more modest: it keeps the parties to their contract.'[198]

Despite its pretentions to neutral non-interference, liberal individualism 'contemplates a relatively large space . . . for governmental moralising'.[199] This can be seen in the notorious 'gay cake' litigation from Northern Ireland, *Lee* v. *Ashers Baking Company Ltd & Others*.[200] The facts were these. Mr Gareth Lee ordered a cake from Ashers Baking (run by Mr and Mrs McArthur) which was to be emblazoned with 'Support Gay Marriage'. Ashers initially accepted the order, but they later rescinded it, apologised and refunded Mr Lee because they thought of themselves as 'a Christian business' and as such could not print such a slogan. Mr Lee was able to get another cake from a different bakery in time for his event, but he claimed that he had been discriminated against either on grounds of sexual orientation or on grounds of religious belief or political opinion. The Supreme Court held that the bakers' objection to the slogan was dissociable from these protected characteristics and so could not be direct discrimination.[201] Lady Hale further explained that, despite the possibility that Mr Lee was discriminated against based on his political beliefs, the law 'must not be read or given effect in such a way as to compel providers of goods, facilities and services to express a message with which they disagree, unless justification is shown'.[202] This prompted Mr Lee's Equality Commission for Northern Ireland (ECNI) representative to claim that 'this judgment appears to say that companies are allowed to have beliefs, not the individuals but the companies, and that somehow that belief trumps, takes precedence over,

193 Para. 42. 194 Para. 43. 195 Para. 46.

196 *Craigdallie* v. *Aikman* (1813) 1 Dow 1, 14–16 at para. 51. 197 Para. 47. 198 Para. 48.

199 James E. Fleming, 'Taking Responsibilities as well as Rights Seriously' (2010) 90 *Boston University Law Review* 839–55, pp. 840, 843.

200 [2018] UKSC 49. 201 Per Hale LJ at paras. 21–3, 33–4. 202 Para. 56.

the beliefs, if any, of people looking for the service'.[203] The judgment was explicit that this was not the case: 'In holding that the company is not liable, this court is not holding that the company has rights under Article 9; rather, it is upholding the rights of the McArthurs under that article.'[204] Though an eventual victory for the bakers, this row over a £36.50 cake took more than four years of litigation and incurred over £500,000 in costs, half of which was public money spent by the ECNI.[205] The case has even now been referred to the European Court of Human Rights.[206] Final outcome pending and aside, the litigation is a striking example of moral aggression. One eminent liberal commentator's interpretation is illustrative in this regard: 'The issues on which Christians particularly tend to rest their case for intolerance and persecution turn out to be, in any sane historical perspective, absurdly tiny – the possibility, for instance, that a fundamentalist baker might be forced to bake a gay cake.'[207] In other words, those who dissent from the principles of public egalitarianism are parochial bigots labouring under trivial religious delusions, deserving to be hit by the full force of the state. That this jeopardises protections for conscientious objectors, and that public funds were wasted on quixotic moralising, and that the whole sequence of litigation was grossly disproportionate to the inconvenience suffered are all concerns that pass liberal individualism by.

Second, the attempt to treat matters involving collective liberty as purely individualistic phenomena does not explain the law and creates major problems for religious organisations because religious liberty is not only for individuals.[208] Numerous scholars have shown that individual rights inadequately explain important aspects of the current law and cannot afford adequate protection to religious communities.[209] Yet the diminutive size and the relative obscurity of this material are further proof that collective liberty

203 Lauren Harte, 'Equality Commission Boss Defends £500,000 Legal Bill for Ashers Gay Cake Case' (*Belfast Telegraph*, 11 October 2018), 'Video: Statements after Supreme Court Victory for Ashers in Gay Cake Case'.

204 Para. 57.

205 BBC News, 'Ashers "Gay Cake" Row: Bakers Win Supreme Court Appeal' (*BBC News*, 10 October 2018).

206 BBC News, 'Ashers "Gay Cake" Row Referred to European Court' (*BBC News*, 19 August 2019).

207 Adam Gopnik, *A Thousand Small Sanities: The Moral Adventure of Liberalism* (New York: Basic Books, 2019), p. 137. See also Mel Cousins, 'Taking Equal Protection beyond Its Proper Scope? Why People With Sincere Religious Beliefs Can Continue to Discriminate' (2019) 41(2) *Journal of Social Welfare and Family Law* 222–4, pp. 223–4 which accuses Lady Hale's judgment of being 'the court's worst equality ruling in recent decades' and an example of 'British elites supporting religious intolerance'.

208 Rivers, *Law of Organized Religions*, p. 317.

209 Ibid., pp. 318–22; Nicholas Aroney, 'Freedom of Religion as an Associational Right' (2014) 33 (1) *University of Queensland Law Journal*, pp. 153–86; Rex Adhar and Ian Leigh, *Religious Freedom in the Liberal State* (2nd ed., Oxford: Oxford University Press, 2015), ch. 11; Jane Calderwood Norton, *Freedom of Religious Organizations* (Oxford: Oxford University Press, 2016).

and groups as such are but a curious afterthought in a thought-world so utterly dominated by liberal individualism. Regardless, on the former point, modern law certainly recognises a collective dimension to religious liberty. The UN's Universal Declaration of Human Rights Article 18 holds: 'Everyone has the right to freedom of thought, conscience and religion; this right includes freedom to change his religion or belief, and freedom, either alone or *in community with others* and in public or private, to manifest his religion or belief in teaching, practice, worship and observance' (emphasis added). Article 9(1) of the European Convention on Human Rights (ECHR) provides for 'the right to freedom of thought, conscience and religion; this right includes freedom to change his religion or belief, and freedom, either alone or *in community with others* and in public or private, to manifest his religion or belief, in worship, teaching, practice, and observance' (emphasis added), while Article 11(1) establishes 'the right to freedom of peaceful assembly and to freedom of association with others'. Religious organisations can be victims for the purposes of Article 34 ECHR and are able to bring claims for alleged breaches of their human rights regardless of whether or not they have legal personality.[210] In *Metropolitan Church of Bessarabia and Others* v. *Moldova*, the Court stated:

> [S]ince religious communities traditionally exist in the form of organised structures, Article 9 must be interpreted in the light of Article 11 of the Convention, which safeguards associative life against unjustified state interference . . . Indeed, the autonomous existence of religious communities is indispensable for pluralism in a democratic society and is thus an issue at the very heart of the protection which Article 9 affords.[211]

Likewise, in *Hasan and Chaush* v. *Bulgaria*, the Court recognised that 'religious communities traditionally and universally exist in the form of organized structures . . . Participation in the life of the community is thus a manifestation of one's religion, protected by Article 9.'[212] In *Ahmad* v. *UK*, the Court stated that 'the right to manifest one's religion "in community with others" has always been regarded as an essential part of the freedom of religion'.[213] On this point, 'legal entity status for religious communities is a prerequisite to genuine freedom of conscience'.[214]

The UK's Human Rights Act (HRA) 1998 section 13(1) holds: 'If a court's determination of any question arising under this Act might affect the *exercise by a religious organisation (itself or its members collectively)* of the Convention

[210] Julian Rivers, 'Religious Liberty as a Collective Right' in Richard O'Dair and Andrew Lewis (eds.), *Law and Religion* (Oxford: Oxford University Press, 2001), p. 228; *X & Church of Scientology* v. *Sweden*, No 7805/77, 16 DR 68 (5.5.79); *Christian Association of Jehova's Witnesses* v. *Bulgaria*, No 28626/95, 90 DR 77 (3.7.97.).

[211] (2001) no 45701/99 2001 at para. 118. [212] (2000) HUDOC (ECHR) at para. 62.

[213] (1981) 4 EHRR 165 (ECHR) at para. 41.

[214] A. Lekhel quoted in Peter W. Edge, *Religion and Law: An Introduction* (London: Ashgate, 2006), p. 42.

right to freedom of thought, conscience and religion, it must have particular regard to the importance of that right' (emphasis added). Section 11 establishes that HRA 1998 should not endanger the traditional rights, liberties and privileges which pre-date it. This is especially significant in the law of charities under which religious associations can benefit from significant financial advantages seeing as section 3(1)(c) of the Charities Act 2011 recognises 'the advancement of religion' as a legitimate charitable purpose.[215] In brief, religious associations have basic rights to legal entity status (although not necessarily corporate personhood) and internal structural autonomy (internal ordering and regulation), as well as to select, train, appoint and dismiss leaders; establish places of worship and meeting; raise funds; uphold religious community life; access restricted institutions such as schools, hospitals and prisons; provide educational, charitable and humanitarian institutions such as schools; enjoy a public presence through activities such as printing and disseminating religious material; and enjoy protection from hostile acts of third-party individuals or groups as well as from the state.[216] Organised religions also enjoy a range of exemptions from discrimination and equality law.[217] More specifically, religious associations, unlike individuals, are denied the right to freedom of conscience, although 'it is far from clear why a freethinking individual should be able to object to a church tax on the grounds of freedom of thought, conscience and religion, but a freethinking association is unable to object'.[218] They have also been denied the right to privacy, even though 'cases could arise in which confidential information is held primarily about the activities of an organisation, and in which the association might be the proper victim' in the event of a breach.[219]

As regards the latter point, an overemphasis on individualism can be detrimental to faith communities and undermine their protection. Numerous problems for religious associations arise from this attitude as individualised rights are 'inherently weak' in their ability to protect religious liberty.[220] For one, they require the courts to balance individual and public interest: the general rules which might burden the religious individual by making it difficult for them to practise are formulated to maximise public interest and so decisions tend to go against the individual. Also, the courts treat as equal the representatives of religious collectives and individuals who simply hold unconventional beliefs along with 'all the weakness in position [for the

215 Rivers, 'Religious Liberty as a Collective Right', p. 237.

216 Rivers, *Law of Organized Religions*, pp. 56–69.

217 Hill et al., *Religion and Law*, pp. 79–80; Sandberg, *Law and Religion*, pp. 117–28; Rivers, 'Religious Liberty as a Collective Right', pp. 233–6.

218 Rivers, *Law of Organized Religions*, p. 69; Rivers, 'Religious Liberty as a Collective Right', p. 228 footnote 10; *Verein 'Kontakt-Information-Therapie' and Hagen* v. *Austria*, no. 11921/86 (1988).

219 Rivers, *Law of Organized Religions*, p. 70; *Church of Scientology of Paris* v. *France*, No. 19509/92 (1995).

220 Rivers, *Law of Organized Religions*, pp. 320–2.

believer] which this implies'.[221] Further, individual rights were historically envisaged as rights against the state, 'yet were cast in universal terms' and now 'double up as rights against everyone' so that there is now 'a presumption that non-state actors should respect these rights as well'.[222] This has had the effect of generating 'a growing assumption that everyone who wishes should be able to join any religious body, or that membership tests are suspect' and so the individual, not the religious body, determines their qualification for membership.[223] This 'individualising of religious liberty against the religious community', a doctrine once intended for 'state-versus-individual' disputes, has come to be 'potentially destructive of the identity of non-state collectivities' and the ethos of civil society more generally.[224]

For Julian Rivers, *Kustannus* v. *Sweden* represents 'a clear example of a failure to recognise collective religious liberty'.[225] The Commission here held that a humanist association was not a religious community or non-profit organisation for Article 9 when it objected to a Swedish law which required it, as majority shareholder in its own company, to pay a church tax against its conscience (even though individuals would have been protected from this). Yet Rivers observes that a more conspicuous example of a neglect of collective religious liberty occurred in *Serif* v. *Greece*.[226] In this case, a man claimed to be the proper Chief Mufti of Rodopi in Thrace in opposition to the Greek government's appointed mufti and was convicted of various offences including usurping the functions of a religious minister. The Court completely missed the point as it accepted that the man's religious liberty had been breached and asked whether or not his conviction was necessary under Article 9(2). He had not sought to officiate at weddings, etc., so his conviction rested on the fact that he merely wore the clothes associated with the office and issued spiritual advice. Even though he wasn't the official mufti, his conviction on these bases was an unjustifiable breach of liberty. Rivers notes that this amounts to saying merely that 'people have the right to pretend to be clergy if they wish' and that the real issue was in fact about who had the right under Greek law to appoint the chief mufti and whether the Muslim community had a collective right under the ECHR to elect their own spiritual leader. In short, 'the Court ducked that central issue'.[227]

An interesting and relevant recent example can be drawn from the Canadian Supreme Court decision in *Loyola High School* v. *Quebec (Attorney General)*.[228] In this case, a Catholic school sought from the relevant minister an exemption from a general law which required all schools to deliver a neutral programme of religious education which did not favour a particular belief system unless they could show that their alternative scheme was 'equivalent' to

[221] Ibid., p. 321. [222] Ibid. [223] Ibid. [224] Ibid., p. 322.

[225] Rivers, 'Religious Liberty as a Collective Right', p. 230; (1996) No. 20471/92 (15.4.96); *Kustannus Oy Vapaa Ajattelija Ab* v. *Finland* (Application No 20471/92).

[226] (1999) No. 38178/97; Rivers, 'Religious Liberty as a Collective Right', pp. 230–1.

[227] Rivers, *Law of Organized Religions*, p. 52. [228] (2015) SCC 12.

the state programme. The exemption request was refused because significant parts of the school's scheme would be taught from a Catholic perspective when it should, according to the minister, be neutral in its entirety. The Loyola school launched an action for judicial review. It was held that the minister's decision was not reasonable as it did not proportionately balance the need to promote tolerance with the need to ensure adequate provision for religious freedom. Significantly in this case, the court stressed the collective institutional aspect of religious freedom. Justice Abella held that the court must 'account for the socially embedded nature of religious belief, and the deep linkages between this belief and its manifestation through communal institutions and traditions'.[229] She quoted Justice LeBel in recognising that '[r]eligion is about religious beliefs, but also about religious relationships'.[230] As such:

> These collective aspects of religious freedom – in this case, the collective manifestation and transmission of Catholic beliefs through a private denominational school – are a crucial part of Loyola's claim ... The Minister's decision therefore demonstrably interferes with the manner in which the members of an institution formed for the very purpose of transmitting Catholicism[] can teach and learn about the Catholic faith.[231]

Chief Justice Moldaver pointed out that the court had previously affirmed that freedom of religion 'has both an individual and a collective dimension [which are] indissolubly intertwined. The freedom of religion of individuals cannot flourish without freedom of religion for the organizations through which those individuals express their religious practices and through which they transmit their faith.'[232] In sum, 'the collective aspect of freedom of religion should find protection'.[233]

Finally, there are signs that liberal individualism has become a victim of its own success and is declining in influence. Katrina Forrester suggests a twofold problem.[234] First, that modern liberalism established such a durable monopoly over political discourse that it was mistaken for common sense itself. Every potential rival – from progressive feminism to neo-liberal conservativism – had to contort itself to fit with rights-based egalitarianism before it could be regarded as serious or decent.[235] Beyond the Overton Window, however, alternative visions for social order were incubating even as it became 'increasingly difficult even to define critical questions, let alone debate and resolve

[229] Para. 60. [230] Para. 59. [231] Para. 61. [232] Paras. 92–4. [233] Para. 97.

[234] See generally Katrina Forrester, *In the Shadow of Justice: Postwar Liberalism and the Remaking of Political Philosophy* (Princeton, NJ: Princeton University Press, 2019).

[235] See also Katrina Forrester, 'The Future of Political Philosophy' (*Boston Review*, 17 September 2019); Katrina Forrester, 'The Crisis of Liberalism: Why Centrist Politics Can No Longer Explain the World' (*The Guardian*, 18 November 2019); Anne Schult and Jonas Knatz, '"We'll Need More Than Rawlsianism Can Offer": Katrina Forrester on John Rawls and Anglo-American Political Philosophy after 1945' (Journal of the History of Ideas Blog, 18 December 2019); Florence Sutcliffe-Braithwaite and Katrina Forrester, 'Liberal Egalitarianism: What's Worth Salvaging?' (*Renewal: A Journal of Social Democracy*, 10 January 2020).

them'.[236] The resulting torpor built for decades until 2016, when all manner of competitors – from 'luxury communism' to Traditionalism – burst back upon the scene to the shock and horror of the political establishment.[237] Second, Rawls and Dworkin were so effective as theorists that practical utility and historical contingency were neglected for abstract coherence. Despite his ardent justification for the right to free speech, for example, Dworkin signally failed to defend its exercise when it mattered most in the face of murderous fanaticism during the Danish Cartoons controversy.[238] Further, the attractiveness of liberal individualism has been heavily dependent on the unprecedented prosperity and security of property-owning democracies. So long as these conditions lasted, liberals could safely assume that political disagreement had been confined to minor quibbles over rights, internationalism, social welfare and diversity promotion. Once these fortunate circumstances began to wane, the ominous historical developments whose significance they obscured – financial deregulation, privatisation, rising house prices, intergenerational discord, terror attacks by non-state actors – compounded to make modern liberalism appear morally and intellectually bankrupt.[239] This much is evident from the cross-partisan reaction against the 'strident language of rights'.[240] For Mary Ann Glendon, 'rights talk' is characterised by 'its starkness and simplicity, its prodigality in bestowing the rights label, its legalistic character, its exaggerated absoluteness, its hyperindividualism, its insularity, and its silence with respect to personal, civic, and collective responsibilities'.[241] For the Marxist scholar Alan Hunt, it also places 'unwarrantable confidence in the capacity of law to realise the political and ethical goals of community and fraternity', while, for Nigel Biggar, it endangers the defences of the very nations championing it.[242] These concerns are starting to enter English law. At the time of writing, the Overseas Operations (Service Personnel and Veterans) Bill, which will restrict claims against the Armed Forces in the wake of multiple scandals involving false allegations and vexatious litigation, is working its way through Parliament.[243] The government has also established an independent

[236] Mary Ann Glendon, *Rights Talk: The Impoverishment of Political Discourse* (New York: Free Press, 1991), p. x.

[237] Aaron Bastani, *Fully Automated Luxury Communism: A Manifesto* (London: Verso, 2019); Benjamin R. Teitelbaum, *War for Eternity: The Return of Traditionalism and the Rise of the Populist Right* (London: Allen Lane, 2020); Joshua Green, *Devil's Bargain: Steve Bannon, Donald Trump, and the Nationalist Uprising* (2nd ed., London: Penguin, 2018).

[238] Ronald Dworkin, 'The Right to Ridicule' (*New York Review*, 23 March 2006).

[239] See Joel Harrison, *Post-Liberal Religious Liberty: Forming Communities of Charity* (Cambridge: Cambridge University Press, 2020); Patrick J. Deneen, *Why Liberalism Failed* (London: Yale University Press, 2019); John Milbank and Adrian Pabst, *The Politics of Virtue: Post-Liberalism and the Human Future* (Lanham, MD: Rowman & Littlefield, 2016); Giles Fraser, 'A Post-Liberal Reading List' (*Unherd*, 22 November 2019).

[240] Glendon, *Rights Talk*, p. x. [241] Ibid.

[242] Hunt, *Reading Dworkin Critically*, p. 13; Nigel Biggar, *What's Wrong with Rights?* (Oxford: Oxford University Press, 2020), chs. 10 and 12.

[243] Claire Mills and Joanna Dawson, 'Overseas Operations (Service Personnel and Veterans) Bill 2019–21' (House of Commons Library: Briefing Paper Number 8983, 22 September 2020).

judicial review panel with further promises to scrutinise the HRA 1998 and 'activist lawyers'.[244] Tellingly, an elegiac Festschrift for Dworkin recently conceded that the 'noble dream' and the 'golden age' of rights have given way to a terminal crisis.[245] The lesson for the jurist, seemingly, is this: study law, history, economics, politics and sociology in equal measure or risk losing all relevance in the real world.[246]

1.4 Conclusion

The English law of religion is heavily indebted to liberal individualism. The Dworkinian formula explains the main trends and remains the dominant ethos behind much contemporary jurisprudence: the inflation of protectable beliefs, a reluctance to become involved in internal religious affairs, translating collective liberty into rights claims. Regulating religion on these grounds provides systematic coherence and uncompromising safeguards against the power of church and state. These concrete benefits are indispensable components of the law of religion. That said, liberal individualism does not explain everything and is not without practical difficulties. One drawback is the relatively clumsy approach to neutrality as regards disputes within religious groups and objections to the scope of equality law. Its most consequential defect, however, is an impoverished conception of groups. The law cannot, and does not, rely upon a framework of purely individual and derivative rights as collective religious liberty is not simply an aggregation of individual members' interests; it is a set of rights, immunities, privileges and powers held by a religious association as such.[247] Treating non-state entities as a mere aggregation of individuals whose existence depends on legal recognition is both 'descriptively inaccurate and prescriptively unappealing' – it points towards a kind of statism that threatens the integrity of groups which challenge state power or adhere to an ethos that runs against public-sphere egalitarianism.[248] As shall be seen, it also makes it difficult to understand collective agency whenever informal-but-tangible groups are involved in harmful activities. These problems seem to have contributed to the recent and possibly irreversible slump in its fortunes. As Lord Denning once noted about religious liberty: 'As so often happens with high-sounding principles, they have to be brought down to earth.'[249] Liberal individualism is just not the best way to do it.

[244] Ministry of Justice, 'Government Launches Independent Panel to Look at Judicial Review' (HMG, 31 July 2020); BBC News, 'Boris Johnson and Priti Patel "Should Apologise for Lawyer Attacks"' (*BBC News*, 26 October 2020).

[245] Zucca, 'Exit Hercules: Ronald Dworkin and the Crisis of the Age of Rights', pp. 313–32.

[246] Forrester, *In the Shadow of Justice*, pp. 278–9.

[247] Rivers, 'Religious Liberty as a Collective Right', p. 231.

[248] Rivers, *Law of Organized Religions*, p. 322.

[249] *Ahmad* v. *Inner London Education Authority* [1978] QB 36 at 41.

2

Multiculturalism

The analysis was the most difficult of the three by all odds. When Holk, after two days of steady work, succeeded in eliminating meaningless statements, vague gibberish, useless qualifications – in short, all the goo and dribble – he found he had nothing left. Everything cancelled out.[1]

2.1 An Introduction to Bhikhu Parekh and Tariq Modood

Multiculturalism has two distinct meanings. The first is purely descriptive – it denotes the uncontentious fact of cultural diversity whereby a multitude of different cultures exist within a single society. The second is normative – it refers to a prescriptive programme aimed at promoting such diversity for its own sake through a process of institutionalisation involving the recognition, accommodation and endorsement of these different cultural identities as equals. This is multiculturalism as 'a new ideology or political theory – it is the latest "ism"'.[2] This chapter is concerned with the latter usage (and hereafter the term 'multicultural' will be used to denote policies or laws inspired by, or falling within, this tradition). This is chiefly because British multiculturalism was developed to guide government policy towards Islam following large-scale Muslim immigration to the UK in the post-war period. More than any other group, Muslims have 'become central to the merits and demerits of multiculturalism as a public policy'.[3]

Normative multiculturalism is an unmistakable product of the 1990s and is now best accessed through this milieu. Though not far distant in time, it was a very different age from today. An infectious sense of optimism and boundless possibility pervaded politics to a degree now unimaginable. The collapse of the Soviet Union in 1991 had removed the last truly existential threat to Western societies. The end of history was proclaimed and liberal intervention abroad had yet to be discredited. China was viewed as a promising partner on the international stage. At home, energy and property were as cheap as politics was stable and mundane. The KLF took Dadaism and cultural appropriation to new heights. The biggest domestic concerns were football hooliganism, illegal

[1] Isaac Asimov, *Foundation* (London: Folio Society, 2012), p. 73.
[2] Paul Kelly (ed.), *Multiculturalism Reconsidered* (Cambridge: Polity Press, 2002), p. 4.
[3] Tariq Modood, *Multiculturalism: A Civic Idea* (2nd ed., Cambridge: Polity Press, 2013), p. 4.

raves and the Millennium Dome. Bowl cuts and block colours were in vogue. Cool Britannia ruled the airwaves, the BBC's *This Life* made solicitors temporarily glamorous and *Loaded* magazine gleefully popularised lad culture. Tabloid journalism was at its pungent best. The Union Jack became an icon and celebrities wanted to be seen with politicians. Once the stuffy Major premiership was blown away by the 'geezer' Tony Blair and his Third Way, things could only get better. Lingering racial injustices – typified by the disastrous investigation into the murder of Stephen Lawrence – were to be attacked head on and righted. Britain would be opened up to business and the world through generous immigration reforms. The new Briton could be anyone from anywhere so long as they gave themselves and their heritage over to the diversification programme. The decade had begun with 'no real mood to catch', but it ended with New Labour in power and pressing ahead with its reformation of national identity and public values.[4]

Multiculturalism was both a driver and a beneficiary of this moment. Fittingly, it was championed by two nationalised migrants who had come to Britain a generation earlier and distinguished themselves as academics. Bhikhu Parekh (as he then was) was born in Gujarat, India in 1935. He was educated at the University of Bombay before moving to England with his wife in 1959 to pursue a doctorate at the London School of Economics. Thereafter, he studied and taught political theory at various universities, spending most of his career at the University of Hull. His work was recognised with appointments to various commissions (Racial Equality, Future of Multi-Ethnic Britain, Religion and Belief in British Public Life), prestigious fellowships and a seat in the House of Lords from 2000.[5] Tariq Modood was born in Karachi, Pakistan in 1952 before migrating to London with his family at the age of eight. He combined his studies at the Universities of Durham, Cardiff and Swansea with anti-racist activism. His sociological work on racial equality and British Muslims led to various positions on influential policy committees, academic fellowships, an MBE and a professorship at the University of Bristol.[6] In 1998, the Runnymede Trust think tank established the Commission on the Future of Multi-Ethnic Britain as a response to the 'many varieties of racism and exclusion that disfigure modern Britain', in

[4] This account is drawn from the following sources: Daniel Rachel, *Don't Look Back in Anger* (London: Trapeze, 2019); Richard Power Sayeed, *1997: The Future that Never Happened* (London: Zed, 2017); Alwyn W. Turner, *A Classless Society: Britain in the 1990s* (London: Aurum Press, 2014) pp. 7–8; John Harris, *The Last Party: Britpop, Blair and the Demise of English Rock* (London: Harper Perennial, 2004); John Higgs, *The KLF: Chaos, Magic and the Band Who Burned a Million Pounds* (London: W&N, 2012); Helen Thompson, 'The Illusions of the 1990s Have Been Shattered but the Decade Is Still Distorting World Politics' (*New Statesman*, 28 August 2019); Ben Sixsmith, 'I Hate the Nineties' (*Spectator USA*, 15 June 2020).

[5] Maya Jaggi, 'First Among Equalisers' (*The Guardian*, 21 October 2000).

[6] Damián Omar Martínez, 'Intellectual Biography, Empirical Sociology and Normative Political Theory: An Interview with Tariq Modood' (2013) 34(6) *Journal of Intercultural Studies* 729–41, pp. 730–1.

particular, 'aggressive hostility to Islam'.[7] Led by Parekh and advised by Modood, it completed its work in 2000 by publishing what is commonly referred to as the *Parekh Report*, which is perhaps 'the best public policy statement on multiculturalism in Britain'.[8] Through this and their other work, they would define multiculturalism for a generation and exert considerable influence over government policy towards religious minorities.

In contrast to liberalism, multiculturalism has no real equivalent of a canon. It is not, by Modood's own admission, 'a political philosophy in its own right, if by that is meant a comprehensive theory of politics'.[9] The closest it has come to that is in Bhikhu Parekh's *Rethinking Multiculturalism*, which Modood describes as a 'tour de force', although Parekh himself suggests that it is neither 'a political doctrine with a programmatic content nor ... a philosophical theory of man and the world'.[10] Taken as a whole, Parekh's work is more conceptual and self-contained within three major books, whereas Modood's writing is generally more applied and fragmentary, being scattered across numerous essays and collections. There is also a clear chain of transmission from Parekh to Modood and beyond. Modood acknowledges that Parekh 'is really the leading British theorist of multiculturalism'[11] and cites him as a 'mentor and role model'.[12] Parekh has in turn hailed Modood as a 'major theorist' whose essays 'amply justify his reputation'.[13] Together with various disciples who work on more specific issues, they make up the Bristol School of Multiculturalism (BSM).[14] The hub of this movement is the Centre for the Study of Ethnicity and Citizenship founded at the University of Bristol in 1999 and directed by Modood.[15] All members are united by a set of basic concerns about racism, social justice and empowerment.

Several features distinguish this school from its relatives. Though a broad, global church, multiculturalism is a hybrid 'child of liberal egalitarianism' and postmodernism in that it attempts to extend the principles of autonomy and equal treatment to cultural groups as well as to individuals.[16] Canada has

[7] Bhikhu Parekh et al., *The Future of Multi-Ethnic Britain: The Parekh Report* (London: The Runnymede Trust and Profile Books, 2000), p. 10.

[8] Modood, *Multiculturalism*, p. 16; Rumy Hasan, *Multiculturalism: Some Inconvenient Truths* (London: Politico Press, 2010), p. 24.

[9] Modood, ibid., p. 6.

[10] Ibid.; Bhikhu Parekh, *Rethinking Multiculturalism: Cultural Diversity and Political Theory* (2nd ed., London: Palgrave Macmillan, 2006), p. 336.

[11] Tariq Modood, 'The Best Books on Multiculturalism Recommended by Tariq Modood' (*Five Books*, 1 December 2010).

[12] Martinez, 'Intellectual Biography', p. 739.

[13] Cover endorsement on Tariq Modood, *Essays on Secularism and Multiculturalism* (Colchester: ECPR Press, 2019).

[14] Geoffrey Brahm Levey, 'The Bristol School of Multiculturalism' (2019) 19(1) *Ethnicities* (2019) 1–27.

[15] Geoffrey Brahm Levey, 'The Bristol School of Multiculturalism' (Research Outreach, February 2020) https://researchoutreach.org/wp-content/uploads/2020/02/Geoffrey-Levey-1.pdf.

[16] Nasar Meer and Tariq Modood, 'Theorising Intercultural Citizenship' in Nasar Meer, Tariq Modood and Ricard Zapata-Barrero (eds.), *Multiculturalism and Interculturalism: Debating the Dividing Lines* (Edinburgh: Edinburgh University Press, 2016), p. 2; James Tully,

produced an especially strong clutch of advocates, including Charles Taylor and Will Kymlicka. As a general rule, these liberal multiculturalists are concerned with improving outcomes for individuals as members of cultural minorities, typically within the North American context where the First Nations and Quebecois feature prominently. The aim is to accommodate their identities within the liberal value system by recognising group rights and designing welfare policies to conserve their practices. Although the practical differences may be overstated, the Bristol School rejects any 'liberal bias' whatever and purports to offer a more radical solution.[17] Parekh and Modood are concerned with groups first and individuals second. Their interest in 'the situation of flesh and blood people seeking recognition and inclusion' is on account of their being carriers of a particular cultural tradition.[18] Put simply, British multiculturalism in the abstract is 'a plea for equality of cultures';[19] in practice, it insists that 'cultural minorities need to pursue and assert their cultural interests and that governments should develop policies that accommodate these interests'.[20]

Multiculturalism may also be distinguished from interculturalism. The latter claims to be a 'more sophisticated phase' of multiculturalism 'which demands greater interethnic dialogue and interaction' than is required by its direct forerunner.[21] It has a range of distinguished advocates around the world and in Britain.[22] It is intended to be an 'emergent process with no necessary end point' that stresses dialogue and interconnectedness over separateness and exceptionalism.[23] Identity is considered to be plural, dynamic and fluid instead of being a rigid absolute to be celebrated for its own sake.[24] This means fostering constructive encounters between cultural groups and state provision for their respective institutional forms.[25] Taken as a whole, the movement is essentially a cosmetic rebranding exercise which attempts to strip away the most toxic aspects of multiculturalism while retaining its 'laudable

'The Illiberal Liberal' in Kelly, *Multiculturalism Reconsidered*, p. 102; Varun Uberoi and Tariq Modood, 'The Emergence of the Bristol School of Multiculturalism' (2019) 19(6) *Ethnicities* 955–70, p. 957.

17 Will Kymlicka, 'Deschooling Multiculturalism' (2019) 19(6) *Ethnicities* 971–82.

18 Levey, 'The Bristol School of Multiculturalism' (Research Outreach, February 2020).

19 Parekh quoted in Jaggi, 'First Among Equalisers'.

20 Levey, 'The Bristol School of Multiculturalism' (Research Outreach, February 2020).

21 Ali Rattansi, *Multiculturalism: A Very Short Introduction* (Oxford: Oxford University Press, 2011), pp. 5–6.

22 Ibid.; Martha C. Nussbaum, *Cultivating Humanity: A Classical Defense of Reform in Liberal Education* (Cambridge, MA: Harvard University Press, 1998), p. 82; Ricard Zapata-Barrero, 'Theorising Intercultural Citizenship' in Meer, Modood and Zapata-Barrero (eds.), *Multiculturalism and Interculturalism*, ch. 6; Ted Cantle, 'About Interculturalism' (author's website, accessed 15 February 2021) http://tedcantle.co.uk/publications/about-interculturalism/.

23 Rattansi, *Multiculturalism*, pp. 153–8, 162–4.

24 Ted Cantle, 'Interculturalism: For the Era of Globalisation, Cohesion & Diversity' (2012) 3(3) *Political Insight* 38–41; Ted Cantle, 'National Identity, Plurality and Interculturalism' (2014) 85 (3) *Political Quarterly* 312–18.

25 Rattansi, *Multiculturalism*, pp. 152, 162–4.

sensitivities' and trying 'to avoid the charge of assimilation'.[26] The two have been treated synonymously by the Parliamentary Assembly of the Council of Europe and, as the multiculturalists themselves point out, it is very hard to see what this vague and seemingly effete offshoot contributes.[27] Interesting familial ties aside, however, the Bristol School must here remain the primary object of study.

2.2 Abstract Multiculturalism

Bhikhu Parekh has written widely on political philosophy and multiculturalism. *Rethinking Multiculturalism* is by far his most important book, although several articles, including 'A New Politics of Identity' and 'Ethnocentric Political Theory', also make noteworthy contributions to his corpus. The first of these is a comprehensive restatement of multicultural doctrine. Though it does discuss practical issues, it is largely a philosophical work which lays out the conceptual framework of the movement.

The moral foundations of multiculturalism rest on a standard critique of liberal individualism. Parekh argues that culture precedes justice in that social consensus is possible only if people living together accommodate one another's ways of life. In time, this openness to compromise will generate a level of commonality sufficient to stabilise society and sustain agreement on the requirements of justice. The 'settled convictions' of different groups must not be excluded or 'radically reinterpreted' to fit within a rationalistic liberal order but should be accommodated through alternative principles of justice designed to sustain social cooperation in myriad inclusive forms.[28] He rejects the liberal claim to neutrality by pointing out that it depends upon the privileging of a rationalistic conception of man which requires cultural groups to 'abstract away their comprehensive doctrines'.[29] There is no guarantee that such a political system will remain stable when swathes of the population with strong non-liberal beliefs are labelled unreasonable by an establishment prepared to ignore deep discontentment. Neutrality masks 'a large hidden agenda' of liberal reordering whereby all alternative worldviews across every area of life are subsumed and rendered anodyne. This process 'can easily violate the integrity of the texts and the tradition' and subordinates them to the political ends of the state.[30] Parekh further notes that liberalism constricts diversity by placing society under a regime of individual rights which operate to the disadvantage of non-conformist ways of life. If cultural minorities cannot use their traditional forms or see their deep convictions respected, 'such

[26] Cantle, 'Interculturalism', pp. 38–41; Hasan, *Multiculturalism*, pp. 194–5.

[27] Dorota A. Gozdecka, 'Religious Pluralism as a Legal Pluralism' in Russell Sandberg (ed.), *Religion and Legal Pluralism* (Farnham: Ashgate, 2015), p. 182; Nasar Meer and Tariq Modood, 'How Does Interculturalism Contrast with Multiculturalism?' (2011) 33(2) *Journal of Intercultural Studies* 175–96.

[28] Parekh, *Rethinking Multiculturalism*, pp. 85–6. [29] Ibid. [30] Ibid., pp. 86–8.

persons are likely to feel deeply alienated and unjustly treated, and might reject the society that has no space for them'.[31] Liberal individualism, in other words, ignores the cultural aspirations of communities and lacks the intellectual resources to accommodate their demands for differential treatment.[32] Britain is better thought of as 'both a community of citizens and a community of communities, both a liberal and a multicultural society, and needs to reconcile their sometimes conflicting requirements'.[33]

From this oppositional stance, Parekh builds his account of multicultural morality. Relativism is said to be an 'incoherent doctrine' because it disregards human universals and objective moral values; moral monism is likewise rejected because it insists that the good and the truth are singular and uniform rather than culturally constituted and mediated.[34] Humans are culturally embedded beings so it would be unjust to pass judgement on them 'without taking full account of the system of meaning, traditions, temperament and the moral and emotional resource of the people involved'.[35] Dworkin's idea of value as an integrated whole is 'naïve' because different ways of life are incommensurable.[36] In reality, Parekh suggests, universal values and the entrenched moral traditions of different societies are engaged in creative interplay, 'the latter domesticating and pluralizing the former and being in turn reinterpreted and revised in their light, thus leading to ... pluralist universalism'.[37] This hybrid doctrine is said to break the 'tired and dubious dichotomy' between the equally untenable poles of relativism and universalism.[38] He further explains that universal values do exist but their meaning, weight and applicability vary across the world, meaning that they must be contextualised and 'even relativized'.[39] On this basis, he elucidates a theory of 'global ethics' based on culturally contextualised rationality and cross-cultural dialogue.[40] These ethics are likewise to be treated as historically contingent so that they 'leave sufficient space for and respect the diversity of moral traditions'.[41] Human rights are analysed in much the same way. They are a 'precious and fragile achievement' with 'cross-cultural validity' and may provide 'valuable insights', but they can become 'hegemonic' by 'delegitimizing and even undermining the integrity of many valuable forms of moral and political sensibility' when their own 'meanings and implications are culturally mediated and ... their universality is appropriated and realised in culturally distinct forms'.[42] In the end, political concepts or institutions – values, law, rights, ethics – are valid only if they are 'widely accepted' as

[31] Ibid. [32] Ibid., pp. 89–90. [33] *Parekh Report*, p. ix.

[34] Parekh, *Rethinking Multiculturalism*, pp. 16, 127. [35] Ibid., p. 47. [36] Ibid., p. 48.

[37] Ibid. [38] Ibid., pp. 127, 349. [39] Ibid., pp. 358–9.

[40] Bhikhu Parekh, *A New Politics of Identity: Political Principles for an Interdependent World* (London: Macmillan International, 2008), pp. 178, 214.

[41] Ibid., p. 208.

[42] Bhikhu Parekh, 'Finding a Proper Place for Human Rights' in Kate E. Tunstall (ed.), *Displacement, Asylum, Migration* (Oxford: Oxford University Press, 2006), pp. 18–19.

part of a 'cross-cultural consensus' so that the rights are 'not culturally parochial or peculiarly liberal or Western'.[43]

The intelligibility of multicultural moral theory is open to question and it has been variously interpreted as 'profoundly conservative',[44] 'radical'[45] and broadly liberal.[46] One critic concludes: 'It may not be altogether Parekh's fault that his arguments are unconvincing and not altogether consistent. It may be that the whole "multi-cultural" project of equally respecting different cultures and ways of life in the same place is deeply flawed.'[47] Another detects an air of 'feigned innocence' hanging over Modood's work as a result of it being written in a deliberately obfuscatory way.[48] The seriousness of these charges and the scope for confusion can be seen in several of Parekh's speeches on female genital mutilation (FGM). In one speech he stated that 'we all know that female genital mutilation is a horrendous practice', but also that 'we should bear in mind how deeply seated in the consciousness of this community this practice is'.[49] In another he exclaimed that 'prosecution has to be far more vigorous than it has been', but then 'it is quite important to bear in mind that we are not objecting to female genital mutilation per se'.[50] It would be a mistake to look for Dworkinian coherence in these pronouncements or to doubt that Parekh sincerely believes all these things at once. They, and the moral core of multicultural theory, are best interpreted as expressions of emotivism as outlined by A. J. Ayer in *Language, Truth and Logic*.[51] Put briefly, it holds that there are no moral truths because one cannot go from facts to values and vice versa. When one expresses an ethical statement, it is no more than a proclamation of disapproval followed by an exhortation not to engage in frowned-upon behaviour. It can be made more emotionally emphatic, but it cannot be validated as a precept of justice. It follows that laws and policies are simply expressions of collective moral sentiments and will be instituted and enforced depending on popular feeling. Criminalising FGM does not make it wrong; it just indicates that it is strongly disapproved of within that society. This is colloquially known as the hurrah/boo theory and it enables adherents to hold contradictory beliefs, make self-negating statements or espouse an erratic kind of empathy while

43 Ibid., p. 25. 44 Hasan, *Multiculturalism*, p. 24.

45 David Goodhart, 'Wishful Thinking and Unresolved Tensions' (2019) 19(6) *Ethnicities* 983–90, p. 985.

46 Kymlicka, 'Deschooling Multiculturalism'.

47 Roger Trigg, 'Review of *A New Politics of Identity* by Bhikhu Parekh' (2009) 84(3) *Philosophy* 450–4, pp. 453–4; see also Goodhart, 'Wishful Thinking', p. 984.

48 Brian Barry, *Culture and Equality: An Egalitarian Critique of Multiculturalism* (Cambridge: Polity Press, 2001), p. 28 on Modood.

49 Bhikhu Parekh, *Hansard*, HL, Vol. 728, 30 June 2011, Debate on Female Genital Mutilation: https://hansard.parliament.uk/lords/2011-06-30/debates/11063052000909/FemaleGenitalMutilation.

50 Bhikhu Parekh, *Hansard*, HL, Vol. 750, 4 December 2013, Debate on Female Genital Mutilation: https://hansard.parliament.uk/Lords/2013-12-04/debates/13120487000081/details#contribution-13120491000013.

51 (London: Penguin, 2001), pp. 110–12.

remaining committed to all of them.[52] Whether or not the resulting laws are coherent, contribute anything positive or make things worse is beside the point. That diversity for its own sake may lead to increasing authoritarianism is beside the point.[53] The rules are that there are no rules, objective good is a contradiction in terms, universalism is pretentious and only authenticity and strength of feeling matter.

In practical terms, pluralised universalism requires an uncompromising commitment to compromise.[54] With this comes an aversion to eristic discourse, or the Socratic method. For Parekh, those who engage in it are indecent 'exhibitionists' taking 'perverse pride in knocking established values';[55] for Modood, there must be 'personal and institutional self-restraint . . . to avoid disrespect, offence and provocation, and to prevent fear and humiliation' as well as 'to show courtesy, civility and respect'.[56] The latter even claims that his students 'are dismayed that philosophy can be so barren and surprised that Socrates does not sometimes get a physical beating . . . [because] the logos is used to break up the opponent's understanding'.[57] Argumentative questioning and creating a scene are thus to be discouraged at all costs. Whenever social tensions arise, Parekh suggests that there must be 'practical deliberation' between the parties aimed at achieving consensus. This dialogue cannot occur in the media because it is too sensationalist; it cannot occur in Parliament because that is too unrepresentative of minorities, too divided along party lines and allegedly 'unused to debating large questions'; and it cannot occur in the courts as 'they are generally adversarial, extremely expensive, and unused to public debates'.[58] He suggests that some kind of new public institution be created to act as a forum for community representatives to meet and explore contentious issues. The process would be designed to sensitise each group to the anxieties of the others with a view first to mutual understanding and then, if possible, to consensual resolution.[59] Modood likewise wishes for moral judgement to be removed from questions of religious difference; the state must go beyond mere toleration by actively encouraging cultural difference for its own sake in order to fully support marginalised identities so that they are put on an equal footing with the

[52] See further Paul Bloom, *Against Empathy: The Case for Rational Compassion* (New York: Vintage, 2018).

[53] Oded Galor and Marc Klemp, 'Roots of Autocracy' (NBER Working Paper No. 23301, March 2017).

[54] Mary Anne Case, 'Feminist Fundamentalism as an Individual and Constitutional Commitment' (2011) 19(2) *American University Journal of Gender, Social Policy and the Law* 549–76, p. 553.

[55] Parekh, *Rethinking Multiculturalism*, pp. 318–19.

[56] Tariq Modood, 'Censor or Censure: Maintaining Civility' in Robin Griffith-Jones (ed.), *Islam and English Law* (Cambridge: Cambridge University Press, 2013), p. 221.

[57] Tariq Modood, *Multicultural Politics: Racism, Ethnicity, and Muslims in Britain* (Edinburgh: Edinburgh University Press, 2005), p. 125.

[58] Parekh, *Rethinking Multiculturalism*, pp. 306–7. [59] Ibid.

majority culture.[60] The Cairo Declaration on Human Rights in Islam (CDHRI) is a good example. It aims to provide 'general guidance . . . in the field of human rights' for subscribing states. Article 1 declares: 'All human beings form one family . . . [and] are equal in terms of basic human dignity and basic obligations and responsibilities.' However, Article 24 qualifies this by stipulating: 'All the rights and freedoms stipulated in this Declaration are subject to the Islamic Shari'ah.'[61] In effect, it is meaningless – a statement of universal principle culturally mediated and negated by unlimited qualification via local interpretations of religious law. Even so, it is an eye-catching emotive declaration which fits the multicultural spirit of compromise and comes from a desire to avoid conflict and state moralising.

Parekh also provides a definition of culture and an account of its relationship with human nature. He views culture as a way of life: 'a body of beliefs and practices in terms of which a group of people understand themselves and the world and organize their individual and collective lives. Unlike differences that spring from individual choices, culturally derived differences carry a measure of authority and are patterned and structured by virtue of being embedded in a shared and historically inherited system of meaning and significance'.[62] Against this, it must be remembered that all cultures are subject to contestation, change, redefinition and reconstitution and therefore have a 'relatively loose and alterable' structure. He likens them to individuated languages: distinct from yet influenced by and sharing aspects of others, as well as providing context, structure and continuity while permitting change and creativity.[63] In short, they are 'comparatively stable as well as open and fluid'.[64] As to their relationship with human nature, Parekh explains that individual personalities are given shape and content by the cultures they inhabit. The worldview, values, mores, taboos and prejudices of their particular group 'strike deep roots and become an inseparable part of their personality'.[65] Their identity and self-respect are thus grounded in, and bound up with, their given community and the regard shown to it by others.[66] This embeddedness entitles each individual to demand respect not just for themselves as human beings but also 'for the collective memories and heritage in terms of which he defines his identity'.[67] Cultural traits are as integral to human beings as their very biology, whereas historically and culturally contingent ideas such as individuality, autonomy and equality are not.[68]

From this, Parekh argues, cultures must have agency and rights. He is clear that they have a real existence and are possessed of 'dignity and moral status'.[69]

[60] Modood, *Multiculturalism*, pp. 58–9.

[61] Organisation of Islamic Cooperation, 'Cairo Declaration on Human Rights in Islam' (Cairo, 5 August 1990): http://hrlibrary.umn.edu/instree/cairodeclaration.html.

[62] Parekh, *Rethinking Multiculturalism*, pp. 2–3. [63] Ibid., pp. 152–3.

[64] *Parekh Report*, p. ix. [65] Parekh, *Rethinking Multiculturalism*, pp. 155–6. [66] Ibid., p. 314.

[67] Bhikhu Parekh, 'The Rushdie Affair and the British Press: Some Salutary Lessons' (Commission for Racial Equality, 1990), p. 13; Kenan Malik, *Multiculturalism and Its Discontents* (Calcutta: Seagull Books, 2013), p. 20.

[68] Parekh, *New Politics of Identity*, p. 210. [69] Ibid., p. 215.

Agency is ascribed to cultural communities because they seemingly have decision-making procedures and act via representatives. Groups can be subjects of justice and make claims upon their members, each other and wider society; they do this through collective action and struggle in pursuit of collective remedies.[70] Individual rights are inadequate to this end and so group rights and representation are essential components of justice and equality.[71] Collective rights in the multicultural context can be justified as derivative, intrinsic and practically necessary.[72] What Parekh calls 'derivative collective rights' arise from two foundational assumptions: i) individuals choose to collect and alienate their rights for the community's sake; ii) culture is constitutive of the individual and so, in order to adequately protect the individual, one must protect culture also. What he calls 'primary collective rights' come from the fact that culture has a real existence and possess rights for its own sake, *sui generis*. Third, collective rights protect community interests and are crucial to ensuring that the nation is 'peaceful and not torn by conflicts'.[73] Regardless of their justification, the fact that cultures possess rights means that 'attacks on the culture or its denial constitute an attack on the persons of the bearers of that culture'.[74]

Modood's work, which mostly consists of scattered or collected essays on Muslim affairs, adds little to Parekh's philosophical exposition.[75] He admits as much and declares his lack of interest in abstract philosophy.[76] Modood's collected output is probably best understood as a series of personal reflections on what it means, or should mean, to be Muslim in modern Britain. This is reflected in his major books as sole author such as *Not Easy Being British* (1992), *Still Not Easy Being British* (2010), *Multicultural Politics* (2005), *Multiculturalism* (2007, 2013) and *Essays on Secularism and Multiculturalism* (2019). His academic career appears to have been driven – not unusually – by a mixture of bravado, intellectual insecurity, parental influence, playground trauma and a desire to reconnect with his heritage.[77] These very personal concerns matter because they set him on a particular course with a number of related priorities such as religious identity politics, advocacy for Muslim interests and an opening out of the concept of Britishness. Modood's primary contribution is to be found in the way he applies multicultural theory to the affairs of British Muslims, the group to which he has a 'special commitment' and to which he has given a 'special focus'.[78]

[70] Ibid., pp. 54, 214. [71] Parekh, 'Finding a Proper Place for Human Rights', p. 37.
[72] Parekh, *New Politics of Identity*, pp. 213–19. [73] Ibid.
[74] Kelly, *Multiculturalism Reconsidered*, p. 7.
[75] See generally Tariq Modood, 'Anti-essentialism, Multiculturalism & the Recognition of Religious Groups' (1998) 6(4) *Journal of Political Philosophy* 378–99, p. 382; Modood, *Multiculturalism*, pp. 7, 20–33; Tariq Modood, 'Hate Speech: The Feelings and Beliefs of the Hated' (2014) 13(1) *Contemporary Political Theory* 104–9, pp. 105–8.
[76] Modood, *Multiculturalism*, pp. 60–1.
[77] Martinez, 'Intellectual Biography', pp. 730–2, 739–40. [78] Ibid., p. 729.

2.3 Applied Multiculturalism

Both Parekh and Modood take a broadly anti-essentialist line as regards the definition of culture. They deny that it has any fixed, a priori essence comparable to an ascertainable individual, corporation or state. In practice, this means that diverse groups such as 'Muslims' cannot be homogenised and treated as monolithic blocs. It follows that their accommodation within British society cannot take the form of 'corporatist inclusion'. This is especially true of Muslims who generally lack unified hierarchical structures and therefore cannot be treated in the same manner as institutionalised churches. The state must not seek to impose 'its own template, plans, modes of partnership and chosen imams and leaders' on the community. Instead, it should adopt an approach that is 'less corporatist, less statist and less churchy – in brief, less French' by allowing the incremental dynamics of civil society to shape a pragmatic accord. In short, 'suck it and see'.[79] This approach is reminiscent of the Ottoman millet system of religious regulation whereby each faith community is governed separately by its own norms and community leaders with very little intervention from central government.[80] Both Parekh and Modood implement their vision by assigning two types of collective rights to cultural communities.

2.3.1 The Right of Groups to Integrity

Cultural communities are to enjoy a general right to collective integrity. This requires a guarantee against state interference and protection against outside hostility. As to the former, groups must be allowed to police and prescribe the behaviour of their members without interference from external authorities. For Parekh, this may include the Catholic Church's freedom to deny its members divorce or excommunicate them.[81] More strikingly, it extends to cover communities that practice or facilitate female genital mutilation (FGM) – a serious offence under English law since 1985[82] – in which case 'all that society is entitled to insist upon is that it should be done by qualified people under public supervision and medically acceptable conditions'.[83] Such practices and others – including forced marriage and polygamy – cannot be objected to per se because they are integral to the communities that engage in them.[84] Instead, the state must allow for differential treatment. This will typically take the form of

[79] Modood, *Multiculturalism*, pp. 74–5.

[80] Roger Scruton, *The West and the Rest: Globalization and the Terrorist Threat* (London: Continuum, 2003), pp. 26–8.

[81] Parekh, *Rethinking Multiculturalism*, p. 218.

[82] See, respectively, the Prohibition of Female Circumcision Act 1985 and the Female Genital Mutilation Act 2003 as amended by the Serious Crime Act 2015.

[83] Parekh, *Rethinking Multiculturalism*, p. 276.

[84] Parekh, *Hansard*, FGM Debate 4 December 2013; Bhikhu Parekh, 'A Varied Moral World' in Susan Moller Okin (ed.), *Is Multiculturalism Bad for Women?* (Princeton, NJ: Princeton University Press, 1999), pp. 71–2.

exemptions from the general law of the land. The exemptions of Sikhs from laws mandating motorbike helmets and hard hats are classic examples of this, as are the Roman Catholic Church's exemptions from anti-sex-discrimination laws.[85] The idea behind this is that difference-blind approaches to equality and social inclusion do not work.[86] Different communities have different priorities when it comes to many social issues such as family structure, employment preferences, educational attainment, personal independence, gender roles, cultural identity, religiosity, and so on. General laws and equality policies are invariably coloured by the cultural norms of those who created them. This leads to favouritism in practice and means that the situation of disadvantaged communities is often worsened by the very measures designed to help them. Thus, Parekh argues, 'there must be a commitment to go beyond the racism- and culture-blind strategies of social inclusion ... [by maintaining] an explicit focus on race equality and cultural diversity'.[87] In other words, general laws and universal principles disadvantage members of different cultural communities because they do not accommodate their practices within the general regulatory framework and consequently lead to exclusion and alienation. The integrity of these communities can be maintained only if they have some leeway against the stringent dictates of uniform law.

As regards the latter, communities must be afforded protection against hostility from within and without. Such attacks threaten the group's integrity and may be perpetrated physically, verbally or intellectually. In specific cases, hostility is categorised as treason or even sexual assault; more often, accusations are framed as racism/Islamophobia. To begin with the former, Parekh cites Professor Ali Mazrui, who charged Salman Rushdie with 'cultural treason', as well as Edward Said, who accused him of a 'lack of loyalty' to Islam.[88] Notwithstanding the murderous fanaticism on display during the *Satanic Verses* Affair, Parekh argues, novelists cannot override the moral obligations entailed by their membership of a given cultural community. Artistic freedom 'cannot include infantile iconoclasm and mindless mud-slinging'.[89] Modood likewise regards the matter as 'a betrayal of one's community' whereby Rushdie can be thought of as a 'coconut', a 'class traitor' or a 'collaborator', or indeed all three. Private belief and personal freedom were not the issue; Western cultural domination and Rushdie's contribution to it were.[90] Even more dramatically, Modood likens the novel to a mass sexual assault against Muslims because 'the eroticisation of the sacred' left them all 'culturally naked'.[91] One Islamic scholar, whom Modood regards as 'the most learned Muslim theologian in Modern Britain',[92] went further still and claimed in *The Guardian* that '[w]hat [Rushdie] has written is far worse than if he had

85 Parekh, *Rethinking Multiculturalism*, pp. 218, 243. 86 Modood, *Multiculturalism*, p. 77.
87 *Parekh Report*, pp. 107, 84. 88 Parekh, *Rethinking Multiculturalism*, p. 159.
89 Parekh, 'The Rushdie Affair and the British Press', p. 13.
90 Tariq Modood, 'Kymlicka on British Muslims: A Rejoinder' (1993) 15(1) *Analyse & Kritik* 97–9, p. 98.
91 Modood, 'Censor or Censure', p. 223. 92 Modood, *Multiculturalism*, p. 131.

raped one's own daughter. Muslims seek Muhammad as an ideal on whom to fashion our lives and conduct, and the Prophet is internalized into every Muslim's heart. It's like a knife being dug into you – or being raped yourself.'[93] With language such as this, the overall point is perhaps best put in operatic terms: Rushdie's work was 'O statua gentilissima' in novel form – tempting, if not choosing, his fate.

There are countless examples of this kind of thinking in other contexts. Take, for example, Peter Thiel, the Republican-supporting entrepreneur who has himself stated, 'I am proud to be gay.'[94] In the leading American LGBT magazine, *Advocate*, Professor Jim Downes posed the question 'But is he gay?' and answered it thus: 'By the logic of gay liberation, Thiel is an example of a man who has sex with other men, but [is] not a gay man. Because he does not embrace the struggle of people to embrace their distinctive identity.' He simultaneously claimed: 'This does not mean that LGBT culture is homogenous [*sic*] or that all LGBT people have the same ideological viewpoints or values, but it does mean that they all understand, on some level, the notion of gay culture.'[95] Professor Deepa Kumar has lectured on 'Neoconservatives, Zionists, the Christian Far Right, Ex-Muslims and other "native informants"' in which she upbraided such people for being 'the new McCarthyites'.[96] She subsequently clarified: 'I didn't say that all ex Muslims [*sic*] are native informants but a particular group which is closely tied to the far right.'[97] The celebrated journalist and author Nesrine Malik adopted this terminology to criticise several Muslim-heritage authors for their 'careerism' and 'conscious complicity' with 'the forces of reaction' as 'Islam's New "Native Informants"'.[98] She has also claimed that, by supporting immigration reform, the Conservative ministers Priti Patel and Sajid Javid had disavowed their parents' generation and were 'brownwashing' the government's 'apartheid' agenda.[99] In June 2020, Patel even received a letter from various Labour politicians denouncing her for using her 'heritage and experiences of racism to gaslight the very real racism faced by black people and communities across the UK'.[100] Relatedly, Professor Kehinde Andrews has claimed that 'Whiteness is a psychosis' and explains that 'Critical

[93] Zaki Badawi quoted in Griffith-Jones (ed.), *Islam and English Law*, p. 213 footnote 8.

[94] Alina Selyukh, '"I Am Proud to Be Gay," Tech Investor Peter Thiel Tells GOP Convention' (NPR, 21 July 2016).

[95] Jim Downes, 'Peter Thiel Shows Us There's a Difference between Gay Sex and Gay: When You Abandon Numerous Aspects of Queer Identity, Are You Still LGBT?' (*Advocate*, 14 October 2016).

[96] Quoted in Benjamin Jones, 'Anti-Muslim Bigotry and the Problem with "Islamophobia"' (National Secular Society, 11 June 2015).

[97] Deepa Kumar, 'A Tweet' (Twitter, 11 June 2015 at 11.12 a.m.): https://twitter.com/professorkumar/status/608939845730361345?lang=en.

[98] Nesrine Malik, 'Islam's New "Native Informants"' (*New York Review*, 7 June 2018).

[99] Nesrine Malik, 'Immigrants Built Britain. Now Their Conservative Children Are Disowning Them' (*The Guardian*, 24 February 2020).

[100] Josh Halliday and Heather Stewart, 'BAME MPs Accuse Priti Patel of Gaslighting in Racism Debate' (*The Guardian*, 11 June 2020).

Whiteness studies' is about 'forcing White people to confront their complicity in the system' of global oppression by the West and 'to make them reborn as allies to the dark oppressed peoples of the world'.[101] He also believes that Black, Asian and minority ethnic (BAME) cabinet members are 'a set of token figures' who 'do not represent Britain's Black and Asian communities' but rather 'meaningless racial symbolism'. As such, 'a cabinet packed with ministers with brown skin wearing Tory masks represents the opposite of racial progress'.[102] Conversely, having an 'unexpected and strange crush' on one of them could be a fetish 'rooted in sexual racism'.[103] It would be easy to dismiss this kind of thinking as 'polytechnic sociology',[104] but it is better to understand where it comes from.

Treating categories of people as rights-bearing units has several consequences. It also assumes that such categories can in principle be represented. It follows that this group must have a representative mindset and that someone, or some organisation, can speak on its behalf. This means that there is a 'true' or 'legitimate' or 'mainstream' set of views for the individuals comprising that category to hold, and a corresponding 'false' or 'disqualifying' set that they cannot or must not hold. If an individual or subset within the larger category diverges from what is deemed proper for that category, it means that they must not in fact be part of it and are disqualified from speaking as a member of it. More than that, it means that their dissent or nonconformity constitutes an attack on the group from which they have become detached or been expelled. That they have freely diverged from the presumed or accepted tenets of their community is inconceivable because as humans they are, by nature, socially embedded beings whose identities are inseparable from their given biological and cultural background. This can only mean that they have been corrupted by, and are in league with, the impersonal dark forces arrayed against the collectivity from which they came. Individuality is no defence – deviant personal opinions or success on terms other than those ascribed to the community cannot be authentic and, by extension, constitute a threat to its integrity. Deviants are 'traitors' or 'rotten coconuts' or 'collaborators' or 'Uncle Toms' or 'native informants' and it is by no means 'brazenly racist' to refer to them as such. As the writer and comedian Shazia Mirza explains: 'When I refer to Sajid Javid as a coconut, I am not referring to his skin colour; I am referring to his lack of loyalties and patriotism towards a group of people from the same background.'[105] It follows that attacks on their character,

[101] Kehinde Andrews, 'The Psychosis of Whiteness: The Celluloid Hallucinations of *Amazing Grace* and *Belle*' (2016) 47(5) *Journal of Black Studies* 435–53, pp. 435–7.

[102] Kehinde Andrews, 'Don't Be Fooled by Johnson's "Diverse" Cabinet. Tory Racism Hasn't Changed' (*The Guardian*, 25 July 2019).

[103] Diyora Shadijanova, 'Your "Strange" Crush on Rishi Sunak Could Actually Be a Racist Fetish' (*The Independent*, 9 April 2020).

[104] Roger Scruton, 'Let's Face It – Ray Honeyford Got It Right on Islam and Education' (*The Spectator*, 5 July 2014).

[105] Shazia Mirza, 'Oh, What a Rotten Bunch of Coconuts' (author's website, 8 April 2019): www.shazia-mirza.com/oh-what-a-rotten-bunch-of-coconuts/.

career decisions and choice of associates are justified reactions by the wronged group as it seeks to assert itself and reverse the victimisation it has suffered. This chain of thought follows a coherent internal logic so long as one accepts that broad categories of people are meaningfully unified.

More generally, however, attacks against cultural communities are said to be manifestations of racism. This is to be understood capaciously. 'We need', Modood says, 'a concept of race and racism that can critique sociocultural environments that devalue people not only because of their origins but also because of their membership in a cultural minority.' Oppression is most severe when a victimised group has its most cherished beliefs attacked. It follows that 'antiracism begins (i.e. ought to begin) by accepting oppressed groups on their own terms'. These terms can then form the basis for a just resistance struggle against the group's oppressors.[106] Such a concept is provided by the *Parekh Report*, which defines racism 'either as division of humankind into fixed, closed and unalterable groups or as systematic domination of some groups by others'.[107] Though subtle and complex, 'all racisms have two separate but intertwining strands'. The first involves 'physical or biologically derived signs', whereas the second 'uses cultural features, such as ways of life, customs, language, religion and dress' to reinforce prejudice.[108] This includes 'East–West racism', 'Europe–Orient racism' and 'Christendom–Islam' racism. It may be committed by individuals or it may have been institutionalised. It can be explicit and intentional, it may be unintentional and thoughtless, or it might be well intentioned but patronising. It may take the form of violence, open discrimination, insensitivity, rudeness, ignorance, bureaucratic incompetence, unequal power relationships, exclusionary practices, or unseemly 'attitudes, narratives and discourses'. In most cases it is rooted in 'in imperialism, anti-Muslim hostility and the slave-trade, and in often strident opposition to immigration'. It is representative of a 'Rule Britannia mindset' which is 'given full-blown expression at the Last Night of the Proms' on an annual basis.[109] Both Parekh and Modood are agreed that Islamophobia is the most pressing kind of cultural racism and that 'there must be a sustained and fearless attack on all forms of racial injustice'.[110] In order to protect cultural communities from external assailment, they favour the promulgation of group defamation or hate speech laws.[111] Modood explains that such laws will further the goal of securing civility and respect for non-dominant cultures.[112]

2.3.2 The Right of Groups to Representation

Cultural communities are also to enjoy a general right to representation. As groups, they have agency and can be legitimately represented. Parekh argues that this agency is evident from collective decision-making procedures and the

[106] Modood, *Multicultural Politics*, p. 104. [107] *Parekh Report*, p. ix. [108] Ibid., pp. 62, xvi.
[109] Ibid., pp. 70–5, 57. [110] Ibid., p. 296; Modood, *Multiculturalism*, p. 41.
[111] Parekh, *Rethinking Multiculturalism*, ch. 10, pp. 313–17.
[112] Modood, *Multiculturalism*, p. 52; Modood, 'Censor or Censure'.

appointment of accredited representatives to advance the collective interests of that community.[113] As such, they are entitled to positive support from the state in order to tackle exclusion and alienation. This right involves a claim to empowerment via inclusion, endorsement, representation, preservation and support. The exercise of this right is commonly known as identity politics or the politics of recognition.[114] Cultural collectivities seek to win recognition by demanding things such as 'anti-discrimination measures, culturally sensitive interpretations and applications of laws, exemptions from certain rules and practices, group-sensitive application of public policy, additional rights and resources, fostering public respect for marginalised identities, ensuring their adequate representation in public institutions, and when appropriate acknowledging their presence in the definition of national identity'.[115] The state must therefore do all it can to institutionalise respect for groups by empowering them to make public claims; if it does not, they will have been 'demeaned, inferiorised, or denied the opportunity to speak in their own voices and define their identities'.[116] Such claims may be made and recognised in one of two main ways.[117] The first is the 'voice of the community' approach whereby the state adopts a 'take me to your leader' strategy and approaches the largest Muslim umbrella group to speak for Muslims as such on their common interests. The second is issue-by-issue representation via a 'democratic constellation' or 'Muslim industry' of organisations and individuals competing to be the voice of 'mainstream' Muslim opinion on any given concern.[118] Whatever the difficulties with either approach, the state should recognise that 'unelected civil society representatives can act as an important supplement to elected representatives' and not look too closely at 'the personal connections and sectarian affiliations of specific Muslim organisations and individuals'.[119] What matters most is that authentic and legitimate Muslim voices are heard by and within government whenever common interests are at stake and a broad consensus exists.[120]

The implication of this group right is that national identity must be remade to accommodate different cultural communities and their identity narratives. Modood notes that the liberal individualistic conception of equal citizenship

[113] Parekh, *Rethinking Multiculturalism*, pp. 214–15.

[114] Parekh, *New Politics of Identity*, p. 43. [115] Ibid., p. 42. [116] Ibid., p. 54.

[117] Stephen H. Jones, Therese O'Toole, Daniel Nilsson DeHanas, Tariq Modood and Nasar Meer, 'A "System of Self-Appointed Leaders"? Examining Modes of Muslim Representation in Governance in Britain' (2015) 17(2) *British Journal of Politics and International Relations* 207–23, p. 220.

[118] Sayeeda Warsi, *The Enemy Within: A Tale of Muslim Britain* (London: Penguin, 2018), pp. 249–61. See also 'New Board of Scholars Is Unifying Fragmented Muslim Communities' (Religion Media Centre, 11 January 2021), https://religionmediacentre.org.uk/news/new-board-of-scholars-is-unifying-fragmented-muslim-communities/.

[119] Jones et al., 'System of Self-Appointed Leaders?', p. 220.

[120] Ibid., p. 214; Therese O'Toole, Daniel Nilsson DeHanas, Tariq Modood, Nasar Meer and Stephen H. Jones 'Taking Part: Muslim Participation in Contemporary Governance' (University of Bristol, 2013), www.bristol.ac.uk/ethnicity/projects/muslimparticipation/documents/mpcgreport.pdf, p. 6.

mandates cultural assimilation, with difference tolerated only in the private sphere. He argues instead for a politics of recognition that encompasses 'public ethnicity' by redefining equality 'as not having to hide or apologise for one's origins, family or community but requiring others to show respect for them and adapt public attitudes and arrangements so that the heritage they represent is encouraged rather than contemptuously expected to wither away'.[121] In order to occupy the same political space without conflict, people must refrain from criticising one another's fundamental beliefs.[122] Modood thus favours an 'open-textured' citizenship and national identity which celebrates diversity while recognising difference and relating it to the things the population has in common.[123] Citizenship should therefore be viewed 'in a plural, dispersed and dialogical way and not reduced to legal rights, passports and the franchise'.[124] Multiculturalism involves 'remaking the national story' by ensuring that public institutions and schools treat 'Muslim history as European history'.[125] He concludes by suggesting that 'strong multicultural identities are a good thing – they are not intrinsically divisive, reactionary or fifth columns – but they need a framework of vibrant, dynamic, national narratives and the ceremonies and rituals which give expression to a national identity ... [which] is respectful of and builds upon the identities that people value and does not trample on them'.[126]

The task as regards religion and Islam is to reaffirm 'a plural, changing, inclusive British identity, which can be as emotionally and politically meaningful to British Muslims as the appeal of jihadi sentiments'.[127] Any suggestion that Muslims are an alien wedge must be part of an 'exclusivist and racist' ideology that seeks to undercut 'the efforts to build cross-cutting connections, syntheses, alliances and so on which multicultural citizenship facilitates and needs'.[128] It must be repeatedly and publicly stressed that there is no problem with Islam in particular or religion in general.[129] At the same time, however, Modood accepts that 'some versions of Islamism are not sufficiently respectful of fellow British citizens and the aspiration of a plural Britain and have to be challenged'.[130] Such Islamists, Parekh clarifies, have nothing to do with mainstream Islam and are merely a few eccentrics to be discouraged.[131] Extremists and suicide bombers are best dealt with indirectly by crafting a reasonable and just accommodation with British Muslims. Meeting their demands is not antithetical to progressive politics and can be achieved through dialogue and inclusive negotiations over multicultural citizenship and nationality. 'That is

121 Tariq Modood, 'Introduction' in Tariq Modood and Pnina Werbner (eds.), *The Politics of Multiculturalism in the New Europe: Racism, Identity and Community* (London: Zed Books, 1997), pp. 19–20.

122 Modood quoted in Kenan Malik, *From Fatwa to Jihad: The Rushdie Affair and Its Legacy* (London: Atlantic Books, 2010), p. 155.

123 Modood, *Multiculturalism*, pp. 9, 135. 124 Ibid., p. 135. 125 Ibid., p. 78.

126 Ibid., pp. 137–9. 127 Ibid., p. 139. 128 Ibid., p. 121. 129 Ibid., p. 122.

130 Ibid., p. 121.

131 Parekh, *Rethinking Multiculturalism*, p. 90; Parekh, *New Politics of Identity*, pp. 168–9.

the best way to overcome the present state of fear, polarization and ultimately suicide bombings in our cities.'[132] That, and a campaign to defeat 'the neo-conservative US-UK international project of controlling Muslims' which has led to 'the victimization and humiliation of Muslims in places such as Palestine, Bosnia, Kashmir, and Afghanistan'.[133] Parekh similarly maintains that the Unites States and Islamic terrorists are the 'mirror image' of each another and are jointly engaged in a project to 'create global fear'. This conflict can end only once the terrorists' grievances have been redressed.[134]

2.4 Multicultural Law and Policy in Britain

Unlike comparable Anglospheric countries such as Canada and Australia,[135] the UK has never officially declared itself to be multicultural despite powerful recommendations to this effect.[136] This does not mean that multiculturalism has had a negligible impact in terms of getting the English law of religion to reflect some of its key concerns with respect to Islam and Muslims. The collective rights ascribed to cultural communities by Parekh and Modood have had a noticeable impact on law and policy. To explain this, it is helpful to divide the history of British multiculturalism into three periods: pre-1997 (emergence), 1997–2005 (zenith) and post-7/7 (decline).

2.4.1 Emergence

Recognisably multicultural policies have existed for quite some time in Britain. They have always proved controversial. In the beginning they did not form part of an explicit ideology and were limited to the bare management of post-war immigration. Many more commonwealth immigrants arrived to settle than had been expected under the British Nationality Act 1948: by 1962, approximately 600 million people had the right to enter and reside lawfully in the UK.[137] As large minority communities began to develop across Britain, racial tensions rose. In response, increasingly tough legislation was passed to dampen down the discord and tackle pervasive discrimination.[138] Such measures were typically components of a top-down strategy with the ultimate aim of preventing widespread public disorder. They targeted the worst abuses and

[132] Modood, *Multiculturalism*, p. 142.

[133] Modood, ibid., pp. 121, 142; Modood, *Multicultural Politics*, p. 166. For a detailed and accurate overview of neoconservative theory and practice, see Douglas Murray, *Neoconservatism: Why We Need It* (New York: Encounter Books, 2006).

[134] Parekh, *New Politics of Identity*, pp. 168–9.

[135] Canadian Charter of Rights and Freedoms (1982), s. 27; Canadian Multiculturalism Act 1988; Parekh, *Rethinking Multiculturalism*, p. 5.

[136] *Parekh Report*, p. 296.

[137] Eric Fripp (ed.), *The Law and Practice of Expulsion and Exclusion from the United Kingdom: Deportation, Removal, Exclusion and Deprivation of Citizenship* (Oxford: Hart, 2015), p. 7.

[138] Race Relations Acts 1965, 1968, 1976; Hasan, *Multiculturalism*, p. 7.

formal discrimination, but did not, for the most part, seek to empower minority communities. Prior to the 1980s, British Muslims did not define themselves predominantly in terms of religion. Though pious, many drank, fasted rarely, prayed infrequently and few women wore headscarves or face-veils. Islam was not generally regarded as some 'sacrosanct public identity' or 'all-encompassing philosophy'. Many simply put up with the discrimination and worked to get on in life as best they could. Those who were politically active tended to be young secular socialists who were self-consciously Western. They saw themselves as Black, which was understood as a political badge rather than an ethnic label.[139] This changed during the 1980s with the fallout from a series of race riots, the culmination of a century of literary scandals, and case law that denied Muslims the status of a protected racial group under the Race Relations Act 1976 while granting it to Sikhs and Jews.[140]

By the early 1990s, the Muslim population of Britain had grown considerably and the Islamic revival triggered by the Iranian Revolution a decade earlier had begun to assert itself.[141] Whereas the umbrella term 'Black British' had once provided some form of unity expressed by non-whiteness, it began to take on a different meaning which stressed the distinctness and difference of each minority sub-category. 'Radical' came to mean someone who is 'a religious fundamentalist, someone who is anti-Western, who is opposed to secularism'.[142] This dynamic was intertwined with the introduction by successive governments of 'pork-barrel' policies, whereby resources were given to particular groups in exchange for political benefits and votes. The resulting divisions caused an intensification of demands for public recognition of cultural or faith-based differences and 'increasing levels of segregation and concomitant ghettoization in many inner areas of towns and cities'.[143] Kenan Malik points to an illustrative example of this counterproductive transition: the 2005 riots in Birmingham between Blacks and South Asians who had previously rioted together against the police back in 1985. After a Jamaican girl was allegedly gang-raped by Pakistanis, Blacks and South Asians fought each other over the course of a weekend, resulting in the murder of a young Black man. Malik observes that Birmingham Council's long-standing drive to engage self-appointed community groups in democratic life by having them compete among

[139] Malik, *Multiculturalism*, pp. 39–41; Hasan, ibid.

[140] See, respectively, (i) Hasan, ibid., pp. 7–8; (ii) Ray Honeyford, 'Education and Race: An Alternative View' (Salisbury Review, 1984); Kritan Tetens, 'The Lyceum and the Lord Chamberlain: The Case of Hall Caine's *Mahomet*' in Richard Foulkes (ed.), *Henry Irving: A Re-evaluation of the Pre-eminent Victorian Actor-Manager* (Farnham: Ashgate, 2008), pp. 49–64; Theodore Dalrymple, *Migration: Multiculturalism and Its Metaphors* (Brisbane: Connor Court Publishing, 2016), pp. 15–29; Malik, *From Fatwa to Jihad*; (iii) *Mandla* v. *Dowell Lee* [1983] ICR 385; *Seid* v. *Gillette Industries Ltd* [1980] IRLR 427; *Tariq* v. *Young EOR Discrimination Case Law Digest No 2*.

[141] See generally Christian Caryl, *Strange Rebels: 1979 and the Birth of the 21st Century* (New York: Basic Books, 2013).

[142] Malik, *Multiculturalism*, p. 42.

[143] Hasan, *Multiculturalism*, pp. 7–8; Malik, *Multiculturalism*, pp. 41–3, 56.

each other for resource allocation had served only to divide the minority populations along ethno-religious lines and entrench the divisions and tensions among them.[144] In short, the acceleration of societal fragmentation following the introduction of multicultural policies ratcheted up inter-communal tensions and incentivised increasingly aggressive demands from unaccountable 'community representatives'. Hence the incident which occurred in 1992 when another head-teacher changed a classroom alphabet display so that 'P for pig' became 'P for pencil' in a bid to placate distressed Muslim parents. This story was picked up by *The Sun*, which ran an article outlining 'a new alphabet tailored to the needs of Muslim pupils' starting with 'A is for Ayatollah' and ending with 'Z is for Zionist Imperialist Aggressor Running Dogs of the Great Satan'.[145] This auspicious controversy roughly coincided with the first use of the word 'Islamophobia' by a British writer (Modood himself) in an attempt to raise awareness of cultural racism and the importance of religious sensitivities.[146] Although such considerations were initially ignored by policy-makers, it would not be long before government policy towards Islam took a decidedly multicultural turn.

2.4.2 Zenith

The high watermark of multiculturalism began in 1997. The first facet of multicultural doctrine to be accepted by government was the right of the Muslim community to be represented. In the years between the Rushdie Affair and the Blair era, Britain had become 'a sandbox for Muslims to play at developing their ideologies, philosophies, and eventually movements'.[147] Multifarious individuals and campaign groups began to coalesce and organise in a serious way throughout 1996–7 with assistance from the Muslim Brotherhood, the largest global movement dedicated to the creation of a worldwide Caliphate, and Jamaat-e-Islami, another highly influential network committed to revolutionary Islam.[148] This was prompted by New Labour's interfaith agenda, which sought to establish a dialogue with Islamic organisations it deemed to be representative of 'moderate, mainstream' Muslims.[149] By far the most successful of these was the Muslim Council of Britain (MCB). It achieved 'the greatest degree of non-factionalism and non-sectarianism' even though its parent group controls less than 4 per cent of all UK mosques.[150] Its primary purpose was to

[144] Malik, ibid., pp. 58–65. [145] Richardson, 2010: ix. [146] Richardson, 2010: x.

[147] C. Scott Jordan quoted in Jenny Taylor, 'The Most Important Muslim That Britain Has Never Heard Of' (*Unherd*, 6 December 2019).

[148] Martyn Frampton, *The Muslim Brotherhood and the West: A History of Enmity and Engagement* (Cambridge, MA: Harvard University Press, 2018), p. 402; Innes Bowen, *Medina in Birmingham, Najaf in Brent: Inside British Islam* (London: Hurst & Co Ltd, 2014), pp. 2–3, 83–99.

[149] Bowen, ibid., p. 89.

[150] Bowen, ibid., pp. 2, 7; Madeleine Bunting, 'A Dialogue of the Deaf' (*The Guardian*, 12 July 2007).

'represent mainstream Muslim opinion' and 'lobby on behalf of Muslims in the corridors of power'.[151] In terms of structure, it took inspiration from Jewish representative bodies such as the Board of Deputies which had, according to Sayeeda Warsi, proved 'effective in engaging lazy officialdom'.[152] As such, it was established as an umbrella body for a broad coalition of Muslim organisations and quickly came to be treated as the 'lead national moderate organisation' and 'the single most representative and successful national Muslim organization'.[153] Blair's government accepted it as the pre-eminent consultee on Muslim affairs and by the end of his first term in office in 2001, 'it had achieved its aim of having Muslim issues and Muslims as a group recognized separately from issues of race and ethnicity; and of being itself accepted by government, media and civil society as the spokesperson for Muslims'.[154] The MCB's notable policy successes included the introduction of state-funded Muslim schools and the inclusion of a religious question on the national census so that future policies could be designed especially for British Muslims.[155] It was also able to obtain major legal reforms in religious discrimination law and, most visibly of all, the introduction of religious hatred offences. In short, the MCB's privileged status was living proof of the practical potency of multicultural collective rights.

Reforms to anti-discrimination law gave effect to the right to collective integrity. The Anti-Terrorism, Crime and Security Act 2001 introduced religiously aggravated offences[156] and the Employment Equality (Religion or Belief) Regulations 2003[157] first made religion or belief a protected characteristic for the purposes of employment law. These protections were consolidated, harmonised and extended by the Equality Act 2006 (Part 2) and are now to be found within the Equality Act 2010, where they are virtually on par with the protections for traits such as race, gender, sexual orientation, age and disability.[158] This legislation was passed primarily because Muslim activists convinced New Labour that they were being unfairly excluded from the existing discrimination law and the existing racial discrimination legislation.[159] Indirect discrimination law – as opposed to direct discrimination law, where an individual's liberty is affected by unfavourable treatment on account of a protected personal characteristic –

[151] Modood, *Multiculturalism*, p. 172. [152] Warsi, *The Enemy Within*, p. 252.

[153] Tariq Modood, *Still Not Easy Being British: Struggles for a Multicultural Citizenship* (Stoke: Trentham Books, 2010), p. 11; Modood, *Multiculturalism*, p. 76; Tariq Modood, 'Multiculturalism Is Not Dead in the UK' (*The Guardian*, 6 October 2010).

[154] Modood, *Multiculturalism*, pp. 172–3. [155] Ibid.

[156] S. 39. For a discussion of CPS policy towards such cases, see Paul Iganski, Abe Sweiry and Jonathan Culpepper, 'A Question of Faith? Prosecuting Religiously Aggravated Offences in England and Wales' (2016) 5 *Criminal Law Review* 334–48.

[157] (SI 2003/1660), implementing EU Employment Directive (Council Directive 2000/78/EC).

[158] Rivers, *Law of Organized Religions*, p. 125; Sandberg, *Law and Religion*, p. 101; Sandra Fredman *Discrimination Law* (2nd ed., Oxford: Oxford University Press, 2011), p. 84.

[159] Neil Addison, *Religious Discrimination and Hatred Law* (London: Routledge-Cavendish, 2007), pp. 27, 61.

grew in step with the multicultural emphasis on collective equality over individual liberty. Indirect discrimination occurs when the equal application of a provision, criterion or practice (PCP) unjustifiably puts an individual or other persons of his or her religion or belief at a disadvantage compared with those not of that religion or group.[160] This necessitates a group-based comparison because 'treatment is no longer personalised, it is collective and only relates to individuals in terms of their real or assumed affiliation to a protected group. This shift from the individual to a group is strictly analogous to the operations carried out by statistics: impersonal aggregates that highlight a collective situation.'[161] Several key cases illustrate the issues and principles at stake.[162]

Both *Eweida* v. *British Airways*[163] and *Chaplin* v. *Royal Devon & Exeter NHS Foundation Trust*[164] involved Christians who wore crosses in contravention of their respective employers' uniform policies. In the former, it was held that there was no indirect discrimination because there was no evidence that practising Christians deemed the wearing of a cross to be a requirement of Christianity – it was the personal choice of the individual concerned. In the latter case, it was held that, even though another nurse had been told to remove a crucifix, the religious beliefs of the nurse in question were not so strong as to lead her to refuse to comply with the policy and so 'persons' had not been disadvantaged. Sandberg notes that these cases are 'particularly troubling' because 'even if it is accepted that the courts are entitled to conclude that a ban on wearing a cross would not disadvantage Christians as a whole, these cases suggest that beliefs held by a few individuals (including beliefs held by a minority of believers within a larger religious group) will not be protected'.[165] A comparison between two other cases reinforces the importance of the collective dimension of indirect discrimination. *R (Watkins-Singh)* v. *The Governing Body of Aberdare Girls' High School*[166] concerned a female Sikh pupil who sought to wear a Kara bangle, in contravention of her school's uniform policy, because she believed it to be 'central to her ethnic identity and religious observance as a Sikh'.[167] Justice Silber accepted that the uniform policy would have a disparate impact upon those who shared the girl's race and religion because of the 'exceptional importance' of the Kara to Sikhs.[168] *R (Playfoot) (A Child)* v. *Millais School Governing Body*[169] involved a schoolgirl who, in contravention of her school's uniform policy, wished to wear a purity ring to symbolise her commitment to premarital celibacy. The presiding judge, Michael Supperstone QC, held that 'the Claimant was under no obligation, by reason of her belief, to wear the ring' and so has not suffered

[160] Rivers, *Law of Organized Religions*, p. 126; Sandberg, *Law and Religion*, pp. 104–17.
[161] P. Simon quoted in Fredman, *Discrimination Law*, p. 183.
[162] Sandberg, *Law and Religion*, pp. 112–14; Mark Hill, Russell Sandberg and Norman Doe, *Religion and Law in the UK* (2nd ed., Alphen aan den Rijn: Kluwer Law International, 2014), pp. 150–2.
[163] [2010] EWCA Civ 80. [164] [2010] ET Case Number: 17288862009.
[165] Sandberg, *Law and Religion*, pp. 113–14. [166] [2008] EWHC (Admin) 1895.
[167] Para. 11. [168] Paras. 46, 56B, 63–66. [169] [2007] EWHC (Admin) 1698.

discrimination on account of the uniform policy which she had also 'voluntarily accepted'.[170] Further, there were 'other means open to her to practice her belief without undue hardship or inconvenience'.[171] The basic point is that the burden imposed by the PCP will appear more onerous in collective contexts given that a religious obligation will look much more like an obligation if everyone in a group does it than if it's one individual's own choice.[172]

Another prime example of the multicultural ethos of religious liberty under the European Convention on Human Rights (ECHR) can be seen in *R (Begum)* v. *Headteacher and Governors of Denbigh High School*.[173] In this related case, a Muslim pupil, Shabina Begum, wished to adhere to her understanding of sharia law by wearing a long jilbab instead of the shorter shalwar kameez permitted by her school's uniform policy. This Luton school was not a faith school and had a diverse, though Muslim-majority, intake. It refused Begum's demand, which had been couched threateningly in terms of human rights proceedings, arguing that the school must remain an inclusive institution that promoted a sense of communal identity across religious, cultural and ethnic lines. Begum was ordered to return home and change into the prescribed uniform. She refused to attend school again until she was allowed to wear the jilbab. Though she eventually lost her claim under Article 9(2) (the right to manifest religious belief) and Article 2 of the First Protocol (the right to education) in the House of Lords, the judgment is instructive. Lord Bingham accepted 'the value of religious harmony and tolerance between opposing or competing groups and of pluralism and broad-mindedness [as well as] the need for compromise and balance' in 'sensitive' cases such as this.[174] He also drew attention to the fact that the school's 'rules were acceptable to mainstream Muslim opinion'.[175] Lord Hoffman then rebuked Begum for her lack of 'common civility' when she 'sought a confrontation' with the school and refused to accept that 'people sometimes have to suffer some inconvenience for their beliefs'.[176] He went on to stress the 'expectation of accommodation, compromise and, if necessary, sacrifice in the manifestation of religious beliefs' that permeated the jurisprudence of the European Court of Human Rights (ECtHR) and, by extension, that of the English courts.[177] Lord Scott issued a similar denunciation of Begum's 'quite unnecessarily confrontational' approach towards the school, which he praised in turn for showing 'no unnecessary rigidity'.[178] Lady Hale lauded the school for designing a uniform to 'suit the social conditions in that school, in that town, and at that time'.[179] She even approvingly cited Parekh twice to make two oppositions highlighting the complexity

[170] Paras. 23, 32. [171] Para. 32. [172] Rivers, 2010: 321. [173] [2006] UKHL 15.
[174] Paras. 32, 34. [175] Para. 34. [176] Para. 50. [177] Para. 54. [178] Paras. 79, 80, 83.
[179] Para. 98.

of the question before her, namely, that traditional religious dress may worn as an 'autonomous act intended to use the resources of the tradition both to change and to preserve it', and that it 'may be used to legitimise power structures rather than to promote ethical principles, and may foster bigotry, sectarianism and fundamentalism'.[180] Taken in the round, the judgment suggests that 'the British value of reasonable compromise', rather than a principled commitment to liberal secularism, underpins leading judicial thinking on religious freedom.[181]

In *Mba* v. *Mayor and Burgesses of the London Borough of Merton*,[182] the Court of Appeal made a conscious attempt to steer the law away from collectivism towards a more individualistic understanding of indirect discrimination. Mrs Mba was a practising Christian who sincerely believed it to be a requirement of her faith that she should not work on Sundays. She was a care assistant at a children's home and her employment contract stated that she would be expected to work outside normal working hours, including bank holidays and weekends. Her claim of indirect discrimination failed on the basis that the interference with her belief was justified, but what matters for present purposes is what the Court had to say about the group dimension of indirect discrimination. Lord Kay held that the employment tribunal had been wrong to give weight to the fact that Mrs Mba's belief 'is not a core component of the Christian faith' because only 'some Christians' adhere to it.[183] He noted that this 'opened the door to a quantitative test on far too wide a basis' when the Court's job was to accommodate 'pluralistic tolerance'.[184] He added that the law's 'sensitivity to the diversity of beliefs between and within religions is something which flows from the respect that is accorded to the range of sincerely held religious beliefs'.[185] Lord Elias further stated that 'it cannot in any way weaken her case with respect to justification that her beliefs are not more widely shared or do not constitute a core belief of any particular religion'.[186] Similarly, Lord Vos held that '[t]he question of whether Mrs Mba's belief was widely held might, in theory and absent Article 9, be relevant to the proportionality question for the reasons I have given. But there is no reason why [the relevant regulation] cannot be equally well read to exclude such a consideration on the ground that Article 9 does not require any test of group disadvantage, and concentrates only on the religious freedom of the individual concerned.'[187] In sum, this case is significant because it represents a clear retreat from multicultural collectivist philosophy and suggests that the law of indirect discrimination is starting to settle into a liberal individualistic mould. This view found support in *Pendleton*

[180] Paras. 94, 95.

[181] For a discussion of this and comparable judgments from around Europe, see Mary Anne Case, 'Feminist Fundamentalism as an Individual and Constitutional Commitment' (2011) 19(2) *American University Journal of Gender, Social Policy and the Law* 549–76, pp. 552–3, 556; Christopher McCrudden, 'Dignity and Religion' in Griffith-Jones (ed.), *Islam and English Law*, pp. 94–106, at p. 101.

[182] [2013] EWCA Civ 1562. [183] Paras. 13–14. [184] Paras. 17, 19. [185] Para. 14.

[186] Para. 35. [187] Para. 41.

v. *Derbyshire County Council & Anor (Religion or Belief Discrimination)*[188] where it was noted that 'a PCP that requires a religious believer to act contrary to conscience' would also amount to a particular disadvantage.[189] Regardless of all this, however, Lord Elias in *Mba* cautioned against taking individualism too far in this area of law, suggesting that 'an evaluation of the impact [of a PCP] must include its extent' and that, in his view, 'it is simply not possible to read down the concept of indirect discrimination to ignore the need to establish group disadvantage'.[190]

The right to collective integrity was enshrined most visibly in the Racial and Religious Hatred Act 2006. The story of the Act's conception and passage is long and dramatic. It is a direct result of the failure of Muslim activists to silence Salman Rushdie in 1989.[191] The most articulate expression of the protestors' demands came in the form of a private prosecution for blasphemous libel. In the decade before the *Satanic Verses* Affair, the offence had been revived thanks to the campaigns of Mary Whitehouse.[192] In 1979, she brought a successful prosecution against *Gay News* for publishing James Kirkup's poem *The Love That Dares to Speak Its Name.*[193] A subsequent appeal by *Gay News* to Strasbourg failed, demonstrating that the offence was compatible with ECHR Article 9.[194] Prior to this litigation, the offence had been policed extralegally through 'the fears, anxieties and sensitivities of individuals'.[195] The *Satanic Verses* protestors clearly saw this as an opportunity when they sought to have the offence extended to non-Christian religions.[196] Though unsuccessful, they had a technical point – that the offence did not protect Muslims – and began to strategically rearticulate their demands. The objective, as Modood notes, remained the same: to ensure that 'Muslim impulses and sensibilities' became part of the fabric of British nationality and public life. Yet this was more likely to be achieved by translating allegations of apostasy and blasphemy into 'contemporary western civic discourses and practices', namely 'the policy goal of creating a legal offence of incitement to religious hatred', which got around 'the inefficacy (and Christian-centricity) of blasphemy laws'.[197] The

188 [2016] UKEAT 0238 15 2903. See also Lady Hale's judgment in *Doogan* v. *Greater Glasgow & Clyde Health Board* [2015] AC 640 SC.

189 Para. 18. 190 Paras. 32, 35. 191 Modood, *Multiculturalism*, p. 173.

192 Russell Sandberg and Norman Doe, 'The Strange Death of Blasphemy' (2008) 71(6) *Modern Law Review* 971–86, pp. 974–5. For an even-handed appraisal of Mary Whitehouse and a selection of her letters, see Ben Thompson, *Ban This Filth! Letters from the Mary Whitehouse Archive 1963–2001* (London: Faber & Faber, 2013).

193 *R* v. *Lemon, R* v. *Gay News* [1979] AC 617.

194 *Gay News Ltd* v. *United Kingdom* (1983) 5 EHRR 123.

195 Sandberg and Doe, 'Strange Death', pp. 974–5. The last successful prosecution had been *R* v. *Gott* (1922) 16 CR App R 87.

196 *R* v. *Chief Stipendiary Magistrate ex parte Choudhury* [1991] 1 QB 429 at 448; *Choudhury* v. *United Kingdom* (1991) 12 HRLJ 172.

197 Modood, *Multiculturalism*, pp. 131, 173; Geoffrey Brahm Levey and Tariq Modood, 'Liberal Democracy, Multicultural Citizenship and the Danish Cartoon Affair' in Geoffrey

United Kingdom Action Committee on Islamic Affairs (UKACIA) was the first and slickest among the many lobby groups created for this purpose. It had declared *The Satanic Verses* to be 'the most offensive, filthy and abusive book ever written by any hostile enemy of Islam' and subsequently morphed into the MCB.[198] This chimed with Modood's own view of the novel – 'culturally low and backward and lacking in sensibility'[199] – and he became 'a friend of the Muslim Council of Britain'.[200] New Labour's policy of treating the MCB as the representative of British Muslims provided them with the opportunity to make good the earlier failure over Rushdie's novel.

In 2001, the Home Secretary announced that the government wished to see blasphemy replaced with new incitement to religious hatred laws which covered all religions equally.[201] This was mirrored by the MCB, which stated: 'The Muslim community would like to see the early introduction of a law that makes it a criminal offence to vilify any religious belief.'[202] Several early attempts to introduce religious hate speech laws – in 2001, 2002 and 2004 – were all defeated in the House of Lords and withdrawn. The final attempt began after the 2005 general election and, 'very strongly supported' by the MCB, the government threatened to use the Parliament Act to force through the Racial and Religious Hatred Bill. It encountered fierce opposition 'from an unusual coalition of comedians, Evangelical Christians and atheists' who feared the chilling effect it would have on their freedom to disagree with and criticise other religions.[203] The Bill was again defeated in the Lords and significantly modified to remove 'abusive or insulting' words of behaviour from the original *actus reus*, remove the dual *mens rea* which also included an alternative recklessness component, remove the 'likely' to stir up religious hatred component, separate the offences of racial and religious hatred and also to insert a free speech protection clause.[204] The government did not wish to accept these compromises and tried to restore the original bill. It was defeated by a single vote in the Commons on 31 January 2006 because Tony Blair left early.[205] That the Act has a turbulent and chequered history serves only to illustrate that it could easily have been, and very nearly was, significantly more potent.[206] In the event, an official review of these offences from 2011 found that there had been only one successful conviction and two people charged

Brahm Levey and Tariq Modood (eds.), *Secularism, Religion & Multicultural Citizenship* (Cambridge: Cambridge University Press, 2009), p. 231.

198 Quoted in Malik, *Fatwa to Jihad*, p. 3; Modood, *Multiculturalism*, p. 172; Bowen, *Medina in Birmingham*, pp. 89–94.

199 Modood, 'Censor or Censure', p. 221.

200 Quoted in Martinez, 'Intellectual Biography', p. 736.

201 BBC News, 'Blasphemy Laws Set to Be Repealed' (*BBC News*, 18 October 2004). The offence was finally abolished by the Criminal Justice and Immigration Act 2008, s. 79.

202 MCB, 'Response to House of Lords Select Committee on the Religious Offences Bill' (MCB, 7 August 2002), p. 3.

203 Addison, *Religious Discrimination*, pp. 139–40.

204 Addison, ibid., p. 140; Sandberg, *Law and Religion*, pp. 142–4.

205 Addison, ibid.

206 Hill et al., *Religion and Law*, p. 164; Addison, *Religious Discrimination*, p. 140.

(with one acquitted upon prosecution and all charges dropped against the other).[207] To date, these offences concerning religious hatred appear not to have been the subject of any major litigation and thus have had no direct further judicial treatment whatsoever.[208] The Crown Prosecution Service (CPS) has also acknowledged that it is 'more difficult to prosecute for inciting religious hatred as opposed to racial hatred'.[209]

The Act's dilution remains 'an open wound' for some Muslim lobby groups like the MCB who wish to see it strengthened along the lines of racial equality laws.[210] Despite this and the fact that it may not have even caught *The Satanic Verses*, the legislation represented a signal achievement for the MCB and multiculturalism.[211] The 2006 Act was the 'legal crescendo' of a process whereby religion came to be redefined as 'an inherent source of identity and not merely a system of belief'.[212] The given definition of religious hatred is the very epitome of a right to collective integrity: 'hatred against a group of persons defined by reference to religious belief or lack of religious belief'.[213] It seemingly does not apply to individual believers who are not identifiable with a wider group.[214] In other words, the multiculturalists had successfully co-opted the language of liberal individualism to ensure that discrimination and hatred laws originally intended to deal with racial identity came to cover group religious identity as well.[215]

2.4.3 Decline

The long 1990s came to an end with 9/11. Though multiculturalism was still at its most influential and many of its successes lay ahead, the ground was beginning to shift. The raw optimism that had once characterised New Labour's approach to religious diversity quickly began to fade as Blair realised, 'No, life's not like that. There's plenty of bad things out there that could happen, and one of them has.'[216] His government thereafter began to view religion, and Islam in particular, as 'a social problem to be controlled'.[217] The final turning point was 7/7. The coordinated suicide attacks on London in 2005 were 'the first incidents of religious warfare in England since the end of the seventeenth century'.[218] They also seem to have

207 Home Secretary, 'Memorandum to the Home Affairs Committee: Post-Legislative Scrutiny of the Racial and Religious Hatred Act 2006' (HMG, Cm 8164, August 2011), p. 7.

208 Ibid., p. 2.

209 Crown Prosecution Service (CPS), 'Racist and Religious Crime – CPS Guidance' (HMG, 2007 Edition).

210 Khadijah Elshayyal, *Muslim Identity Politics: Islam, Activism and Equality in Britain* (London: I.B. Tauris, 2020), pp. 173, 124–6, 199–200, 203.

211 Modood, *Multiculturalism*, pp. 172–3.

212 Addison, *Religious Discrimination*, p. xxiii.

213 Public Order Act 1986, s. 29A.

214 Sandberg, *Law and Religion*, p. 143.

215 Addison, *Religious Discrimination*, p. xxiii.

216 Tony Blair quoted in Rachel, *Don't Look Back in Anger*, p. 437.

217 Sandberg, *Law and Religion*, p. 141 footnote 66.

218 Addison, *Religious Discrimination*, p. xxiii.

done for multiculturalism what the Manson murders did for the 1960s and the hippies: buried an era and tainted an entire movement.[219] From then on, successive governments sought to distance themselves.[220] In December 2006, Blair gave a speech in which he reaffirmed his support for a 'multicultural, multi-faith Britain'. However, he accepted that the bombings had thrown 'into sharp relief' multicultural policies that did not stress shared values or integration and denounced the 'new and virulent form of ideology associated with a minority of our Muslim community'.[221] More than a decade later, he reiterated his regret that 'multiculturalism has been misinterpreted as meaning a justified refusal to integrate when it should never have meant that'.[222] Blair's immediate successor, Gordon Brown, made similar noises[223] before David Cameron went further and declared that the 'doctrine of state multiculturalism' had failed and that 'frankly, we need a lot less of the passive tolerance of recent years and much more active, muscular liberalism'.[224] These statements were indicative of a greater resolve by government to override the multicultural right to collective integrity. This manifested most clearly in revisions to the CONTEST Strategy for countering terrorism and extremism which became more aggressively interventionist in promoting 'British values'.[225] Throughout this period, namely the declining years of New Labour, the MCB likewise fell from grace and with it went any official commitment to the right to collective representation. This was largely owing to its inconveniently vocal opposition to the Iraq War and the growing realisation that it was neither very moderate nor very representative of British Muslims.[226] By 2009, it had lost its privileged position as the government's go-to consultee for Muslim affairs and regular contact was cut off by Hazel Blears, then Secretary of State for Communities and Local Government.[227]

Although multiculturalism has long since lost its favoured status, it left an indelible mark on English law and has never completely died out. Traces

[219] See generally James Riley, *The Bad Trip: Dark Omens, New Worlds and the End of the Sixties* (London: Icon Books, 2019).

[220] Modood, *Multiculturalism*, p. 144; Catherine Curran-Vigier, 'From Multiculturalism to Global Values: How New Labour Set the Agenda' (2008) 5 *Observatoire de la société britannique* 65–80.

[221] Tony Blair, 'Speech on Multiculturalism and Integration' (No. 10 National Archies, 6 December 2006).

[222] Tony Blair, *The Glue That Binds: Integration in a Time of Populism* (Tony Blair Institute for Global Change, 21 April 2019), pp. 3–4.

[223] Derek McGhee, *End of Multiculturalism: Terrorism, Integration and Human Rights* (London: Open University Press, 2008) p. 132; Gordon Brown, 'Speech on Britishness and Immigration Policy' (*The Guardian*, 27 February 2007).

[224] BBC News, 'State Multiculturalism Has Failed, Says David Cameron' (*BBC News*, 5 February 2011).

[225] HMG, 'Prevent Strategy' (London: HMG, Cm 8092, June 2011).

[226] Modood, *Multiculturalism*, p. 173; Bowen, *Medina in Birmingham*, pp. 2–3.

[227] Vikram Dodd, 'Muslim Council Accuses Government of Undermining Independence' (*The Guardian*, 26 March 2009).

remain in many areas. The police and the CPS continue to use a subjective definition of race/religion to identify racial/religious incidents/crimes: 'Any incident/crime which is perceived by the victim or any other person to be motivated by hostility or prejudice based on a person's race/religion or perceived race/religion.'[228] As regards collective representation, the government has expanded its consultations with a greater range of groups since letting go of the MCB. Although the focus has shifted from 'which group speaks for Muslims?' to 'what is the mainstream Muslim opinion on this particular issue?', the working assumption is still that Muslims can in some way be represented as a group.[229] The MCB successfully re-established relations with the Labour Party under Jeremy Corbyn and his successor, Keir Starmer.[230] There has also been considerable pushback against perceived government attempts to interfere with the collective integrity of British Muslims. This is most evident in the furious debate over the Prevent Strategy, which seeks to combat extremism and pre-emptively stop people from becoming terrorists.[231] The most obvious legacy item, however, is the entrenchment of racial and religious identity politics in the public square such that rows over racism and Islamophobia are now rarely out of the media.[232] The use of the term 'Islamophobia' by academics grew exponentially during the 2010s, with 1,613 papers on it through to 2018 compared to only 310 papers throughout the 2000s.[233] Much the same is true of 'racist', which reached 'near-saturation in the humanities and soft social sciences by the 2010s' before surging yet again and exploding in the media from 2014 onwards.[234] While success on this scale is unlikely to be fleeting, there are signs that these words – once damaging charges to be refuted at all costs – are becoming worn out and contemptible in the world beyond academia and the 'Brahmin Left'.[235] This problem is not new and can happen to even the most straightforward terms. The Roman republic (*res publica*), for example, had become so ineffectual by the time of Caesar

[228] CPS, 'Racist and Religious Hate Crime – Prosecution Guidance' (HMG, 2020 Edition).

[229] O'Toole et al., 'Taking Part', p. 6; Jones et al., 'System of Self-Appointed Leaders?', pp. 214–15.

[230] MCB, 'All Labour Leadership Candidates Sign Up to MCB's Ten Key Pledges' (MCB, 16 January 2020).

[231] For an overview, see Steven Greer and Lindsey Bell, 'Counter-Terrorist Law in British Universities: A Review of the "Prevent" Debate' (2018) *Public Law* 84–105.

[232] See generally Tariq Modood, 'The Strange Non-death of Multiculturalism' (European University Institute Max Weber Lecture Series, 2013/03, 20 February 2013); Tariq Modood, 'Understanding "Death of Multiculturalism" Discourse Means Understanding Multiculturalism' (2014) 9(3) *Journal of Multicultural Discourses* 201–11.

[233] All Party Parliamentary Group on British Muslims (APPGBM), 'Islamophobia Defined: Report on the Inquiry into a Working Definition of Islamophobia/Anti-Muslim Hatred' (APPGBM, 27 November 2018), p. 27.

[234] Eric Kaufmann, *Whiteshift: Populism, Immigration and the Future of White Majorities* (London: Penguin, 2019), pp. 322–3; Eric Kaufmann, 'Why the Left Is Losing' (*Law & Liberty*, 13 February 2020), fig. 2.

[235] See Thomas Piketty, *Capital and Ideology* (Cambridge, MA: Harvard University Press, 2019), pp. 807–61.

that he could describe it as 'nothing, merely a word without form or substance'.[236] Barbara Tuchman similarly observed that 'natural human functioning' undermined a key tenet of medieval thought: 'Chivalry, the dominant idea of the ruling class, left as great a gap between ideal and practice as religion … When the gap between ideal and real becomes too wide, the system breaks down. Legend and story have always reflected this; in the Arthurian romances the Round Table is shattered from within.'[237] The point is simply this: words, phrases and concepts can become so elastic, so liberally applied or so removed from reality, that their descriptive value abates. This often has unsettling practical consequences.

Contrast the following from the political sphere. In 2006, Nigel Farage, then an MEP for the United Kingdom Independence Party (UKIP), unsuccessfully demanded an apology from then-leader of the Conservative Party David Cameron for calling UKIP 'fruitcakes and loonies and closet racists mostly'. Farage stated: 'We don't mind name-calling, it's politics, but in this day and age there are things you can't call people and racist is one of them … Fruitcakes and loonies we can live with – we have a sense of humour – but we draw the line at his unfounded accusations of racism.'[238] This is indicative of the gravity that a charge of racism once possessed. Things look very different now. In 2018, Steven K. Bannon, a friend and ally of Farage, was met with rapturous applause when he addressed the French National Front on the tactics of globalist elites: 'Let them call you racist. Let them call you xenophobes. Let them call you nativists. Wear it as a badge of honour. Because every day we get stronger and they get weaker.'[239] This televised pronouncement suggests that accusations of racism are no longer to be feared and are increasingly regarded either as a joke or as mere partisan tactics.[240] This trend is also beginning to filter through English law. In one of the leading decisions on electoral fraud, Mr Commissioner Richard Mawrey QC lamented that '[a]ccusations of racism were the common currency of left/right infighting in the Labour Party but, viewed objectively, none of the participants was remotely racist in any sense that would be understood by a person not in the emotionally over-heated committee rooms in the Town Hall … [A] feature of all these left/right disputes is the ubiquity of the phrase "dogwhistle politics".'[241] He went on to explain that the relevant issues had 'absolutely nothing to do with racism whatsoever'[242] and that

[236] Quoted in Suetonius, *De Vita Caesarum* at 77.1, translated by Lucca Fezzi in *Crossing the Rubicon: Caesar's Decision and the Fate of Rome* (London: Yale University Press, 2019), p. 5.

[237] Barbara Tuchman, *A Distant Mirror: The Calamitous 14th Century* (London: Penguin, 2017), p. xxvi.

[238] Ros Taylor, 'Cameron Refuses to Apologise to Ukip' (*The Guardian*, 4 April 2006).

[239] Morgan Winsor, 'Steve Bannon: "Let Them Call You Racist … Wear It as a Badge of Honor"' (*abcNews*, 10 March 2018).

[240] For a historical perspective on this phenomenon, see Tom Holland, 'Tom Holland over hoe het christendom het Westen vormde' (De Ongelooflijke Podcast, 28 February 2020).

[241] *Erlam & Ors* v. *Rahman & Anor* [2015] EWHC 1215 (QB), paras. 195–6.

[242] Para. 195.

> [t]he advantage of the cliché is that one may take a completely innocent, indeed anodyne, statement of a political opponent and claim that it contains a 'coded' message often, as Wikipedia remarks, of a racist nature. It is a cliché much employed by the media-political class but it must be remarked that, in real life, it is usually invoked to accuse political opponents of saying something which they had not said and had had no intention of saying. In short, the 'code' often exists only in the mind of the person crying 'dog-whistle politics' at his adversary.[243]

What is more, it is becoming increasingly risky to level such accusations. In October 2016, the US-based Southern Poverty Law Centre (SPLC) published a 'Field Guide to Anti-Muslim Extremists'. This organisation claims to 'monitor hate groups and other extremists throughout the US and exposes their activities to law enforcement agencies, the media and the public'.[244] This document included the British broadcaster, author and activist Maajid Nawaz, who describes himself as 'a secular liberal Muslim' and 'counter-extremist'.[245] Nawaz and his Quilliam Foundation obtained a $3.375 million settlement and public apology from the SPLC, which stated that he had 'made valuable and important contributions to public discourse, including by promoting pluralism and condemning both anti-Muslim bigotry and Islamist extremism ... [T]hey are most certainly not anti-Muslim extremists.'[246] The news agencies CNN and *The Washington Post* recently and respectively settled $275 million and $250 million defamation suits launched by a high school student, Nick Sandmann, who was misleadingly portrayed as the aggressor in an allegedly racist and widely televised confrontation with a Native American man in Washington DC in January 2019.[247] In 2018, under Scots law, a former SNP Councillor won £40,000 in damages for an 'implausible and inherently unlikely' accusation of racism against Pakistanis, which was 'activated by malice and ill-will as part of a campaign directed against the pursuer by the opposing faction within the local SNP'.[248] These examples from multiple jurisdictions would further suggest that

243 Para. 197.

244 SPLC, 'Fighting Hate' (SPLC website, accessed 17 February 2021) www.splcenter.org/fighting-hate.

245 Quilliam, 'Maajid Nawaz' (Quilliam website, accessed 17 February 2021) www.quilliaminternational.com/about/staff/maajid-nawaz/.

246 SPLC, 'SPLC Apology to Maajid Nawaz and the Quilliam Foundation' (SPLC, 22 June 2018); Quilliam, 'Southern Poverty Law Center, Inc. Admits It Was Wrong, Apologizes to Quilliam and Maajid Nawaz for Field Guide to Anti-Muslim Extremists, and Agrees to Pay $3.375 Million Settlement' (Quilliam, 18 June 2018).

247 Erica Davies, 'Pay Day: CNN settles $275 Million Suit from MAGA Hat-Wearing Covington Catholic Student Nick Sandmann after Stand-Off Video' (*The Sun*, 7 January 2020); Cameron Knight, 'CNN Confirms a Settlement Has Been Reached with Covington Catholic Student Nick Sandmann' (*USA Today News*, 7 January 2020); Emily Crane, 'Kentucky Teen Settles $250m Defamation Lawsuit against Washington Post after Claiming the Outlet Made Him Out to Be a Racist Following His Stand-Off with a Native American at the Lincoln Memorial' (*Daily Mail*, 24 July 2020).

248 *McAnulty* v. *McCulloch* [2018] CSOH 121 at paras. 25, 27, 38.

'racism' and its derivates are now as overbroad as they are overused – the problem being less that they mean nothing and more that they have come to mean anything. In short, the vernacular of multiculturalism is also starting to look like a victim of entropy and its own success.

2.5 Conclusion

The English law of religion has been heavily impacted by multiculturalism in recent decades. Parekh and Modood's thinking informs and explains major developments in legal policy, namely: attempts to redress racial/religious injustice, increasing sensitivity to the collective claims of organised religion, and the de facto recognition of group rights. As theorists, they are right in two important respects: (i) the threat posed by liberal individualist law to the integrity of religious groups; and (ii) the need to treat groups as actors in their own right requiring legal protection. Notwithstanding, multiculturalism is inimical to the effective governance of organised religion. This is primarily owing to Parekh and Modood's crude understanding of groups, which leads them to treat broad categories of people as actors with meaningful agency and rights. The fault does not originate with them as the English language is 'notoriously poor' at signifying different collective entities.[249] The problem is compounded by the Islamic concept of the *umma*, which denotes the fictional unified community of all Muslims across the globe.[250] It has been an ungraspable dream since at least the mid-seventh century when the First Fitna (Muslim civil war) overthrew the Rashidun Caliphate and created permanent schisms within Islam. Nevertheless, the notion of the faith personified as a homogeneous community remains powerful and appealing. In practice, it lends credence to the idea that Islam must be the primary, if not sole, focus of loyalty for all believers. It follows that any attack – verbal or physical – on one Muslim or subset of Muslims, or indeed any of their beliefs, is necessarily an assault upon them all and a slight against the faith itself. In short, the English language and a concept endemic to Islam militate against clear thinking.

The multiculturalists' culpability begins with their preference for style over substance. Combining elements from both classic scholarly definitions of bullshit, multiculturalism is partly Frankfurtian in that it displays indifference to truth and reality, and partly Cohenian in that even its lucid utterances are manifestly unprofound and unclarifiably unclear.[251] In this it is the purest

[249] Antony Black (ed.), 'Introduction' in Otto von Gierke, *Community in Historical Perspective: A Translation of Selections from Das deutsche Genossenschaftsrecht*, Mary Fischer (transl.) (Cambridge: Cambridge University Press, 1990), p. xxxiii.

[250] John L. Esposito, *Islam: The Straight Path* (Oxford: Oxford University Press, 1988), p. 65. The comparable aspiration of a unified 'Christendom' was dealt a fatal blow by the centuries-long wars of religion following the Reformation – see Mark Greengrass, *Christendom Destroyed: Europe 1517–1648* (London: Penguin, 2015).

[251] Harry G. Frankfurt, *On Bullshit* (Princeton, NJ: Princeton University Press, 2005), pp. 33–4, 55, 63; G. A. Cohen, 'Complete Bullshit' in *Finding Oneself in the Other* (Princeton, NJ: Princeton University Press, 2013), pp. 106–7 footnotes 26, 27.

expression of early Blairism: untrammelled idealism, difference splitting, short termism, trite sloganeering, sentimental journeying, thoughtless compromise, conceptual incoherence, erratic emotivism, philosophy by committee. Not to be found in any standard jurisprudence textbook, the scholarship is unrigorous, dodges difficult questions, indulges in half-baked conspiracism about global neoconservatism and is replete with self-negating declarations on tired culture war issues like free speech which would be 'more or less effective for a rally or leaflet'.[252] There is little discernible interest in the unglamorous fields of law reform where the greatest improvements to everyday life can be made. Even as anti-racist advocacy, it 'is ineffective and even destructive when it takes the place of scholarly interpretation or strategic political analysis'.[253] These defects, consequent on its origins in intellectual activism and semi-public committees, resurface time and again in the chapters to follow. Parekh and Modood could be forgiven for unprincipled pragmatism if they had detailed workable reforms on specific social issues; they could be forgiven for not having granular legal knowledge of every relevant field if they had a coherent theory from which one could deduce constructive legal policy; they have neither. It is governance by bromide, if indeed it is governance at all.

Articulation is especially important whenever group rights and wrongdoing with a collective dimension are at issue. The multicultural approach to Muslim representation leaves many unanswerable questions unanswered. For example, the MCB has been at the forefront of various unsuccessful efforts to introduce an actionable official definition of Islamophobia.[254] The latest was designed by Modood and the All Party Parliamentary Group on British Muslims (APPGBM): 'Islamophobia is rooted in racism and is a type of racism that targets expressions of Muslimness or perceived Muslimness.'[255] It comes with a series of fantastical slovenly tests for 'ulterior motives' and 'mutual learning', which only ever generate the answer that 'X *may* be Islamophobic or racist'.[256] Regardless, this racialised definition reflects the multicultural tendency to think of Muslims in class terms and is a well-meaning exercise in self-defeat. The point of the APPGBM project is to refute 'the myth of Islamic uniformity' by addressing prejudicial behaviour which 'essentialises Muslims, locating them in a homogenous [*sic*] group defined by one, single essence that is continuously depicted and perceived as incompatible, or inassimilable, with western societies'.[257] However, when Muslims are attacked as though they

[252] Adolph Reed Jr, 'Antiracism: A Neoliberal Alternative to a Left' (2018) 42 *Dialectical Anthropology* 105–15, p. 105.

[253] Ibid.

[254] See generally APPGBM, 'Islamophobia Defined'; Trevor Phillips, John Jenkins and Martyn Frampton, 'On Islamophobia: The Problem of Definition' (Policy Exchange, 2019).

[255] APPGBM, ibid., p. 50.

[256] Contrast the contradictory instructions on its application in Modood, *Essays on Secularism and Multiculturalism*, pp. 85–6 and APPGBM, 'Islamophobia Defined', p. 36.

[257] APPGBM, ibid., p. 48.

were a racial unit, it does not follow that they can be adequately defended through laws and policies which frame them as such. Treating 'expressions of Muslimness or perceived Muslimness' as though they were immutable racial characteristics (themselves suspect[258]) grants in principle the very premise it seeks to deny.

Further, a recent study of Muslim understandings of Islamophobia found no majority consensus on any of the sample statements. For 'Most Muslims sympathise with terrorists', there was a fifty/fifty split as to whether or not it was Islamophobic; 'British Muslims do not share western values' and 'Muslims often overreact to criticism of their religion' each produced a forty-seven (Islamophobic)/fifty-three (not Islamophobic) split; and 'Muslims have too much influence in Britain' produced a forty-four (Islamophobic)/fifty-six (not Islamophobic) split. Muslims who possessed a degree were 63 per cent more sensitive to such statements than their co-religionists.[259] In other words, the absence of even a bare majority on this issue reflects the fact that there is little that unites Muslims beyond their self-categorisation as such. Even if there were a majority on a given issue – the surest sign of something being mainstream – that is still no reason to grant its wishes. For example, a recent poll found that 52 per cent of British Muslims thought that homosexuality should be made illegal.[260] Similarly, the MCB maintains a policy of refusing membership to Ahmadiyya Muslims on the basis that they are not genuine Muslims.[261] As a religious organisation, it is entirely legitimate for them do so but, so far as the state is concerned, this must automatically disqualify them from official recognition. If the MCB is once more treated as representative, the state would be straying into theological dispute by tacitly granting that the Ahmadiyya are not true or good Muslims. It has no business doing so. Muslim organisations, large and small, are legitimate representatives only of their own and their members' interests. Clearly, the state could not entertain acting upon this just because it is mainstream and some loud activists demand it; just as important are the interests of Ahmadiyya and LGBT citizens and the 48 per cent of Muslims who did not wish to make it illegal. The only way to deal with such matters is on principle, not according to crude majoritarianism. As Michael Sandel notes, it is simply not possible to govern a diverse society or protect minorities within minorities based on 'the idea that rights should rest on the values that predominate in any given community at any given time'.[262]

[258] See generally Adam Rutherford, *How to Argue with a Racist: History, Science, Race and Reality* (London: W&N, 2020).

[259] Julian Hargreaves and L. Daniel Staetsky, 'Antisemitism and Islamophobia: Measuring Everyday Sensitivity in the UK' (2019) *Ethnic and Racial Studies* 1–23, pp. 10–11.

[260] Frances Perraudin, 'Half of All British Muslims Think Homosexuality Should Be Illegal, Poll Finds' (*The Guardian*, 11 April 2016).

[261] MCB, 'Position Statement: The Muslim Council of Britain and Ahmadis' (MCB, 6 April 2016).

[262] Michael J. Sandel, *Liberalism and the Limits of Justice* (2nd ed., Cambridge: Cambridge University Press, 1998), p. x.

Relatedly, it is hard to see where multiculturalism leaves the Armed Forces Muslim Association (AFMA), which strives to 'recognise the contribution [of] Muslim personnel' and make the military 'a welcoming place to work for Muslims'. This is no small task given that more British Muslims have joined ISIS (more than 900)[263] than serve in the UK armed forces (currently 650).[264] AFMA's founder and the British Army's first Muslim chaplain Imam Asim Hafiz OBE has stated unequivocally that he believes 'there is no conflict' between being Muslim and serving in the armed forces.[265] He laments the abundancy of disinformation and has stated:

> There is no doubt a misunderstanding among the Muslim community that this is somehow a war against Islam. The military is out there trying to support Afghanistan and the Afghan people. They are not fighting a religion or a culture. Just because [British Muslims] join the armed forces doesn't mean they lose their soul or lose their faith. I've met many Muslims (in the forces) who are very devout.[266]

Under multiculturalism, any Muslim involvement with the British forces tasked with carrying out a neoconservative agenda would seem, to put it at its mildest, like the worst possible betrayal of Muslims everywhere and a threat to their collective integrity. That serving British Muslims could fight against hostile Muslim forces out of 'love of Allah, Queen and country'[267] does not seem possible on this view despite Modood's wish to create an inclusive national identity. In light of the stakes, it seems fair to say that Britain and British Muslims deserve better philosophising than this.

There is perhaps one final thing to be said in favour of multiculturalism. In a Festschrift in honour of Parekh, Paul Kelly's opening chapter draws attention to the possible indirect and 'unconscious influences' that a forgotten school of thought may have had on multiculturalism.[268] He detects echoes of early twentieth-century pluralism in Parekh's work, and in particular the ideas of Otto von Gierke, Frederic W. Maitland, John Neville Figgis, G. D. H. Cole and Harold Laski.[269] A particularly important affinity is the idea that there is more

[263] Lizzie Dearden and Richard Hall, 'The Britons Who Went to Join Isis: Where Are They Now?' (*The Independent*, 15 February 2019).

[264] AFMA, 'About Us' (AFMA website, accessed 17 February 2021) https://afma.org.uk/about-us/.

[265] Asim Hafiz, 'Muslim Chaplaincy in the UK: The Chaplaincy Approach as a Way to a Modern Imamate' (2015) 43(1) *Religion, State & Society* 85–99; Asim Hafiz, 'Islam and the Armed Forces: Are They Compatible?' (AFMA, 28 March 2017).

[266] Poonam Taneja, 'Army Imam Says British Muslims Can Be Good Soldiers' (*BBC News*, 13 January 2014).

[267] Zaki Cooper, 'For Love of Allah, Queen And Country' (*The Times*, 21 July 2018).

[268] See Varun Uberoi's 'Introduction' to Varun Uberoi and Tariq Modood (eds.), *Multiculturalism Rethought: Interpretations, Dilemmas and New Directions* (Edinburgh: Edinburgh University Press, 2015), p. 16.

[269] Paul Kelly, 'Situating Bhikhu Parekh's Multiculturalism: Bhikhu Parekh and Twentieth-Century British Political Thought' in Uberoi and Modood, *Multiculturalism Rethought*, ch. 1, pp. 33–40, 45–50.

to political life and philosophy than the relations between the individual and the monistic state (contrary to the premises of liberal individualism) because intermediary groups play a central role in mediating this relationship and in so doing shape public culture.[270] Likewise, there is a similar notion that groups, especially religious ones, have some kind of inherent worth and authority over their members against that of the state and that these should not be compelled to secularise in line with the public sphere.[271] In the end, however, neither Parekh nor Modood cites the pluralists in their own work, so any claims made regarding the impact of these on multiculturalism are based on 'at best circumstantial evidence'.[272] Kelly oversteps when he claims that the multiculturalists' superficial account of society as a community of communities and citizens 'could have been lifted directly' from the pluralists, but he is right to suggest that the faint resemblance speaks to the credit of the former.[273] At the very least, it shows that the multiculturalists are dimly aware that any cogent account of the law and religion relationship must contain a robust theory of groups. For that, however, one must look to the pluralists themselves.

[270] Kelly, ibid., p. 33. [271] Ibid., pp. 33–6. [272] Ibid., p. 33. [273] Ibid.

3

Classical Pluralism

In all questions of this nature the practice of mankind ought to have great weight against the theories of individuals.[1]

3.1 An Introduction to Otto von Gierke

Classical pluralism is an ill-fitting label for the thought of Otto von Gierke. First, it seems somewhat improper to employ the term 'classical' when Gierke loathed all things Roman and spent his life fighting the classical inheritance. Second, the term 'pluralism' is anachronistic for Gierke and hence an added insult to the legacy of a meticulous historian.[2] There are no better alternatives, however. These are meaningless mouthfuls for modern English speakers (*Genossenschaftstheorie* or 'Gierkean organismic theory') or misleadingly politicised ('liberal pluralism') or already refer to other distinct movements ('associationalism').[3] Though suboptimal, classical pluralism acknowledges Gierke's original genius as a poet of common law, is comparatively easy to pronounce, carries less baggage, distinguishes Gierkean philosophy from related movements and irrelevant movements such as 'value pluralism' or 'legal pluralism', and alludes to more of the relevant themes than any of its competitors.[4] In subsequent chapters, however, the book will simply adopt the term 'pluralism' when formulating arguments and policies in the spirit of Gierke. The serviceability of this terminology will become clearer as this chapter progresses. Clearer still will be the ways in which Gierke is the ideal philosopher for those who dislike philosophising, the ideal jurist for those who

[1] Alexander Hamilton, 'On the Constitutionality of a National Bank' (23 February 1791) in Carson Holloway and Bradford P. Wilson (eds.), *The Political Writings of Alexander Hamilton, Volume II: 1789–1804* (Cambridge: Cambridge University Press, 2017), p. 77.

[2] It was first coined by Harold Laski in 1915 and never adopted by Gierke himself. See James Kirby, 'History, Law and Freedom: F.W. Maitland in Context' (2019) 16(1) *Modern Intellectual History* 127–54, p. 129.

[3] See, respectively, F. W. Coker, *Organismic Theories of the State: Nineteenth Century Interpretations of the State as Organism or as Person* (New York: Columbia University Press, 1910), pp. 76–80; Rupert Emerson, *State and Sovereignty in Modern Germany* (New Haven, CT: Yale University Press, 1928), pp. 126–54; Paul Q. Hirst, *Associative Democracy: New Forms of Economic and Social Governance* (Cambridge: Polity Press, 1993), pp. 15–16.

[4] On classical German genius and England's troubled relationship with it, see Jonathan Bate, *The Genius of Shakespeare* (London: Picador Classics, 2016), pp. 180–4.

dislike lawyers, the ideal political theorist for those who dislike politicking, and the ideal intellectual for those who care nothing for names, cliques or fashionable opinion.

Born on 11 January 1841 in Stettin, Pomerania (now Szczecin, Poland), Gierke found his formative years and education saturated in Prussian conservatism. Having studied in Berlin to become a Doctor of Law by the age of nineteen, he enjoyed near-lifelong rude health. A polymath of the highest order, he was also known as a consummate socialite with a talent for conversing with all sorts, apparently viewing this as essential to sustaining his charm, literary style and ability to combine theoretical and practical ideas. Like Mozart, he could party late into the night and return straight home to work until dawn. After graduating, he served in the army and began his academic career as an historian and jurist in 1865, interspersed as it was with distinguished service in the artillery during the Austro-Prussian and Franco-Prussian wars. Thereafter he held professorships at Breslau (1872–84), Heidelberg (1884–7) and Berlin (1887–1921). The foundations for his success were laid in 1868 when, at the insistence of Theodor Mommsen, the first of four instalments of Gierke's magnum opus was published, *Das Deutsche Genossenschaftsrecht* ('The German Law of Associations', hereafter *DDG*).[5] The second followed in 1873, the third in 1881, the fourth in 1913. A mooted fifth volume was never written. This series was the culmination of a lifelong endeavour to reconcile unity and plurality as he found them in history. He died from lung complications in Berlin on 10 October 1921.[6]

Gierke's academic life was framed by the struggle between two factions of the Historical School over the formation of the German constitution. This movement arose in reaction to natural law and abstract rationalism. It posited that law, like language and art, was an expression of a people. Friedrich Carl von Savigny (1779–1861) inaugurated the School in 1814 with his seminal essay *On the Vocation of Our Age for Legislation and Jurisprudence*. In this and other works, he urged jurists to study the sources and historical evolution of national law to better understand the present and shape the future in accordance with the character of the people.[7] For Savigny and his disciples, this meant looking back to the reception of Roman law during the fifteenth century, admiring its codified abstractions of public and private, its universalistic

[5] Ewan McGaughey (transl.), '"Introduction" to Otto von Gierke, "The Social Role of Private Law"' (2018) 19(4) *German Law Journal* 1017–1116, pp. 1018–19; Sobei Mogi, *Otto von Gierke: His Political Teaching and Jurisprudence* (London: P.S. King & Son, 1932), p. 15.

[6] See generally Mogi, ibid., pp. 14–15, 17, 24, 27; John D. Lewis, *The Genossenschaft Theory of Otto Von Gierke: A Study in Political Thought* (Madison: University of Wisconsin, 1935; Literary Licensing LLC reprint, 2013), pp. 22–3; Ron Harris, 'The Transplantation of the Legal Discourse on Corporate Personality Theories: From German Codification to British Political Pluralism and American Big Business' (2006) 63 *Washington and Lee Law Review* 1421–78, pp. 1427–31.

[7] For an overview, see R. W. M. Dias, *Jurisprudence* (5th ed., London: Butterworths, 1985), pp. 375–84; G. W. Paton and David P. Derham, *Jurisprudence* (4th ed., Oxford: Clarendon Press, 1972), pp. 19–21.

aspirations and uncompromising individualism, as well as its potential for formalising a legal system across disparate imperial territories. Gierke, however, was a 'determined, fighting Germanist'.[8] These rival historicists saw themselves as heirs to Arminius, animated by the desire to drive alien Roman influences out of German jurisprudence. For them, native medieval common law was the true wellspring of the *Volksgeist* (spirit of the people) and it was imperative that this submerged tradition be recovered. Gierke's mentor was Georg Beseler (1809–88), a founding father of Germanism who instilled in his pupil a deep loathing for imported legal concepts and a love for historical inquiry into associative law.[9] The catalysing moment for these competing schools came in 1888 with the publication of the draft Civil Code (*Bürgerliches Gesetzbuch*). It was a bitter disappointment to the Germanists and they attacked it furiously, winning a substantial rewrite to preserve something of Germany's indigenous communal traditions and preventing a purely Romanist codification.[10] Gierke famously warned:

> The Roman tendency found its chief expression in the systems and experiments of the Communists and Socialists. Although their methods and aims diverged greatly, they all aimed to bring into play the highest universality . . . [while] some aimed towards the despotism of equality – in comparison with which Asiatic despotism would be freedom itself.[11]

Nevertheless, the Germanists ultimately lost when the Code was adopted in 1896 and took effect in 1900. Even at the end of his career, Gierke was still fighting a rearguard action with a three-volume treatise on German private law (1895–1917). He saw the continuation of the struggle as a solemn duty and determined to interpret the Code in accordance with Germanistic ideals, thereby to 'save of the German law and for the German law what could still be saved'.[12]

If Gierke is remembered at all, his reputation is overshadowed by his association with German nationalism. Military service left a deep imprint on Gierke's psyche and he cast the experience of going to war in rapturous terms:

> [T]here are times when the spirit of the community reveals itself to us with an elemental power, in an almost visible shape, filling and mastering our inward being to such an extent that we are hardly any longer conscious of our individual existence, as such. Here, in Berlin, in the Unter den Linden, I lived through such

8 Lewis, *Genossenschaft Theory*, p. 17.

9 See Lewis, ibid., pp. 17–25; Mogi, *Otto von Gierke*, pp. 11–28; McGaughey, 'Social Role of Private Law', pp. 1018–26. Beseler's own masterpiece was *Volksrecht und Jurisrecht [People's Law and Jurists' Law]* (Leipzig: Weidmann, 1843). For an overview of the influences on Gierke, see Michael Dreyer, 'German Roots of the Theory of Pluralism' (1993) 4(1) *Constitutional Political Economy* 7–39.

10 Mogi, *Otto von Gierke*, p. 25; Lewis, pp. 18–19; Harris, 'The Transplantation', p. 1422 footnote 1.

11 Harris, ibid., p. 1438.

12 Lewis, *Genossenschaft Theory*, p. 19.

> an hour of consecration . . . in the year 1870 [when the Franco-Prussian War broke out].[13]

He began to view war as 'most intensely productive of culture' and saw in 1914 an opportunity to unleash the 'world-conquering energy . . . of the German nature' which alone was capable of enlightening the intended subject races of a global Reich.[14] Shortly before the outbreak of the Great War, he had played up the affinities among the three great Teutonic powers – Germany, England, the United States – which shared bonds of 'blood and iron [and] civil war'.[15] As the conflict progressed, however, his fervour increased to the point of unquestioning faith and he was even cited by the US Committee on Public Information as an exemplar of German militarism.[16] He could scarcely console himself once Germany's cause came to grief. In his final public address in 1919, he railed against his countrymen for their 'shameless disavowal of earlier national spirit', 'the rejection by the masses of all thought of their fatherland' and the passing of an age of German heroes.[17] Laced with pathos and conspiracy, these closing words were an ominous portent of what was to come. With Gierke's passing in 1921, the stage was set for the next generation of jurists to pursue notions of German degeneracy, wartime betrayal and revanchism to their logical conclusion. In all this, Gierke was a man of his time and, like so many intellectuals, allowed himself to be swept up by the zeitgeist.[18] This was more than enough to poison his legacy, but the increased popularity of his works during the 1930s and their distortion by the Nazis did for the rest.[19] A century after his death, Gierke is little more than a shade in the academy, a stark reminder that personal politics and posthumous appropriation can descend like thick fog over a life's work, tainting it and obscuring the author's brilliance.

3.1.1 History and Interpretation

Gierke's obscurity among the English-speaking peoples is owing in large part to his elusiveness. Reading him is akin to engaging with scripture or fragments from antiquity. This is especially true of Gierke's political ideas, which were

13 Quoted in A. W. Sparkes, *Talking Politics: A Wordbook* (London: Routledge, 1994), p. 97.

14 Maria Tatar, *Lustmord: Sexual Murder in Weimar Germany* (Princeton, NJ: Princeton University Press, 1997), p. 196 footnote 15; Wallace Notestein and Elmer Stoll, *Conquest and Kultur: Aims of the Germans in Their Own Words* (Washington, DC: US Committee on Public Information, 1918), p. 13.

15 Otto von Gierke, 'German Constitutional Law in Its Relation to the American Constitution' (1910) 23(4) *Harvard Law Review* 273–90, pp. 275, 290.

16 Notestein and Stoll, *Conquest and Kultur*, p. 13.

17 Lewis, *Genossenschaft Theory*, p. 23; McGaughey, 'Introduction', p. 1022.

18 Harris, 'The Transplantation', pp. 1438–40.

19 Antony Black (ed.), 'Introduction' in Otto von Gierke, *Community in Historical Perspective: A Translation of Selections from Das deutsche Genossenschaftsrecht*, Mary Fischer (transl.) (Cambridge: Cambridge University Press, 1990), p. xxiii.

never consolidated into an explicit manifesto. They must instead be distilled from disparate historical studies and the occasional inaugural lecture spread over a half-century. This is a difficult process made harder absent a knowledge of German; the English monoglot is entirely dependent on a handful of translations, introductions and monographs. These are uniformly of a very high standard, although some of the older texts are heavily abridged and presented without comprehensive indexes. The only book-length studies date from the 1930s and are now long out of print. Thus, most of Gierke's huge corpus remains inaccessible and unstudied, the sum total of English translations forming a sliver of the German whole.[20] What is more, each interpreter seems to catch a very different meaning from his texts. To give a sense of scale and inscrutability, Gierke has been variously described as 'a nineteenth-century liberal';[21] 'a romantic counter-individualist ... especially close to Marx';[22] a socialistic 'communitarian';[23] 'a collectivist' justifier of 'absolute totalitarian power';[24] an anti-Western, anti-bourgeois, anti-technocratic, anti-equalitarian revolutionary;[25] 'a conservative and a nationalist';[26] a darling of internationalist progressives;[27] 'a pluralist';[28] not a pluralist;[29] a syndicalist;[30] a 'corporatist and quasi-collectivist';[31] 'a unitarist';[32] a Darwinist;[33] a dogmatist;[34] a patriot;[35] an authoritarian;[36] 'a radical reformer, a reactionary, a jingoist';[37] a realist;[38] a Burkean Tory;[39] 'anti-elitist';[40] a Prussian monarchist;[41] and 'a little too republican'.[42] Others have sought to draw a distinction between his earlier and later works, the former agreeably liberal and rich, the latter barren and infected by 'mystical nationalism'.[43] Yet more have claimed that his political theory 'is really but a by-product of other interests' in jurisprudence and legal history, whereas another asserts that these are merely 'secondary to his political theory

20 See generally Mogi, *Otto von Gierke*, pp. 268–82; Lewis, *Genossenschaft Theory*; Frederic W. Maitland (transl.), 'Introduction' in Otto von Gierke, *Political Theories of the Middle Age* (Cambridge: Cambridge University Press, 1900; Cambridge Paperback Library reprint, 2008).

21 Richard Tuck, *Philosophy and Government 1572–1651* (Cambridge: Cambridge University Press, 1993), p. 158; Black, 'Introduction', p. xix.

22 Black, 'Introduction', pp. xviii, xxv.

23 James Q. Whitman, *The Legacy of Roman Law in the German Romantic Era: Historical Vision and Legal Change* (Princeton, NJ: Princeton University Press, 2014), p. 231.

24 Dias, *Jurisprudence*, pp. 383–4.

25 Ernst Troeltsch, 'The Ideas of Natural Law and Humanity in World Politics' in Otto von Gierke, *Natural Law and the Theory of Society 1500–1800* with 'Introduction' by Ernest Barker (transl.) (Boston: Beacon Press reprint, 1957), p. 210.

26 McGaughey, 'Introduction', p. 1018. 27 Ibid. 28 Mogi, *Otto von Gierke*, p. 120.

29 Lewis, *Genossenschaft Theory*, pp. 24, 64, 87, 91.

30 Dreyer, 'German Roots of the Theory of Pluralism', p. 33. 31 Black, 'Introduction', p. xix.

32 Mogi, *Otto von Gierke*, p. 222. 33 Ibid., p. 233.

34 Lewis, *Genossenschaft Theory*, p. 88; Black, 'Introduction', p. xiv.

35 Paul Q. Hirst (ed.), 'Introduction' to *The Pluralist Theory of the State: Selected Writings of G.D. H. Cole, J.N. Figgis and H.J. Laski* (London: Routledge, 1989), p. 18.

36 Lewis, *Genossenschaft Theory*, p. 91. 37 Ibid., p. 25. 38 Ibid., p. 24. 39 Ibid., pp. 20–1.

40 K. Newton, 'A Critique of the Pluralist Model' (1969) 12(4) *Acta Sociologica* 209–23, p. 209.

41 Lewis, *Genossenschaft Theory*, p. 67. 42 Black, 'Introduction', p. xxv.

43 Black, ibid., pp. xv, xix, xxii; Harris, 'The Transplantation', pp. 1437–40.

agenda'.[44] Dissonance on this scale might suggest vacuity in the source material as with multiculturalism, or it could mean that attempts to pin Gierke to the Bed of Procrustes are missing the point.

Many scholars have noticed the ease with which Gierke can be misread and the fruitlessness of attempts to assign accurate labels to his theory.[45] There are three reasons for this. The first is stylistic: he frequently employed poetic language after the romantic fashion. This 'slightly mystical' rhetoric 'invites misinterpretation' via selective quotation.[46] Second, Gierke's personal beliefs are often mistaken for an integral part of his political philosophy. One must distinguish between the contingent prejudices of a Victorian man and the enduring value of his works. As already outlined, Gierke began as a Prussian patriot and died a conspiratorial German nationalist. His political theory makes no such journey and was continuously enriched throughout Gierke's lifetime. Antony Black, in his otherwise excellent primer, errs on this. He makes two claims: that Gierke 'never substantially modified his theory' and that 'after 1868 he made hardly any noteworthy contribution to the question of how state and association are related'.[47] The former is a misleading half-truth, the latter straightforwardly false. The essence of Gierke's theory did not morph or degenerate over time, but most of his greatest contributions came after the supposed watershed moments of 1868 or 1870–1. The subsequent volumes of *DDG* aside, his definitive accounts of law and state, social law, and the nature of associations did not appear until, respectively, 1874, 1889 and 1902.[48] It would also be difficult to explain his international, cross-partisan appeal to later scholars if his work were as parochial as is sometimes made out. Third, and most importantly, Gierke's versatility serves to obscure his primary vocation as an historian. He went so far as to apologise for departing from 'the spirit of historical analysis' on the rare occasions when he did reveal his own philosophical position.[49] When this is forgotten or downplayed, his ideas seem to license as many interpretations as there are points on the political spectrum.

The key to Gierke is his historicism.[50] All of his ideas – sociological, jurisprudential, political – came to him from history.[51] The starting point for

[44] Lewis, *Genossenschaft Theory*, p. 89; Harris, ibid., p. 1437.

[45] David Runciman, *Pluralism and the Personality of the State* (Cambridge: Cambridge University Press, 1997), pp. 62–3; Black, 'Introduction', p. xiv; Lewis, *Genossenschaft Theory*, pp. 25, 64; Mogi, *Otto von Gierke*, pp. 222–67.

[46] Lewis, *Genossenschaft Theory*, p. 25. [47] Black, 'Introduction', pp. xxx, xxii.

[48] See Runciman, *Pluralism*, p. 61 footnote 52; McGaughey, 'Introduction'; Gierke 'The Nature of Human Associations' (Appendix C) and 'The Basic Concepts of State Law and the Most Recent State-Law Theories' (Appendix D) in Lewis (transl.), *Genossenschaft Theory*, pp. 139–57, 158–85.

[49] Gierke, *Natural Law*, p. 226.

[50] Meaning 'the tendency to regard historical development as the most basic aspect of human existence, and historical thinking as the most important type of thought' as per the non-pejorative third definition in Angus Stevenson (ed.), *The Shorter Oxford English Dictionary* (6th ed., Oxford: Oxford University Press, 2007), p. 1255.

[51] Runciman, *Pluralism*, p. 4.

any investigation into human nature had to be historical experience rather than any set of cherished beliefs. This would reveal that humans and their ideas were, everywhere and always, to be found embedded within groups. These were historically given, not rationally chosen from birth. By tracing the history of communal life and its myriad manifestations back to the earliest times, the historian could illuminate the evolution of ideas and thereby gain insight into the human mind itself. Only when this task was complete could sociology and jurisprudence take over to postulate general rules of human interaction. Without this grounding in reality, political theory was little better than irresponsible speculation upon wishful thinking. Gierke's goal was to produce 'the widest-ranging of all histories of ideas ... [spanning] the whole history of Western political life and thought'.[52] This would have been an unlikely ambition but for the fact that Gierke was a peerless synthesiser of historical knowledge and contemporary law.[53] In this he was the equal of his more famous disciple, Frederic William Maitland.[54] Their common historical method married thoroughness with vision, worldliness with empathy, and directness with erudition. They were what might now be called applied legal historians, interested chiefly in those parts of the past that spoke to present predicaments. The granular details of medieval law were worth mastering because they provided the best defence against naivety. Realism and systematic thought were in history's gift; taking the past seriously was the only way through contemporary social problems.[55]

To challenge Gierke, one must meet him on equal terms as an historian. To defeat the *Genossenschaftstheorie*, it must be shown that Gierke is fundamentally mistaken about the patterns he identifies in past social relations and the conclusions he derives about humanity. Caricatures based on his personal politics will not suffice. Neither will convenient generalisations drawn from over-emphasised or isolated statements.[56] Each of Gierke's ideas formed part of a life-spanning tapestry of thought from which no strand can be unpicked without defacing the whole. Gierke himself often lost sight of this. This is what makes him dangerous and attractive in equal measure, but it is also where his true value lies. Reconstructing Gierke's political philosophy is always a creative act. Anyone who comes to Gierke for answers can find them, whatever their own motivations or prejudices. This is neither good nor bad in itself. Like the whisky distillation process, the final product may be shallow or complex, sharp or smooth, unstable or balanced. Each new interpreter will emphasise or downplay different aspects of his thought, infuse elements of their own, and put him to use for wildly different agendas. Nevertheless, his theory transcends any search for ideological purity and the tribalism of party politics. It creates the space for political disagreement while guaranteeing the legal framework

52 Ibid. 53 Ibid.; Lewis, *Genossenschaft Theory*, p. 20.
54 G. R. Elton, *F.W. Maitland* (London: Weidenfeld and Nicolson, 1985), p. 12.
55 Lewis, *Genossenschaft Theory*, pp. 20–2. 56 Ibid., pp. 25, 64, 85.

under which these discussions can continue to take place. This non-/cross-partisan quality is one of the most refreshing dimensions of his philosophy which, properly understood, must always be taken and implemented as whole. If nothing else, Gierke took ideas seriously; it is only right that his own are given the same courtesy.

3.1.2 Philosophical Tenets

For many, the Middle Ages are a world lit only by fire and George R. R. Martin.[57] Gierke knew better. He had no qualms whatever about drawing from the medieval mind to furnish his own, and proudly admitted to being 'genuinely medieval'. Accordingly, he 'starts from the Whole, but ascribes an intrinsic value to every Partial Whole, down to and including the Individual'.[58] His theory proceeds from the assumption that human nature is dualistic: everyone lives as an individual and as one of a kind, each a world unto himself and each a part of higher unities capable of outlasting him. Man is by nature a social creature.[59] Humans begin life as products of the most fundamental of all groups – the family – and subsequently seek fulfilment in the company of others.[60] Over time, family life generates the tribes, communities and nations that give meaning to a person's life and make viable the very possibility of history. This is because the creation of associations bonds the living to each other as well as to generations past and as yet unborn. Associations draw people out of the confines of our own lives and outlast them, making possible continuity over time and space. Without them, social coherence would be unattainable and each generation's achievements would vanish upon their passing, going unrecorded for posterity. Current and future generations would have no way of knowing about the deeds of their ancestors and, crucially, no means of avoiding past mistakes.[61]

While associations make historical development possible, the driving force is generated by the productive tension between the principles of unity and plurality. If unity dominates, intellectual life is stifled, human excellence atrophies and society descends into absolutism. If plurality triumphs, social consensus becomes impracticable, intellectual life disintegrates and politics relapses into factionalism. Whichever overwhelms the other, it will tyrannise society mercilessly while attempting to preclude the rebirth of its rival, likely without long-term success and potentially at the cost of civil peace. Rather, an accord must be struck and symmetry maintained between the two so that the

[57] William Manchester, *A World Lit Only by Fire: The Medieval Mind and the Renaissance, Portrait of an Age* (London: Little Brown, 1993); George R. R. Martin, *A Song of Ice and Fire* (London: HarperCollins, 1992–?).

[58] Gierke, *Political Theories*, p. 7.

[59] Black, 'Introduction', p. xxi note 19; Gierke, 'Social Law', p. 1034.

[60] Gierke, ibid.; Kirby, 'History, Law and Freedom', p. 130.

[61] Mogi, *Otto von Gierke*, pp. 29–30; Gierke, *Community in Historical Perspective*, p. 2.

particular can exist within the general, the state can defend the whole, civil society can flourish within the state, and individual liberty is protected by law. The state, the association, the individual – each has intrinsic worth, each its own rights and competencies, each keeps the others in check, and together they facilitate social progress. Unlike conventional liberal theories of groups, Gierke regarded their value and vitality as being independent of whether or not they enhanced or detracted from individual autonomy and well-being.[62] When these components are arranged harmoniously, freedom results and society thrives. If not, well, then history is littered with collapsed empires, failed states and ruined peoples.[63] This value conflict has universal application and has been long recognised outside the West. Take, for example, the opening lines of *Romance of the Three Kingdoms* from fourteenth-century China: 'The empire, long divided, must unite; long united, must divide. Thus it has ever been.'[64]

Gierke was adamant that any theory that failed to properly explain and recognise groups was defective. His prime target in this regard was fiction theory, derived from highly individualistic Roman jurisprudence. It holds that groups have mere fictitious personalities, existing only as creatures of state law. Their personality is but a concession of the sovereign and their continued existence depends on the state's sufferance. They assume a unity that is nothing more than a useful pretence as they have no soul, no character, no mission, no true nature, no agency, no independent existence and hence no natural rights. Another of Gierke's targets was contract theory. This held that groups are merely aggregates of the individuals involved in setting them up by contract. Thus, if ten people came together to set up a group, the nature of their connection is a rationally chosen partnership implemented via contract. When the group appears to act as a unity, it does so via an appointed representative chosen by the other nine members to act on their behalf. The membership is thus simply a collection of separate individuals bracketed together and renamed as one for convenience, though in truth the whole is no more than the sum of the parts. In both of these theories, the only subject of rights and duties is the individual person. Groups are not in any real sense comparable to persons even when they are treated as corporate bodies under the law. Gierke considered this to be both inaccurate and a straightjacket on associational life, hampering group independence and rendering groups vulnerable to the whims of the state.[65]

62 For a general and specific example of such, see, respectively, Christopher Heath Wellman, 'The Paradox of Group Autonomy' in Ellen Frankel Paul, Fred D. Miller Jr and Jeffrey Paul (eds.), *Autonomy* (Cambridge: Cambridge University Press, 2003), pp. 265–85; and Farrah Ahmed, 'The Liberal Defence of Religious Freedom' (2017) 42(1) *Australian Journal of Legal Philosophy* 266–9.

63 Gierke, *Community in Historical Perspective*, pp. 1–3.

64 Luo Guanzhong, *Three Kingdoms, A Historical Novel: Complete and Unabridged*, Moss Roberts (transl.) (Berkeley: University of California Press, 2004, Vol. 1 of 2), p. 3.

65 Gierke, *Community in Historical Perspective*, p. 5. See also Barker, 'Introduction', pp. lxiv–lxvi; Maitland, 'Introduction', pp. xviii–xxv; Black, 'Introduction', p. xvii; Harris, 'The Transplantation', pp. 1428–9; Mark H. Hager, 'Bodies Politic: The Progressive History of

Central to Gierke's theory was the concept of real group personality. This essentially means that when people organise, the emergent group acquires a will and personality of its own, over and above the distinct wills and personalities of its individual members. These group-persons are not fictions, symbols, aggregates, collective names or apparatuses of the state. Rather, they are living organisms arising naturally from man's consciousness and associative urge.[66] They can will and act of their own accord and do so via the body of members who function as its organs.[67] State law does not create the entity, which is both pre-legal and extra-legal, but ought simply to recognise and respect its real existence.[68] Thus, as Roger Scruton notes, corporate groups can make decisions; act as free and responsible agents; possess moral and legal rights and duties; promulgate laws for themselves and their members; be objects of praise, blame, loyalty, pride, anger, resentment, hate and affection; have habits of mind, including vices and virtues; stand in personal relations and assume many of the roles undertaken by human individuals; and live as historical beings which flourish and decline over time subject to circumstance and their ability to achieve their purposes.[69]

At a glance, real group personality may seem abstruse or, as Dworkin thought, spooky. Not so. Gierke conceded that biological imagery had its limits and should not be pushed too far. He warned against assigning gender to groups or taking allegorical representations of the state (e.g. Britannia or Germania) seriously. Organismic analogy served to clarify and illustrate but could not fully explain group-beings with scientific accuracy. The natural sciences could furnish interesting comparisons, but were too mechanistic and impersonal to deal with a phenomenon bound up with the ethical, spiritual and philosophical activities central to the human experience. The farthest one should have taken organicism was to say that social groups are living unities composed of diverse living parts, namely human beings, which are linked by more than just physical or natural bonds.[70] He acknowledged that there was 'no direct proof' for the existence of group-beings, but went on to explain that this was not fatal:

> That which we recognise as real must find a place in our rational world, even though its real nature is unexplained and perhaps impossible of explanation. The puzzle of the [group] organism is identical with the puzzle of life. We do not know what life really is. But we cannot for that reason exclude the concept of life from science. For we know that life exists. Moreover, we can describe and delimit the phenomena of life ... We notice that [any bearer of life] is an organised unit containing differentiated parts, and maintaining itself by the

Organizational "Real Entity" Theory' (1989) 50(2) *University of Pittsburgh Law Review* 575–654, pp. 579–80.

66 George Heiman, 'Introduction' in Otto von Gierke, *Associations and Law: The Classical and Early Christian Stages* (Toronto: University of Toronto Press, 1977), p. 9.

67 Maitland, 'Introduction', p. xxvi. 68 Harris, 'The Transplantation', pp. 1424, 1429.

69 Roger Scruton, 'Corporate Persons' (1989) 63 *Proceedings of the Aristotelian Society, Supplementary Volumes* 239–66, p. 245.

70 Heiman, 'Introduction', pp. 7–8.

> purposive cooperation of those parts; and that this unity, constant in spite of changes in its parts, and working together with the parts, is not identical with the sum of its parts . . . This concept is just as suitable scientifically as any other concept that is reached by accurate abstraction from the known facts in the case, and likewise expresses a reality. Its legitimacy does not depend upon the ability to explain the reality upon which it is based . . . Direct proof for the existence of living social units is not to be found. But neither is the individual living unit directly demonstrable. We may well, however, infer indirectly the existence of such units from their actions.[71]

In other words, we do not need to know why or how life exists to know that it does. Even then, we cannot perceive its every aspect or fullness through our physical senses alone.[72] The language employed to discuss it has simply to be clear and workable – good enough is fair enough. This is equally true for individuals and group persons: the lives of both are ascertainable by observing their behavioural traits, pronouncements, deeds and social interactions. History, jurisprudence and social science are thus for groups what biography, biology and psychology are for individuals. Thus, the law of associations simply paints 'a legal portrait of a real being'.[73] Interestingly, Gierke's concept of real group personality appears to receive retroactive support from the maturing science of 'emergence'.[74] Emergence is 'the arising of novel and coherent structures, patterns and properties during the process of self-organization in complex systems'.[75] Emergent phenomena occur on the macro level rather than the micro level of their constituent parts. They can be found both in nature (e.g. flocking, ant colony constructs or the physical property of 'wetness') and human society (e.g. mob sentiments, spontaneous market behaviour or viral internet trends). In all cases, as John H. Holland explains, emergence 'is a property without a sharp demarcation' but can be summarised as 'the action of the whole is more than the sum of the actions of the parts'.[76] Without making too much of it, Gierke may have been on to something with a grounding in the natural, as opposed to purely social, sciences.

[71] Gierke, 'The Nature of Human Associations' in Lewis, *Genossenschaft Theory*, pp. 148–52. See also Barker, 'Introduction', pp. lxvii–lxix.

[72] Lewis, *Genossenschaft Theory*, p. 58.

[73] Barker, 'Introduction', p. lxvii.

[74] The Santa Fe Institute, New Mexico is at the forefront of innovation in this field: www.santafe.edu/.

[75] Jeffrey Goldstein, 'Emergence as a Construct: History and Issues' (1999) 1(1) *Emergence* 49–72, p. 49.

[76] John H. Holland, *Complexity: A Very Short Introduction* (Oxford: Oxford University Press, 2014), pp. 1–6. For more detail, see John H. Holland, *Emergence: From Chaos to Order* (Oxford: Oxford University Press, 1998) and Steve Johnson, *Emergence: The Connected Lives of Ants, Brains, Cities and Software* (London: Penguin, 2002).

3.1.3 Group Units

For Gierke, the whole of society – the body politic – was constituted by the *Volk* (people). This was the most capacious and complex form of community. It established the most fundamental of collective identities and encompassed the state itself, every type of association, each individual person and all of their respective and collective achievements. It was moved by its own *Volksgeist* (spirit of the people), was conscious of its own existence and place in the world, deliberated with a common will and acted with a common hand.[77] National character was one manifestation of its existence, just as were the legal, cultural and historical accomplishments of that people. It pre-dated the state and was greater than it or any of its particular decisions or actions. The state as an entity was not the nation; it was merely another expression of that society's history, culture and laws.[78] This resonates with Henry Kissinger's observation that history is to a country what childhood experience is to an individual.[79] Membership of the *Volk* was not racially determined; it rested upon participation in the great historical tradition of the Germanic peoples. This cultural focus seemed to anticipate more recent discoveries about the nature of ancient Germania to which Gierke and the Germanists looked for inspiration. Peter Heather has explained, for example, that these territories may have been dominated culturally and politically by Germanic groups but were in fact ethnically diverse and a far cry from anything like a racially pure proto-fatherland.[80] In this sense, the Gierkean *Volk* was comparable to Hegel's capacious Greek, Roman, Germanic and Oriental 'world-historical realms' rather than the 'blood and soil' *Volksgemeinschaft* of the Nazi era.[81] Ernest Barker, writing at a time when fascists were twisting it beyond all recognition, still felt able to praise Gierke's 'rarefied and qualified doctrine', despite its potential for abuse.[82] In short, Gierke developed the concept of the *Volk* as a group unit to express the idea that a nation and its people are greater than their rulers or any majority of voters.[83] It is above all a unifying concept, and one essential to any democracy. As Roger Scruton put it, the nation is the highest form of shared first-person plural known to political theory.[84] It enables the population to hold together on a more fundamental level as a 'we' despite surface disagreements over religion, government policy or cultural trajectory.

[77] Heiman, 'Introduction', pp. 9, 11–12; Gierke, *Community in Historical Perspective*, p. 93.

[78] Runciman, *Pluralism*, p. 54; Lewis, *Genossenschaft Theory*, p. 63.

[79] Henry Kissinger, *World Order: Reflections on the Character of Nations and the Course of History* (London: Allen Lane, 2014).

[80] Peter Heather, *The Fall of the Roman Empire: A New History of Rome and the Barbarians* (Oxford: Oxford University Press, 2006), p. 53.

[81] Runciman, *Pluralism*, pp. 58 footnote 45, 217–18; Black, 'Introduction', p. xx.

[82] Barker, 'Introduction', p. lxxxiii. [83] Emerson, *State and Sovereignty*, p. 173.

[84] Roger Scruton, 'Should Countries Be More Like Families?' (*BBC Magazine*, 30 August 2013).

Beneath the nation, the state was the highest personality to be found within society. Composed of all the individual and group persons within that community, it is by nature the only communal person that can represent the whole community, a role no other group could fulfil. It is the sovereign and embodied common will of its people which encompasses all other persons and associations within a legal matrix which defines secure spheres for their endeavours. It commands the 'plenitude of powers', reaches 'into every sphere of human social life' and is the only type of organisation that can regulate other associations.[85] However, it is not above but partly constituted by law and must act in accordance with it if it is to remain a 'state of laws'. Hence, it is not absolute, existing for and in itself, but stands in reciprocal relationship with its constituent parts. In this way, the state, though pre-eminent, is no more or less important than the individuals and associations from which it derives its personality. It possesses a unity and life of its own, but is as much a part of the organic whole as any other person or group living within it. As with other groups, it arises not from some rational social contract but rather stems from the natural fact of human sociability.[86] This organismic worldview has roots in classical antiquity, but was given special significance with the advent of Christianity when the early Church, a community of the faithful, began to describe itself as a body composed of many interdependent parts. By late antiquity, the foundations for a conceptually distinct entity, separate from the state, had been laid and over time would acquire increasing legal significance, culminating in the formal separation of spiritual and temporal power.[87] This means that the 'political functions of life' are now marked off from 'other social functions of life' so that neither intrudes upon the other's turf.[88]

The monogamous family, however, was 'the most inner, most full of life, and strongly anchored association, which even today weathers all storms and still constitutes the securest foundation of our society'. Underpinning and predating all other forms of social order, it was in the state's own interest to facilitate the formation of this elementary institution and to promote marriage. Indeed, family law served as 'the nucleus of all social rights' as it went about fulfilling this 'great social role'. As the family unit is held together by far more than 'the sovereignty of the individual', family law had to resist becoming 'a twisted individual law' in thrall to 'the Roman-individualist dogma'. This meant that it could not be 'torn apart into special rights in other people and mechanistically connected property rights and obligations'. Rather, family jurisprudence 'should be founded on the idea of unity and commonality, so that, with the proviso of special rights belonging to each party in the "marriage community", the married couple governs as an entity'. This group entity, the household, is given life when two individuals merge part of their existence into it – acting jointly on all matters of substance, generating a distinct body of

[85] Lewis, *Genossenschaft Theory*, pp. 61–5. [86] Heiman, 'Introduction', pp. 42–4.
[87] Ibid., pp. 144–5. [88] Lewis, *Genossenschaft Theory*, p. 85.

norms governing property disposal and child-rearing, and tending to the goals and interests of the group and each of its constituent members with equal assiduity. Against this, the public and private facets of state law are limited to 'the preservation and consolidation of the elements of the communal body' and can 'never without an emergency let the holy and age-old rights of fathers and mothers go to waste'. Public authorities may legitimately intervene when, for example, a family proves incapable of protecting its members from abuse. Should the marriage fail, the household entity is terminated and its assets and responsibilities become subject to claims from the individuals out of which it was composed.[89] The family had thus to be properly integrated into the state regulatory system but, as an authoritative association with civilisational importance, could only be legitimately interfered with once it began to fail on its own terms. Correcting for entropy is a recurring theme in Gierke's writing.

Beyond the family, Gierkean civil society is best imagined as a teeming ecosystem. Multiple species spring up, compete, coexist, cooperate, interbreed, mutate, decay and die in a display as bewildering as any to be found in nature. To make some sense out of it, Gierke developed an equivalent of the Linnaean taxonomy for the classification of associations. It divides into three categories: the fellowship (*Genossenschaft*), the privileged institution (*priviligierte Korporation*) and the vassal institution (*Anstalt*). Each, along with many hybrids, can be found in modern society at any given time. The highest form is the fellowship, the privileged institution being either an aged version of it or an opportunistic parasite, and the vassal institution subsisting as a pallid appendage to either temporal or spiritual authority.

Of the three, only the fellowship can be properly regarded as a group person. It is a mode of communal life traceable back into the Hercynian Forest of free Germania, sharing an 'equality of origin' with the state and the individual.[90] Gierke defined them as follows: 'a group of wills develop a single, unified will from themselves: here the single wills mould themselves into a new will-unit in relation to that part of themselves which they surrender to the association ... [which is] endowed with an autonomous legal personality'.[91] Put more straightforwardly, it is 'a living organism and a real person, with body and members and a will of its own. Itself can will; itself can act; it wills and acts by the men who are its organs as a man wills and acts by brain, mouth and hand; it is a group-person, and its will is a group-will'.[92] Fellowships grow naturally out of the activity of freely associating individuals and inhabit all corners of society. As associations of free persons, each is limited only by its self-imposed constitution and collective interests.[93] Under English law, they might exist as corporations, unincorporated associations or trusts. Typical examples include

[89] Gierke, 'Social Law', pp. 1096, 1098, 1100, 1112.
[90] Barker, 'Introduction', p. lviii; Mogi, *Otto von Gierke*, p. 70.
[91] Lewis, *Genossenschaft Theory*, p. 60 footnote 21; Heiman, 'Introduction', p. 19.
[92] Maitland, 'Introduction', p. xxvi. [93] Gierke, *Community in Historical Perspective*, p. 46.

city corporations, the Stock Exchange, the Inns of Court, professional guilds, unions, collegiate universities, churches, sports clubs, charities and start-ups. Regardless of type and constitution, fellowships such as these are characterised by their vitality, common purpose and camaraderie. They are as essential to individual fulfilment as they are to the health of free society as a whole. Absent membership in them, man would be unrecognisable and diminished, his participation in and protection from the political life of the state meagre.[94]

The privileged institution bears superficial resemblance to the fellowship and may even have started life as one. Over time, however, it has debased itself by losing sight of its original purpose. To be sure, fellowships sought and received privileges, but when granted they were always issued for the sake of the fellowship itself, not the individuals who led it. This dynamic is reversed in privileged institutions. These organisations exist because of and for the sake of the privilege so that those within the group can maintain, exploit and augment it. Membership is equated with having a share in the group's privilege as a matter of private right and personal enrichment. Unsurprisingly, it is the habit of privileged institutions to disengage with public life. Typical behavioural traits include collective egotism, ravenous monopolisation, out-group hostility, petulant demands for rights shorn of duties, and a determined obliviousness to the common good. For example, a group of men come together in the Middle Ages to found and incorporate a new town. They seek privileges and exemptions from the royal government for the good of the new town. Their demands are met by the king and the town prospers. Several hundred years later, long after the original founders have died, the borough is ruled by an incompetent oligarchy which jealously guards the town's privileges from all comers. Their reason for doing so is because these privileges enrich them and not because the interests of the community as a whole will be served. Another example might be any one of today's predatory, bloated, unscrupulous, conceited, risk-averse universities.[95] Yet another might be the multinational company that dedicates itself to maximising shareholder profits whatever the cost to the environment, its own workers or even the health of its customers.[96] Noisy claims to the contrary, entities such as these exist principally to further the narrow interests of small elites. The practical consequence is that they cease to be, or belong to, a genuine community. Any moral or religious elements the group once had atrophy; they become creative vacuums and roadblocks to further innovation. Operating in this way means that privileged institutions cannot be considered true unities and thus legitimate personalities.[97]

[94] Heiman, 'Introduction', p. 9.

[95] See Lucian J. Hudson and Iain Mansfield, 'Universities at Crossroads' (Policy Exchange, 23 February 2020) and Alexandre Alfonso, 'How Academia Resembles a Drug Gang' (LSE Blog, 11 December 2013).

[96] See, for example, James Bloodworth, *Hired: Six Months Undercover in Low-Wage Britain* (London: Atlantic Books, 2019).

[97] Gierke, *Community in Historical Perspective*, pp. 105–6.

The vassal institution appears when 'a single will injects itself into a group, unifying it'.[98] Its structure is imposed from the top down, generating an artificial unity irrespective of its members' wishes. The hallmarks of its manufacture are Procrustean uniformity and amenability to centralised supervision. Its creation is an act of administration rather than spontaneous social ordering, meaning that it has official functions rather than independent purposes. By its very nature, it cannot tolerate expressions of localism, non-conformity or exclusivity. Roger Scruton uses the Russian 'Potemkin institution' as an illustrative example. In the aftermath of the Bolshevik Revolution, Lenin sought to subvert any non-state actor that threatened to dilute the Party's power. Associations of all kinds were infiltrated, shuttered or otherwise made to conform to state ideology. Their members were hence discharged from the reciprocal bonds that once united them and were instead conscripted by proxy into a cause that was not their own.[99] Less dramatic examples include most public or semi-public organisations, foundations endowed by secular or religious authorities (*Stiftung*) and 'authoritarian unions' (*herrschaftlicher Verband*). All such institutions are mere satrapies of bureaucratic power, docile and lifeless instruments of whichever higher authority created them.[100] Though they are an identifiable group unit, they are most certainly not group beings.[101]

There are some loose groupings, however, that are not really groups at all. They have no claim whatever to unity or personality. These are what Gierke called 'classes', by which he meant broad categories of people or organisations.[102] This would include everything from 'Europeans' to 'women' to 'leftists' through 'immigrants', 'Muslims' and 'Christians' to 'workers', 'the media' and the 'community of nations'. The reason these are not be considered true group units is simply that they are neither meaningfully unified nor concretely organised into anything like a tangible collectivity with a common will. Individuals within these classes might share biological or theological characteristics, for example, but they do not think and act as one. This is because they are really nothing more than abstract, a priori categories imposed from without or accepted by those who self-identify as such. More often than not, they are fiercely contested and the subject of endless debate. Absolute statements, prejudicial or otherwise, that pertain to all members of a class therefore have extremely limited validity and typically require extensive qualification to be of any practical use. It follows that classes should not be treated either morally or legally as agents.[103] They cannot be blamed or punished for the actions of a few

[98] Lewis, *Genossenschaft Theory*, p. 60 footnote 21. [99] Scruton, 'Corporate Persons', p. 262.

[100] Gierke, *Community in Historical Perspective*, pp. 132, 139, 244–5. See also Weigang Chen, *Confucian Marxism: A Reflection on Religion and Global Justice* (Leiden: Brill, 2014), pp. 260–1.

[101] Emerson, *State and Sovereignty*, p. 131.

[102] Gierke, 'The Nature of Human Associations' in Lewis, *Genossenschaft Theory*, p. 151.

[103] Roger Scruton, 'What Is Right?' in Mark Dooley (ed.), *The Roger Scruton Reader* (London: Continuum, 2011), p. 27.

of their members. Their members should not uniformly be assumed to be victims or perpetrators of some sort of injustice. No self-appointed spokesmen or lobby group can be deemed a legitimate representative of the class or its members. What is more, it cannot be said that the class has any interests of its own, as its members are likely to disagree among themselves as to what these are, or may have conflicting interests in their capacity as members of different groups. In short, classes or categories may be used to organise sociological thought, but they do constitute group units.

3.1.4 Law and Authority

Law acts as the connective tissue joining each individual and group organ to one another as well as to the body politic. Gierke viewed law as an integrated unity and warned against allowing it to divide off into silos. Rigid categorisation was a bequest of the Romans who attributed dissimilar purposes to public and private law. The former was for regulating the concerns of the state, the latter for matters affecting the individual. This dichotomy was practical and has helped lawyers manage the normative implications of man's individual and social dimensions. Without it there would simply be an undifferentiated mass of jurisprudence, impenetrable to scholars and practitioners alike, and inhibitive of specialisation and everyday use. Gierke accepted that convenient concepts were a necessity but insisted that they could never be the last word.[104] His real interest lay in the space between ostensible opposites, where insights could be gleaned into the whole of which both are part. This informs his own distinction between 'individual' and 'social' law.[105]

Individual law is straightforward and familiar. It is concerned only with private relations between persons, be they groups or individuals. Its purpose is to establish 'a free sphere of activity in which the individual creates legal relations through his own free act of will'. Thus, persons use contract law to create 'mechanical attachments' between themselves as 'closed units of life'. Each of these units is treated as sovereign and not as an integrated part of one or more higher units.[106] By contrast, social law governs all dimensions of group life, from state–group relations through associational constitutions to membership rights. It translates the norms of communal existence into concrete legal principles, enabling the integration of all into the social whole.[107] Traditional public law falls within this category as it applies both to the state as the highest association as well as to all individuals and groups within it *as members of the state* and hence articulated parts of the whole. Another aspect is the delineation among the spheres of legitimate associational power, the

[104] Gierke, 'Social Law', p. 1034; Gierke, 'The Basic Concepts of State Law and the Most Recent State-Law Theories' in Lewis, *Genossenschaft Theory*, p. 158.
[105] Lewis, *Genossenschaft Theory*, pp. 71–2. Gierke also used modified definitions of 'private' and 'public' law to make the same distinction in slightly narrower terms.
[106] Lewis, *Genossenschaft Theory*, p. 72. [107] Ibid., p. 71.

autonomy of individual members, and third-party rights. Examples might include statutes prescribing the form and structure of non-state organisations, canon law, internal company codes of conduct and the governing documents of a charitable trust. Thus, Gierke explains, social law is not synonymous with state law and

> knows no isolated individuals, but only groups or members of groups. Instead of a world of coordinated and self-encompassed units of will, it postulates a world of social beings in which from the beginning will is determined by its organic relations to other wills; in which the composite unity of the whole is referred to the multiplicity of single wills and the multiplicity of single units is referred to the unity of the general will.[108]

The problem with conventional jurisprudence is that it treats these two branches of law as incongruous abstractions when they are no such thing.

Regardless of provenance, all branches of law share a common dual purpose: to 'build and secure the life of the community as a whole' and to uphold 'each person's unique and immortal worth'.[109] Left to itself, private law becomes indifferent to power disparities. This is because it treats real people as abstractions in a theoretical position of parity when in fact they are often vastly unequal. As a consequence, unbounded contractual freedom becomes a 'fearsome weapon in the fist of the strong, a blunted tool in the clutch of the weak'.[110] Autarkic public law, on the other hand, degenerates into excessive statism and stultifying bureaucracy. Individuals and groups become fungible vessels for state ideology if they are not absorbed completely into the machinery of government. Any protections they might have enjoyed, any spheres or wills of their own, will be dismantled if they prove inconvenient to majoritarian or elite dogma. Gierke's prescription was twofold: 'a drop of socialist ointment' to dilute the excessive individualism of private law and a gust of 'natural law freedom' for any overly administrative public law system.[111]

These were not the only areas afflicted by dangerous abstractions. Gierke noted that modern rights discourse was becoming increasingly frivolous as reciprocal duties were downplayed. This led to conceptual hyperinflation and the translation of all manner of inappropriate issues belonging to the realm of politics or public policy into rights talk. It also encouraged people to demand concessions from others without reflecting on what obligations this might properly confer on them in turn.[112] It was therefore imperative to stress that mutuality was at the very core of civilisation and as such there could be 'no rights without duties'. Thus, rights had to be marked out and guaranteed by law to secure the individual within his sphere of sovereignty. This meant that

[108] Quoted in ibid., p. 72. [109] Gierke, 'Social Law', pp. 1046, 1034. [110] Ibid., p. 1080.
[111] Ibid., pp. 1034, 1036, 1046, 1048, 1050.
[112] See generally Mary Ann Glendon, *Rights Talk: The Impoverishment of Political Discourse* (New York: Free Press, 1993) and Dominique Clément, 'Human Rights or Social Justice? The Problem of Rights Inflation' (2018) 22(2) *International Journal of Human Rights* 155–69.

they were necessarily qualified and none – be it attached to property or human – was more sacrosanct than another or the common good. The focus, as ever, had to be on the social whole and how rights and duties could be woven together into a seamless web 'to protect reasonable interests and the conditions of life of the community'.[113] Likewise, the intelligentsia had betrayed the general public by crawling so far up their own ivory towers that they had nothing worthwhile left to communicate. Whereas ordinary people were patriotic and possessed a latent understanding of organic community, academics revelled in technical cant, foreign law and unbridled statism. So stark had this disconnect become that Gierke raised it to a point of method. While depth of principle and 'transparent clarity of concept [are] the noble goal of every science',[114] one could learn very little about intellectual history or real life from legal scholars. Too many would rather spend their time shoe-horning inconvenient facts into elaborate schema than disturb any of their own assumptions wherever 'the flood of life' might break through.[115] Far better to simply disregard their specious, jargon-addled pedantry and return instead to an everyday understanding of communal life. Only then could the harm be undone and scholarship begin to benefit society.[116]

Gierkean jurisprudence is moved to 'do justice to [law's] nature as an historical manifestation of human corporate spirit'.[117] It works backwards from the facts of real life to create useful concepts; it does not attempt to 'master and model life according to abstract concepts'.[118] In doing so, however, it cannot accept unprincipled compromises for the sake of avoiding unease or disquiet; to do so would invite irrationality and chaos into the very heart of the legal system.[119] For Gierke, the idea of justice was natural in so far that it was immanent in every human heart – it was not the floating cosmic force of traditional natural law theory. It was universal in so far as all humans have the same fundamental needs as individuals of the same social species, but manifested in myriad ways given that all humans lived through shifting historical circumstances across many different cultures. Positive law had to remain alive to contingency while honouring the accumulated wisdom of its traditions. Successful legal systems were justified *and* ancient. In this regard, Germanic common law and the organic fellowship represented the highest form of social organisation to be found anywhere in the world.[120] Societies ordered around

[113] Gierke, 'Social Law', pp. 1058, 1060, 1062, 1064.
[114] Lewis, *Genossenschaft Theory*, p. 21; Mogi, *Otto von Gierke*, pp. 154–9.
[115] Lewis, ibid., pp. 21–2, 159; Emerson, *State and Sovereignty*, p. 50.
[116] Black, 'Introduction', p. xxvii; Gierke, *Community in Historical Perspective*, pp. 235–40, 246–9; Antony Black, *Guild and State: European Political Thought from the Twelfth Century to the Present* (London: Transaction Publishers, 2003), p. 248. The relationship between scholarship and statesmanship is explored in depth by Mary Ann Glendon in *The Forum and the Tower* (Oxford: Oxford University Press, 2011).
[117] Gierke in Lewis, *Genossenschaft Theory*, Appendixes D and C, respectively, at pp. 162, 139.
[118] Ibid., p. 162. [119] Ibid., pp. 162–4; Mogi, *Otto von Gierke*, pp. 156–9.
[120] Black, 'Introduction', pp. xvi, xx; Barker, 'Introduction', pp. 223–6.

these institutions stood the best chance of being able to resolve, or at least manage, the 'primitive human strivings after unity and liberty'.[121] As to the nature of authority, it was similarly embedded within history and social institutions. For Gierke, law and state arose as coevals from primitive associations based on 'purely physical' ties of family, tribe and ethnicity. They exist in a symbiotic relationship, each requiring the other to develop and each realising itself only through the other. The state does not merely preserve and enforce the law but strives 'for the perfection of human society in every aspect'.[122] This was not a prescription for some kind of fixed outcome at the end of history such as a communist revolution and/or perfect social justice. Rather, it was open-ended and entailed the 'longed-for harmony' of discordant social principles (unity and plurality, order and freedom, individual and community). It would be achieved by re-emphasising associational life in the law and politics of the nation. Thus revitalised, society would thrive and be more than capable of navigating the vicissitudes of history and an uncertain future.[123]

The state was not the sole enunciator of law, however, and the law itself was but one manifestation of communal life.[124] All associations generate law, project power, exert influence and build culture.[125] Their own norms, rules and decisions are binding on their members.[126] This authority is derived from the group having been given life by the voluntary combination of its members' wills in pursuit of a common goal. To achieve its ends, the group invariably requires close coordination and discipline. Indeed, communal existence would be unthinkable without law which must bring about an 'ordering of spheres of will'.[127] These collective wills are themselves the culmination of an organic process rather than products of unanimity or majoritarianism. Human sociability leads to the coalescing of individual wills into group wills, both of which then join in unison to form the common will of that nation. The state is the common will incarnate within a territorially demarcated body politic, the highest form of social organism living to carry out the shared purposes of the community. It is empowered to do so with a plenitude of sovereign powers which it uses to order and protect its constituent parts and to engage with other states on the world stage.[128] A legitimate monopoly on force is therefore a 'theoretical assumption for the state', but coercion is not essential to the concept of law: 'Law, with or without means of enforcement, still remains law.'[129] It may be ineffectual without the power and sanctions to back it up, but

[121] Lewis, *Genossenschaft Theory*, p. 68. [122] Ibid., p. 69.
[123] Runciman, *Pluralism*, pp. 57–9; Mogi, *Otto von Gierke*, p. 264; Gierke, *Community in Historical Perspective*, pp. 3, 12.
[124] Lewis, *Genossenschaft Theory*, pp. 61, 69; Heiman, 'Introduction', p. 13.
[125] Gierke, 'The Nature of Human Associations' in Lewis, *Genossenschaft Theory*, p. 156.
[126] Scruton, 'Corporate Persons', pp. 259–60.
[127] Lewis, *Genossenschaft Theory*, p. 72; Heiman, 'Introduction', p. 45.
[128] Heiman, ibid., pp. 44–5; Mogi, *Otto von Gierke*, pp. 163–5.
[129] Lewis, *Genossenschaft Theory*, pp. 70–1; Heiman, ibid., p. 46; Emerson, *State and Sovereignty*, p. 69.

law is still properly so called in their absence. This reflects the organic nature of authority and reaffirms Gierke's position that associations are a genuine source of law. It follows that each group is constrained by its own laws and self-interest. Its own enactments must be, and be seen to be, legitimate expressions of the common will and therefore in the best interests of the whole and its members. If not, the common bond of sociability and shared purpose that unites the organisation will be undone along with its living personality. Further, no state or voluntary association could unmake its own organs without doing fatal damage to itself. Strong protections for individual and group rights are as much in the group's interests as they are in those of the members; each must pay due regard to its own rights, duties and place in society and behave conscientiously in its relations with others.[130] Gierke's jurisprudence builds 'from the bottom up instead of from the top down'[131] and is thus 'to a high degree anti-absolutist and anti-statist'.[132]

In stark contrast stood social contract theory. So far as Gierke was concerned, the tradition that culminated in Jean-Jacques Rousseau's *The Social Contract* (1762) was the enemy of all that was good and a truly 'baneful potion' for inducing permanent revolution.[133] Rousseau's collectivist doctrine required 'the total alienation of each associate with all his rights to the whole community'.[134] Having given themselves over completely to the state, the people of a territory 'concentrated all their wills into one' and formed the 'general will'.[135] This was not simply an aggregated 'will of all' but a distinct volition that expressed itself in laws predicated on the 'absolute omnipotence of the assemblage of the people'.[136] It could not err, could not be bound by its own laws, could not tolerate other sources of authority, and could not permit autonomous associations to offer alternative visions of the good life. Anyone, or any group, that deviated would be 'forced to be free' by being compelled into obedience through the exercise of 'communal strength'.[137] Political power was indivisible and religion inseparable from it. Here, Rousseau admired Muhammad's 'extremely sound' views and the undifferentiated nature of the early Caliphate, which he perceived as being 'wholly united, and in that respect good'. That was, at least, until the Arabs became 'soft and feeble' by permitting a gap to emerge between temporal and spiritual power.[138] Gierke did not just react against Rousseau, however. He detected malevolent features common to every iteration of the social contract, namely ahistoricity; the rejection of real group personality; the failure to appreciate human sociability and its natural

[130] Heiman, ibid., p. 46; Lewis, ibid., pp. 70–4. [131] Emerson, *State and Sovereignty*, p. 129.
[132] Lewis, *Genossenschaft Theory*, p. 69.
[133] Otto von Gierke, *The Development of Political Theory*, Bernard Freyd (transl.) (London: Routledge Revivals, 2018), pp. 18, 98.
[134] Rousseau quoted in ibid., p. 109.
[135] Jean-Jacques Rousseau, *The Social Contract*, Christopher Betts (transl.) (Oxford: Oxford World Classics, 1999), p. 55.
[136] Gierke, *Development of Political Theory*, p. 98; Runciman, *Pluralism*, pp. 42–3 footnote 17.
[137] Rousseau, *The Social Contract*, pp. 58–9, 70. [138] Ibid., pp. 79, 160–1.

expression through associational activity; the primacy of coercion in contractarian legal theory; the general disregard for individual worth; the contempt for historical tradition; the tendency towards collectivisation, centralisation and 'all-devouring despotism'; and the unremitting hostility towards autonomous groups.[139]

Even so, Gierke was alive to the dark side of group life and accounted for groups' ability to endanger individuals and society itself. He stipulated that they must be prevented from encroaching upon each other's autonomy as well as that of their members. They must not be allowed to subsume the whole of a person's life, for example, and can be stopped from doing so by enforcing the individual rights of their members. Their power is also limited by the reciprocal social duties attaching to their own rights.[140] Collectivist doctrines which sought to dissolve all trace of the person (individual or group) into a homogeneous mass were antithetical to Gierke's philosophy.[141] Associational relationships must be characterised neither by 'ruthless egoism nor passive subjection' but rather by harmonious voluntary agreement.[142] There is a tacit point here about Gierke's vision for the good life: one should not give oneself over completely to any singular cause or group, and no group should seek to consume its members' entire lives and individual excellence.[143] It is not healthy, for example, to invest every waking hour working for a law firm at the expense of one's family, friendship and other passions. Likewise, if a fanatical religious movement claims absolute allegiance from its members in all things, isolates them from the rest of society and attacks other groups for not conforming to its demands. Gierke is implying that the lives of individuals and groups must be authentic but also varied, rounded and integrated. The one type of ideology his pluralism cannot accommodate is absolutism, and the one type of person it will not abide is the one-dimensional bore.

3.1.5 Summing Up

Gierke's thought, though rich and deserving of lengthy exposition, can be concentrated into the following set of propositions:

Human nature is dualistic: each person is at once unique and merely one among many. This generates the productive tension between the principles of unity and liberty which drives human history. Every society is coloured by historical precedent and should be understood as an organic whole. All levels of communal life – state, association, individual – are organs of equal worth

[139] Heiman, 'Introduction', p. 5; Mogi, *Otto von Gierke*, pp. 62, 206–12; Gierke, *Community in Historical Perspective*, p. 116; Gierke, *Development of Political Theory*, pp. 18, 109–10, 175, 181, 247–8, 273, 319; Barker, 'Introduction', p. xlv; Gierke, *Natural Law*, pp. 101, 106, 108, 128–36, 149–50, 166–7.

[140] Black, 'Introduction', p. xix. [141] Heiman, 'Introduction', pp. 12, 44–5.

[142] Lewis, *Genossenschaft Theory*, pp. 60–1.

[143] Mogi, *Otto von Gierke*, pp. 162–3; Heiman, 'Introduction', pp. 8–9.

but with different purposes. Groups are themselves persons created by human sociability. They have inherent value and are instrumental in facilitating individuals' engagement with the state. The family and voluntary associations are vital to the health of society, although they can become corrupted and harmful. Classes or categories of people are not genuine groups and have neither agency nor personality. Every group has a sphere of autonomy and authority which must be protected alongside individual rights. Communal living, let alone social cohesion, would be impossible without law. Law is itself a unity, although it divides into two broad categories: individual and social. The former regulates relations between complete units (group–group, individual–individual, etc.) whereas the latter regulates relations between parts of the whole (group–member, state–group, etc.). Social law is binding on its members but only as members of that group. Each group up to and including the nation has a common will formed by the shared wills of its members. Each whole, and each partial whole, cannot devour its constituent organs (be they individuals or group persons or both) without harming itself. Systematic thinking, realism and the pursuit of coherence are prerequisites for a functioning justice system. It pays to be cautious when looking to reform the constitution of an entity as complex as modern society. The first, best and last instructor is history. None of these propositions can be thought of or applied in isolation from the others when deployed to solve contemporary socio-legal challenges.

Gierke thus made four signal contributions to political theory:[144]

(i) *A dualistic philosophy of unity and plurality*
   - Gierke's medievalism led him to reconcile the social and individualistic dimensions of human nature and fit them into a coherent political schema. In doing so, he bridged the gap between natural and positive law, universality and particularity, community and liberty, continuity and change.

(ii) *An emphatic defence of associational life and group rights*
   - Gierke did away with the traditional binary of individual–state relations. He recognised the inherent value of voluntary associations and insisted upon their protection as real persons. He also acknowledged the need to regulate group activities and define their spheres of authority so that neither they nor the state could acquire omnicompetence across all aspects of human life.

(iii) *A refined typology of non-state groups*
   - The German language is 'notoriously rich' in words denoting different sorts of group.[145] Gierke's historically informed classificatory system

[144] Alternative summaries of his contributions can be found in Mogi, *Otto von Gierke*, pp. 261–2 and Roger Scruton, *The Philosopher on Dover Beach: Essays* (Manchester: Carcanet Press, 1990), p. 59.

[145] Black, 'Introduction', p. xxxiii.

reflects this. Thanks to his translators, this extraordinarily versatile vocabulary is now at the disposal of English jurisprudence.

(iv) *An organic theory of law and authority*

- Gierke stressed the 'intimate connection' between legal and political philosophy.[146] The crux of this connection lay in group dynamics rather than command and coercion. Binding social law could therefore be generated naturally by associations other than the state.

3.2 The Golden Age of Pluralism

Despite the absence of an explicit manifesto for a pluralist political project, Gierke's ideas took off in spectacular fashion at the turn of the twentieth century; during the first two decades, pluralism enjoyed a short international heyday and became the dominant influence in political theory. Treated as central to any serious political analysis and the subject of numerous books, pluralism touched almost all aspects of intellectual life.[147] At this time, Western states were beginning to expand and centralise in a recognisably modern way. Bureaucratisation was strengthening its grip and pluralism arose both as a reaction against this and as a corrective to theories which ignored the role of groups in the political process and communal life.[148] In real terms, it was of 'considerable practical, legal and political importance' as Europeans and Americans wrestled with fundamental questions about the power and nature of associations as well as the extent and type of legal protection afforded them by the state.[149]

That Gierke ever had an English reception was owing entirely to Frederic Maitland, who translated and introduced part of *DDG* as *Political Theories of the Middle Age* ('*PTMA*', 1900). It is extremely unlikely that anyone else could have done for Gierke what Maitland did. The latter's peerless learning, scholarly temperament and stately elegance made German legal theory seem like native common sense.[150] Gierke had nothing but contempt for those who neglected history; Maitland could not stand to see it abused. By all accounts a mild and delightful man, Maitland took an extremely dim view of academic activism and fled from it 'as from the hateful thing'.[151] He insisted instead upon rigour and empathy, which are on full display in his writing on religious

[146] Gierke, *Natural Law*, p. 36.

[147] Runciman, *Pluralism*, p. 195; Avigail I. Eisenberg, *Reconstructing Political Pluralism* (New York: SUNY Press, 1995), p. 63.

[148] Runciman, ibid., p. 197; Jane Stapleton, 'Barker, Sir Ernest (1874–1960)' (Oxford: Oxford Dictionary of National Biography, 2010), p. 2; David Nicholls, *Three Varieties of Pluralism* (London: MacMillan Press, 1974), p. 5.

[149] Kirby, 'History, Law and Freedom', pp. 130–1; Law Daly, *God's Economy: Faith-Based Initiatives and the Caring State* (Chicago: Chicago University Press, 2009), pp. 163–7.

[150] For a comparison between the two, see Elton, *F.W. Maitland*, p. 12.

[151] Quoted in Henry Arthur Hollond, *Frederic William Maitland, 1850–1906: A Memorial Address* (London: Quaritch, 1953), p. 18.

toleration. Despite his own liberal sensibilities, he refused to judge the dead by these standards when they had laboured under very different assumptions and faced down the mortal dangers of their own day. To do otherwise would be as sterile as it was patronising. For example, notwithstanding the gradual abandonment of attempts to impose religious conformity from the late seventeenth century, Roman Catholicism continued to be seen 'not as a mere religious error, but as a grave political danger'.[152] Major restrictions and disqualifications were retained well into the Victorian era, but Maitland concluded that 'considering the risings of 1715 and 1745, we are perhaps not justified in condemning that treatment'.[153] It was vital 'to prevent the intrusion of untimely ideas' upon past lives and vanished worlds, else 'we shall be doing worse than if we armed Hengist and Horsa with machine guns or picturing the Venerable Bede correcting proofs for the press'.[154] Orthodox scholarship was plainly 'a contradiction in terms ... [for] if we try to make history the handmaid of dogma she will soon cease to be history'.[155] In other words, the nostrums of contemporary academia – whatever they may be – have no place in serious historical inquiry. They are antithetical to genuine insight and say far more about the limited intellects of their hosts than any subject they purportedly enlighten.

As early as 1890, Maitland had written to Sir Frederick Pollock announcing that 'for six weeks past I have had "juristic persons" on my mind, have been grubbing for the English evidence and reading the Germans, in particular Gierke's great book (it is a splendid thing though G. is too metaphysical)'.[156] Following a critical review of the first edition (1895) of his sensational *The History of English Law* by a Germanist historian, Maitland revised it and adopted wholesale Gierke's theory of real group personality in the second edition (1898).[157] He also demonstrated that this concept was not critical to the practical application of Gierke's theory.[158] As regards the protection of groups in law, form mattered far less than substance. Gierke wrote to Maitland confessing, 'I do not understand your law of trusts.'[159] Whereas he assumed that corporate law was essential to the protection of associations, Maitland demonstrated that trusts were equally effective despite the 'wholesome English contempt for legal technique'.[160] Commenting on 'the most specifically

[152] Frederic W. Maitland, *The Constitutional History of England*, H. A. L. Fisher (ed.) (Cambridge: Cambridge University Press, 1961 reprint), pp. 514, 516–17.

[153] Ibid., p. 517.

[154] Frederic W. Maitland, *Frederic William Maitland, Historian: Selections from His Writings*, Robert Livingston Schulyler (ed.) (Berkeley: University of California Press, 1960), p. 35.

[155] Elton, *F.W. Maitland*, p. 21.

[156] Quoted in Alan MacFarlane, *F.W. Maitland and the Making of the Modern World* (London: Palgrave, 2002), p. 17.

[157] Kirby, 'History, Law and Freedom', p. 139.

[158] Black, 'Introduction', p. xvii.

[159] Quoted in Jonathan Garton, *Moffat's Trusts Law: Text and Materials* (6th ed., Cambridge: Cambridge University Press, 2015), p. 1053.

[160] Frederic W. Maitland, *Selected Essays*, Harold Dexter Hazeltine, Gaillard Thomas Lapsley and Percy Henry Winfield (eds.) (Cambridge: Cambridge University Press, 1936), p. 236.

English of all our legal institutes', Maitland observed that 'the device of building a wall of trustees enabled us to construct bodies which were not technically corporations and which yet would be sufficiently protected from the assaults of individualistic theory. The personality of such bodies . . . though explicitly denied by lawyers, was on the whole pretty well recognised in practice.'[161] English law thus 'muddles along with semi-personality and demi-semi-personality towards convenient conclusions'.[162] The late Roger Scruton further noted 'that trusts arose precisely because the law has an inbuilt tendency to recognise personality, whether or not under that description'.[163] Regardless of the precise method, robust legal safeguards were essential to the preservation of social liberty as groups are most vulnerable to the state. This is because law can exert only external control over individuals – it cannot rewrite their DNA or forcibly reform their character. Each collective entity, however, organically generates legal norms as it 'sets up within its own circle a special law corresponding to its concrete individuality'.[164] So, in addition to its activities being controlled, it is also at risk of having its internal order – its very personality – restructured by state diktat. Without the ability to establish its own membership criteria, define its purposes or appoint chosen spokesmen, the group will cease living.

Maitland's *PTMA* acted as the stimulus and transmitter for the liberal, socialist and Christian variants of pluralism which later spread across Britain and America.[165] John Neville Figgis seems to have been the index case in this regard, having become entranced by his mentor's enthusiasm for Gierke and *Genossenschaftstheorie*.[166] Indeed, Maitland would tell him that Gierke's work was the greatest he had ever read.[167] This relationship, the paramount non-theological influence on Figgis' thought, was at least partially reciprocal as he is acknowledged in Maitland's *Introduction* with 'thanks for many valuable suggestions'.[168] Figgis built on Maitland's insights and adapted Gierke for 'the profoundest of all the problems of men's life together', namely church–state relations under English law.[169] His purpose was to account for the unavoidable tension between the religious and the secular by reaching a workable compromise through principled reciprocity. He was alive to the

[161] Ibid., p. 235. [162] Ibid., p. 237. [163] Scruton, 'Corporate Persons', pp. 246–7.

[164] Quoted in Lewis, *Genossenschaft Theory*, p. 59.

[165] See R. H. Tawney's *Religion and the Rise of Capitalism* (London: Verso, 2015 reprint) for an interesting hybrid. For an overview of the international movement during this period, see Marc Stears, *Progressives, Pluralists, and the Problems of the State: Ideologies of Reform in the United States and Britain, 1909–1926* (2nd ed., Oxford: Oxford University Press, 2006). The historical legacies of these variants are debated in Mark Bevir (ed.), *Modern Pluralism: Anglo-American Debates since 1880* (Cambridge: Cambridge University Press, 2012).

[166] Runciman, *Pluralism*, p. 124.

[167] Maitland, 'Introduction', p. xlv footnote 5; Maurice G. Tucker, *John Neville Figgis: A Study* (London: S.P.C.K., 1950), p. 58.

[168] Hirst, *The Pluralist Theory*, p. 10; Maitland, 'Introduction', p. xvl footnote 5.

[169] John Neville Figgis, *Churches in the Modern State* (London: Longmans, Green & Co., 1913), p. xi.

dangers that the English political tradition could pose to communal life. Hobbes was particularly troubling in this regard, having described corporate bodies as 'many lesser Commonwealths in the bowels of a greater, like worms in the entrails of a natural man'.[170] Figgis feared the elective despotism of a Parliament with Hobbesian sovereignty which could tamper with the inner lives of religious groups at will. Like Gierke, he viewed society in organismic terms and understood the church, by which he meant any religious body, as 'a social union with an inherent original power of self-development, acting as a person with a mind and will of its own'.[171] In his own words:

> We do not find a sand-heap of individuals, all equal and undifferentiated, unrelated except to the state, but an ascending hierarchy of groups, family, school, town, county, union Church, etc., etc. All these groups (or many of them) live with a real life; they all need to be allowed reasonable freedom, but must be restrained from acts of injustice towards one another or the individual; they are all means by which the individual comes to himself. For in truth the notion of isolated individuality is the shadow of a dream, and would never have come into being but for the vast social structure which allows a few individuals to make play, as though they were independent, when their whole economic position of freedom is symbolic of a long history and complex social organisation. In the real world the isolated individual does not exist; he begins always as a member of something, and his personality can develop only in society, and in some way or other he always embodies some social institution. I do not mean to deny the distinctness of individual life, but this distinction can function only inside a society. Membership in a social union means a direction of personality, which interpenetrates it, and according to your predilection, you may call either an extension or a narrowing; it is both true. You cannot be a member of any society and be the same as though you were not a member; it affects your rights and duties, limits at once and increases your opportunities; and makes you a different being although in many different degrees, according to the nature of the society and the individual members ... All these groups and unions have their effect, and limit and develop your life, make you do, or refrain from doing, what otherwise you would not, and in so far prevent you being a free and untrammelled citizen of the state. More than that, they penetrate your imagination and your thought and alter not only what you do but what you want to do.[172]

While religious groups possessed inherent rights as group persons to meet, discipline members and develop doctrine, Figgis was conscious of the need to prevent religious groups from attempting to interfere with or persecute others.[173] Again, in his own words:

> We cannot eat our cake and have it. We cannot claim liberty for ourselves while at the same time proposing to deny it to others. If we are to cry 'hands off' to the

[170] Thomas Hobbes, *Leviathan*, ch. XXIX, para. 21 (London: Folio Society, 2012), p. 239.
[171] Figgis, *Churches in the Modern State*, pp. viii, 99. [172] Ibid., pp. 87–90.
[173] Tucker, *John Neville Figgis*, p. 64.

> civil power in such matters as marriage, doctrine, ritual, or the conditions of communion inside the church – and it is the necessary condition of a free religious society that it should regulate these matters – then we must give up attempting to dictate the policy of the secular state in regard to the whole mass of its citizens.[174]

He continues:

> We do not need to deny the due rights of civil power . . . We shall do no good by claiming for the church powers which it is either inexpedient or unfair for it to exercise. We need enquiry. We must know the limits as well as the province of the church within the modern state . . . [which must also] learn that she must tolerate not merely individual liberty but the religious society, must know that its life is real and must develop, and cannot (and must not) be stopped. This is our task; it is hard, but it is high. We have to do with the real facts of human society, not with prescriptive claims or traditional rights.[175]

In the end:

> All we can claim, all we can hope for, is freedom for ourselves as one society among many. It seems to me in a high degree dishonest, and even more impudent, to go about and proclaim the rights of freedom and variety . . . if in other matters we seek to deny it. Liberty does not mean the right to punch the heads of those who disagree with you.[176]

Between them, Maitland and Figgis turned the University of Cambridge into the global hub of pluralism. Attending Maitland's Ford Lectures at Oxford in 1897 was a young Ernest Barker, the future Rockefeller Chair in Political Science at Cambridge. He left deeply impressed and would later translate another part of Gierke's *DDG*, published in 1934 as *Natural Law and the Theory of Society*.[177] He lauds Maitland on the first page, stating that he cannot 'claim, in any way, to inherit the prestige or carry the authority which the weight of Professor Maitland's learning, and the arresting power of his style, have justly won for *Political Theories of the Middle Age*, and especially for its *Introduction*'.[178] Figgis in his turn inspired the founders of guild socialism, G. D. H. Cole and Harold Laski, the latter paying tribute to the 'brilliant volumes of Figgis' as well as 'Gierke's magisterial survey of German association'.[179] As a sign of their relative importance, however, Pollock thought it 'an ill day for [Laski] when he fell into the hands of Figgis. (There was a distinct cranky element in F. which became crankier in his later work. Once I caught him misunderstanding Maitland.)'[180]

174 Figgis, *Churches in the Modern State*, pp. 112–13.
175 Extracted in David Nicholls, *The Pluralist State* (2nd ed., London: Palgrave, 1994), pp. 158–9.
176 Figgis, *Churches in the Modern State*, p. 120.
177 Stapleton, 'Barker', p. 2; Runciman, *Pluralism*, p. 64.
178 Barker, 'Introduction', p. ix.
179 Hirst, *Pluralist Theory*, p. 10; Tucker, *John Neville Figgis*, p. 108.
180 Frederick Pollock in *The Pollock-Holmes Letters: Correspondence of Sir Frederick Pollock and Mr Justice Holmes 1874–1932* (Cambridge: Cambridge University Press, 2015 reprint, Vol. 2 of 2), p. 25; Nicholls, *The Pluralist State*, p. 51.

The first American to write on Gierke was the German-educated Ernst Freund in his *The Legal Nature of Corporations* (1897).[181] Yet it was Maitland, even then regarded as 'the greatest legal historian of the era', who had far greater influence across the United States and was chiefly responsible for Gierke's reception there.[182] Maitland's translation was read by Mr Justice Holmes, who then incorporated Gierke's ideas on organic social relations into one of the most famous judicial dissents in American history.[183] The philosopher John Dewey, who had also read Maitland, formulated an American variant of pluralism which held that the state was instrumental to the promotion and protection of other voluntary forms of associations.[184] Dewey's work focused heavily upon the themes of education and civil society as the means by which to further individual development and sustain liberal democracy as a way of life.[185] Although the Anglo-German branch was by far the most significant, a parallel wave of pluralistic scholarship sprang up around Europe at roughly the same time. In Holland, for example, the neo-Calvinist prime minister Abraham Kuyper pressed for the pillarisation of Dutch society. In essence, this meant that all intermediate bodies were to enjoy 'sphere sovereignty' over their relevant sectors and that each faith community was entitled to run its own institutions with aid from the government.[186] In France, a slightly later movement known as the French Institutionalists, led by Maurice Hauriou, Georges Renard and Joseph T. Delos, argued that the individual is 'a social being, as needing for growth and fulfilment the structure of institutionalised relationships'.[187] For them, the creation of law and state was preceded by the coalescing of individuals into cooperative organisations and institutions which, guided by a pursuit of a common endeavour, develop into a powerful driving force in society.[188] Neo-Thomistic in nature, Hauriou's theory held that positive law is derived from institutions rather than vice versa. This is

181 (Chicago: University of Chicago Press.) See David Gindis, 'Ernst Freund as Precursor of the Rational Study of Corporate Law' (2020) 16(5) *Journal of Institutional Economics* 597–621, pp. 599, 606.

182 Harris, 'The Transplantation', pp. 1431–2.

183 *Mount Vernon Cotton Co* v. *Alabama Power Co*, 240 US 30, 32 (1916); McGaughey, 'Introduction', p. 1021.

184 Nicholls, *Three Varieties of Pluralism*, p. 22.

185 Eisenberg, *Reconstructing Political Pluralism*, p. 27.

186 See Michael Wintle, 'Pillarisation, Consociation and Vertical Pluralism in the Netherlands Revisited: A European View' (2000) 23(3) *West European Politics* 139–52; Kent A. Van Til, 'Subsidiarity and Sphere Sovereignty: A Match Made In . . .?' (2008) 69(3) *Theological Studies* 610–36; Kyle David Bennett and Jeppe Bach Nikolajsen, 'The Practice of Pluralism: Jeffrey Stout and Abraham Kuyper on Religion and Civil Solidarity' (2014) 8(1) *International Journal of Public Theology* 67–84. For a modern parallel, see Hans-Martien ten Napel, *Constitutionalism, Democracy and Religious Freedom: To Be Fully Human* (London: Routledge, 2017).

187 William W. Bassett, 'Review of Alan Broderick (ed.), *The French Institutionalists: Maurice Hauriou, Georges Renard, Joseph T. Delos*' (1971) 35(2) *The Thomist: A Speculative Quarterly Review* 324–8, p. 542.

188 Ibid., p. 543.

because institutions are collective undertakings ordered in such a way that they can realise particular goals. As such, they foster a sense of unity to provide meaning and win social acceptance for the rules they create in order to attain their objectives.[189] French Institutionalists also valued the idea of societal progress, which they believed was driven by the rational development of ideas in the light of natural law principles such as order, justice and liberty and the practical need for the balancing of powers.[190] In short, Gierke's reception was a three-stage process. He first passed through Maitland to Figgis (the classical English pluralists), then to Cole, Laski and Barker (the later English pluralists) and finally abroad to America and Europe (the international pluralists).

3.3 Eclipse

Despite its attractions and runaway success, pluralism did not long enjoy its boom years. Its influence collapsed suddenly around 1920, leading David Runciman to conclude that 'the single most striking feature of the pluralist movement in English political thought is the abrupt way in which it ends'.[191] The explanation is threefold. First, there is the blunt practical point that the classical pluralists were all dead by the beginning of the 1920s – Maitland in 1906, Figgis in 1919 and Gierke in 1921 – and their best years were over much earlier. That their influence in England did not long outlast their death is further vindication of their emphasis on the importance of institutions as vectors of ideas and sustainers of missions throughout history. As Runciman notes, it is significant that none of them 'succeeded in founding a school of like-minded historians to pursue their interest in group personality'.[192] Gierke's best student, Hugo Preuss (1860–1925), was to draft the Weimar Constitution but outlived him by only four years. He was also Jewish, more of a democrat and less of an historian than Gierke – a combination which respectively consigned him to 'complete negligence' within the Second Reich and meant that his ideas did not travel well beyond its borders or down through time.[193] Perhaps the greatest 'what if' was the premature death of Mary Bateson in November 1906, mere weeks before Maitland's own.[194] An accomplished and promising medievalist, Bateson was a disciple of Maitland and his co-author on many projects. He adored and admired her in equal measure, writing an obituary just prior to his final departure for the Canary Islands in which he praised her 'hunger and thirst for knowledge, the keen

[189] Martin Loughlin, 'Modernism in British Public Law, 1919–79' (2014) *Public Law* 56–67, p. 65.
[190] Bassett, 'Review', p. 543. See also Cecile Laborde, *Pluralist Thought in the State in Britain and France 1900–25* (London: Macmillan, 2000).
[191] Runciman, *Pluralism*, p. 195. [192] Ibid., p. 195.
[193] Dreyer, 'German Roots of the Theory of Pluralism', pp. 23–35.
[194] Mary Dockray-Miller, 'Bateson, Mary (1865–1906)' (Oxford: Oxford Dictionary of National Biography, 2004).

delight in the chase, the good-humoured willingness to admit that the scent was false, the eager desire to get on with the work, the cheerful resolution to go back and begin again, the broad good sense, the unaffected modesty, the imperturbable temper'.[195] It is impossible to say whether she would have taken up the vacant mantle of pluralism, but with these qualities she may well have matched Maitland had she outlived him. All this was lamented by Laski in 1925: 'men like Maitland – perhaps the greatest legal genius in England since Bentham – were never able to gather around them disciples to carry on their work'.[196]

Second, history overtook pluralism and turned the late pluralists off their own movement. The success of the Bolsheviks in the Russian Revolution in 1917 revitalised political theories concerned primarily with state–individual relations while the simultaneous growth of the Labour Party, the trade union movement and the welfare state refocused attention away from groups towards the increasing role of the state. During the same period, the philanthropic faith-based welfare system that existed in Britain had begun to break down owing to overwhelming demand. It was increasingly apparent that 'resources were too slender to turn the provision of welfare services into a competition between rivals' and that the state would need to drastically increase its involvement if the needs of the population were to be met effectively.[197] All this seemed to prompt the left-wing pluralists Laski and Cole to lose interest in the basic tenets of pluralism and gravitate towards socialist political theory during the 1920s.[198] In Germany, Carl Schmitt started questioning the very legitimacy of liberalism as well as its ability to hold society together in the face of attacks from warring groups of communists and Nazis.[199] He would go on to become an enthusiastic advocate for dictatorship and the Nazi Party's foremost jurist.[200] Barker, a liberal pluralist, was dismayed with 'the great tide of Romantic thought ... which has flowed in Germany ... and has risen to a *fluctus decumanus* in this year of grace 1933'.[201] He rightly recognised as a grave threat during the inter-war period the spread of Romanticist groups in Europe – Hitler's Germany and Mussolini's Italy in particular – which took racial exclusiveness and the Rousseauian general will as their foundational principles.[202] The grave danger posed by such groups was that they engulfed

[195] Quoted in C. H. S. Fifoot, *Frederic William Maitland: A Life* (Cambridge, MA: Harvard University Press, 1971), pp. 277–8 and H. A. L. Fisher, *Frederick William Maitland: A Biographical Sketch* (Cambridge: Cambridge University Press, 1910), p. 172.

[196] Quoted in Runciman, *Pluralism*, p. 195.

[197] Julian Rivers, *The Law of Organized Religions: Between Establishment and Secularism* (Oxford: Oxford University Press, 2010), p. 272.

[198] Runciman, *Pluralism*, pp. 195–6.

[199] See Carl Schmitt, *Legality and Legitimacy*, Jeffrey Seitzer (transl.) (Durham, NC: Duke University Press, 2004 reprint) and *Dictatorship*, Michael Hoetzl and Graham Ward (transl.) (Cambridge: Polity Press, 2013 reprint).

[200] See generally Yvonne Sherratt, *Hitler's Philosophers* (London: Yale University Press, 2013), ch. 4.

[201] Barker, 'Introduction', p. liii.

[202] Runciman, *Pluralism*, pp. 217–18.

individual lives and individuality itself, ending 'in little more than the brute and instinctive automatism of the hive'.[203] After the Great War, many theorists, Barker included, were primarily concerned with preventing a second and so began to focus upon practical developments in the field of international relations instead of the fundamental questions surrounding associational activity.[204] Ultimately, Runciman points out, these inter-war socialist and liberal themes edged out and left no room for political pluralism.[205] In short, there was a shift in intellectual priorities caused by the failure of voluntary welfare provision and the historical events of the Great War and the inter-war period.

Third, the late pluralists abandoned their former convictions 'because they no longer believed that political pluralism could be made to work'.[206] Classical pluralism was simply another casualty of the Great War as, in the words of D. H. Lawrence: 'All the great words were cancelled out for that generation.'[207] The chasm could never be recrossed or the disillusionment dispelled – the timeless certainties of a society reliant upon men and groups organising themselves for the betterment of all were seemingly gone forever.[208] As Figgis himself put it: 'Much that we deemed so secure is gone, the serene and gracious harmonies of ten years back are not for us . . . Progress, with a capital P, was torpedoed by the man who sank the *Lusitania*.'[209] The pluralists themselves felt powerless to effect change through the spontaneous workings of civil society in the aftermath. Figgis quite literally lost his mind having 'worked too hard and thought too much';[210] the rest were persuaded that progress could only be legislated for by an increasingly powerful state.[211] History had changed not just itself but the pluralists' entire perspective on it.[212] In short, the new intellectual trends of socialism (for Laski and Cole) and liberal individualism (for Barker) led the late pluralists to find in pluralism 'a limited, and limiting, view of political life . . . [which] prevented the political theorist from expressing himself at all'.[213] Laski came to see liberty as inseparable from equality, the absence of which pervaded society and its myriad institutions. He surmised that state power alone could make this good, and began to advocate for 'a party, armed with a doctrine and a programme, to take control of government and direct the process of

203 Barker, 'Introduction', p. xvii. 204 Runciman, *Pluralism*, p. 196. 205 Ibid.
206 Ibid., p. 210.
207 Quoted in Barbara Tuchman, *The Guns of August* (New York: Library of America, 2012), p. 486.
208 Runciman, *Pluralism*, p. 210. Figgis seemed to have seen it coming: *Civilisation at a Crossroads* (London: Longmans, Green & Co., 1913), p. ix; *Antichrist and Other Sermons* (London: Longmans, Green & Co., 1913), pp. 30–1.
209 Quoted in Mark Chapman, *The Coming Crisis: The Impact of Eschatology on Theology in Edwardian England* (London: Bloomsbury, 2001), pp. 132–3.
210 Tucker, *John Neville Figgis*, p. 22.
211 Stapleton, 'Barker', p. 2; Tucker, ibid., pp. 21–2; Robert E. Dolman, 'Forgotten Man of the Church of England John Neville Figgis as Preacher' (1996) 107(6) *Expository Times* 169–72, p. 170.
212 Runciman, *Pluralism*, pp. 210, 197–8. 213 Ibid., pp. 198–9.

reform'.[214] Similarly, Cole turned to Marx's account of historical development for answers and came away thinking that the job of the political theorist was to expose the vested interests in politics and counter them through involvement in the business of the state.[215] Marxism was, of course, particularly hostile to free association which diluted state power. Lenin's 'brilliant invention', the Potemkin institution (the purest form of Gierkean vassal institution), was an association infiltrated by, and made subservient to, the party which terminated its autonomy and squelched any signs of initiative. Churches, universities, schools, clubs and societies were all either destroyed outright or reconstituted as appendages of the party and the state.[216] Barker, on the other hand, felt that pluralism had proved itself inadequate when confronted by the malignant tendencies of groups during the inter-war period when they demonstrated their 'capacity to browbeat both members and non-members alike'.[217] In short, classical pluralism came to be seen by the later pluralists as incapable of delivering an intellectual and political response to post-war historical developments.

3.4 A Silver Age

Despite its precipitous collapse more than a century ago, pluralism has survived, unacknowledged, in scattered fragments within the works and concerns of later political theorists. It has resurfaced explicitly several times in a periodic cycle of rebirth and death. At no point since, however, has pluralism reached the heights attained during its classical phase under Gierke. The golden age has lapsed into a silver age which, if not quite a 'rank, weed-grown garden', is nevertheless marked by 'lassitude and enervation'.[218]

3.4.1 Echoes and Fragments

Michael Oakeshott (1901–90) drew upon aspects of pluralism to elucidate his own theory of state–association relations. His two modes of association, the rule-articulated civil association (*societas*) and the purpose-driven enterprise association (*universitas*), were taken from Gierke.[219] In Britain, these stand in 'a relationship of unstable equipoise' and the unresolvable tension between

[214] Michael Newman, '*Laski, Harold Joseph (1893–1950)*' (Oxford: Oxford Dictionary of National Biography, 2011), p. 3.

[215] Runciman, *Pluralism*, pp. 209–11.

[216] Scruton, 'Corporate Persons', p. 262.

[217] Stapleton, 'Barker', pp. 2–3.

[218] Wilhelm Sigismund Teuffel and Ludwig Schwabe, *Teuffel's History of Roman Literature: Revised and Enlarged, The Imperial Period* (London: George Bell & Sons, 1892, Vol. 2 of 2), p. 192. See the distinction drawn between Golden and Silver Latin in Charles Thomas Cruttwell, *A History of Roman Literature from the Earliest Period to the Death of Marcus Aurelius* (London: Charles Griffin & Co., 1877).

[219] Paul Franco, *Michael Oakeshott: An Introduction* (London: Yale University Press, 2004), p. 165.

them is highly productive, enabling the nation to emerge victorious from the Second World War with its traditional freedoms intact.[220] Oakeshott sympathised with Barker and admired Maitland, sharing their dislike of excessively interventionist authority and accepting that rich associational life was a condition of metaphysical unity.[221] However, he departed from pluralism when it came to real group personality on account of his deep distrust of mass mentalities and anything that smacked of anti-individualism. He feared any kind of morality that implied submission to a moral leader who acted as the managing director of a community whose resentments were stoked for instrumental ends. This fear became so great that he came to regard groups 'as the nemesis of an order constituted by self-determining individuals'.[222] However, in 1982, at the age of eighty-one, he wrote: 'I have just got a book by a Harvard chap, M J Sandel, called *Liberalism and the Limits of Justice* . . . [It seems to be] the book I have been waiting for . . . [and] it begins with the best criticism I have seen of Rawls and Dworkin.'[223] The higher forms of communitarianism evidently resonated with Oakeshott as indeed they do with the themes and concerns of pluralism.

In the preface to the second edition of his *Liberalism and the Limits of Justice*, Michael Sandel registers his unease with easy labels.[224] Communitarian thought goes wrong, he suggests, when it descends into relativism or majoritarianism. Individual freedom and universal rights are essential to the health of society and are not what is wrong with liberal individualism; rather, it prioritises the right over the good and purports to be neutral towards competing worldviews which it merely seeks to regulate. This does nothing more than keep a lid on major disagreements; it downplays shared obligations and empties politics of substantive moral content, which becomes about shallow moralising and increasingly hollow calls for civility. All this creates space and opportunity for fundamentalists who 'rush in where liberals fear to tread'.[225] To avoid this, society must foster a strong sense of citizenship, sacrifice, service and moral engagement by providing 'inadvertent civic education' in the form of participation in common institutions such as schools and public debates.

220 Richard Mullender, 'Transmuting the Politico-Legal Lump: Brexit and Britain's Constitutional Order' (2018) 39(3) *Cardozo Law Review* 1019–38, p. 1024; Franco, *Michael Oakeshott*, pp. 162–6.

221 Luke O'Sullivan, *Michael Oakeshott: Selected Writings Collection* (Luton: Andrews UK Ltd, 2014), ch. 2 [pages unnumbered].

222 Jane Stapleton, *Group Rights: Perspectives since 1900* (Bristol: Thoemmes Press, 1995), pp. xxviii–xxix; Paul Franco, *The Political Philosophy of Michael Oakeshott* (London: Yale University Press, 1990), p. 201; O'Sullivan, *Michael Oakeshott*, note 18[A].

223 Quoted in Franco, *Michael Oakeshott*, pp. 173, 199 footnote 18.

224 Michael J. Sandel, *Liberalism and the Limits of Justice* (Cambridge: Cambridge University Press, 1998), p. ix.

225 Michael J. Sandel, *Justice: What's the Right Thing to Do?* (London: Penguin, 2010), p. 243. See also Michael J. Sandel, *Public Philosophy: Essays on Morality in Politics* (Cambridge, MA: Harvard University Press, 2006), pp. 54–5, 156–73; Sandel, *Liberalism and the Limits of Justice*, pp. ix–x.

This process of 'soulcraft' is inescapably judgemental, but it generates civility as a by-product as people learn the virtuous habits and qualities that make for effective citizens and neighbours. True socialisation takes place through persuasion and habituation rather than coercion and haranguing.[226] Sandel's ultimate message is that, whether we like it or not, we are all engaged in a common project: making society as much as our own lives as good as they might possibly be. The failure to even think about embarking on this task has created a culture best described by Sir Billy Connolly as 'beige' and a politics dominated by 'beigists'. The first task of political philosophy is therefore to eliminate the creeping beigism that has taken hold of the West. The state is not sufficient to do this on its own. The atomised individual cannot achieve it. Only civil society can 'draw us out of our private, self-interested concerns and get us in the habit of attending to the common good'.[227] It is remarkable and encouraging that these ideas are gaining traction in China where Sandel is now hailed as an intellectual rockstar.[228]

Michael Walzer likewise stresses the importance of civil society and pluralised sources of authority to the maintenance of a just and free society. In *Spheres of Justice*, he argues that modern democracy requires the boundedness provided by the nation-state which is entitled to determine the admissions criteria for and restrict immigration.[229] The political community was properly a world of common meanings in which 'language, history, and culture come together [...] to produce a collective consciousness'.[230] Politics strengthens these bonds by enabling the resident population to exercise its collective right to shape and preserve itself.[231] The cohesion and integrity of the whole can be achieved only if justice is itself bounded within different spheres, each with its own internal moral logic. In order for these spheres to function properly on their own terms, their integrity must be guaranteed by the state whose job it is to police the boundaries of the different spheres and prevent them from collapsing into one another.[232] The legal sphere, for example, deals with security, due process and welfare, while the religious sphere is concerned with the distribution of divine grace and the salvation of souls. The state must therefore ensure that law and law enforcement agencies are up to the Lockean task of procuring, preserving and advancing citizens' civil interests while excluding itself entirely from salvific activities. People are, of course, free

[226] Sandel, *Justice*, pp. 263–9; Sandel, *Public Philosophy*, pp. 55–6; Michael J. Sandel, *Democracy's Discontent: America in Search of a Public Philosophy* (Cambridge, MA: Belknap Press, 1996), pp. 317–21.

[227] Sandel, *Public Philosophy*, pp. 55–6.

[228] Michael J. Sandel and Paul J. D'Ambrosio (eds.), *Encountering China: Michael Sandel and Chinese Philosophy* (Cambridge, MA: Harvard University Press, 2018).

[229] Michael Walzer, *Spheres of Justice: A Defense of Pluralism and Equality* (New York: Basic Books, 1985), p. 39.

[230] Ibid., p. 28. [231] Ibid., pp. 29, 32, 52.

[232] Margo Trappenburg, 'In Defence of Pure Pluralism: Two Readings of Walzer's Spheres of Justice' (2000) 8(3) *Journal of Political Philosophy* 343–62, p. 344.

to acknowledge religious hierarchies and norms, but these are not legally imposed or legally binding.[233] Sandel's reading of Walzer is that he advances a vision of community which cultivates the common life of its members and in which justice, which begins with membership, is concerned not only with distribution but with the moral conditions necessary for acceptance as a member.[234] These are precisely the concerns and desires which animated Gierke. Nevertheless, there is a slight glibness to communitarianism. It asks all the right questions and identifies all the major problems, yet it provides no concrete programme of action for addressing them. Indeed, Sandel himself admits that 'I don't have a fully worked out answer' to the question of what sort of political discourse would be necessary to create the ideal communitarian society.[235]

In recent years, there has been a great flowering of what might be called the Institutional School of history, which argues that institution building is the driving force behind Western history. Many prominent scholars advocate this applied approach which relates to classical pluralism in two important respects.[236] First, their works tend to be holistic in scope and take the form of a grand, arcing narrative. Second, they emphasise the importance of institutionalising ideas, the value of differentiating between the spiritual and the temporal spheres, and the historic significance of the rise of the nation-state. The two most relevant exemplars are Harold J. Berman and Niall Ferguson, given the former's focus on medieval law and the latter's interest in the wider themes of civil society and Western progress after 1500.

Berman adopted a holistic definition of law encompassing positivism, natural law and the historical school of law as social action, or the idea that it is 'the actualizing of law that is its most essential feature'.[237] He also believes that the Western tradition is in danger and takes stock of our current predicament:

> This, indeed, is the crisis of our legal tradition: We are at the end of one era and at the beginning of another. We are at the end of an era in which world history was centred upon Western history and at the beginning of an era in which Western history is centred in world history. With respect to law, the sense of ongoingness, of progress, of destiny and mission, which has characterised the Western legal tradition for some nine centuries, and which has given the political and moral aspects of that tradition their dynamic impulse, has diminished substantially.[238]

[233] Walzer, *Spheres of Justice*, pp. 85, 245.
[234] Sandel, *Public Philosophy*, pp. 177–8.
[235] Sandel, *Justice*, p. 261.
[236] See, for example, Walter Scheidel, *Escape from Rome: The Failure of Empire and the Road to Prosperity* (Princeton, NJ: Princeton University Press, 2019); Daron Acemoglu and James A. Robinson, *Why Nations Fail: The Origins of Power, Prosperity and Poverty* (London: Profile Books, 2013) and *The Narrow Corridor: How Nations Struggle for Liberty* (London: Penguin, 2020).
[237] Harold J. Berman, 'Toward an Integrative Jurisprudence: Politics, Morality, History' (1988) 76 (4) *California Law Review* 779–801, p. 782.
[238] Ibid., pp. 799–800.

A view of law and society as being a connected whole, seeing the potency of law as an active institution for giving ideas real force in the world, and a distinct feeling that something of immeasurable value is in grave danger of being lost, are the very essence of classical pluralism. Berman expanded upon these facets in both volumes of his masterwork *Law and Revolution*. He concluded that the separation of spiritual and secular authority during the eleventh century was 'the first of the great revolutions of Western History … [which had] the character of total change'.[239] The partitioning of law from theology and liturgy came with the legal revolution of the twelfth century and served to cement the divide between religious and posited law while feeding the rivalry between secular and religious courts.[240] The Reformation and the English Revolution were of similar magnitude because they 'transferred spiritual authority and spiritual responsibilities to the secular lawmakers of the various principalities and nation-states, whose supreme authorities now embraced all the jurisdictions that had previously been autonomous'.[241] In short, law and history are inseverable and the health of Western societies depends upon the perspective and sense of purpose they provide.

Ferguson takes a holistic approach to history and outlines, *via negativa*, the methodology necessary to understanding it: history is not just 'a handful of fucking things in no particular order'; rather, in the spirit of Alan Bennett's trilemma, it is 'a mode of contrarian argumentation, a communion with past Truth and Beauty'.[242] If done properly, it should be applied to contemporary problems.[243] He laments the 'decline and fall of history' as enrolment in the subject drops and its academic practitioners cocoon themselves in activism, political orthodoxy and the trivialities of obscure subgroups.[244] He is certainly not alone in noticing the race to the marginal and the dismaying reality that most historians now 'spend their lives learning more and more about less and less'.[245] The aim of his book *Civilisation* is to answer the question: 'Just why, beginning around 1500, did a few small polities on the western end of the Eurasian landmass come to dominate the rest of the world, including the more populous and in many ways more sophisticated societies of Eastern Eurasia?'[246] The answer, he explains,

239 Harold J. Berman, *Law and Revolution: The Formation of the Western Legal Tradition* (Cambridge, MA: Harvard University Press, 1983, Vol. 1 of 2), p. 520.

240 Ibid., p. 531.

241 Harold J. Berman, *Law and Revolution: The Impact of the Protestant Reformation in the Western Legal Tradition* (Cambridge, MA: Harvard University Press, 2006, Vol. 2 of 2), pp. ix–x.

242 Niall Ferguson, *Civilization: The Six Killer Apps of Western Power* (London: Penguin, 2011), p. xix.

243 The Belfer Centre's 'Applied History Project' at the Harvard Kennedy School is at the forefront of innovation in this field: www.belfercenter.org/project/applied-history-project.

244 Niall Ferguson, 'The Decline and Fall of History' (Washington, DC: American Council of Trustees and Alumni, 28 October 2016).

245 Bagehot, 'The Study of History Is in Decline in Britain' (*The Economist*, 18 July 2019); Eric Alterman, 'The Decline of Historical Thinking' (*The New Yorker*, 4 February 2019).

246 Ferguson, *Civilization*, p. xv.

is to be found in the 'Six Killer Applications' instituted by the Western nations over the past half-millennium: competitive capitalism, scientific innovation, laws of private property, medicine, consumerism and the work ethic fostered by Western religious ideas. Like Berman, he believes that the West's vibrancy is currently under threat and that 'we are living through the end of 500 years of Western ascendancy'.[247] In the 2012 Reith Lectures, he sets out to diagnose the problem and finds that the pillars of West European and North American societies – representative government, the free market, the rule of law and civil society – have begun to degenerate as part of a wider process of institutional decay. In America and Britain, for example, 'social capital' (i.e. membership of voluntary associations) has declined drastically in recent decades and has 'manifestly accelerated'.[248] All this matters because these are the very institutions which made the West great and make it work today. His suggested remedy is for the government to establish a Council of Historical Advisers 'to illuminate current challenges and choices by analyzing precedents and historical analogues'.[249]

This approach asks big questions and yields intriguing results. For example, one of the most interesting questions in comparative history is why modernity was ushered in by the West rather than by Islam during its Golden Age. Like Alexander Demandt's 210 different reasons for the decline and fall of Rome, the possible explanations are myriad.[250] One of the most compelling is that medieval Islam was unable to sustain its intellectual vitality because sharia law lacks a meaningful equivalent of corporate personality.[251] The House of Wisdom (*Bayt al-Hikmah*) in Abbasid Baghdad fostered a dazzling cast of scholars and was one of the world's foremost centres of learning during its heyday in the late eighth and early ninth centuries.[252] The problem as regards long-term development was that it was essentially a Gierkean vassal institution dependent on the goodwill and resources of its patron, the Caliph. So long as

[247] Ibid.

[248] Niall Ferguson, *The Great Degeneration: How Institutions Decay and Economies Die* (London: Penguin, 2012), p. 119.

[249] Graham Allison and Niall Ferguson, 'Why the U.S. President Needs a Council of Historians' (*The Atlantic*, September 2016). Again, he is not the only one to have suggested something like this: Anthony Seldon, 'Why Every Government Department Needs a Resident Historian' (*Prospect*, 1 May 2020); Daniel Steinmetz-Jenkins, 'Beyond the End of History' (*Chronicle of Higher Education*, 14 August 2020); James Hankins, 'How to Renew Traditional Historical Study in Graduate Schools' (James G. Martin Centre for Academic Renewal, 19 August 2020).

[250] From Alexander Demandt, *Der Fall Roms: Die Auflösung des römischen Reiches im Urteil der Nachwelt* (Munich: C.H. Beck, 1984). For the full list in English, see https://courses.washington.edu/rome250/gallery/ROME%20250/210%20Reasons.htm.

[251] See generally Malise Ruthven, *Islam in the World* (3rd ed., Oxford: Oxford University Press, 2006); Wael B. Hallaq, *An Introduction to Islamic Law* (Cambridge: Cambridge University Press, 2011), pp. 38, 47.

[252] See Jim Al-Khalili, *Pathfinders: The Golden Age of Arabic Science* (London: Penguin, 2012) and *The House of Wisdom: How Arabic Science Saved Ancient Knowledge and Gave Us the Renaissance* (London: Penguin, 2012); S. Frederic Starr, *Lost Enlightenment: Central Asia's Golden Age from the Arab Conquest to Tamerlane* (Princeton, NJ: Princeton University Press, 2015).

the ruler endorsed its activities, it flourished; once Caliphal support was withdrawn, it declined rapidly and was being overtaken by the new European universities long before the Mongols finally destroyed it in 1258.[253] Similarly, the *Muqaddimah* (*Introduction to World History*) of Ibn Khaldun (1332–1406) did not gain much traction in the Islamic world because it was not widely adopted and transmitted by educational establishments.[254] Khaldun was, however, openly contemptuous of unworldly scholars and their abstractions.[255] Among his many merits, he is interesting for his discussion of the role of *asabiyyah* (group solidarity) in history as cohesive groups overcome decadent empires before declining in turn.[256] In other words, the absence of corporate personality ensured that intellectual brilliance remained sporadic rather than self-sustaining. It also prevented the various functions of government being separated out into differentiated institutions with compartmentalised jurisdictions. Exciting new scholarship indicates that these structural deficiencies are the chief reason for the chronic under-development and persistent authoritarianism in the modern Middle East.[257] Summing up, the Institutional School takes history as its starting point and integrates policy into a comprehensive vision of Western society and civilisation. The insights it provides, not to mention its potential for broad public appeal, make it the strongest modern contender for Gierke's mantle and the most promising carrier of the classical pluralist remnant.

3.4.2 False Dawns

Classical pluralism has come down to the twenty-first century in the inexplicit, parasitical forms discussed in this chapter. For the most part, it has been without committed defenders willing or able to refit and relaunch it as a distinct, comprehensive and viable tradition. Nevertheless, academic interest in pluralism has surged periodically since the 1970s, though often without much mention of Gierke himself. The first of these short-lived revivals began

[253] Robert Irwin, *Ibn Khaldun: An Intellectual Biography* (Princeton, NJ: Princeton University Press, 2018), pp. 162–3.

[254] Ibn Khaldun, *The Muqaddimah (An Introduction to History): The Classic Islamic History of the World*, Franz Rosenthal (transl.) and N. J. Dawood (ed.) (Princeton, NJ: Princeton Classics, 2015).

[255] Irwin, *Ibn Khaldun*, p. 38. [256] Ibid., pp. 45–7.

[257] There are various angles on this theme: Timur Kuran, *The Long Divergence: How Islamic Law Held Back the Middle East* (Princeton, NJ: Princeton University Press, 2013); Jared Rubin, *Rulers, Religion and Riches: Why the West Got Rich and the Middle East Did Not* (Cambridge: Cambridge University Press, 2017); Jean-Phillippe Platteau, *Islam Instrumentalised: Religion and Politics in Historical Perspective* (Cambridge: Cambridge University Press, 2017); Toby E. Huff, *The Rise of Early Modern Science: Islam, China, and the West* (3rd ed., Cambridge: Cambridge University Press, 2017); Ahmet T. Kuru, *Islam, Authoritarianism and Underdevelopment: A Global and Historical Comparison* (Cambridge: Cambridge University Press, 2019); Joseph Heinrich, *The Weirdest People in the World: How the West Became Psychologically Peculiar and Particularly Prosperous* (London: Allen Lane, 2020).

with David Nicholls's *Three Varieties of Pluralism* (1974) and *The Pluralist State* (1975). The former is a slight volume that establishes the typical form for subsequent books on the subject. Nicholls begins by noting the ambiguity and disputed nature of pluralism as well as the very loose way in which it tends to be applied by all manner of theorists across all kinds of contexts for all sorts of purposes. He then focuses in upon pluralism as a socio-political theory before introducing English pluralism as well as its American colonial and post-colonial variants. The central theme of his analysis is that each of these related branches of socio-political pluralism stems from the same neglected intellectual concern, which is the relationship between unity and diversity in modern society and the way in which this is and ought to be structured and institutionalised. *The Pluralist State* is a more substantial survey of socio-political pluralism with a strong emphasis on its classical English exponents, three of whom (Figgis, Laski and Maitland) are excerpted as appendices. George Heiman's translation of another small section of Gierke's *DDG*, to complement Maitland and Barker's earlier efforts, appeared in Canada in 1977.[258] The publication of these books in the mid-1970s marks a major milestone because Nicholls and Heiman were the only academics since the 1930s to devote any sort of attention to pluralist thinkers, let alone translate or undertake a systematic survey of their ideas. Interestingly, they made very little impression at the time. In the second edition of *The Pluralist State* (1994), Nicholls recalls that a reviewer wrote of the original that its core themes and, by extension, the tenets of pluralism, 'do not strike the modern reader as questions of immediate note'.[259] One of Heiman's reviewers upbraided him for assuming that readers would have heard of Gierke by omitting from the introduction an account of his life and importance. The review concludes that the book was 'overpriced' and that Heiman was unable to explain 'why should one read Gierke?'[260] More than a decade would pass before pluralism resurfaced again.

The second pluralist revival was a sustained transatlantic effort beginning in 1989 and lasting into the early 2000s. It began as reaction to the 'torpor in political theory' induced by the long rivalry between liberal individualism and socialism which left vacant the middle ground between 'a false individualism and a mechanical collectivism'.[261] The scholarship took two forms. One strand furnished a major new translation of Gierke's *DDG*, surveyed earlier pluralists and produced the first comprehensive intellectual history of pluralism.[262] The other sought to rejuvenate democracy by reconstructing political pluralism as a viable modern theory in its own right. This strand subdivided into left-liberal

[258] See Heiman, 'Introduction'. [259] J. Weeks quoted on p. ix footnote 1.

[260] Fred Vaughan, 'Review of *Associations and Law: The Classical and Early Christian Stages*' (1979) 12(1) *Canadian Journal of Political Science* 165–7.

[261] See Hirst, *The Pluralist Theory*, pp. 1–2 and Nicholls, *The Pluralist State*, p. xx.

[262] See, respectively, Gierke, Black (ed.) and Fischer (transl.), *Community in Historical Perspective* (1990); Hirst, *The Pluralist Theory of the State* (1989); Nicholls, *The Pluralist State* (1994); Stapleton, *Group Rights* (1995); Gregor McLennan, *Pluralism* (Minneapolis: University of Minnesota Press, 1995); Laborde, *Pluralist Thought* (2000); Runciman, *Pluralism* (1997).

and social democratic branches. The former emanated from the United States and was championed by Robert A. Dahl, Avigail I. Eisenberg and William A. Galston. Put crudely, these pluralists rejected the Marxian concept of class agency, adhered to an instrumental understanding of the value of groups in democratic societies, and favoured a bare minimum of state intrusion into private and group life.[263] The social democratic branch was developed by Paul Q. Hirst, Joshua Cohen and Joel Rogers. They were primarily interested in economic associations and reducing the democratic deficit in bureaucracies, advocating for associative democracy based on the devolution of decision-making and the strengthening of trade unions and other voluntary associations as a counterweight to state power.[264] Against the backdrop of history's end, neo-liberalism and intensifying cultural change – most notably the 'active and vociferous' demands from Muslim groups[265] – the enormous salience and the contemporary relevance of political pluralism were all but assured.[266] Nevertheless, interest began to ebb as the millennium drew near. For the most part, the 1980s/'90s revival took little from Gierke directly and its emphases and divisions echoed those of the second generation of English pluralists (i.e. Figgis, Laski and Cole). Compared with Gierke's, the resulting theories are largely uninterested in history, maintain a much narrower focus on democratic revitalisation and limit themselves politically with their concern for fitting into liberal or progressive traditions. Their fading was likely not a coincidence as pluralism tends to flower only during times of great optimism and possibility. As multicultural identity politics took over and the spirit of the 1990s died away, disillusionment returned and political theory lapsed back into pontification and pessimism.[267]

The latest resurgence of pluralism began in Canada in 2014 with the publication of Victor Muniz-Fraticelli's *The Structure of Pluralism: On the*

[263] See Robert A. Dahl, *Dilemmas of Pluralist Democracy: Autonomy vs. Control* (New Haven, CT: Yale University Press, 1982) and *Democracy and Its Critics* (New Haven, CT: Yale University Press, 1989); Avigail I. Eisenberg, *Reconstructing Political Pluralism* (1995) and 'Pluralism and the Authority of Groups to Discriminate' (2019) *Critical Review of International Social and Political Philosophy* 1–22; William A. Galston, *Liberal Pluralism: The Implications of Value Pluralism for Political Theory and Practice* (Cambridge: Cambridge University Press, 2002) and *The Practice of Liberal Pluralism* (Cambridge: Cambridge University Press, 2005). For a critique, see Newton, 'A Critique of the Pluralist Model', pp. 209–23.

[264] See Paul Q. Hirst, Associative Democracy (1993), *From Statism to Pluralism: Democracy, Civil Society and Global Politics* (London: Routledge, 1997), *Reinventing Democracy* (ed.) (Hoboken, NJ: Wiley-Blackwell, 1996) and 'Statism, Pluralism and Social Control' (2000) 40 (2) *British Journal of Criminology* 279–95; Joshua Cohen and Joel Rogers, 'Secondary Associations and Democratic Governance' (1992) 20(4) *Politics & Society* 393–472 and *Associations and Democracy: The Real Utopias Project Vol. I*, Erik Olin Wright (ed.) (London: Verso, 1995). For a critical overview, see Rodney Barker, 'The Pluralism of British Pluralism' (2009) 14(1) *Journal of Political Ideologies* 31–45. For a pluralist critique, see Victor Muniz-Fraticelli, *The Structure of Pluralism: On the Authority of Associations* (Oxford: Oxford University Press, 2014), pp. 81–98.

[265] Nicholls, *The Pluralist State*, p. xvi.

[266] Hirst, *The Pluralist Theory*, p. 8; Nicholls, *The Pluralist State*, p. ix.

[267] Stears, *Progressives, Pluralists, and the Problems of the State*, pp. vii–viii.

Authority of Associations, followed a year later by Jacob T. Levy's *Rationalism, Pluralism, and Freedom*.[268] Both are committed to a distinctive pure form of pluralism which proceeds from value pluralism and develops into a holistic account of the triadic relationship among individual, association and state. Muñiz-Fraticelli explicitly rejects multiculturalism as inadequate because it does not distinguish between self-regulating associations capable of taking corporate action (churches, universities, etc.) and broad groupings that are little more than general categories of people (ethnicities, cultures, etc.). The latter cannot logically claim allegiance, let alone monopolise it, as 'it is possible to disobey an association, but it is not possible to disobey a culture'.[269] He also accepts the need to institutionalise abstract principles if they are to have any real impact in the world and places a strong emphasis on 'concrete legal and political institutions that can structure interaction and intercourse both among associations and between them and the state'.[270] Levy is alive to the blind spots of liberalism (overbearing statism) and multiculturalism (destabilising factionalism, in-/inter-group oppression, self-imposed community isolation, the growth of parallel political cultures and the potential of particularly powerful groups to capture the state itself).[271] He also regrets that rationalistic liberalism favouring equality and universalism has triumphed so completely over the pluralistic strain which favoured the concrete freedoms enshrined in voluntary associations.[272] There is a strong historical turn in both works which marks them out as especially significant. Muñiz-Fraticelli locates the authority of groups in medieval constitutionalism, whereas Levy situates pluralism within the wider currents of liberal thought, devoting more than half the book to the history of pluralism from the 'birth of intermediacy' in eleventh-century Europe.[273] Their signal accomplishment is thus to reconfirm that historical inquiry is a fit and proper aid to the construction of serious political philosophy. Nevertheless, the authors' rejection of any unified system of value and authority renders their brand of pluralism unnecessarily modest: they are unable to offer more than limited guidance as to how social conflicts might be resolved rather than merely lived with, let alone advise on how the relationships among individuals, groups and the state could be optimised.[274] Had they started from the practices of mankind itself rather than an a priori commitment to value pluralism, they might have matched Gierke's achievement. Even so, interest in classical pluralism appears to have been rekindled and other scholars have since translated another important component of Gierke's legal philosophy,[275] explored the scale of his impact on Maitland's political

[268] (Oxford: Oxford University Press, 2015.)

[269] Muñiz-Fraticelli, *Structure of Pluralism*, pp. 38, 51. [270] Ibid., p. 3.

[271] Levy, *Rationalism, Pluralism, and Freedom*, pp. 3, 239. [272] Ibid., pp. 2–3.

[273] Ibid., pp. 89–91.

[274] See P. S. Nash, 'Review of *The Structure of Pluralism: On the Authority of Associations* by Victor M. Muñiz-Fraticelli; *Rationalism, Pluralism & Freedom* by Jacob T. Levy' (2017) 6(1) *Oxford Journal of Law and Religion* 220–3.

[275] McGaughey, 'Introduction' to Gierke, 'Social Law' (2018).

thought,[276] applied his ideas to the history of English corporations and appraised his legacy in continental jurisprudence.[277] There is seemingly little to connect these three waves of pluralism except to note that they appeared just prior to major political upheavals (1979, 1989, 2016). This suggests that the common thread may be a search for answers that conventional political theory, or 'jurisprudence as usual',[278] cannot supply in times of dissatisfaction with the status quo.

3.5 Conclusion

The last time Gierke featured in his own right in a standard jurisprudence textbook was in 1985. Even then he was just 'another writer of whom some mention should be made' in two short paragraphs tagged on to a few short pages on the Romanist Historical School.[279] This seems wholly unjustified if entirely understandable. His personal politics, fragmentary reception and dualistic philosophy militate against easy acceptance today. Despite this, he is a rewarding jurist with permanent relevance. His classical pluralism, as it is here so gracelessly called, overcomes every major flaw in liberal individualism and multiculturalism. Over the former, it guarantees rights without deifying them, restores the prestige of civil society, protects intellectual and religious diversity, and offers a national vision capable of transcending tribal politics. Over the latter, it offers a far more sophisticated account of collective entities, a philosophical dualism without self-negation or relativism, and a realistic approach to the dangers posed by group life. Gierke is now even more salient in the post-2016 world. It is telling that modern students of pluralism view the new populism as 'how democracy ends' and even as 'antipluralism'.[280] In this, they are the heirs to Figgis and Laski rather than Gierke, their pluralist sympathies ranking behind their commitments to liberalism and other progressive traditions.[281] In a sense, this makes them unduly conservative, wishing as they seem to for the return of centrist politics. Reading Gierke closely, however, would suggest that populism is as much a fulfilment of political pluralism as it is a threat to it. The disconnect between Western peoples and their governments over economics and culture was evidently too great to persist. Traditional politics proved incapable of addressing the most basic

276 Kirby, 'History, Law and Freedom'.

277 Henry S. Turner, *The Corporate Commonwealth: Pluralism and Political Fictions in England 1516–1651* (Chicago: Chicago University Press, 2016), pp. 21–3; Mariano Croce and Marco Goldoni, *The Legacy of Pluralism: The Continental Jurisprudence of Santi Romano, Carl Schmitt, and Constantino Mortati* (Stanford, CA: Stanford University Press, 2020), pp. 20–6.

278 Dreyer, 'German Roots of the Theory of Pluralism', p. 18.

279 Dias, *Jurisprudence*, pp. 383–4.

280 David Runciman, *How Democracy Ends* (London: Profile Books, 2019); William A. Galston, *Antipluralism: The Populist Threat to Liberal Democracy* (London: Yale University Press, 2020).

281 See, for example, Runciman's 'Preface' to *Pluralism*, pp. xi–xiv.

social problems and it was only a matter of time before a major realignment took place. This is nothing especially new.[282] The great promise of populism is, of course, that it will restore the bond between government and the governed. If it succeeds, a very Gierkean vision will have been realised; if it overpromises and fails to deliver, or descends into raw majoritarianism, the health of society will suffer accordingly.

In the end, Gierkean method is straightforward. One always starts with history. Along with law, it forms part of a seamless web that cannot be rent without losing sight of the whole.[283] It must be approached fearlessly and humbly, requiring mastery of the detail as well as vision. One's own political views have no place in the past and must be left behind, for culture war proselytising precludes genuine empathy and insight into the human condition. History will not provide ready-made answers to contemporary problems, 'but it has its hour when the long-expected solutions of social and political science fail to materialise'.[284] Done properly, historical inquiry provides perspective, a sense of proportion, and freedom from 'repeating some questions again and again, running in circles unproductively'.[285] In short, it reveals more about human behaviour than abstractions ever could. Even so, 'we live some theory all the time' as our lives unfold in and around institutions embodying our most important ideas.[286] To function effectively, these institutions require legitimacy and stability, which are themselves dependent upon a coherent set of rules and principles, which in turn require some sensible generalisations and categorisations. Too often, nice-sounding ideas are flung from the sociology floor of the ivory tower and expected to fly. With very few exceptions, they plummet noisily to earth and land in a great mess, harming bystanders and besmirching scholarship in the process. Viable theories – as much as the institutions they shape – are already grounded, entirely unsentimental and coherent. They exist not to serve as proof of urbanity but to explain things as they are in plain language. As such, all parts should be held in balance and work in unison for the good of human understanding. One need not disagree with Marx's injunction to change the world, but to do this for the better one must first take the world as one finds it and interpret it accordingly. As regards law reform, then, it is essential to keep in mind Thomas Carlyle's attribution of the insights of genius to 'cooperation with the tendency of the world'.[287] The best law is as simple as possible, but no simpler. It can achieve this only if it is

[282] Niall Ferguson, 'Populism as a Backlash against Globalization: Historical Perspectives' (2016) 8 *Horizons: Journal of International Relations and Sustainable Development* 12–21.

[283] Frederick Pollock and Frederic W. Maitland, *The History of English Law before the Time of Edward I* (2nd ed., Cambridge: Cambridge University Press, 1968 reprint, Vol. 1 of 2), p. 1. It seems likely that Ronald Dworkin got this well-used phrase from Maitland.

[284] Istvan Hont, *Jealously of Trade: International Competition and the Nation-State in Historical Perspective* (Cambridge, MA: Harvard University Press, 2005), p. 156.

[285] Ibid. [286] Sandel, *Democracy's Discontent*, p. ix.

[287] Quoted by Christina Sommers in 'Feminism and Freedom' in Roger Scruton (ed.), *Liberty and Civilization: The Western Heritage* (New York: Encounter Books, 2010), p. 106.

rooted in ordinary life and built from the ground up around everyday problems. Like history, it is both a unity and a partial whole, which must encompass life at every level – individual, civil society, state, society – and provide the scaffolding for joined-up thought and sound judgement. Like classical pluralism, it is made to be applied. In this respect, Gierke is the common law jurist par excellence and it is impossible to fully appreciate him in isolation from the most important legal challenges of the day. The remainder of this book will therefore endeavour to deploy him 'in context' as a field guide to the most fraught issue in law and religion: the relationship between British Islam and English law.

Part II
Practice

Introduction to Part II

Part I introduced the two dominant models hitherto used to articulate and address tensions between English law and religion. It highlighted their multifarious inadequacies and then recovered for modern jurisprudence the lost pluralism of Otto von Gierke. Part II will apply these theories to social problems in five sectors which are critical to the structure and functioning of British Islam. The subjects – banks, charities, schools, elections, clans – have been selected because they have been overlooked by law and religion scholars in favour of more glamorous culture-war issues, and because they present exciting opportunities for productive reform. In so doing, it will not attempt to put words into the mouths of theorists who are either long-dead or have never written on the given subject. In the absence of evidence, it will avoid arguing, for example, that 'liberal individualism or the multiculturalists say X about Y and would therefore do Z in this case' or that 'classical pluralism requires this to be thought and done about that problem'. Instead, it will examine the workings of each sector, flag the main problems, and show how and why approaching them from each theoretical perspective helps or hinders understanding. In each chapter, the interpretive limitations of liberal individualism and multiculturalism in the given context are made explicit before the author's recommendations, inspired and assisted by Gierkean concepts, are set out in response to the presenting issues of that chapter. The cumulative effect illustrates the sharpness of pluralistic diagnoses, the prudent remedies that flow from them, and the practical utility of Gierke's thought. A light-based analogy may help to get this point of method across. Attempting to solve social problems using liberal individualism or multiculturalism is like shining a coloured spotlight on a dark stage: a certain aspect of a certain subject is illuminated in a certain light in a theatrical way, distorting its true colours and leaving much else in the dark. Solving problems with pluralism is more like lamping rabbits: the full-spectrum glare of a bank of floodlamps suddenly lighting up the field and everything in it from every angle all at once, leaving nothing unexposed and making it much easier to clean up. Many of the field's startled denizens will not take kindly to such treatment, but that is not for them to decide and they will suffer what they must. Some of the social problems encountered in Part II are fairly unexciting and technical; others are outrageous and utterly grotesque. Regardless, by the end of the part, the reader should have a good sense of what the problems with British Islam actually are, where they come from and how they can be solved. Virtually all of them have a neglected collective dimension. Perhaps the most surprising find, which was not anticipated by the author at the outset, is that the corruption emanating from Muslim clans is quite so pervasive. There is evidence for this in every chapter and a key aim of this part is to build the case for their dissolution. This is laid out explicitly and in full at the end of Chapter 8. The reader should come away from Part II feeling even more optimistic than when they left Part I, having had the main problems clarified for them and the optimal solutions explained to them. More than that, however, they will have acquired the theoretical resources and techniques to enable them to rethink every other aspect of the relationship between English law and British Islam not covered in these pages. For the author to someday witness that would be success indeed.

4

Banks

4.1 Introduction

This chapter addresses the growth of Islamic banks and finance in the UK. It begins with a brief historical overview of the informal forerunner institutions' development into Islamic banks and then into a thriving global industry in which the UK is a leading player. It proceeds to survey the distinguishing features of Islamic banking and typical financial products before charting the innovative regulatory reforms that permitted the industry to expand. Section 4.5 on the small volume of English case law highlights the standard but manageable issues arising from its continuing organic growth. The subsequent section (4.6) models the two conventional theoretical approaches to the rise of Islamic banks and the regulatory means used to achieve it, as well as the problems with these interpretations. The final section (4.7) sets out a pluralist response offering the best explanation and justification for these developments. It concludes with an appraisal of the problem of informal financial instruments and an optimistic assessment of the industry and the new formal institutions created, falling as they do within the general regulatory framework of the UK's financial system.

4.2 A Brief History of Islamic Banking in the UK

The modern Islamic finance sector has its roots in unregulated, peer-to-peer savings clubs called *kameti* or *bisi* and informal, trust-based money transfer networks known variously by region as *hawala*, *hundi* or *xawala*, both of which date back to the Middle Ages.[1] The first generation of Muslim immigrants to the UK did not typically have any knowledge of, opportunity to access or urgent desire for sharia-compliant banking in either their country of origin or their host society. At the time, workers in Britain were paid in cash and most

[1] For an overview, see, respectively, Seth B. Carpenter and Robert T. Jenson, 'Household Participation in Formal and Informal Savings Mechanisms: Evidence from Pakistan' (2002) 6(3) *Review of Development Economics* 314–28; Nicholas Dylan Ray, 'The Medieval Islamic System of Credit and Banking: Legal and Historical Considerations' (1997) 12(1) *Arab Law Quarterly* 43–90.

modern financial institutions and instruments (such as credit cards, instantaneous international money transfer and globalised stock markets) either had not yet been invented or were the special preserve of the wealthy. The Islamic financial services industry has not been 'transmitted unchanged from a village in Pakistan to Canary Wharf'; it is less a product of Muslim assertiveness than it is an adaptable mechanism for meeting practical needs.[2] The early *kameti* functioned as follows: a closely connected group of workers pooled part of their earnings to collectively buy one house – usually for the first or founder member – where they all could live until the scheme had carried on and each member owned a house. This helped to provide greater economic security for devout working mothers in particular and has resulted in higher rates of property ownership among Pakistani families.[3] However, owing to discrimination and a desire to keep the extended family together, they have become concentrated in undesirable and deprived areas. As time wore on and the bonds requiring sustained trust in the *kameti* weakened owing to increasing integration, decreasing discrimination and a growing culture of homeownership, the need for a replacement service and bespoke products began to build throughout the 1980s.[4] However, the *hawala* system remains a popular method of transferring remittances overseas at low cost via middlemen (*hawaladars*) to extended family and other associates.[5]

Formal Islamic banking did not have an auspicious start. The first Muslim-owned bank which targeted Muslim custom, the Bank of Credit and Commerce International (BCCI), collapsed in 1991 'amid allegations of large-scale fraud' and made regulators suspicious of any financial institution aimed explicitly at the Muslim market.[6] The first Islamic bank properly-so-called, Al-Baraka, was owned entirely by the Saudi Sheikh Saleh Abdullah Kamel and also closed in 1993 despite claiming £3 million annual profits in its final year of business. This was because it failed to comply with the Bank of England's order that it diversify its ownership (based on regulations introduced after the BCCI's collapse governing oversight and exposure to unacceptable risk) and so surrendered its licences to offer banking services. A great deal of the bank's customers displayed unusual loyalty with many refusing to remove their funds and some even offering financial assistance, a fact probably owing to their suspicions that the closure of a profitable bank amounted to prejudice against Islamic institutions.[7] These events in the early history of UK Islamic banking

[2] Elaine Housby, *Islamic Financial Services in the United Kingdom* (Edinburgh: Edinburgh University Press, 2011), pp. 23–4.

[3] Abigail Woodward, 'Exploring Economic Inactivity through Lived Experiences of British Pakistani Muslim Women' (Bridge Institute, November 2018), pp. 2–3, 9–11.

[4] Housby, *Islamic Financial Services in the United Kingdom*, pp. 24–5; UK Government, 'UK Excellence in Islamic Finance' (HMG, October 2014), pp. 8–10.

[5] See Roger Ballard, 'Coalitions of Reciprocity and the Maintenance of Financial Integrity within Informal Value Transmission Systems: The Operational Dynamics of Contemporary *hawala* Networks' (2005) 6(4) *Journal of Banking Regulation* 319–52.

[6] Housby, *Islamic Financial Services in the United Kingdom*, pp. 24–5.

[7] Ibid., pp. 25–7.

are significant because they contributed to an emerging sense of Muslim identity which demanded its own tradition of financial services, raised awareness of the emerging phenomenon among policy-makers, and encouraged the authorities to continually attempt to demonstrate inclusivity while dispelling Muslim perceptions of unfair targeting.[8]

Despite its troubled beginnings, the British Islamic finance industry took off in the late 1990s and expanded enormously throughout the first decade of the twenty-first century.[9] In 1997, the United Bank of Kuwait introduced an Islamic home purchase finance plan; in 2003, HSBC introduced Islamic home purchase and personal finance products as well as branches of its Islamic division across most UK towns; in 2004, the first independent Islamic bank, the Islamic Bank of Britain, was authorised by the Financial Services Authority (FSA) to offer a full range of sharia-compliant banking services; in 2005, Lloyds TSB started to offer Islamic current accounts and home purchase schemes in its branches, which served large Muslim populations; and in 2006–7, the FSA approved the first independent Islamic corporate investment banks, respectively, the European Islamic Investment Bank, and the Bank of London and the Middle East.[10] The UK is a global centre for Islamic finance and the main hub of activity outside the Muslim world, with five licensed Islamic banks and English law being the most popular municipal legal system for cross-border transactions.[11] It is also the leading provider of Islamic finance courses, with eighty in operation, and the government has plans for a system of 'alternative sharia-compliant' student finance.[12] The global market for the industry was worth around $2.4 trillion in 2017 with sharia-compliant banking assets constituting around 6 per cent of the world total.[13] There are at least nineteen billion dollars' worth of reported sharia-compliant assets in the UK alone, the total value having grown by 150 per cent between 2006 and 2014, with steady growth thereafter.[14] The global industry is projected to reach around $3.8 trillion in value by 2023 and expand further from there.[15] In short, Britain acted early to capture a booming market and now enjoys

[8] Ibid., pp. 28–9; Martin Harrison, 'Islamic Finance and the UK' (GOLCER and Lancaster University, May 2018), pp. 7–8.

[9] Ibid., pp. 28–41, 173. [10] Ibid., pp. 28–34, 40–1.

[11] Ibid., pp. 42–3; UK Government, 'UK Excellence in Islamic Finance', pp. 1–3; TheCityUK and DDCAP, 'The UK: Leading Western Centre for Islamic Finance' (TheCityUK, November 2015); John Dewar and Munib Hussain, 'The Islamic Finance and Markets Review' (*Law Reviews UK*, 4th ed., October 2019), p. 10; Zulkifli Hasan and Mehmet Asutay, 'An Analysis of the Courts' Decisions on Islamic Finance Disputes' (2011) 3(2) *ISRA International Journal of Islamic Finance* 41–71, p. 54.

[12] UK Government, 'Fulfilling Our Potential: Teaching Excellence, Social Mobility and Student Choice' (HMG, November 2015), pp. 40–1; TheCityUK, 'Global Trends in Islamic Finance and the UK Market 2019' (TheCityUK, April 2019), pp. 3, 8–9.

[13] TheCityUK, ibid. [14] UK Government, 'UK Excellence in Islamic Finance', p. 3.

[15] TheCityUK, 'Global Trends in Islamic Finance and the UK Market 2019', pp. 8–9; Shereen Mohamed and Jinan Al Taitoon, 'ICD-REFINITIV Islamic Finance Development Report 2019' (ICD-REFINITIV, 2019).

precedence over its Western competitors.[16] In many respects, the emergence of Islamic finance as a specific object of research mirrors the growth of the industry itself. Nicholas Foster was the first to conceptualise Islamic finance law in 2007, arguing that it was a composite legal order and a distinct field of practice.[17] It is only within the last decade that a small cadre of specialists have produced the main practitioner's guide and several major studies.[18]

4.3 Distinguishing Features of Islamic Finance

Islamic finance is closely tied up with the ethical ideals of a faith which seeks to establish 'a social order capable of providing social justice along with economic prosperity'.[19] Although Islam is by no means the only religion with implications for the economic sphere, the industry's popularity has formed part of a wider religious revival which looks back to early Islam as a golden age and quests for non-Western alternatives deemed to be more compatible with this religious ethos.[20] Thus, when Muslims opt for Islamic finance products or services, they may well do so out of a sincere belief that this will help them to lead good, pious lives and avoid 'the evils associated with immoral forms of economic gain'.[21] However, research into their motivations is very limited and Islamic banking may be largely to do with the spread of consumerism and brand-consciousness among the growing Muslim middle class.[22] To a certain extent, sharia-compliant banks are alien institutions to English law as they use very different rules and financial products to achieve broadly similar objectives to standard banking.[23] The UK government notes that although modern Islamic finance is effectively 'at the beginning of its lifecycle[,] . . . the underlying financial principles of the industry remain unchanged since their origin over 1,400 years ago'.[24] As such, several typical and common sharia-compliant instruments set it apart from conventional finance.

16 TheCityUK, 'Global Trends in Islamic Finance and the UK Market 2019', pp. 13, 36.

17 Nicholas Foster, 'Islamic Finance Law as an Emergent Legal System' (2007) 21 *Arab Law Quarterly* 170–88.

18 See Craig R. ott and David M. Eisenberg (eds.), *Islamic Finance: Law and Practice* (Oxford: Oxford University Press, 2012; 2nd ed., 2020) and the scholars references throughout this chapter.

19 Timur Kuran, *Islam and Mammon: The Economic Predicaments of Islamism* (Princeton, NJ: Princeton University Press, 2006), p. ix. For a brisk overview, see Abdul Karim Aldohni, 'The Quest for a Better Legal and Regulatory Framework for Islamic Banking' (2015) 17 *Ecclesiastical Law Journal* 15–35.

20 Kuran, ibid., pp. ix–xi; Elaine Housby, *Islamic and Ethical Finance in the United Kingdom* (Edinburgh: Edinburgh University Press, 2013), pp. 1–4.

21 Kuran, ibid., p. ix.

22 Housby, *Islamic Financial Services*, pp. 10–12; Philip Lewis and Sadek Hamid, *British Muslims: New Directions in Islamic Thought, Creativity and Activism* (Edinburgh: Edinburgh University Press, 2018), p. 209. See also Vali Nasr, *Meccanomics: The March of the New Muslim Middle Class* (London: Oneworld, 2010).

23 Abdul Karim Aldohni, *The Legal and Regulatory Aspects of Islamic Banking: A Comparative Look at the United Kingdom and Malaysia* (London: Routledge, 2011), p. 152.

24 UK Government, 'UK Excellence in Islamic Finance', p. 7.

Islamic finance is governed by a set of strict economic principles derived from religious doctrine. First, the 'most characteristic feature of Islamic banking' is the prohibition on usury or paying/taking interest-payments, which is usually called *riba*.[25] This is because sharia does not treat money as valuable in itself and thus asserts that no charge should be made for its use.[26] It is also forbidden to trade or invest in pork products and alcohol among other things such as, generally speaking, gambling services and commodified sex.[27] There is also a prohibition on uncertainty/speculation (*gharar*), that is, 'aleatory' contracts involving outcomes dependent upon chance, such as the sale of unborn animals or as-yet-unripe fruit, or goods not under the seller's control such as runaway animals or stolen cars, or transactions where the price of the goods is not specified or certain at the time of agreement (i.e. contracts which refer to 'current market value' would be impermissible). This has meant that insurance – life insurance in particular – is problematic for many conservative Muslims because it involves considerable uncertainty with regard to whether a claim will ever be made and, if one is, how it will relate to the amount paid in premiums.[28] Further, 'any risk in a transaction must be shared between at least two parties, meaning that investors and entrepreneurs alike must bear the business risk for a share in the profit'.[29]

As a result of such principles, a number of particular methodological instruments have become popular for use in the modern financial context. The *sukuk* is essentially a type of Islamic bond which represents the holder's ownership in the underlying asset. The *ijara* is a leasing contract whereby the bank purchases an asset such as a house and leases it to the customer over a specified period. The *murabaha* is a combination of contracts (usually for home purchase) for purchase and immediate resale to the customer at an agreed increased price. The *musharaka* is for business finance through an investment partnership (like a joint venture scheme) whereby multiple parties contribute capital to a venture, then agree upon and share the proportion of profits and losses attributable to the sum invested. The *mudaraba* is also for business finance and is a partnership-financing contract whereby one party supplies the capital while the other provides the labour and the profits are shared in agreed proportions.[30] The *wakalah* is an agency contract whereby one party authorises another to perform services on its behalf. The *takaful* is a form of Islamic insurance involving mutual assurance. The *tawarruq/bay' al-inah* is a combination of contracts for the deferred sale and immediate

[25] Housby, *Islamic Financial Services*, pp. 16–19.

[26] UK Government, 'UK Excellence in Islamic Finance', p. 7.

[27] Housby, *Islamic Financial Services*, p. 13. [28] Ibid., pp. 14–16.

[29] UK Government, 'UK Excellence in Islamic Finance', p. 7.

[30] See Abdul Karim Aldohni, 'Islamic Banking and the UK New Legal and Financial Regulatory Architecture: The Potential Challenges Ahead' (2016) 31(3) *Banking & Finance Law Review* 443–65 for a discussion of the potential difficulties posed to this mechanism by the ring-fencing of retail banking to protect it from the excesses of investment banking under the Financial Services (Banking Reform) Act 2013.

purchase of the same goods where the price difference essentially amounts to a loan. The *bay' salam* is a type of sale involving advance payment for future delivery. The *qard hasan* is the only kind of permissible loan; with it, only the principal is repaid without any additional interest. These various instruments are common within the Islamic finance sector and are designed to meet the demands of traditional sharia as well as the contemporary globalised markets.[31] The precise theological justifications for these instruments in any given context will depend on the particular tradition of Islamic jurisprudence adhered to by the bank and its customers, but the general principles and formal methods will be broadly similar.[32]

4.4 The Regulation of Islamic Finance in the UK

All financial regulation has three central objectives: (i) maintaining the stability of the economic system; (ii) making financial institutions viable and safe; and (iii) protecting consumers.[33] This generates 'prudential regulation' designed to ensure the stability and soundness of financial institutions and 'conduct of business regulation' which focuses on firms' business conduct towards their customers.[34] The coalition government abolished the old Financial Services Authority (FSA) in 2013 and replaced it with two new regulatory institutions, each responsible for the pursuit of distinct objectives: (1) the Financial Conduct Authority (FCA) is responsible for 'promoting effective competition and conduct of business regulation'; and (2) the Prudential Regulatory Authority (PRA) has a higher degree of authority in overlapping matters and is 'concerned with the safety and soundness of the financial system and the securing of an appropriate degree of protection for policyholders'.[35]

Islamic finance began to receive significant attention from law- and policymakers at the turn of the millennium. In 2001, the Bank of England set up a Working Group – with all kinds of representatives from the Treasury, the FSA, major banks and Muslim organisations – under Lord Edward George to examine the obstacles and difficulties hindering the development of a flourishing Islamic finance industry.[36] In 2003, the joint HM Treasury and HM Revenue & Customs Tax Technical Group was created to work out the specific technical details and potential problems of Islamic finance within the UK.[37] In a speech that same year, Lord George explained that competitive Islamic finance

[31] UK Government, 'UK Excellence in Islamic Finance', p. 7; Housby, *Islamic Financial Services*, pp. 193–7; Hasan and Asutay, 'An Analysis of the Courts' Decisions on Islamic Finance Disputes', p. 57.

[32] Housby, *Islamic Financial Services*, p. 18.

[33] Jonathan Ercanbrack, *The Transformation of Islamic Law in Global Financial Markets* (Cambridge: Cambridge University Press, 2015), p. 175.

[34] Ibid. [35] Ibid., p. 188.

[36] Housby, *Islamic Financial Services*, p. 35; UK Government, 'UK Excellence in Islamic Finance', p. 11.

[37] UK Government, ibid.

products were not so dissimilar from conventional products that they could not conceivably be accommodated within the existing regulatory framework were a satisfactory degree of consistency, standardisation and specification to be achieved. He saw no reason why the 'essential legal framework needed to be disturbed or why our economic or social objectives needed to be adversely affected on this basis' and suggested that, 'as a matter of general principle, a wider range of financial products would benefit the whole of our community and . . . Islamic products could prove to be attractive beyond the purely Muslim sector'.[38] In accordance with liberal free-market principles and with the proper regulatory oversight, there was nothing particularly controversial or dangerous about encouraging the growth of Islamic finance so that the British economy could exploit this lucrative and rapidly expanding global industry.

Regulation dealing specifically with Islamic finance began to be introduced from 2003 to meet certain government objectives and overcome various problems. In 2006, then-Chancellor Gordon Brown stated his desire for London to become 'the gateway to Islamic finance and trade'.[39] In 2008, the Labour government set out its twin objectives which were 'to enhance the UK's competitiveness in financial services by establishing the UK as a gateway for international Islamic finance; and to ensure that everybody, irrespective of their religious beliefs, has access to competitively priced financial products'.[40] The attainment of these was to be guided by the principles of fairness (no 'extending special favours' to Islam and 'no faith-based requirements for the take-up of Islamic products' so that there is a 'a level playing field established for Islamic finance'); collaboration ('a collaborative approach between the Government, industry and the third sector'); and commitment (to 'promoting the industry and engaging more closely with practitioners').[41] In 2014, then-Prime Minister David Cameron expressed his 'delight' at the successful expansion of the industry and stated that its future 'looks bright', indicating that more would be done in future to promote 'excellence' in the sector.[42] To this end, the UK became the first Western country to launch sovereign *sukuk* bonds to the sum of £200 million in June 2014; the initiative proved highly successful with orders in excess of £2 billion, and a second sovereign *sukuk* bond worth £500 million was launched in March 2021.[43] The Al Rayan Bank, the UK's largest Islamic bank, launched the first public *sukuk* (£250 million) to be issued in a non-Muslim country in 2018.[44]

[38] Edward George, 'Speech by the Governor of the Bank of England to the Islamic Home Finance Seminar' (London: Bank of England, 27 March 2003), p. 2.

[39] Quoted in Housby, *Islamic Financial Services*, p. 42.

[40] UK Government, 'The Development of Islamic Finance in the UK: The Government's Perspective' (HM Treasury, December 2008), p. 13.

[41] Ibid., pp. 13–14.

[42] UK Government, 'UK Excellence in Islamic Finance', p. 1.

[43] HM Treasury and George Osborne, 'Government Issues First Islamic Bond' (*UK Government News*, 2014); HM Treasury, 'UK Bolsters Islamic Finance Offering with Second Sukuk' (*UK Government News*, 25 March 2021).

[44] Al Rayan Bank, 'Al Rayan Bank (UK) Issues Largest Ever Sterling Sukuk for £250m' (Al Rayan Bank, 14 February 2018).

There is every reason to believe that Islamic finance will continue to be promoted by successive UK governments for the foreseeable future.

The authorities have long recognised the fact that Islamic instruments are hindered by strict conventional regulation. The Labour government's policy towards Islamic finance identified four key obstacles to the further development of the industry: (i) taxation; (ii) standardisation; (iii) awareness; and (iv) skills.[45] Each shall be taken in turn. Regarding taxation, the government stressed the need to 'ensure that Islamic finance arrangements are taxed neither more harshly nor more lightly than equivalent structures'.[46] It is therefore unsurprising that 'legislative measures have largely focused on amending tax provisions for Islamic financial structures'.[47] Throughout the relevant legislation and policy documents, Islamic finance is referred to as 'alternative finance' in the interests of neutrality.[48] The Finance Act 2003 removed the double charge for stamp duty land tax (SDLT) incurred by Islamic mortgages when a bank buys a property and resells it to an individual customer.[49] The *murabaha* is the 'most utilised structure' in Islamic finance and the Finance Act 2005 also removed SDLT from equity-sharing arrangements.[50] Both kinds of SDLT relief were extended to corporate entities by the Finance Act 2006.[51] The Finance Act 2007 clarified the taxation and regulation of various Islamic products with special focus upon *sukuk*.[52] However, few regulations were created to address the unique contractual features of Islamic finance and the old FSA was simply expected to apply its 'conventional risk-based approach to the industry, which stresses economic substance over legal form'.[53] In short, the period 2003–7 saw considerable legislative activity aimed at integrating Islamic finance into the UK's economy and regulatory regime, a task which 'is very much work in progress'.[54] Although there are apparently no plans for major legislative amendments in the near future, incremental changes are expected in order to make Islamic finance viable and competitive within the UK.[55] The Bank of England, for example, accepts that Islamic banks face continuing problems with cash reserves and liquidity as they have had to develop costly ways to get around interest-dependent mechanisms while satisfying liquidity requirements. In

[45] UK Government, 'The Development of Islamic Finance in the UK: The Government's Perspective', p. 15.

[46] Ibid.

[47] Jonathan Ercanbrack, 'The Regulation of Islamic Finance in the UK' (2011) 13(1) *Ecclesiastical Law Journal* 69–77, p. 70.

[48] Ercanbrack, 'The Regulation of Islamic Finance in the UK', p. 73. [49] Ss. 72–3.

[50] Ercanbrack, 'The Regulation of Islamic Finance in the UK', p. 70. [51] S. 168. [52] S. 53.

[53] Ercanbrack, 'The Regulation of Islamic Finance in the UK', pp. 70–1.

[54] Jonathan Ercanbrack, 'Islamic Finance: Law and Practice' (2013) 5 *Journal of Business Law*, pp. 164–7; Natalie Schoon, *Islamic Banking and Finance* (London: Spiramus Press, 2010), pp. 155–8; Michael Ainley, Ali Mashayekhi, Robert Hicks, Arshadur Rahman and Ali Ravalia, 'Islamic Finance in the UK: Regulation and Challenges' (London: Financial Services Authority, November 2007), p. 8.

[55] Dewar and Hussain, 'The Islamic Finance and Markets Review', p. 10.

response, it is creating a non-interest-based alternative liquidity facility (ALF) to enable Islamic banks to 'hold a reserves-like asset in a non-interest based environment' whereby 'participant deposits will be backed by a fund of assets, the return from which, net of hedging and operational costs, will be passed back to depositors in lieu of interest'. The aim is to promote flexibility, efficiency and simplicity so that the industry is placed 'on a more level footing with the rest of the market, giving firms here greater flexibility in meeting their liquidity requirements, and helping them to compete with conventional peers while staying true to their founding principles'.[56]

As regards standardisation, the government noted that a 'lack of commonly accepted standards for products and practices in any industry can be a barrier to development' and that, in the context of Islamic finance, this problem is exacerbated by what it calls 'the dynamic nature of Shariah interpretation'.[57] In other words, the various divergent schools of Islamic jurisprudence make it hard to achieve the adequate standardisation of industry practice. Further, the government appreciates the difficulty and has declared that the UK authorities do 'not intend to adopt a state-led approach' because they 'are secular bodies, not religious regulators' and should thus remain neutral.[58] At present, the state 'takes no responsibility for problems of choice of evaluative criteria such as whether an Islamic financial product or service complies with the Sharia' and so 'individual financial institutions are wholly responsible for determining whether the products and services they offer comply with the principles and tenets of the Sharia'.[59] In most institutions, this is typically done via specialist consultancy services or through a supervisory board of sharia scholars (SSB) who, if they occupy an executive role in the firm, are themselves subject to general regulatory 'Approved Persons' requirements, which are designed to ensure that they are fit and proper for the job.[60] Given the absence of a hierarchical authority within Islam and the anarchic nature of sharia law, the involvement of religious scholars in financial institutions is widely recognised as a significant and unique liability. Their destabilising effect stems in large part from the fact that incompetence or perceived disregard for sharia principles on their part will make customers highly sceptical of the institution's claims to provide products with sharia authenticity.[61]

Ercanbrack highlights the uncertainty, the lack of consistency and the dangers to confidence and reputation posed by religious scholars' involvement and points to 'serious concerns regarding a conventional regulator's ability to

[56] Andrew Hauser, 'Why Islamic Finance Has an Important Role to Play in Supporting the Recovery from Covid – and How the Bank of England's New Alternative Liquidity Facility Can Help' (London: Bank of England, 2 December 2020), pp. 8–9.

[57] UK Government, 'The Development of Islamic Finance in the UK: The Government's Perspective', p. 19.

[58] Ibid. [59] Ercanbrack, 'The Regulation of Islamic Finance in the UK', p. 74.

[60] Ibid., pp. 74–5; Ercanbrack, *The Transformation of Islamic Law in Global Financial Markets*, pp. 204–7.

[61] Ibid., p. 77; ibid., pp. 200–4, 234.

deal with them'.[62] There are also problems of independence / conflicts of interest given that most scholars are appointed by the firm's management and thus have an economic stake in the business.[63] That a sharia adviser should be competent in Islamic jurisprudence, finance and accounting creates a major problem of being able to certify genuine expertise across the industry.[64] There is a general lack of transparency surrounding the sharia supervisory process itself as full disclosure/publication of the 'duties, competence, composition and decision making of the SSB, including the publication of all fatwas' and reasoning is irregular to non-existent.[65] In addition, Housby looks to the fact that, among British Muslims, there appears to be a 'clear preference for recruiting from their country of origin rather than among religious scholars trained in Britain' and that many imams 'are not well adapted to British life' with only 8 per cent born here and a mere 6 per cent having English as their first language.[66] This raises competency and suitability issues around the use of such scholars in an institutionalised setting. There have been a number of recent initiatives aimed at cultivating common industry standards and reducing uncertainty. A variety of widely recognised and respected international organisations have been set up in the attempt to create global common standards in Islamic finance. The most prominent examples are bodies such as the Accounting and Auditing Organisation for Islamic Financial Institutions (AAOIFI), the Islamic Financial Services Board (IFSB) and the International Islamic Financial Market (IIFM). Despite receiving widespread recognition and support, these boards' recommendations are not mandatory beyond a small number of jurisdictions where their take-up is compulsory.[67] In the UK, the industry has been largely left to its own devices in this regard, with little formal state intervention, although the government does endorse the further consolidation of international standards and the promotion of general good practice.[68] Regional developments such as EU regulatory harmonisation have pushed the industry in the direction of increasing transnational coherence, as have global initiatives such as the Basel Committee on Banking Supervision (BCBS).[69]

Finally, the government has also been supportive of campaigns to raise awareness of the Islamic financial services industry and its products as well as training initiatives designed to provide the high-quality professional skills,

[62] Ibid., p. 75; ibid., pp. 200, 202; Ercanbrack, 'Islamic Finance: Law and Practice', p. 171.

[63] Ercanbrack, *The Transformation of Islamic Law in Global Financial Markets*, p. 200.

[64] Ibid., pp. 201–2. [65] Ibid., pp. 202–3.

[66] Housby, *Islamic Financial Services in the United Kingdom*, p. 9.

[67] On their commendable efforts to institutionalise and standardise practice, as well as the ongoing challenges, see Jonathan Ercanbrack, 'The Standardization of Islamic Financial Law: Lawmaking in Modern Financial Markets' (2019) 67(4) *American Journal of Comparative Law* 825–60.

[68] UK Government, 'The Development of Islamic Finance in the UK: The Government's Perspective', pp. 20–1.

[69] Ercanbrack, *The Transformation of Islamic Law in Global Financial Markets*, pp. 207–22.

qualifications and expertise prized in the industry.[70] The considerable and increasing number of recognised educational establishments offering specialised courses, as well as the many banks, consultancies and law firms which offer industry-related services, suggest that this policy has been broadly successful.

4.5 English Case Law on Islamic Finance

There is a general scarcity of English case law on Islamic finance. This may be owing to the reluctance of firms to develop innovative structures that might expose them to litigation and the fact that, in any event, 'plain vanilla financial transactions have generally become non-litigious'.[71] Another factor is likely to be the growth of alternative commercial dispute resolution under the Arbitration Act 1996. This allows Islamic tribunals to issue legally binding judgments in accordance with religious principles under certain conditions.[72] The parties may agree, for example, to appoint an arbitrator holding specific religious beliefs and empower him or her to apply religious law.[73] This flexible system enhances economic freedom for businesses and enables them to resolve their differences confidentially, meaning that many disputes never reach the courts. Even so, the few recorded English cases illustrate the main issues in Islamic finance law.

Islamic Investment Co Ltd v. *Symphony Gems NV* (2002) ALL ER (D) 171 was the first Islamic financial transaction to be decided in a Western court. It concerned a *murabaha* financing agreement made 'in accordance with the Islamic Shariah' but explicitly 'governed by and construed according to English law'.[74] The parties were in dispute as to whether the agreement was in fact a sharia-compliant *murabaha* contract. The High Court did not concern itself with the legal issue of whether the contract was sharia-compliant and confined itself instead to construing the agreement in terms of English contract law.[75] The judgment, as Ercanbrack notes, was entirely consistent with the standard English doctrine of upholding the freedom to form properly agreed contracts and 'reasonable business practices' so that commercial interests are safeguarded.[76] This approach was followed and expanded upon in *Shamil Bank* v. *Beximco Pharmaceuticals Ltd* (2004) EWCA Civ 19, which involved another *murabaha* agreement. Neither party was based in England, yet the

[70] UK Government, 'The Development of Islamic Finance in the UK: The Government's Perspective', pp. 21–7; Ercanbrack, 'Islamic Finance: Law and Practice', p. 165.

[71] Ercanbrack, *The Transformation of Islamic Law in Global Financial Markets*, p. 223.

[72] Julian Rivers, *The Law of Organized Religions: Between Establishment and Secularism* (Oxford: Oxford University Press, 2010), p. 101. For a detailed guide to policy, procedure and practice, see Susan Blake, Julie Browne and Stuart Sime, *A Practical Approach to Alternative Dispute Resolution* (6th ed., Oxford: Oxford University Press, 2021).

[73] *Jivraj* v. *Hashwani* (2011) UKSC 40; *Halpern* v. *Halpern* [2008] QB 195; *Musawi* v. *RE International (UK) Ltd & Ors* (2007) EWHC 2981 (Ch).

[74] Ercanbrack, *The Transformation of Islamic Law in Global Financial Markets*, p. 224.

[75] Ibid., p. 225. [76] Ibid., p. 226.

contract contained the following clause: 'Subject to the principles of the Glorious Sharia'a, this Agreement shall be governed by and construed in accordance with the laws of England.' The appellants argued that the agreement was enforceable only if it complied with both sharia (which they argued should take precedence) and English law.[77] The Court of Appeal's decision established a number of principles: (i) that the religious principles agreed upon and used at the time of signing to certify that the contract was sharia-compatible could not later be changed; (ii) that a contract could not simultaneously be governed by two legal systems, so the English jurisdiction must prevail; and (iii) that general references to sharia principles did not identify which specific aspects of religious law were to be incorporated into the contract terms.[78] Thus, the doctrine of incorporation of foreign law into an agreement as contractual terms can function only when that law is amenable to it, meaning that it must possess 'specific "black letter" provisions'.[79] This follows a long line of authority which has consistently held that sharia cannot 'reasonably be said to exist' or at least 'contains no precise rule' concerning any particular contract, meaning that 'Islamic law' cannot reasonably be used as the governing law unless it is sufficiently certain.[80] Clearly, English courts cannot, as a matter of fact, determine what something as broad as the 'Glorious Sharia' actually is, but they are perfectly able to apply principles and rules which have been freely agreed upon within the parameters set out under English law and are certain enough for application in the given case.

In *The Investment Dar Company KSCC* v. *Blom Developments Bank SAL* (2009) EWHC 3545 (Ch), a Kuwaiti investment company, The Investment Dar (TID), argued that it had not performed its obligations to Blom Bank because their *wakalah* contract was void on account of not being sharia-compliant, which was itself an ultra vires issue. Leave to appeal was granted – TID later withdrew its case owing to financial distress – by the judge, who commented that there was 'an arguable case' on the question of religious principles. Although the case went no further and had no precedential value, it caused 'much consternation' in the industry because it suggested that English courts might conceivably attempt to adjudicate upon religious disputes and again highlighted the risks of sharia non-compliance.[81] These risks resurfaced again in *Dana Gas PJSC* v. *Dana Gas Sukuk Ltd & Ors* [2017] EWHC 2928 (Comm). Dana Gas, a United Arab Emirates (UAE) energy company, informed its investors that it would stop making payments on its restructured *sukuk*

[77] Ibid., pp. 227, 229; Housby, *Islamic Financial Services in the United Kingdom*, p. 38.

[78] Housby, ibid.; Ercanbrack, ibid., p. 230.

[79] Ercanbrack, ibid., pp. 229–30.

[80] *Petroleum Development Ltd* v. *Sheikh of Abu Dhabi* [1951] 18 ILR 144; *Ruler of Qatar* v. *International Marine Oil Company Ltd* [1953] 20 Int LR 534; *Saudi Arabia* v. *Arabian American Oil Co (Aramco)* [1958] 27 Int LR 117; Ercanbrack, 'The Regulation of Islamic Finance in the UK', p. 76.

[81] Housby, *Islamic Financial Services in the United Kingdom*, pp. 38–9; Ercanbrack, *The Transformation of Islamic Law in Global Financial Markets*, pp. 233–4.

insurance because it was no longer compliant with the sharia prohibition on *riba* and hence UAE law as well. Had this been allowed to stand, it would have 'set an odious precedent' and threatened the entire industry by allowing firms to escape their debt obligations by pleading sharia non-compliance.[82] In the event, the High Court ruled against Dana Gas and confirmed that English courts will consider Islamic finance instruments governed by English law as questions of English contract law only.[83] This limited body of case law is beneficial to the industry because it provides a measure of clarity as to jurisdiction and which legal principles the English courts will apply.[84] Nevertheless, the cases highlight the risks that arise from controverted interpretations of religious principles in a commercial context; the indeterminate and contentious nature of sharia strictures and interpretations; the jurisdictional difficulties in complex conflict of laws cases; and the need for, and the benefits to be derived from, further standardisation efforts.[85]

4.6 Interpreting Islamic Banks and Finance

Several scholars are concerned that the growth of Islamic banking has 'fostered an environment conducive to Islamist militancy' by promoting segregation and sectarianism so that Muslims become 'reluctant to deal with conventional banks'.[86] The attendant problem of informal under-/unregulated Islamic financial organisations then becomes much more serious as it creates opportunities for criminal/terrorist financing by those seeking to exploit the wishes of observant Muslims.[87] The financial services sector is at high risk from these threats and Al Rayan Bank, for example, has been accused of providing services to a variety of organisations with alleged links to alleged terrorist and Islamist organisations (allegations it disputes).[88] While these are valid general concerns, it is important to clarify that the problem is not with Islamic finance per se. There is undoubtedly a pressing need to combat social segregation and dangerous Islamic groups – the threat underlying these academic concerns – and

[82] Jonathan Ercanbrack, 'Islamic Financial Law and the Law of the United Arab Emirates: Disjuncture and the Necessity for Reform' (2019) 33 *Arab Law Quarterly* 152–78, p. 155.

[83] Dewar and Hussain, 'The Islamic Finance and Markets Review', p. 9. [84] Ibid.

[85] Ercanbrack, *The Transformation of Islamic Law in Global Financial Markets*, pp. 231–2. These will primarily be directed at securities, enforcement mechanisms and increased coordination between municipal legal systems facilitating Islamic finance (Ercanbrack, 'Islamic Financial Law and the Law of the United Arab Emirates', pp. 152, 177–8).

[86] Kuran, *Islam and Mammon*, p. ix; Aldohni, *The Legal and Regulatory Aspects of Islamic Banking*, p. 23.

[87] Aldohni, ibid., pp. 23–4.

[88] HM Treasury and Home Office, 'National Risk Assessment of Money Laundering and Terrorist Financing 2020' (HMG, December 2020), pp. 54–5; Andrew Norfolk, 'Al Rayan Bank: Clients Include "Terror" Group and Abu Hamza's Former Mosque' (*The Times*, 5 August 2019). The ongoing dispute seems to have resulted in a partial settlement: Bryan Cathcart, 'Another Anti-Muslim Piece in Murdoch's Flagship Paper Ends in a Libel Settlement' (*Byline Times*, 23 July 2020).

English law has a big part to play in that struggle. It is often suboptimal in this regard and, as shall be discussed in subsequent chapters, could be drastically improved in many areas. There is also a role for civil society groups which target the funding of hateful organisations by putting public pressure on their banks and advertisers to withdraw. Nevertheless, it is difficult to view the accommodation and assisted development of the Islamic finance industry within the UK as anything other than a success story. An appeal to two key measurements justifies this conclusion.

In today's world, having a bank account is every bit as essential to everyday life as having running water or central heating. One obviously cannot bank as an individual person as this activity is dependent upon having access to competitive financial institutions. Devout Muslims wishing to live authentic Islamic lives by forgoing standard commercial options and opting instead for religious banking services will be prevented from doing so for as long as the law does not allow for the survival of the necessary institutions. Thus, prior to the relevant amendments to English tax law, the domestic market environment was utterly hostile, not neutral, towards Islamic banking. Yet, now the enormous size of the industry, its projected expansion and the fact that the UK currently dominates the Western market stand as testament to the commercial viability, vitality and potential of Islamic finance. It has already been used to finance a range of iconic London landmarks from the Shard to the Olympic Village, and the industry looks set to play an important role in the UK's economic recovery from Brexit and the Covid pandemic.[89] Furthermore, this has been achieved in an incredibly short space of time with relatively little legislative intervention beyond small-but-significant amendments to the tax regime. The industry is evidently coping very well under the conventional regulatory regime, which itself appears to have experienced no real difficulties in incorporating Islamic finance within its general provisions. Given that Islamic finance has now gone global, there would be no sense in the government attempting to exclude British business from its lucrative potential, an endeavour which would no doubt prove futile in any event.

Banks and other financial institutions can now come to obtain an Islamic character if they wish; they may decide what products to offer and enjoy great leeway to decide upon the religious stringency of their packages, while any individual, regardless of their religion, may choose to avail themselves of these products. The overall regulatory framework is geared towards securing objective and neutral values and purposes – simplicity, clarity, certainty and the protection of the vulnerable – which happen to coincide with the broad Islamic emphasis on social justice and equality, which underpins the products to begin with. This neutral structure itself permits and sustains a hugely diverse range of institutions with considerable variations in doctrine and religiosity among

[89] Alicia Buller, 'How Islamic Finance Could Help Pull the UK out of Its Brexit and Covid Slump' (*Arabian Business*, 16 December 2020).

them. Housby remarks that to assume that 'all those of Muslim heritage actively desire sharia compliant products' would constitute 'sheer laziness of thought', given the diversity of the population and the general lack of serious studies on this question.[90] This question really is neither here nor there as liberal economics and the globalised free market rely upon a number of key principles – free choice, free trade and fair competition – which are entirely compatible with the emergence of new products, new avenues for dispute resolution and new markets for anyone who wishes to use them. For instance, more than 80 per cent of Al Rayan Bank's fixed-term deposit customers are non-Muslim, which suggests that anyone in search of a good deal can benefit from the industry.[91] The very rationale of free market capitalism is that, subject to consumer protection considerations and the demands of general institutional stability, one is free to offer and accept and profit from virtually any kind of service or product that one wishes. So long as it remains subject to the general, neutral and equitable regulations of the UK jurisdiction (which is explicit government policy anyway), Islamic finance is perfectly welcome as it provides employment, generates expertise, increases competitiveness in the wider industry, enhances consumer choice, promotes English law in world markets and bolsters national wealth. However, it is hard to explain or justify the success of Islamic banks using either liberal individualism or multiculturalism.

4.6.1 Via Liberal Individualism

Liberal individualism is uncharacteristically unclear on this subject as it overlooks important collective aspects of the phenomenon. On one hand, Islamic finance helps to secure personal choice as well as substantive equality for those whose religious beliefs preclude or discourage them from utilising standard financial products. Dworkin was supportive of affirmative action to 'dissolve balkanization' in other contexts, and economic liberalism – capitalism for the allocation of resources and the production of wealth – is a pillar of any liberal society.[92] On the other hand, this is achieved by tax exemptions (albeit it within a more general framework of 'alternative finance') which would seem to undermine the law's integrity as regards formal equality. For the most part, however, a purely liberal individualistic framework would not recognise the need to make these sorts of accommodative arrangements within the general law of commerce in order to permit the growth of viable religious financial services. So long as Muslims could bank somewhere and were not

[90] Housby, *Islamic Financial Services in the United Kingdom*, pp. 10–11.

[91] Amir Firdaus, 'The UK Can Be a World Leader in Islamic Finance' (*The Telegraph*, 10 May 2019).

[92] See Ronald Dworkin, 'Affirmative Action: Is It Fair?' (2000) 28 *Journal of Blacks in Higher Education* 79–88, p. 88 and *Justice for Hedgehogs* (Cambridge, MA: Harvard University Press, 2011), pp. 357–8.

discriminated against by standard institutions, there would be no real issue so far as this theory is concerned. What is missing from the reductive approach is a capacity to analyse the purposes of institutions beyond securing individual choice and equality under the state. Islamic banks are more than mere vehicles for personal wealth and religious preferences, and these cannot be secured without first providing for the institutional liberty upon which they rely.

4.6.2 Via Multiculturalism

The British multiculturalists pay comparably little attention to Islamic banking. This is likely because it is a rather dull technical subject lying far beyond the expertise of sociologists concerned only with broad themes of religious identity. There are a few scattered comments from Parekh which speak unequivocally in its favour and confirm the basis of this support. His position is that Islamic banking ought to be thought of first and foremost as an expression of Muslim culture which will 'add to the richness and vitality of society'.[93] This is reason enough to support it and, as far as possible, the industry should be left to develop on its own terms, perhaps with its own parallel regulatory structure if demanded. In other words, British Muslims are exercising their class agency by creating financial institutions to act as an appendage to their will in the economic sphere, meaning that Islamic banks are Gierkean vassal institutions of that faith. There is a lot more to the law than this, and maintaining such a narrow focus on the empowerment of Muslims again obscures the point of these institutions as well as the benefits they confer on the UK. However, it is significant that there are no decisive objections to the accommodation of Islamic finance and commercial arbitration from either a Dworkinian or a multicultural perspective. Although the growth of this industry seems like a relatively quick and easy win for both sides, we are not yet furnished with adequate reasons for supporting it.

4.7 A Pluralist Response to Islamic Banks and Finance

It is far easier to understand and appreciate the success of Islamic banks with reference to pluralism. Historical insight into the origins and regulation of banks serves to frame the analysis. The ultimate point of money is to make the production and exchange of resources more efficient than mere subsistence and barter; the ultimate point of banks is to securely and profitably store, move and invest money for individuals, organisations and states; the ultimate point of the banking system is to supervise and organise all of this activity into a stable, prosperous and dynamic economy.[94] Western banking originated with Jewish

[93] See Bhikhu Parekh, 'Feeling at Home: Some Reflections on Muslims in Europe' (2009) 8 *Harvard Middle Eastern and Islamic Review* 51–85, p. 71 and *A New Politics of Identity: Political Principles for an Interdependent World* (London: Macmillan, 2008), p. 118.

[94] Thomas Sowell, *Basic Economics: A Common Sense Guide to the Economy* (5th ed., New York: Basic Books, 2015), 363–91.

moneylenders in medieval Italy who, being free from the Church's ban on usury, could finance and insure risky ventures from benches (*banci*) in their ghettos.[95] Stimulated by the Crusades, banking soon religion-hopped as Christian families invented legal fictions to bypass the prohibition on interest and institutionalised financial services.[96] Many of the most successful instruments ended up being falsely attributed to Jews.[97] These early dynastic banks enriched themselves, their own city-states and European culture (by paying for the Renaissance).[98] By the seventeenth century, the Bank of England and a regulated, recognisable banking system had emerged in England, capable of financing everything from personal projects through business ventures to national defence.[99] Thereafter, the products and attendant regulatory apparatus simply became more sophisticated as modern capitalism developed through periods of crisis and prosperity.[100] There are two points to take from this summary. First, inventing complicated financial instruments to work with or around religious doctrine is neither new nor alarming – the West's unprecedented wealth has its origins in that very business. Second, for banks to function effectively, they must be regulated as purposeful actors in their own right with the potential to do good and ill at every level of society: individual, intermediate, national, international. While broadly similar in form and function, each institution will have its distinct character and internal rules – it can thrive, ail and die as much as any organic entity affected by internal and external conditions. Financial institutions are about far more, in other words, than the facilitation of individual choice or the embodiment of a culture. They are true Gierkean fellowships.

The same cannot be said for *kameti* and *hawala*. These networks are difficult to define with precision for legal purposes as they are built around kinship groups and rely on a closed circuit of trusting personal relationships at each stage of every transaction.[101] They are especially popular wherever income and literacy are lowest.[102] *Hawala* are illegal in parts of the USA and in India, while in the UAE and Pakistan they are ostensibly

[95] Niall Ferguson, *The Ascent of Money: A Financial History of the World* (2nd ed., London: Penguin, 2019), p. 35.

[96] Ibid., pp. 42–8.

[97] See generally Francesca Trivellato, *The Promise and the Peril of Credit: What a Forgotten Legend about Jews and Finance Tells Us about the Making of European Commercial Society* (Princeton, NJ: Princeton University Press, 2019).

[98] Ferguson, *The Ascent of Money*, pp. 42–8. [99] Ibid., pp. 49–50.

[100] See generally Ranald C. Mitchie, *British Banking: Continuity and Change from 1694 to the Present* (Oxford: Oxford University Press, 2016); David Kynaston, *Till Time's Last Sand: A History of the Bank of England 1694–2013* (London: Bloomsbury, 2017); Youssef Cassis, Richard S. Grossman and Catherine R. Schenk (eds.), *The Oxford Handbook of Banking and Financial History* (Oxford: Oxford University Press, 2016).

[101] Nikos Passas, 'Demystifying Hawala: A Look into Its Social Organization and Mechanics' (2006) 7(1) *Journal of Scandinavian Studies in Criminology and Crime Prevention* 46–62; Woodward, 'Exploring Economic Inactivity through Lived Experiences of British Pakistani Muslim Women', pp. 5–6.

[102] Carpenter and Jenson, 'Household Participation in Formal and Informal Savings Mechanisms: Evidence from Pakistan', pp. 325–7.

regulated quite heavily.[103] In the UK, *hawala* are subject to the same legal requirements as conventional money service businesses (MSBs) and risk-based supervision by HM Revenue and Customs (HMRC), which also provides specific compliance advice to MSBs engaged in this type of money transmission.[104] There is even a '*hawala* defence' to money laundering at common law whereby the accused can assert that they had 'no knowledge or suspicion that money laundering was taking place and that the transactions had the appearance of genuine *hawala* transfers'.[105] In practice, however, financial transactions through these networks are traceless, lack meaningful safeguards and are typically 'operated from unlicensed and unregistered store-fronts in Western Europe, North America and elsewhere'.[106] One scholar has suggested that 'the central purpose of contemporary *hawala* systems is to facilitate the transfer of value between one currency and another on a global scale', and that only 'conspiracy theorists' and 'paranoid' peddlers of a 'mindless moral panic' would seek to suppress them.[107] As an expert witness, he contributed to the defeat of two criminal prosecutions concerning alleged conspiracies to launder money of illicit origin using this argument, and by suggesting that the defendants' use of *hawala* made it less likely that criminally acquired funds could enter a system so dependent upon reputation and trust.[108] Others have argued that regulating *hawala* is 'important and necessary', but that it 'should not be stereotyped as a criminal financing mechanism' because 'there is no evidence that *hawala* is used more often [than formal banking] for illegitimate purposes'.[109] Rather, the development of 'a light-touch regulatory framework for low value remittances' would lessen

[103] Patrick M. Jost and Harjit Singh Sandhu, 'The Hawala Alternative Remittance System and Its Role in Money Laundering' (FinCEN, INTERPOL and FOPAC, undated, accessed 28 February 2021): www.treasury.gov/resource-center/terrorist-illicit-finance/documents/fincen-hawala-rpt.pdf, p. 11; Adil Anwar Daudi, 'The Invisible Bank: Regulating the Hawala System in India, Pakistan and the United Arab Emirates' (2005) 15(3) *Indiana International and Comparative Law Review* 619–54.

[104] See, respectively, House of Lords European Union Committee, 'Money Laundering and the Financing of Terrorism – Nineteenth Report, Session 2008–09' (House of Lords, HL132, July 2009), ch. 5: 'Current Threats, Alternative Remittance Systems', paras. 147–56 and HMRC, 'Business Sector Specific Guidance: Money Service Businesses: Introduction – Money Transmitters' (HMRC, MLR3C10125, 3 July 2017); David Faulkner, 'UK Regulation of Money Service Businesses' in IMF, 'Regulatory Frameworks for Hawala and Other Remittance Systems' (IMF, 2005), pp. 42–6.

[105] *R* v. *H/J (November 2019) [unreported]*; details in Narita Bahra, QC, 'Narita Bahra QC Successfully Defended in £11M Money Laundering Trial' (2 Hare Court, 19 November 2019).

[106] Ercanbrack, *The Transformation of Islamic Law in Global Financial Markets*, p. 149.

[107] Roger Ballard quoted in Marina B. V. Martin, '*Hundi/Hawala*: The Problem of Definition' (2009) 43(4) *Modern Asian Studies* 909–37, pp. 932–3; Roger Ballard, 'Hawala: Criminal Haven or Vital Financial Network?' (October 2006) *Newsletter of the International Institute of Asian Studies* 1–9, pp. 7–8 and 'Coalitions of Reciprocity and the Maintenance of Financial Integrity within Informal Value Transmission Systems', p. 321.

[108] Martin, '*Hundi/Hawala*: The Problem of Definition', pp. 932–3.

[109] See Narita Bahra, QC and Jonathan Ercanbrack, 'Hawala Money Transfer Systems: Debunking the Presumption of Illegitimacy' (2 Hare Court, 19 November 2019).

the risks and enable *hawala* to continue serving as 'a vital means of poverty alleviation and financial inclusion' across South Asia, where overseas remittances account for a large proportion of household incomes and in total often exceed formal foreign investment and aid.[110] Indeed, some societies have become so dependent on *hawala* remittances that they would likely collapse altogether if these were somehow abruptly cut off.[111] There is some merit in these arguments, but ultimately they are unpersuasive.

It is certainly not paranoid to harbour misgivings about the continuing legality of *hawala*. Although the UK government's 'approach to regulating *Hawala* can sometimes seem to be a little hesitant', it has long recognised that 'by its nature *Hawala* is more susceptible to misuse'.[112] Every UK national risk assessment of money laundering and terrorist financing has rated the MSB sector as being at high risk from money laundering and terrorist financing.[113] There are numerous recorded instances of funds reaching terrorists in Syria and Somalia via *hawala*, and, at the most recent estimate, it was thought 'highly likely' that these networks 'launder over £2 billion per year in the UK'.[114] The obvious reason why there is not more evidence is that there is rarely any to be gathered from informal multinational transactions with little to no paper trail.[115] On top of this, *hawala* is rarely the only or even the primary activity of MSBs, which makes it harder for prosecutors to prove elements of the relevant offences.[116] As a general rule – and recurring theme throughout this

[110] Bahra QC and Ercanbrack, ibid.; Ayako Kageyama, 'Extent of Poverty Alleviation by Migrant Remittances in Sri Lanka' (2008) 28(1) *South Asia Research* 89–108.

[111] See, for example, Manuel Orozco and Julia Yansura, 'Keeping the Lifeline Open: Remittances and Markets in Somalia' (Oxfam America, 2013); HMG and Beechwood International, 'Safer Corridors Rapid Assessment: Case Study of Somalia and UK Banking' (Beechwood International, September 2013); Monika H. Mali, 'Regulating *Hawala*: Thwarting Terrorism or Jeopardising Stability?' (unpublished thesis, Naval Postgraduate School, Monterey, CA, December 2019), pp. 15–25.

[112] See, respectively, Mark Jenner, 'Why Hawala Is Detrimental for Our Financial Safety? [*sic*]' (Mark Jenner & Co., 10 February 2021); HMG, 'Government Reply to the Nineteenth Report from the House of Lords European Union Committee Session 2008–09 HL132' (HMG, October 2009), p. 17.

[113] HM Treasury and Home Office, 'National Risk Assessment of Money Laundering and Terrorist Financing 2015' (HMG, October 2015), pp. 93–4; HM Treasury and Home Office, 'National Risk Assessment of Money Laundering and Terrorist Financing 2017' (HMG, October 2017), pp. 68–9; HM Treasury and Home Office, 'National Risk Assessment of Money Laundering and Terrorist Financing 2020', pp. 118–20.

[114] See, respectively, HM Treasury and Home Office, 'National Risk Assessment of Money Laundering and Terrorist Financing 2015', pp. 93–4 and HM Treasury and Home Office, 'National Risk Assessment of Money Laundering and Terrorist Financing 2020', p. 120. For documented examples, see BBC News, 'Travel Agent Jailed in £500m Scam' (*BBC News*, 17 April 2007) and *United States* v. *Moalin* No. 13–50572 (9th Cir. 2020). For more detail on the role of *hawala* in financial crime, see Financial Action Taskforce (FATF), 'The Role of Hawala and Other Similar Service Providers in Money Laundering and Terrorist Financing' (FATF, October 2013).

[115] See Jenner, 'Why Hawala Is Detrimental for Our Financial Safety?'.

[116] Jost and Sandhu, 'The Hawala Alternative Remittance System and Its Role in Money Laundering', p. 11.

book – English law struggles with loosely defined groups and networks. Its response to the *hawala* system is no exception: a slew of failed prosecutions followed by a 'growing regulatory tsunami' followed by rising compliance costs for conventional banks passed on to customers who turn in greater numbers to cheaper and riskier *hawala* followed by costly expansions of state apparatus to deal with ever more individual transactions involving insignificant sums of money, ad infinitum.[117] The rise of virtual currencies and end-to-end encrypted communications has only made things harder for the authorities.[118] This vicious cycle shows every sign of accelerating and, as one beneficiary gleefully put it, 'ensures a constant stream of work for the forensic accountant specialising in fraud and money laundering!'.[119] It is also true that the sources, ends and applications of *hawala* funding, as well as the kinship networks through which it moves, are neither necessarily nor thoroughly criminal. *Hawala* may be used by rich and poor alike for legitimate and even laudable purposes – family remittances, humanitarian relief, business trading, personal expenditure, etc. – as well as illegitimate and dangerous ones – tax evasion, political corruption, money laundering, terrorist financing, trafficking and smuggling.[120] Again, there is no sure way to tell which or which combination is involved in any given transaction because the *hawala* does not really have a *central* purpose beyond the facilitation of any and all transactions of network members. To insist that it must is to impose inappropriate Western-centric assumptions on this phenomenon. This all-purpose system is difficult for outsiders, including criminal outsiders, to penetrate, but there is no clear internal distinction between legal and illegal cross-border enterprises.[121] The only way around this is to insist on well-regulated, differentiated institutions dedicated to each legitimate purpose: banks for finance, charities for humanitarian relief, and so forth. To some extent, it is up to these institutions and market forces to drive the development of accessible low-cost financial products attractive to rich and poor alike; the rest will be determined by effective domestic regulation and international standardisation. Some progress has been made since 9/11 in this regard.[122] However, there will always be a limit to what direct state regulation can achieve, light-touch or otherwise, against vassal institutions such as *kameti* and *hawala*. Nevertheless, with patience and a pluralist strategy, it is possible to chart a way forward.

It is singularly unhelpful to frame *kameti* and *hawala* in terms of individual autonomy or community culture: they have micro- and macro-level

[117] Martin, '*Hundi/Hawala*: The Problem of Definition', pp. 929–34; Nikos Passas, 'Fighting Terror with Error: The Counter-Productive Regulation of Informal Value Transfers' (2006) 45 (4) *Crime Law and Social Change* 315–36, pp. 321–3.

[118] Genesis J. Martis, 'A Guidance [*sic*] to Understand *hawala* and to Establish the Nexus with Terrorist Financing' (ACAMS, March 2018), pp. 7, 17.

[119] Jenner, 'Why Hawala Is Detrimental for Our Financial Safety?'.

[120] Daudi, 'The Invisible Bank', pp. 619, 629.

[121] Martin, '*Hundi/Hawala*: The Problem of Definition', p. 933.

[122] See generally Daudi, 'The Invisible Bank'.

importance and must be met with joined-up thinking and a systematic response. Recent historical experience suggests that draconian crackdowns via outright bans and aggressive de-risking (i.e. refusal of banking services) have little impact on these adaptable informal networks and drive them further underground.[123] Even if a specialised light-touch regulatory framework were introduced, it would still face the same evidential difficulties and perpetuate the vicious cycle of failing enforcement, bureaucratic expansion and further incentivising *hawala* usage. There are certainly regulatory improvements to be made – greater transparency requirements in the MSB sector, better information sharing and coordination among better-resourced enforcement agencies, improved literacy around the nature and functioning of *hawala*[124] – but even these can do only so much so long as the transnational kinship networks upon which these MSBs depend remain operational. These clans and their financial instruments undermine the very concept of nationhood by undermining allegiance to the law of the land and the state's ability to supervise monetary activity.[125] They are especially detrimental to the economic development of poorer countries by denying them revenue and facilitating systemic corruption.[126] The evidence relating to terrorist financing, money laundering, tax avoidance, fraud and corruption identified in this chapter joins the body of evidence presented in subsequent chapters to justify the dissolution of this kind of endogamous group unit (the privileged institution par excellence). The legal means of doing so are presented in Chapter 8. This being done, the costs of compliance and doing finance are likely to decrease with positive knock-on effects for access to formal banking. Even so, the government would need to develop an international aid strategy to wean other societies off *hawala* and address their macroeconomic issues through the alleviation of poverty, illiteracy, corruption and financial dysfunction. Banks must themselves shoulder their global civic responsibility by improving access to their services for the world's poor, regardless of nationality or creed. In the meantime, philanthropists and organised charities would need to continue their vital humanitarian work and ramp it up further to deal with any emerging difficulties. In short, the end of *hawala* would merely be the end of the beginning as regards fostering responsible international finance.

In terms of domestic policy, this all translates into offering the UK's Islamic banks enthusiastic but conditional support. It matters not at all whether the industry is intrinsically innovative or whether it is simply an ingenious purveyor of doctrine-compliant instruments. The banks themselves should be viewed as

123 See generally Ballard, 'Coalitions of Reciprocity and the Maintenance of Financial Integrity within Informal Value Transmission Systems'; Passas, 'Fighting Terror with Error: The Counter-Productive Regulation of Informal Value Transfers'; Daudi, 'The Invisible Bank', pp. 640–54; UKNRA 2015, pp. 49, 94–5; UKNRA 2017, p. 69; UKNRA 2020, pp. 115, 118–20.

124 See generally Oliver Kraft, 'Money Service Businesses in the UK: Improving the Conditions for Effective Financial Crime Supervision and Investigations' (RUSI, January 2018).

125 Ercanbrack, 'The Regulation of Islamic Finance in the UK', p. 72.

126 Daudi, 'The Invisible Bank', pp. 633–4.

voluntary associations first and as expressions of Muslim culture only incidentally. Banks which constitute themselves Islamically are not mere appendages of Muslim culture; they are living group units, regardless of whether their staff and customers happen to be Muslim. As organisations, their conduct is not simply a reflection of the faith and so cannot be attacked or defended on this basis; they are to be judged as individual organisations with the capacity to determine and pursue their own interests. Thus, on the individual level, these institutions and products support free choice and help to improve the financial situations of those who wish to bank according to their religious beliefs. On the civil society level, they have intrinsic worth as legitimate fellowship institutions while serving to enhance the vibrancy of civil society and as viable competitors to regular banks. The state retains an interest in regulating them and taxing their activities accordingly, as it does with other financial institutions. On the national level, the industry accords with Britain's historical tradition as a great trading power, advancing the national interest, fostering world-beating expertise and projecting commercial clout around the world. If the industry in general or any particular bank were to begin to enrich a dangerous geopolitical rival, or if the financial system were to require a general overhaul, the level of support could be revised and readjusted to fit the new reality. Otherwise, the industry should be left to compete and develop organically under the general regulatory system with light-touch interventions as and when required.

A pluralist emphasis on institutionalisation will only enhance the governance of Islamic finance. A consistent problem recognised by successive governments and scholars in the field is the lack of standardisation in industry standards and practices. There are undoubtedly limits to what the law (or, indeed, any government) can achieve, given the demands of secular neutrality and the fact of globalisation, which severely curtails extraterritorial authority. Even so, if Islamic finance develops a more corporate structure with official encouragement, many of the problems relating to underground practices, uncertain religious principles, irreconcilable and disputatious authority figures and the effective training and accreditation of professional sharia experts will be lessened.[127] A final point is that the brevity of this chapter should not be taken as a sign of its insignificance. This particular case study demonstrates that the regulation of Islamic finance is an exemplary instance of English law's relationship with British Islam under a pluralist framework.

[127] Aldohni, *The Legal and Regulatory Aspects of Islamic Banking*, pp. 23–4.

5

Charities

5.1 Introduction

This chapter addresses the abuse of charitable religion. It begins with a brief history of the abuse of religious charities. This draws out the entrenched legal requirements for charities to guard against administrative and purposive abuse, and highlights the resourcing and remit issues the Charity Commission has faced since its inception. It notes the general success of Muslim or Muslim-led charities to contextualise five pressing contemporary concerns: Charity Commission effectiveness, unregulated domestic fundraising, terrorist financing, foreign funding and extremist exploitation. Taking these in order of difficulty, it acknowledges the 'faith factor' where relevant and notes the need for theory when addressing unresolved policy questions about potentially dangerous foreign and non-state influence over important domestic institutions. The penultimate section (5.4) models the two conventional theoretical interpretations of these issues and their attendant problems. The final section (5.5) offers a pluralist response and details the most sensible reforms.

5.2 A Brief History of the Abuse and Regulation of Religious Charities

The concept of charity began in ancient times as *caritas*, the Latin for esteemed costly objects and a sense of benevolence. Under the influence of Christianity, it took on a devotional aspect and came to denote either the distribution of alms or an institution dedicated to such good works.[1] During the Middle Ages, organised charity revolved around the Church and lesser corporate institutions – hospitals, schools, military orders, monasteries – which carried out a range of exclusively pious and more practical activities. Despite all manner of specific objectives and structures, religious idealism – serving God through the transfer of wealth – gave charities coherence and clout as a social force, incentivising the rich to give more and the pious to join up.[2] Early English law was especially

[1] James William Brodman, *Charity and Religion in Medieval Europe* (Washington DC: Catholic University of America Press, 2009), pp. 3–4.

[2] Ibid., pp. 2–3.

conducive to their proliferation and enrichment – the ecclesiastical courts obtained exclusive jurisdiction over the testament of personal property, generous rules of construction cured seemingly uncertain or indefinite legacies, and the Church had perpetual existence, which enabled it to accumulate vast landholdings free of the usual feudal duties and charges.[3] Privilege and power on this scale, tied as they were to corruption and abuse, inevitably attracted state attention. Special licences granted at royal discretion were introduced as early as 1006 to limit the amount of land being removed from the feudal economy through gifts to the Church. However prudent, they failed to prevent excessive Church landholdings, causing a fatal shortage in Anglo-Saxon tax revenues and knights prior to the Battle of Hastings in 1066, making the Norman Conquest easier than it might have been. These restraints were reinforced in Magna Carta while a raft of mortmain ('dead hand') legislation over subsequent centuries sought to curtail further gifts to the Church and other corporations.[4] Enforcement varied according to the religiosity of the monarch and his power relative to the Church and Parliament.[5]

The privileges of religious charities also affected the laity, who resented the delays, fees, malfeasance and ineffective remedies attendant on litigation in the ecclesiastical courts. In response, they began to petition the Chancellor, whose jurisdiction over charitable legacies was established and entrenched during the fifteenth century.[6] By Tudor times, monasteries were notorious for sybaritic greed – especially for neglecting their obligations to provide poor relief – before Henry VIII had them dissolved following a comprehensive survey of their assets.[7] Put crudely, these problems can be classified as 'administrative abuse' encompassing the acquisition and disposal of assets and the management of religious charities. The main questions for the law were practical in nature: 'How should charitable fundraising and spending be regulated?' and 'Are religious charities actually fulfilling their pious and practical objectives?' In such a religiously cohesive society there was little need to ask whether these objectives were valid and desirable in themselves.

The Reformation shattered the medieval consensus on charitable religion. As confessional diversity and conflict deepened, as the English came to reflect 'less on the fate of their souls and became more concerned with the worldly

[3] Gareth Jones, *History of the Law of Charity, 1532–1827* (Cambridge: Cambridge University Press, 1969), pp. 4–5; Mary F. Radford, 'The Case against the Georgia Mortmain Statute' (1992) 8(2) *Georgia State University Law Review* 313–61, pp. 317–18.

[4] Kerry O'Halloran, Myles McGregor-Lowndes and Karla W. Simon, *Charity Law and Social Policy: National and International Perspectives on the Law Relating to Charities* (New York: Springer, 2008), pp. 134–5.

[5] Radford, 'The Case against the Georgia Mortmain Statute', p. 319.

[6] Jones, *History of the Law of Charity*, pp. 5–6.

[7] For a measured view of monastic corruption and the *Valor Ecclesiasticus* of 1535 ('church valuation'), see Neil S. Rushton, 'Monastic Charitable Provision in Tudor England: Quantifying and Qualifying Poor Relief in the Early Sixteenth Century' (2001) 16(1) *Continuity and Change* 9–44.

needs of their fellow men', so the Church's grip on charities slackened.[8] The law of charities, confronted with new purposive questions as well as practical ones, began to realign with the priorities of secular government.[9] The Henrician crackdown on religious corporations led to the rise of 'uses', which became the preferred vehicle for charitable gifts.[10] This device was developed in large part to evade mortmain legislation and assist in fraud.[11] Its success led directly to the Statute of Elizabeth (Charitable Uses Act 1601) which sought to restrict administrative abuses, including 'frauds, breaches of trust, and negligence', but 'unintentionally created a definition of charity that resonates in the law today'.[12] The famous Preamble set out the purposes that would be accepted as charitable and in so doing 'laid down an agenda for what was thereafter to become a public benefit contract between the state and charity'.[13] Every subsequent expansion, summary or update of these purposes has fallen broadly within the 'equity' or 'spirit and intendment' of that Statute.[14] For example, while the Preamble references charitable religion only obliquely – 'maintenance of ... churches' – it was eventually made explicit into one of the principal headings of charity as 'trusts for the advancement of religion'.[15] Tudor charities legislation was part of a wider reaction against the Roman Catholic Church, which menaced Protestant England from within and without for centuries.[16] This threat took a variety of forms – religious massacres, invasion scares, assassination attempts, bomb plots, propaganda campaigns – which were countered only through constant vigilance and ruthless determination.[17] Elizabethan intelligence was especially sophisticated and adept at tracking foreign funds destined for religious subversives.[18] In this febrile atmosphere, charity law had to determine the permissible object of religious charities and what to do about those whose ends were unacceptable or dangerous.

As regards the former, 'the only permissible object of a religious charity was an endowment for the national Church', as 'all other gifts or purposes intended

[8] Jones, *History of the Law of Charity*, p. 10.

[9] Kerry O'Halloran, *Religion, Charity and Human Rights* (Cambridge: Cambridge University Press, 2014), p. 47.

[10] O'Halloran et al., *Charity Law and Social Policy*, p. 135. [11] Ibid.

[12] Jones, *History of the Law of Charity*, p. 26; James J. Fishman, 'The Political Use of Private Benevolence: The Statute of Charitable Uses' (Pace Law Faculty Publications Paper 487, 2008), p. ii.

[13] O'Halloran, *Religion, Charity and Human Rights*, p. 50.

[14] Jamie Glister and James Lee, *Hanbury and Martin: Modern Equity* (21st ed., London: Sweet & Maxwell, 2018), p. 361.

[15] *Special Commissioners of Income Tax* v. *Pemsel* [1891] AC 531. Since codified in statute in s. 2(4)(b) and (c) Charities Act 2006 and now s. 3(1)(m)(ii) and (iii) Charities Act 2011.

[16] See, for example, John Bellamy, *The Tudor Law of Treason* (London: Routledge, 1979).

[17] See Jessie Childs, *God's Traitors: Terror and Faith in Elizabethan England* (London: Vintage, 2015) and Stephen Alford, *The Watchers: A Secret History of the Reign of Elizabeth I* (London: Penguin, 2013).

[18] Christopher Andrew, *The Secret World: A History of Intelligence* (London: Allen Lane, 2018), pp. 164–5.

for religious ends were not only not charitable, they were illegal'.[19] As regards the latter, draconian measures culminating in the Clarendon Code of the seventeenth century introduced numerous criminal offences, search and seizure powers, restrictions on gatherings, and religious tests designed to achieve religious homogeneity and suppress rebellion against the Crown.[20] While repression eventually gave way to toleration – 'a slow transition from the maintenance of one true religion to the principle that there is, in law, no false religion'[21] – this post-Reformation body of law left one important legacy. The Toleration Act 1688, which legalised assemblies of Protestant dissenters, did so only on the condition that the doors of their meetings were not 'locked, barred or bolted'.[22] This provision enshrined the expectation that religious groups should demonstrate a reasonable degree of openness in their activities and that the state will not interfere so long as there is no danger of sedition or treason.[23] In short, early modern charity law had not only to cope with standard administrative abuses but also to address deep moral questions as to what religious charity was for and how it might be exploited by hostile ideologues.

The Industrial Revolution brought Great Britain untold power and wealth.[24] It also brought into sharp relief the grinding poverty of the toiling masses, prompting the Victorian elite to revolutionise philanthropy just as they had manufacturing.[25] Commissioners with the power to inspect and supervise charities were yet another Tudor creation and had been placed on a statutory footing by the Statute of Elizabeth in 1601.[26] Despite this, and the introduction of a registry of charities in the late eighteenth century, 'old corruption' survived well into the nineteenth century.[27] It was not until the Brougham Inquiry (1819–37) resulted in the prosecution of 400 charities that the need for an independent standing Commission was accepted by government.[28] After several unsuccessful attempts at reform, and the realisation that 'it was impossible, through the Court of Chancery, to obtain redress for the abuses of charitable institutions', the Charitable Trusts Act 1853 created

[19] O'Halloran, *Religion, Charity and Human Rights*, pp. 48–50.

[20] Julian Rivers, *The Law of Organized Religions: Between Establishment and Secularism* (Oxford: Oxford University Press, 2010), pp. 13–14 and ch. 1 on the Corporations Act 1661, the Act of Uniformity 1662, the Quakers Act 1662, the Conventicles Act 1664, the Five Mile Act 1665, the Conventicles Act 1670 and the Test Acts of 1673 and 1678.

[21] Ibid., p. 24. [22] Section IV.

[23] For a modern restatement of this principle, see Gallagher (Valuation Officer) v. Church of Jesus Christ of Latter-Day Saints (2008) 1 WLR 1852 per Lord Scott at paras. 43–51.

[24] On the conditions and system of concepts that made it possible, see, respectively, Roger Osborne, *Iron, Steam and Money: The Making of the Industrial Revolution* (London: Pimlico, 2013) and William Rosen, *The Most Powerful Idea in the World: A Story of Steam, Industry and Invention* (London: Pimlico, 2011).

[25] See Charles Dickens, *Hard Times* (London: Penguin Classics, 2003).

[26] Diarmaid MacCulloch, *Thomas Cromwell, A Life* (London: Allen Lane, 2018), pp. 274–5; Jones, *History of the Law of Charity*, ch. 3.

[27] O'Halloran et al., *Charity Law and Social Policy*, pp. 136–8.

[28] Jones, *History of the Law of Charity*, ch. 11 and O'Halloran et al., ibid., pp. 138–9.

the first permanent Commission responsible for the regulation of charities.[29] Now called the Charity Commission for England and Wales ('the Commission'), its basic functions have always included 'inquiry and advice, property transactions, sanctioning judicial proceedings and remedial schemes' and its powers have frequently been extended to help it carry these out more effectively.[30] Interestingly, the regulator was plagued from its very inception by accusations that it was simply not up to the task of identifying and dealing with the abuse of charities.[31] Fishman notes that 'there were three continuing foci of criticism: the selection of the Commissioners, their perceived lack of aggressiveness, and the slow pace of reform'.[32] In 1854, for example, *The Times* claimed that 'the Commissioners lacked vision, decisiveness, and talent to cope with the array of abuses, and strictly construing their charge'.[33] In the paper's own words:

> Abuses sleep as soundly as they did before the Commission was established, for the Commission has been too well bred to wake them. All that we have gained by our great legislative effort and the expenditure of many thousands a year is the making comfortable provision for several very respectable persons at the public expense, and the providing an ever ready answer to anyone who shall be indiscreet enough to . . . drag to light the misappropriation of charitable funds.[34]

The Commission, it seems, has always been stuck in an impossible and uncertain political position. It is nearly always seen as being 'too Tory for the Radicals and too Radical for the Tories' or as too interventionist or not proactive enough.[35] The widespread perception that it is 'a wholly unpopular body lacking political support' is clearly nothing new; even during the Victorian era,

> [t]he body never was granted sufficient authority or resources to rationalize all charitable endowments in need of reform. Nor could it ever garner public or parliamentary support. The Commission's efforts were resisted by trustees of charities. It became a symbol of meddling government. By the end of the century, the office seemed to lose vigour and initiative . . . and was viewed as a government bureaucracy doing routine things in a routine way.[36]

The Commission's role developed considerably during the late nineteenth century as the English education system, then run almost entirely by charities, came under fire for being inefficient and unfit for the purposes and needs of

[29] Sir Samuel Romilly quoted in James J. Fishman, 'Charitable Accountability and Reform in Nineteenth-Century England: The Case of the Charity Commission' (2005) 80(2) *Chicago-Kent Law Review* 723–78, pp. 728, 724–30. On the notoriety of the Court of Chancery at this time, see Charles Dickens, *Bleak House* (London: Penguin Classics, 2003).

[30] See Peter R. Elson, 'The Origin of the Species: Why Charity Regulations in Canada and England Continue to Reflect Their Origins' (2010) 12(3) *International Journal of Not-for-Profit Law* 75–89; part II Charities Act 2011.

[31] Fishman, 'Charitable Accountability and Reform in Nineteenth-Century England', pp. 749–50.

[32] Ibid. [33] Ibid. [34] Quoted in ibid., p. 749 footnote 142. [35] Ibid., pp. 769–70.

[36] Ibid., pp. 770, 774.

modern society. As the state began to assume ever-greater responsibility for the substance and provision of education, it was increasingly felt that the charitable sector had to be rationalised in order to meet demand. Indeed, the very 'ideology of philanthropy and the role of charity also changed' throughout this period: whereas, before, charities were seen as being the 'principal source of assistance', with the state occasionally bringing up the shortfall, they eventually came to be seen as supplementary to permanent state involvement in the provision of education and welfare.[37] All this led to the expectation that the Commission should play a greater role in rationalising, scrutinising and collecting information about the administration of charities.[38] This was not matched by any corresponding increase in resources, staffing or assistance from Parliament and, for the most part, the Commission and the myriad issues confronting it were largely ignored well into the twentieth century.[39] In short, 'the failure of the Charity Commission in some sense reflected the failure of nineteenth-century liberalism and its replacement by the modern welfare state'.[40]

In general, however, the involvement of government in charities was still quite limited from the mid-nineteenth century until the 1960s. The original Charity Commissioners had a fairly restricted jurisdiction over largely self-regulated religious charities 'out of a concern for autonomy from Government interference'.[41] As Rivers points out, 'the basic policy was that where adequate oversight was provided by a religious denominational structure, that of the Charity Commissioners was not necessary'.[42] The principal effect of the Charities Act 1960 was to compel non-exempt charities to register and then subject them all to the powers and oversight of the Commission.[43] It effected a substantial reordering of the law of charities and established the broad basis of the regulatory regime which, with various amendments and consolidations, persists to this day.[44] The Charities Act 2006 is the only comparably transformative statute of more recent times: it incorporated the Commission as a corporate body with statutory objectives, functions, duties and defined powers; created the Charity Tribunal to streamline appeals against the Commission's decisions; codified and occasionally extended the existing common law on charitable purposes and status; and created a new incorporated legal vehicle for charity, the Charitable Incorporated Organisation (CIO). In the end, the historic problems faced by the Commission – a 'lack of resources, inadequate legislative support, too broad a mandate with too many organizations to oversee' – have remained constant, as have, largely, its expected functions of enforcement and education.[45] It must combat misconduct, establish order and instil a sense of responsibility into the sector while enduring

[37] Ibid., pp. 757–66. [38] Ibid., pp. 768–9. [39] Ibid., pp. 774–5. [40] Ibid., p. 776.
[41] Rivers, *Law of Organized Religions*, p. 161. [42] Ibid., p. 167. [43] Ibid.
[44] Ibid.; Public Administration Committee, 'The Role of the Charity Commission and "Public Benefit": Post-Legislative Scrutiny of the Charities Act 2006' (House of Commons, 21 May 2013), ch. 2.
[45] Fishman, 'Charitable Accountability and Reform in Nineteenth-Century England', pp. 777–8.

chronic under-resourcing ascribable to the fact that 'charitable accountability is not of central importance to government or politics and is marginal to the overall [economic] health of society'.[46]

5.3 Contemporary Challenges

It has been argued, often without substantiation, that Muslims are a 'securitised suspect community' targeted en bloc by state authorities and the Prevent counter-extremism programme.[47] While this mode of thinking has percolated into debates about religious charities, it is more productive to reframe the issues as technical challenges set in historical perspective. Although Islamic charities (*waqf/awqaf*) have historically taken a quite different form from English ones, the problem is not one of adaptation or access or lack of enthusiasm as British Muslims give more to charity than those of any other faith in the UK.[48] Rather, the main issues are non-novel and non-specific; many of the concerns surrounding Muslim or Muslim-led charities are simply subsets of more general issues in the sector. The discussion dispatches each matter in ascending order of difficulty. The hardest purposive questions on foreign funding and extremism are outlined at the end of this section but addressed in the theoretical sections that follow (Sections 5.4 and 5.5).

5.3.1 Charity Commission Capability

5.3.1.1 Criticisms and Improvements

In recent years, the Charity Commission's effectiveness as a watchdog has been called into question yet again. A review of the charity sector, published by the National Audit Office (NAO) in 2012, found that the Commission 'takes a risk-based approach to regulation, whereby it focuses its resources on those areas it considers are the greatest threat to public trust and confidence. Declining resources mean that it increasingly relies on self-help measures for charities ... [and] relies mainly on external reporting, for example from trustees, to identify when charities are not complying with charity law.'[49] The review questioned 'whether the Commission can maintain public trust and confidence in charities, given its declining resources'.[50] A year later, the NAO published a scathing report highlighting a plethora of concerns. It found

46 Ibid.

47 Helen and David Fenwick, 'Prevent, Free Speech, "Extremism" and Counter-Terrorism Interventions: Exploring Narratives about Chilling Expression in Schools' (2020) *Public Law* 661–79, p. 668.

48 See variously Ruth Gledhill, 'Muslims "Are Britain's Top Charity Givers"' (*The Times*, 20 July 2013); John L. Esposito, *Islam: The Straight Path* (Oxford: Oxford University Press, 1988), p. 206; Roger Scruton, *The West and the Rest: Globalization and the Terrorist Threat* (London: Continuum, 2003), p. 98.

49 National Audit Office (NAO), 'Regulating Charities: A Landscape Review' (NAO, July 2012), p. 5.

50 Ibid.

that the Commission was barely using its statutory enforcement powers and was very slow to act, if it did at all, when serious regulatory concerns were raised.[51] This was largely because it depended on the good faith and timely co-operation of trustees 'intent on abusing charitable status'.[52] It rarely gathered its own information to identify risk and monitor compliance, relying almost exclusively on external sources to trigger investigations.[53] What is more, the resources, equipment and staffing available to the Commission were found to be worryingly inadequate.[54] In short, the NAO concluded bluntly that the Commission 'is not regulating charities effectively' and 'is not delivering value for money'; these findings were confirmed by the Public Accounts Committee chaired by Margaret Hodge MP, which determined that 'the Charity Commission is not fit for purpose' on much the same grounds.[55] It has also been accused, not least by Baroness Sayeeda Warsi, of practising 'McCarthyism' with a 'disproportionate' focus on Muslims, and of being 'Islamophobic' or 'anti-Muslim'.[56]

The NAO's follow-up review in 2015 found that the Charity Commission had undertaken a sweeping programme of improvements aimed at improving its effectiveness as a watchdog. For example, it had secured additional funding from the Treasury; taken on new board members with expertise in areas such as 'fraud prevention, counterterrorism, data mining and risk management'; begun the process of developing a more effective risk assessment model with increasing resources being devoted to high-risk cases; started coordinating its efforts with those of other authorities more effectively; found better ways to use its statutory powers; and begun improving its capacity to undertake investigations and monitor continuing compliance.[57] It concluded that the Commission had 'made good, early progress' albeit with considerable scope for further improvement.[58] A subsequent report into public and industry perceptions found a high degree of confidence and trust in the Commission's role, fairness and effectiveness as well as very high levels of support for its new powers granted under the Charities (Protection and Social Investment) Act 2016 to ensure that it could do more to regulate and enforce compliance within the sector.[59] This represented a marked improvement in

[51] NAO, 'The Regulatory Effectiveness of the Charity Commission' (NAO, December 2013), p. 7.
[52] Ibid., p. 8. [53] Ibid. [54] Ibid.
[55] Ibid., p. 9; House of Commons Committee of Public Accounts, 'The Charity Commission: Forty-Second Report of Session 2013–14' (House of Commons, January 2014) and 'Charity Commission Not Fit for Purpose' (House of Commons, February 2014).
[56] Quoted in Kirsty Weakley, 'Baroness Warsi Criticises Commission Chair over Muslim Charities' (*Civil Society News*, 22 November 2017); Atif Imtiaz, 'An Examination of the Inquiries Conducted on British Muslim Charities by the Charity Commission' (2020) 2 *The Forum: The Journal of the British Muslim Charity Sector* (Muslim Charities Forum) 11–13, pp. 11, 13.
[57] NAO, 'Follow-Up on the Charity Commission' (NAO, January 2015), pp. 6–9.
[58] Ibid., p. 10.
[59] Charity Commission and Populus, 'Trust and Confidence in the Charity Commission: Research Study Conducted by Populus on Behalf of the Charity Commission' (Charity Commission, June 2015), pp. 5–7.

the Commission's public profile and sense of direction, although public confidence dropped to its lowest point in 2018 before rising again through to 2020.[60] The most recent NAO review, published in 2017, acknowledged that the Commission had 'improved significantly' under the stewardship of William Shawcross (Chairman, 2012–18).[61] It had become more efficient and proactive as a risk-based regulator, but continued to be hampered by inadequate resources and data collection.[62]

5.3.1.2 Budget and Record Keeping

The Charity Commission's budget for 2019–20 was £29.3 million to regulate a sector populated by 168,000 registered charities with an annual income of £81.2 billion and expenditure of £78.7 billion.[63] Around 34,800 charities (20 per cent of all charities) conduct religious activities, which are the sole activity of 12,000 (7 per cent of all charities).[64] In 2007, there were 1,373 registered Muslim charities with a collective worth of £218.5 million, and a more recent estimate from 2016 put the total at 2,054 (4.7 per cent of all faith-based charities) worth over £542 million.[65] Statistics on the regulation of religious charities are sparse as the Commission's record keeping is patchy at best. The figures for 2007–8 show that 14 of the 42 published statutory inquiries (the most serious kind for high-risk cases) and 33 of the 145 published non-statutory compliance cases (the most common type of advisory investigation) involved charities with a religious core purpose.[66] In 2013–14, the first and only year for which figures on specific religions are available from the Commission, there were 23 statutory inquiries (11 per cent of the total number of inquiries) into registered charities with a religious classification and, of these, 9 (39 per cent) were Muslim.[67] There were also 241 operational compliance cases into religious charities (23 per cent of the total number of cases) and, of these, 49

[60] Ibid., pp. 8–9; Charity Commission and Populus, 'Trust in Charities 2020 – Overview of Findings' (Charity Commission, June 2020), p. 4.

[61] NAO, 'Charity Commission: Progress Report' (NAO, November 2017), p. 5.

[62] Ibid., pp. 7–8; William Shawcross, 'What's Changing at the Charity Commission?' (Charity Commission, 8 March 2016).

[63] Charity Commission, *Charity Commission Annual Report 2019–2020* (Charity Commission, HC 507, July 2020), pp. 10–12.

[64] Jessica Nicholls and Russell Hargrave, 'Questions of Faith' (NPC, 2014); National Secular Society (NSS), 'For the Public Benefit? The Case for Removing "the Advancement of Religion" as a Charitable Purpose' (NSS, February 2019), pp. 8, 13.

[65] Charity Commission, 'Working with Faith Groups – Feedback from Muslim Charities' (Charity Commission, October 2007); David Bull, Lucy de Las Casas and Rachel Wharton, 'Faith Matters: Understanding the Size, Income and Focus of Faith-Based Charities' (NPC, June 2016), pp. 3–4.

[66] Charity Commission, 'Charities Back on Track 2007–08: Themes and Lessons from the Charity Commission's Compliance Work' (Charity Commission, 2008), pp. 32, 36.

[67] Charity Commission, 'Tackling Abuse and Mismanagement: Report of Charity Commission's Investigations and Compliance Case Work 2013–14' (Charity Commission, 2014), pp. 40, 51, 54.

(20 per cent) were Muslim.[68] A freedom of information request by one transient think tank found that 38 per cent of statutory inquiries opened between December 2012 and May 2014 concerned Muslim charities; another found that of the 286 statutory inquiries ongoing between April 2016 and March 2017, only 2 of the 14 religious charities investigated were Muslim; of 335 operational compliance cases into religious charities in the 2014–15 financial year, 77 were Muslim.[69] A more comprehensive study covering every accessible report on the Commission's website found that out of a total of 296 inquiries into charities of all kinds between 2008 and 2019, 59 concerned Muslim-led charities.[70] In short, it would be unwise to draw any firm conclusions from these figures as the records are too poor and fragmentary; the Commission itself admits that it 'do[es] not have reliable data' on charities and cases connected with any particular religion.[71]

Inadequate funding is the underlying issue here. For almost two centuries, the Charity Commission has faced an impossible task from an impossible position. It would be unfair to demand miracles. Nevertheless, it would undoubtedly benefit from greater resources and much better record keeping The former could be achieved by a small levy on charitable fundraising and the latter at least has a precedent in the Commission's short-lived Faith and Social Cohesion Unit tasked with research and engagement with Muslim charities.[72] This would all enhance oversight and transparency while improving the state of knowledge of the sector and emerging problems. In the meantime, it would be helpful for the Commission to continually refute misinformation by emphasising that charities are regulated as individual organisations and not suspect sectors or collective faith communities.

5.3.2 Administrative Abuse

5.3.2.1 Unregulated Domestic Fundraising

In December 2015, then-Prime Minister David Cameron launched 'a comprehensive review to root out any remaining funding of extremism within the

[68] Ibid., pp. 39, 54.

[69] See, respectively, Sam Burnes James, 'Charity Commission Anti-extremism Processes Are Unsound, Think Tank Says' (*Third Sector*, 17 November 2014); Emma Webb, 'Wolves in Sheep's Clothing: How Islamist Extremists Exploit the UK Charitable Sector' (Henry Jackson Society, February 2018), p. 11; Tesse Akpeki and Barbara Eze, 'Faith-Based Charities in the Spotlight' (Bateswells, spring 2016), pp. 4–5.

[70] Imtiaz, 'An Examination of the Inquiries Conducted on British Muslim Charities by the Charity Commission', p. 11.

[71] Charity Commission, 'Tackling Abuse and Mismanagement', p. 48.

[72] NAO, 'Charity Commission: Progress Report', pp. 7, 31; Charity Commission, 'Parliamentary Briefing: Survey of Mosques in England and Wales' (Charity Commission, 1 February 2009); Kaye Wiggins, 'Charity Commission Axes "Bold, Innovative" Faith and Social Cohesion Unit' (*Third Sector*, 27 July 2010); Charity Commission, 'Specialist Guidance for Faith-Based Charities' (National Archives, 3 September 2014).

UK'.[73] Although the full report was never published, in July 2017 then-Home Secretary Amber Rudd disclosed that '[t]he most common source of support for Islamist extremist organisations in the UK is from small, anonymous public donations, with the majority of these donations most likely coming from UK-based individuals'.[74] A subsequent investigation found that right-wing extremism is 'highly likely self-funded via legitimate means' as well.[75] Regardless of the definition or type of extremism, this is a straightforward legal problem to solve. House-to-house and street collections require a licence from the local authorities, although in the latter case a loophole exists for direct debit agreements as these are merely promises of money at a later date.[76] There are widespread and severe concerns about aggressive fundraising by charities – 'chugging', in common parlance – so this general issue is not unique to Muslim organisations.[77] For example, unscrupulous tactics and data sharing among charities resulted in the late Olive Cooke receiving thousands of donation requests which led to her feeling 'distressed and overwhelmed'.[78] This sort of problem is not new – medieval and early modern mortmain statutes were aimed at the 'acquisitive hands' of donees rather than the donors themselves.[79]

Nevertheless, these problems are exacerbated by the sociologically distinct character of Islamic charity in which almsgiving, or *zakat*, is a compulsory religious tenet.[80] Over the last decade, the convulsions taking place across the Muslim world have spurred a surge in humanitarian donations (which increase during Ramadan and other Islamic festivals) with the attendant problem of unregulated financial activity.[81] West Yorkshire Police, for example, have reported that community activists use pedestrian-crossing

[73] Hansard, HC, 2 December 2015, Column 321, Daily Hansard Debate on National Security: https://publications.parliament.uk/pa/cm201516/cmhansrd/cm151202/debtext/151202-0001.htm.

[74] 'Statement UIN HCWS39 on Extremism' (House of Commons, 12 July 2017): https://questions-statements.parliament.uk/written-statements/detail/2017-07-12/HCWS39.

[75] HM Treasury and Home Office, 'National Risk Assessment of Money Laundering and Terrorist Financing 2020' (HMG, December 2020), p. 46; see also Tom Keatinge, Florence Keen and Kayla Izenman, 'Fundraising for Right-Wing Extremist Movements' (2019) 164(2) *RUSI Journal* 10–23.

[76] House to House Collections Act 1939, ss. 1–2, 11; Police, Factories, &c. (Miscellaneous Provisions) Act 1916, s. 5.

[77] Public Administration Committee, 'The Role of the Charity Commission and "Public Benefit"', p. 36; Charities (Protection and Social Investment) Act 2016, ss. 13–14; Charity Commission, 'Charities Act 2016: New Fundraising Rules' (Charity Commission, 1 November 2016).

[78] Steven Morris, 'Poppy Seller Who Killed Herself Got 3,000 Charity Requests for Donations a Year' (*The Guardian*, 20 January 2016); Howard Lake, 'FRSB Publishes Results of Olive Cooke Investigation and Related Complaints' (*UK Fundraising News*, 20 January 2016).

[79] Radford, 'The Case against the Georgia Mortmain Statute', p. 316; O'Halloran et al., *Charity Law and Social Policy*, pp. 136–7.

[80] Amy Singer, *Charity in Islamic Societies* (Cambridge: Cambridge University Press, 2008), p. 218; Barnard Lewis and Buntzie Ellis Churchill, *Islam: The Religion and the People* (Upper Saddle River, NJ: Pearson Education, 2009), p. 16.

[81] Hannah Stuart, 'Community Policing and Preventing Extremism: Lessons from Bradford' (London: Henry Jackson Society, February 2015), p. 21.

traffic lights to stop lines of traffic and then seek donations for their 'buckets for Syria', intimidating those who do not give money.[82] Collectors, who are usually known to their targets, also turn up 'week in week out' during the day when the young Muslims and their mothers are at home and demand *zakat* from the often privately reluctant and harassed occupants.[83] It is also extremely difficult to keep track of informal collections and unidentifiable collection pots being placed 'anywhere and everywhere'.[84] The report concludes that fundraisers are aggressively exploiting the injunction to donate *zakat* in a way that places intense spiritual, cultural and communal pressure on local Muslims. Despite efforts by the police and the Charity Commission to promote safe charitable giving within Muslim communities, the local authorities responsible for enforcing the relevant regulations have proven largely ineffective. This is because they merely write advisory or warning letters to registered charities, allowing much of the fundraising to continue unchecked.[85] Comparable concerns have been raised about online crowdfunding platforms and campaigns, which have been described as 'a regulatory black hole' despite the growing importance of this method.[86] None of this should be thought of as a specifically Muslim problem: the issues are to do with 'inconsistent, fragmented, outdated and complex' laws which can be easily fixed; the necessary reforms would improve standards right across the charitable sector.[87]

Going forward, the loophole for direct debit agreements should be closed so that licences become mandatory. Second, the various statutes governing charitable fundraising should be consolidated and regularised with tougher penalties for breaches and primary enforcement responsibilities transferred to the police. Two proposed statutory schemes to achieve this have never been implemented.[88] Third, online crowdfunding and new financial technologies should be brought within the regulatory system.[89] Taken together, these measures would shore up the existing legal framework by promoting transparency and ethical practice. However, there have already been some attempts to address the regulatory aspect of concerns over fundraising. A cumbersome self-regulatory scheme involving three oversight bodies was established in 2006 and has since been replaced by the Fundraising Regulator in 2016.[90]

[82] Ibid., p. 20. [83] Ibid., p. 22. [84] Ibid., p. 21. [85] Ibid., pp. 20–3.

[86] Suzanne McCarthy, 'Fundraising Platforms – Fixing a Regulatory Black Hole' (2018) *Risk & Regulation* 24–7; Charity Commission, 'Government Response: Online Charitable Giving Summit: Statement of Meeting' (Charity Commission, 3 October 2017).

[87] Home Office, 'Public Collections for Charitable, Philanthropic and Benevolent Purposes: Consultation Paper' (HMG, September 2003), p. 5.

[88] See Practical Law Private Client, 'Charity Fundraising: Public Charitable Collections Practice Note' (Thomson Reuters, accessed 23 February 2021), pp. 1–15, which covers the proposed amendments contained in the Charities Act 1992, ss. 65–74 and Charities Act 2006, ss. 45–66.

[89] See Matthew Robert Shillito, 'Regulating the Digital (Currency) Revolution: Unravelling the Technological Challenge Faced by Charities' in John Picton and Jennifer Sigafoos (eds.), *Debates in Charity Law* (Oxford: Hart, 2020), ch. 12, pp. 257–78.

[90] Lord Hodgson, 'Trusted and Independent: Giving Charity Back to Charities – Review of the Charities Act 2006' (HMG, July 2012), pp. 87–104; Sir Stuart Etherington, Lord Leigh, Baroness Pitkeathley and Lord Wallace, 'Regulating Fundraising for the Future: Trust in

Membership of this consolidated body remains voluntary, but take-up has increased steadily year by year.[91] It maintains a 'Code of Fundraising Practice' which stipulates that face-to-face fundraisers must carry ID and comply with local authority requirements.[92] It investigates complaints by members of the public and if recommendations are made and ignored, it may refer the matter to the Charity Commission itself.[93] While the scheme represents a significant improvement on what went before, face-to-face and online fundraising remain joint-second among the most complained about methods of fundraising.[94] It is perhaps significant that the 2016 Act provides reserve powers for the government to confer additional powers on the Commission to control fundraising should the existing scheme prove inadequate.[95] Further, despite the existence of a Statement of Recommended Practice for accounting and financial reporting by charities throughout the UK, there are still no common international standards for non-profit organisations, meaning that transparency and accountability remain poor for cross-border activities.[96]

5.3.2.2 Terrorist Financing

Countering terrorist financing is another top priority for the government and the Commission.[97] Compared with the funding of extremism, it is 'a better understood area' and the raft of legislation and regulatory guidance dealing with it is far more sophisticated.[98] Although authorities have traditionally focused on the revenues of Islamic movements, there is a growing awareness that radical right-wing groups pose a serious threat.[99] The charitable and wider

Charities, Confidence in Fundraising Legislation' (NCVO, September 2015); Alison Dunn, 'Eddies and Tides: Statutory Regulation, Co-regulation, and Self-Regulation in Charity Law in Britain' in Oonagh Breen, Alison Dunn and Mark Sidel (eds.), *Regulatory Waves: Comparative Perspectives on State Regulation and Self-Regulation Policies in the Nonprofit Sector* (Cambridge: Cambridge University Press, 2017), ch. 2, pp. 21–44, at pp. 27–8.

[91] Fundraising Regulator, 'Annual Review 2018–19' (Fundraising Regulator, November 2019), p. 2.

[92] Fundraising Regulator, *Code of Fundraising Practice* (Fundraising Regulator, October 2019), part 3, s. 8.

[93] Fundraising Regulator, *Complaints Process* (Fundraising Regulator, 18 September 2020).

[94] Fundraising Regulator, 'Annual Complaints Report 2019–20' (Fundraising Regulator, November 2020), pp. 7–11.

[95] S. 14.

[96] See generally Charity Commission, 'Charities SORP: Accounting and Reporting by Charities: Statement of Recommended Practice Applicable to Charities Preparing Their Accounts in Accordance with the Financial Reporting Standard Applicable in the UK and Republic of Ireland (FRS 102)' (2nd ed., Charity Commission, October 2019); Chartered Institute of Public Finance and Accountancy (CIPFA) 'International Financial Reporting for Non-profit Organisations (IFR4NPO): A Consultation Paper' (CIPFA, January 2021).

[97] UK Government, 'CONTEST: The United Kingdom's Strategy for Countering Terrorism' (HMG, June 2018); Charity Commission, 'Collection: Dealing with Wrongdoing and Harm in Charities' (Charity Commission, 2008–19).

[98] Rudd, 'Statement UIN HCWS39 on Extremism'; Terrorism Act 2000, ss. 15–18; Charity Commission, 'Compliance Toolkit: Protecting Charities from Harm, Chapter One: Charities and Terrorism Summary' (Charity Commission, November 2016).

[99] Keatinge et al., 'Fundraising for Right-Wing Extremist Movements', pp. 10–23.

non-profit sector has been 'formally recognised as a concern, the terrorism threat to the sector remains, and the sector continues to be misused and exploited by terrorist organisations through a variety of means'.[100] Typical abuses include sham charities being used as front organisations for terrorists, lawfully raised funds being diverted for illicit purposes, and 'exploitation of a charitable umbrella, such as through the recruitment and payment of extremists or for the propagation or glorification of a militant ideology'.[101] For more than a decade after 9/11, the global response was uneven and generally lax.[102] Writing in 2014, Professor Clive Walker concluded: 'The United Kingdom approach to those charities assailed by the taint of terrorism funding has been one of considerate understanding if not, at times, downright indulgence ... [The Commission's] serial indulgence of abuses does no favours to charities seeking to engage public support for oppressed people.'[103] This was broadly confirmed in 2015 by the first UK National Risk Assessment (UKNRA) which deemed the risk of terrorist financing via charities to be 'medium-high' despite the rarity of convictions and the difficulty of determining the end destination of funds.[104] However, the next UKNRA in 2017 downgraded the general risk of terrorist financing through the non-profit sector from 'medium-high' to 'low' thanks to increasingly stringent and internationally coordinated counter-measures.[105] The risks to the sector remained 'similar' and 'low' according to the subsequent 2020 report.[106] The Charity Commission's admittedly limited statistics also suggest that terrorist abuse is infrequent compared to more mundane incidents of fraud, safeguarding and mismanagement, which make up the bulk of its compliance cases.[107]

This all comes with the caveat that 'certain parts of the sector [face] significantly higher risks'.[108] Muslim-led humanitarian charities, especially small and inexperienced ones operating in war-torn parts of the Middle East,

[100] Financial Action Taskforce (FATF), 'Risk of Terrorist Abuse in Non-profit Organisations' (FATF, 2014), p. 2.

[101] Clive Walker, 'Terrorist Financing and the Policing of Charities: Who Pays the Price?' in Colin King and Clive Walker (eds.), *Dirty Assets: Emerging Issues in the Regulation of Criminal and Terrorist Assets* (Farnham: Ashgate, 2014), ch. 11, pp. 229–60 at p. 230; Nitsana Darshan-Leitner and Samuel M. Katz, *Harpoon: Inside the Covert War against Terrorism's Money Masters* (London: Hachette Books, 2017).

[102] FATF, 'Risk of Terrorist Abuse in Non-profit Organisations', p. 2.

[103] Walker, 'Terrorist Financing and the Policing of Charities', pp. 255–6.

[104] HM Treasury and Home Office, 'National Risk Assessment of Money Laundering and Terrorist Financing 2015' (HMG, October 2015), p. 94.

[105] HM Treasury and Home Office, 'National Risk Assessment of Money Laundering and Terrorist Financing 2017' (HMG, October 2017), p. 73.

[106] HM Treasury and Home Office, 'National Risk Assessment of Money Laundering and Terrorist Financing 2020' (HMG, October 2020), pp. 124–7.

[107] Andrew O'Brien, 'Review: Wolves in Sheep's Clothing Report – Extremism in Charities' (CFG, 1 March 2018).

[108] HM Treasury and Home Office, 'National Risk Assessment of Money Laundering and Terrorist Financing 2017', p. 73; HM Treasury and Home Office, 'National Risk Assessment of Money Laundering and Terrorist Financing 2020', p. 124.

are among the most vulnerable to exploitation, although this is likely to lessen over time.[109] Intentional wrongdoing, poor practice and inadvertent mistakes undermine public confidence in the entire sector and lend credence to the view that Muslim charities, taken collectively, constitute a major threat.[110] This perception has been exacerbated by libel tourism in the English courts.[111] The partially successful efforts of the now-deceased Saudi Arabian billionaire Khalid bin Mahfouz to suppress at least four major studies linking his financial and charitable activities to terrorism are the most notorious example of this.[112] The correct response to this is simply targeted and proportionate enforcement; regulatory vigilance and adaptability in the face of a continually evolving threat; and, ideally, an overhaul of English defamation law to make it more hospitable to investigative reporting.[113]

5.3.3 Purposive Questions

5.3.3.1 Foreign State Funding

A more difficult unanswered question is the advisability of permitting domestic charities to receive overseas funding from foreign states. There are two main areas of concern. First, many UK universities pursue or accept (directly or indirectly) funding from foreign governments including China, Russia, Iran and the Arab Gulf States.[114] This is typically applied to 'strategically important' courses and institutes dedicated to Islamic or Chinese studies.[115] Sixteen UK universities rely for a fifth of their total fee income on Chinese students, for

[109] HM Treasury and Home Office, 'National Risk Assessment of Money Laundering and Terrorist Financing 2017', pp. 73–4; Imtiaz, 'An Examination of the Inquiries Conducted on British Muslim Charities by the Charity Commission', pp. 11–13.

[110] See generally Jonathan Benthall and Jerome Bellion-Jourdan, *The Charitable Crescent: Politics of Aid in the Muslim World* (London: I.B. Tauris, 2003); Jonathan Benthall, 'The Overreaction against Islamic Charities' (2007) 20 *ISIM Review* 6–7; Jonathan Benthall, *Islamic Charities and Islamic Humanism in Troubled Times* (Manchester: Manchester University Press, 2016).

[111] Nick Cohen, *You Can't Read This Book: Censorship in an Age of Freedom* (2nd ed., London: HarperCollins, 2013).

[112] See Jean-Charles Brisard, *Terrorism Financing: Roots and Trends of Saudi Terrorism Financing. Report Prepared for the President of the Security Council United Nations* (New York: JCB Consulting, 2002); Jean-Charles Brisard and Guillaume Dasquié, *The Forbidden Truth: US–Taliban Secret Oil Diplomacy and the Failed Hunt for Bin Laden* (New York: Nation Books, 2002); J. Millard Burr and Robert O. Collins, *Alms for Jihad: Charity and Terrorism in the Islamic World* (Cambridge: Cambridge University Press, 2006); Rachel Ehrenfeld, *Funding Evil: How Terrorism Is Financed and How to Stop It* (3rd ed., New York: MultiEducator, 2011); Craig Unger, *House of Bush, House of Saud: The Secret Relationship between the World's Two Most Powerful Dynasties* (3rd ed., New York: Gibson Square Press, 2019).

[113] On the need for proportionality in the regulatory struggle against terrorist financing and money laundering, see Warren Barr, 'Shell Charities and Terrorist Financing: A Sledgehammer to Crack a Shell?' (2018) 32 *Trusts Law International* 202.

[114] Lee Jones and Philip Cunliffe, 'Saving Britain's Universities: Academic Freedom, Democracy and Renewal' (CIEO, 2020), pp. 21–2.

[115] Robin Simcox, 'A Degree of Influence: The Funding of Strategically Important Subjects in UK Universities' (Centre for Social Cohesion, March 2009).

example.[116] This money creates leverage and has tangible effects upon its hosts. It helps to stifle discussion of inconvenient topics, realigns university governance with the wishes of donors, subordinates research to political agendas, and operates under conditions of minimal financial transparency.[117] In some cases, Chinese sponsorship of British scientific research has helped China to gain access to sensitive new military technologies.[118] A specific study of Gulf-funded institutes found that they were less likely to raise issues of democracy, human rights and gender inequality than were comparable research centres which did not rely upon such funding.[119]

The second major concern is that many UK mosques are funded at least in part by foreign governments. For example, the new Cambridge 'eco-mosque' was financed by a consortium of Turkish government agencies and opened by President Recep Erdogan himself.[120] Saudi Arabian groups control 6 per cent of UK mosques, but fund hundreds more across Britain and Europe as part of 'a long-term strategy of influence'.[121] The Islamic Centre of England was founded by a proxy of the Supreme Leader of Iran in the 1990s and is required by its governing document to have at all times one trustee who is a representative of the Iranian government.[122] Regardless of any concerns over extremism if and when they arise, the more fundamental question is this: should autocratic foreign states be permitted to establish and exert financial influence over crucial domestic institutions? Should there be any doubt as to the import of this, the journalist Nick Cohen has documented how China bought the silence of Muslim-majority states over its atrocities against Uighur Muslims. These nations – Pakistan, Egypt and Iran among them – who in the past posed as defenders of Islam against novels and cartoons, stay mute and have even blocked a UN investigation because of their dependency upon the 'unadorned and unstoppable' financial influence of the Chinese Communist Party.[123] Though the UK has yet to formulate a coherent

[116] Will Tanner, 'Trading Places: How Universities Have Become Too Reliant on Overseas Students and How to Fix It' (*Onward*, July 2020), pp. 2–4. See also Salvatore Babones, 'It's Time for Western Universities to Cut Their Ties to China' (*Foreign Policy*, 19 August 2020).

[117] Simcox, 'A Degree of Influence', pp. 11–13. Foreign Affairs Select Committee, 'A Cautious Embrace: Defending Democracy in an Age of Autocracies – Second Report of Session 2019' (House of Commons, HC 109, 4 November 2019), pp. 5–10.

[118] Radomir Tylecote and Robert Clark, 'Inadvertently Arming China: The Chinese Military Complex and Its Potential Exploitation of Scientific Research at UK Universities' (*Civitas*, February 2021).

[119] Jonas Bergan Draege and Martin Lestra, 'Gulf-Funding of British Universities and the Focus on Human Development' (2015) 7(1) *Middle East Law and Governance* 25–49.

[120] BBC News, 'Turkey's President Erdogan Opens Cambridge "Eco-mosque"' (*BBC News*, 5 December 2019).

[121] Jessica Elgot, '"Sensitive" UK Terror Funding Inquiry May Never Be Published' (*The Guardian*, 31 May 2017); Innes Bowen, 'Who Runs Our Mosques?' (*The Spectator*, 14 June 2014).

[122] Robert Mendick, 'UK-Registered Islamic Charity Has Described Qassim Soleimani as a "Great Martyr"' (*The Telegraph*, 6 January 2020); David Brown, 'Inquiry into Charity Islamic Centre of England That Called Iran's Soleimani a Martyr' (*The Times*, 7 January 2020).

[123] Nick Cohen, 'Why Do Muslim States Stay Silent over China's Abuse of the Uighurs?' (*The Guardian*, 4 July 2020).

response of its own, other Western countries have already begun to devote serious attention to this very question. Austria has introduced prohibitions against foreign investment in mosques, likely to counter Turkish influence;[124] the Dutch parliament has established a commission to investigate the influx of foreign money into mosques and schools;[125] and the US Department of Education has opened investigations into Harvard and Yale, which it suspects have received undisclosed funds from Saudi Arabia and China.[126] Again, this is not an 'Islam issue' as such, but the way in which it is addressed will have significant consequences for British Muslims as much as anyone else.

5.3.3.2 Defining Extremism

Non-violent extremism is perhaps the most fraught matter of all. There are two legal definitions in circulation, although it is not entirely clear how they relate to one another. The first is to be found in the Prevent Strategy, which defines extremism in general as 'vocal or active opposition to fundamental British values, including democracy, the rule of law, individual liberty and mutual respect and tolerance of different faiths and beliefs . . . [and] calls for the death of members of our armed forces'.[127] All charities are obliged to prevent abuse for extremist purposes and some, including educational charities, are classified as 'specified authorities' with an additional duty 'to have due regard to the need to prevent people from being drawn into terrorism'.[128] The second definition, which does not refer at all to the first, is specifically concerned with Islamic extremism. It is to be found in the High Court judgment of *Shakeel Begg* v. *BBC* [2016] EWHC 2688 (QB), which contains a ten-point definition referring to, among other things, a Manichean worldview, violent jihad, encouraging Muslims to support terrorism, law-breaking interpretations of sharia, and 'extreme Salafist Islamism'.[129] In that case the claimant, the chief imam and a trustee of the Lewisham Islamic Centre, sued the BBC for libel having been called 'an extremist preacher who promotes violent jihad'.[130] He lost and was described by the learned judge as a 'Jekyll and Hyde character' who 'on occasions when it . . . suited him, and he was speaking to predominantly Muslim audiences and/or audiences who might be receptive to his message . . . shed the cloak of respectability and revealed the horns of extremism'.[131] Begg's fellow trustees have rejected this depiction and at

[124] Julian Borger, 'Austria Defends New Law on Foreign Funding of Mosques' (*The Guardian*, 8 March 2015); Reuters, 'Austria to Shut Down Mosques, Expel Foreign-Funded Imams' (*Reuters News*, 8 June 2018).
[125] Dutch News, 'MPs Begin Hearings into Foreign Funding of Dutch Mosques' (*DutchNews.nl*, 10 February 2020).
[126] BBC News, 'US Investigates Harvard and Yale over Foreign Funding' (*BBC News*, 13 February 2020).
[127] HMG, 'Prevent Strategy' (HMG, Cm 8092, June 2011), p. 107.
[128] Charity Commission, 'Guidance: Chapter 5 – Protecting Charities from Abuse for Extremist Purposes' (Charity Commission, 19 November 2018) and Counter-Terrorism and Security Act 2015, s. 26.
[129] Paras. 118–28. [130] *Begg* v. *BBC* [2016] EWHC 2688 (QB) at para. 19. [131] Para. 352.

the time of writing he remains a trustee of the charity.[132] In March 2017, another charity, Citizens UK, referred itself to the Charity Commission for promoting Begg after he was ruled to be an extremist.[133]

As regards charity law, it seems likely that the *Begg* test may be used to clarify whether or not someone is an extremist in future cases involving, for example, Muslim or Muslim-led charities. Regardless, the Prevent definition illustrates the persistent stumbling block of imprecise abstract nouns.[134] It is generally acknowledged that this 'broad definition of extremism has led to confusion and a lack of focus', although it may soon be replaced by the similarly vague notion of 'hateful extremism'.[135] It even seems to have been ineffectual on its own terms in the charity sector.[136] The *Begg* definition raises the constitutional difficulties inherent in any well-meaning state foray into religious affairs. Mr Justice Haddon-Cave strayed into dangerous territory by making statements such as 'It is common ground that Islam is a religion of peace', 'Islam forbids anything extreme' and 'Islam forbids terrorism'.[137] Factual (in)accuracy aside, this is a political definition of religion.[138] The learned judge was trying to define Islam itself, despite it not being an ascertainable entity. This impacts the important constitutional principle that it is not for secular authorities to determine whether someone is good or bad, fringe or mainstream, as measured against the standards of their faith and sect.[139] To do otherwise violates the state's commitment to impartiality and non-intervention in theological controversy. This is a well-recognised principle recently reiterated by Lord Toulson, who stressed that defining religion with reference to 'fine

[132] Tom Wilson, 'Extremism in the Community: The Case of Shakeel Begg' (Henry Jackson Society, March 2017), p. 1.

[133] Liam Kay, 'Citizens UK Reports Itself to Regulator after Criticism of Link to Controversial Imam' (*Third Sector*, 21 March 2017).

[134] See Helen and David Fenwick, 'Prevent, Free Speech, "Extremism" and Counter-Terrorism Interventions: Exploring Narratives about Chilling Expression in Schools' (2020) *Public Law* 661–79, p. 676; Steven Greer and Lindsey Bell, 'Counter-Terrorist Law in British Universities: A Review of the "Prevent" Debate' (2018) *Public Law* 84–105.

[135] Hannah Stuart, 'Counter-Terrorism and Extremism in Great Britain since 7/7' (London: Counter Extremism Group, July 2020), p. 1; Commission for Countering Extremism (CCE), 'Operating with Impunity – Hateful Extremism: The Need for a Legal Framework' (CCE, February 2021), p. 8.

[136] See generally Webb, 'Wolves in Sheep's Clothing'; Usama Hasan, David Toube and Muna Khan, 'Mainstreaming Islamism: Islamist Institutions and Civil Society Organisations' (Quilliam Foundation submission to the Commission for Countering Extremism, September 2019).

[137] Paras. 98, 129, 9.

[138] See Efraim Karsh, *Islamic Imperialism: A History* (2nd ed., London: Yale University Press, 2013). See also the somewhat contradictory acknowledgement at para. 123 that 'advocating armed fighting in defence of Islam' has long been interpreted as a '*collective* religious obligation'.

[139] On this theme, see Peter W. Edge, 'Hard Law and Soft Power: Counter-Terrorism, the Power of Sacred Places, and the Establishment of Anglican Islam' (2010) 12(2) *Rutgers Journal of Law and Religion* 358–82.

theological or liturgical niceties' was 'more fitting for theologians than for the Registrar General or the courts'.[140] In short, these definitions are generating huge amounts of controversy while making it difficult to determine who or what the law should be targeting, why and how.

5.4 Interpreting the Abuse of Charitable Religion

5.4.1 Via Liberal Individualism

Charity is perhaps the hardest sector for the law and the regulator to get right. At least some theory is required to address the underlying moral questions, – What are charities for? What is their place in society? Why should they enjoy tax exemptions, public goodwill and other benefits?[141] – solve the technical ones, – How should fundraising be regulated? What counts as misconduct? Are the Commission's powers fit for purpose? – and make the answers cohere into a functioning system of rules. The principles of liberal individualism offer one interpretive framework with which to do this. On this view, the charity sector produces diverse goods beneficial to the public on a voluntary (distinguishing it from state welfare) and altruistic (distinguishing it from private enterprise) basis. It therefore requires some degree of independence from state control while remaining accountable to stakeholders and the public.[142] Charity law is 'best understood as a set of power-conferring rules' enabling individuals to organise and act in pursuit of goods which 'make a contribution to the conditions for autonomy'. By recognising a plurality of purposes, charity law increases the number of options from which people can choose as they live out their personal visions of the good life.[143] Religious purposes are one such option, even though members of religious groups may not always exercise their legal freedoms to the same extent as non-believers.[144] Toleration matters because a society that allows for a plurality of faiths will ensure that its public culture and individual autonomy 'are substantially enhanced in circumstances where a variety of religious beliefs and practices coexist peacefully'. However, whenever 'religious beliefs or practices' threaten this by enforcing seclusion, attacking other religions or discriminating in ways that affect the conditions for autonomy and equality for all, the state must refuse to promote them through charity law with its attendant benefits.[145] In short, charities are organisations with instrumental worth as semi-autonomous supplements to

[140] *R (on the application of Hodkin and another) (Appellants)* v. *Registrar General of Births, Deaths and Marriages (Respondent)* [2014] AC 610 at para. 63.

[141] See Glister and Lee, Hanbury and Martin: Modern Equity, pp. 362–7.

[142] See Matthew Harding, 'Independence and Accountability in the Charity Sector' in Picton and Sigafoos (eds.), *Debates in Charity Law*, pp. 13–36.

[143] Matthew Harding, 'What Is the Point of Charity Law?' (University of Queensland, 25 May 2011) 1–37, pp. 9–10, 28.

[144] Matthew Harding, *Charity Law and the Liberal State* (Cambridge: Cambridge University Press, 2014), p. 174.

[145] Harding, 'What Is the Point of Charity Law?', p. 34.

the state's basic purpose, which is to guarantee the conditions of individual autonomy including some measure of distributive justice.[146] As Dworkin thought, however, they are not essential for a just and equal society because their contributions are 'limited and arbitrary in the way charity inevitably is'.[147] As group entities, they are each an assembly of individual wills acting in concert in pursuit of shared purpose within a legal form prescribed and recognised by the state.

It is straightforward enough on this view – to protect life, liberty and the integrity of the liberal state – to justify reforms that ensure that fundraising is properly regulated, that the Commission is adequately financed and empowered, and that opportunities for terrorist financing are minimised. It is much less clear what to do with foreign state funding. On one hand, this money may contribute to the recognised charitable purposes and social diversity; on the other, it leaves institutions such as universities and mosques at the mercy of foreign powers who may or may not be working to undermine the national interest. This liberal dilemma makes it very difficult to formulate a coherent policy and the law's current state is likely a product of it. Yet by far the greatest limitation of this approach can be seen in the government's legal and policy response to extremism. For example, scrutiny of actual or alleged extremism tends to address the utterances or behaviour of individual trustees.[148] Similarly, the Casey Review (2016) looked at these issues in aggregate, raising the problem of 'regressive attitudes in some minority religious groups' and 'extremist views [which] will often be seen as uncompromising or intolerant'.[149] These concerns, framed in this way, led to the Charities (Protection and Social Investment) Act 2016, which gave the Commission a range of new powers to remove and disqualify trustees.[150] This includes disqualification for 'continuing conduct by the person, whether or not in relation to a charity, [that] is damaging or likely to be damaging to public trust and confidence in charities generally or in the charities or classes of charity' in question.[151]

The Charity Tribunal decision in *Dr Zakir Abdul-Karim Naik* v. *The Charity Commission for England and Wales* (CA/2019/0014) tested the adequacy of the Commission's new powers. The appellant, an Islamic preacher excluded from the UK over terrorism supportation concerns, unsuccessfully challenged

146 Harding, *Charity Law and the Liberal State*, pp. 113–16. For a robust defence of the general applicability of this approach, see Jane Calderwood Norton, *Freedom of Religious Organizations* (Oxford: Oxford University Press, 2016) and '*Freedom of Religious Organizations*: A Reply' (2017) 42(1) *Australian Journal of Legal Philosophy* 296–308.

147 Ronald Dworkin, *Sovereign Virtue: The Theory and Practice of Equality* (Cambridge, MA: Harvard University Press, 2002), p. 236.

148 See HMG, 'Counter-Extremism Strategy' (HMG, Cm 9148, October 2015), pp. 27–8. For examples, see Webb, 'Wolves in Sheep's Clothing' and NSS, 'For the Public Benefit? The Case for Removing "the Advancement of Religion" as a Charitable Purpose'.

149 Dame Louise Casey, 'The Casey Review: A Review into Opportunity and Integration' (HMG, December 2016), pp. 121–31, 143–5.

150 Ss. 4, 5, 9, 10. 151 S. 10(7)(F).

a decision to disqualify him as a charity trustee generally, which would include being a trustee of Islamic Research Foundation International (IRFI), which is itself the subject of an ongoing statutory inquiry.[152] However, the Tribunal set the tariff at seven and a half years as opposed to the fifteen years proposed by the Commission: it acknowledged that the conduct was serious, but accepted that there were mitigating factors relevant to public trust and confidence in charities in that Naik had acted in good faith and cooperated with the Commission. This in itself raises further questions about the willingness of the Tribunal to impose the strictest penalties in the most severe cases involving matters relevant to the protection of the general public as well as public trust and confidence in charities. Thus, while the 2016 Act does enable the Commission to direct the winding up of a charity if it is a body corporate under certain conditions, namely if it is expedient in the public interest and there has been maladministration, for the most part, and in all other cases, it is the trustees who will be so directed.[153] In any event, the relevant provision has been used only three times up to March 2020.[154] The Commission itself declares that, as regards extremism, its focus is on 'the conduct of the trustees' and 'activities of concern' rather than the charity in its own right; as such, typical remedial action tends to involve the issuing of guidance to trustees or, in severe cases, the appointment of an interim manager to set the charity's affairs in order.[155] In sum, the intellectual resources available to liberal individualism preclude an adequate response to purposive abuses of charity, which require something more sophisticated than policing individual wrongdoing and attacking abstract nouns like 'extremism'.

5.4.2 Via Multiculturalism

While, predictably, there is no specialised multicultural literature on charity law, it is possible to suppose how it might look at its most cogent. Muslim charities, for example, would be understood as appendages of Islamic culture or institutional expressions of the larger rights-bearing unit of 'British Muslims'. Their most important public contribution – beyond the practical benefits accruing from their standard charitable purposes – is to provide an organisational vehicle for the diversification of society. Law and policy must acknowledge all this by supporting Muslim charities and their members as they strive, cooperate and

[152] BBC News, 'Indian Preacher Zakir Naik Is Banned from UK' (*BBC News*, 18 June 2010); John Plummer, 'Regulator Criticised for Not Opening Inquiry into Charity Chaired by Man Barred from UK' (*Third Sector*, 16 December 2019); Charity Commission, 'Charity Watchdog Opens Inquiry into Islamic Research Foundation International' (Charity Commission, 15 May 2020).

[153] Ss. 7–84B(2)(d).

[154] HMG, 'Charities (Protection and Social Investment) Act 2016 Post-Implementation Review' (HMG, CP 225, March 2020), p. 17.

[155] Webb, 'Wolves in Sheep's Clothing', pp. 142–3; Charity Commission, 'Guidance: Chapter 5', para. 15.

compete for resources, legitimacy and public recognition. This might entail the following three steps. First, the presumption of public benefit, abolished by the Charities Act 2006, could be fully restored so that religious charities are automatically presumed to be beneficial to the public.[156] The burden of proof on religious charities would, at least in theory, be lessened and they would enjoy greater leeway both to establish themselves and to operate according to their own vision of the good. This would build on existing achievements in accommodating difference and promoting marginalised communities.[157]

Second, the state should neither pass judgement on the beliefs and attitudes of Muslim charities or their leaders nor favour more cooperative liberal ones over those reputed to have conservative tendencies. Official backing for the Quilliam Foundation, 'the world's first counter-extremism organisation', and the selection of Sara Khan, a 'born human rights activist', to lead the Commission for Countering Extremism might be thought bad practice in this regard.[158] Far better to have a 'grassroots-led response', such as the MCB's proposed counter-radicalisation programme, once touted as a rival to the government's Prevent Strategy.[159] Schemes such as this are positive expressions of Muslim civic virtue. They allow faith communities to define for themselves what counts as dangerous extremism and mobilise their own resources without facing external pressure to liberalise. If the government is to engage with any particular charity, it should not concentrate on 'the personal connections and sectarian affiliations of specific Muslim organisations and individuals' because this has led to 'a large number of Muslim civil society organisations being treated as "toxic"'.[160] This only harms the diversity and the vibrancy of the charitable sector as well as the integrity of the Muslim community itself. One scholar even considers attempts to regulate the charitable status of mosques as running counter to 'the diverse, complex and affective identities of Muslims in Britain' and as engendering 'racialization and orientalism in conceptualizations of non-Christianness'.[161] Likewise,

[156] S. 3(2); Charities Act 2011, s. 4(2). For an argument in favour of doing this anyway, see Debora Morris, 'Public Benefit: The Long and Winding Road to Reforming the Public Benefit Test for Charity: A Worthwhile Trip or "Is Your Journey Really Necessary?"' in Myles McGregor-Lowndes and Kerry O'Halloran (eds.), *Modernising Charity Law: Recent Developments and Future Directions* (Cheltenham: Edward Elgar, 2010), ch. 4, pp. 103–27.

[157] For a general discussion of multiculturalism in the charity sector, see Kerry O'Halloran, *Religion, Charity and Human Rights*, pp. 30–41.

[158] BBC News, 'New Counter-Extremism Tsar Sara Khan Faces Calls to Quit' (*BBC News*, 25 January 2018); Ben Quinn, 'Tommy Robinson Link with Quilliam Foundation Raises Questions' (*The Guardian*, 12 October 2013).

[159] Vikram Dodd, 'Muslim Council of Britain to Set Up Alternative Counter-Terror Scheme' (*The Guardian*, 19 October 2016).

[160] Stephen H. Jones, Therese O'Toole, Daniel Nilsson DeHanas, Tariq Modood and Nasar Meer, 'A "System of Self-Appointed Leaders"? Examining Modes of Muslim Representation in Governance in Britain' (2015) 17(2) *British Journal of Politics and International Relations* 207–23, p. 220.

[161] Suhraiya Jivraj, *The Religion of Law: Race, Citizenship and Children's Belonging* (London: Palgrave Macmillan, 2013), p. 151.

conditional foreign state funding of domestic charities should remain permissible so long as they help the disadvantaged Muslim community and new diasporas entrench themselves and 'get on' in British society. That said, there are no logical objections to having a well-regulated fundraising system, a well-resourced regulator and robust terrorist financing safeguards. Fraud and terrorism endanger Muslims as much as anyone else and threaten the very existence of a multicultural nation. Any wrongdoing by trustees, donors or any member of a charity should continue to be regarded as the work of individuals and it is imperative that it not be used to implicate the Muslim community more generally.

Third, the Charity Commission should evolve out of its current investigatory/enforcement mould into an arm's-length facilitator/educator. As it is, the Commission has faced accusations of excessive interventionism, politicisation and Islamophobia.[162] For example, the manager of one Muslim charity has claimed that 'the scrutiny on Islam risks widening the schism between Muslims and other faiths, leading to further segregation of communities. It makes people feel that there is no place for Muslims in modern Britain and that we are being relegated to second-class citizens.'[163] This sentiment was echoed by Baroness Warsi, who has claimed that 'extremist abuse of the charity sector has [been] and remains negligible', while a murky and now-defunct think tank claimed that 'Muslim charities are being targeted by the Commission' and collectively constitute a 'suspect sector'.[164] If such allegations are to be avoided in future then, short of a deregulation programme leading to self-regulation, the Commission might adopt a co-regulatory approach working with other bodies with relevant expertise. This is already taking root in some areas such as fundraising and might be expanded to religious charities so that they have greater involvement in the oversight process. The result may improve perceptions of the Commission among minority communities and enable it to operate more efficiently on a tight budget.[165]

Summing up, if the foregoing multicultural account of religious charities is true to the founding texts, charities are to be regarded as having intrinsic worth because they, their leaders, their members and their donors are inseparable components and carriers of a living culture with agency and its own ends. Whether or not these align with the state's own purposes or the liberal ethos of

162 See generally Debra Morris, 'The Charity Commission for England and Wales: A Fine Example or Another Fine Mess?' (2016) 91 *Chicago-Kent Law Review* 965.

163 Quoted in Alex Delmar-Morgan, 'Islamic Charities in UK Fear They Are Being Unfairly Targeted over Extremism' (*The Guardian*, 22 July 2015).

164 Baroness Sayeeda Warsi, 'Connections Not Coexistence – Building Bridges between Communities' (NCVO 20th Annual Hinton Lecture, 21 November 2017); Adam Belaon, 'Muslim Charities: A Suspect Sector' (London: Claystone, November 2014), p. 23. For background on the latter, see SW1 Forum, 'Claystone Think Tank' (Substack, 24 November 2020) https://sw1forum.substack.com/p/claystone-think-tank.

165 See Alison Dunn, 'Eddies and Tides: Statutory Regulation, Co-regulation, and Self-Regulation in Charity Law in Britain' in Breen et al. (eds.), *Regulatory Waves*, ch. 2, pp. 21–44 at pp. 27–31.

the public square is beside the point – they should not be interfered with purely for running counter to these. As with any other tradition, Islamic culture is inherently valuable and its integrity – along with that of its agents, individual or collective – must be respected accordingly. This approach mounts some valuable challenges to its liberal individualistic rival. Most notably, albeit for unconvincing reasons, it refocuses attention on charities as group entities in their own right requiring robust safeguards against state interference. It also resists the liberal tendency to draw Manichean distinctions between good and bad Muslims before attempting to save the former from the latter as part of a campaign against abstract nouns.[166] Yet it leaves many important questions unanswered.

It is hard to see, for instance, how the law and policy-makers can avoid drawing moral distinctions between Muslim groups based on their connections, behaviour and objectives. For example, what is to be done with a non-violent group striving to benefit from charitable status to overthrow the nation and establish a global caliphate? Multiculturalism seems to have no convincing answers beyond compromise and recognition for their own sake, yet charity law is inescapably judgemental as the *Goodman Committee on Charity Law and Voluntary Organisations* noted back in 1976: 'however liberal or tolerant a society may be[,] it has the duty to determine what is and what is not beneficial to it; accordingly[,] between good and evil it cannot be neutral. It must exclude from charitable status what it regards as evil just as it can and does outlaw what it regards as detrimental to its moral welfare.'[167] It follows that an opt-in regulatory scheme emphasising self-reliance and self-regulation 'could lead to a loss of public confidence in charities by compromising the credibility and quality of regulation'.[168] Co-regulation through voluntary bodies such as the Fundraising Regulator incurs a variety of risks including regulatory capture by the largest, loudest charities; poor oversight of small, uncooperative charities; irregular fundraising practices; costly bureaucratic duplication; the rise of a parasitic service market to advise on proliferating requirements; a reactive rather than proactive approach to compliance; and general public and sector confusion over the need for and jurisdiction of each regulatory body. Many of these dangers will be amplified if membership remains small and sanctions weak – self-regulation and co-regulation sound nice, but often they amount to de facto deregulation.[169] In short, there are many good reasons to have one independent, proactive regulator with a comprehensive remit, a powerful arsenal of sanctions and universal authority

166 Commission on Religion and Belief in British Public Life, 'Living with Difference: Community, Diversity and the Common Good' (Woolf Institute, December 2015), p. 76.

167 Quoted in Gary Watt, 'Giving unto Caesar: Rationality, Reciprocity, and Legal Recognition of Religion' in Richard O'Dair and A. D. E. Lewis (eds.), *Law and Religion: Current Legal Issues*, Vol. 4 (Oxford: Oxford University Press, 2001), p. 57.

168 Alison Dunn, 'Regulatory Shifts: Developing Sector Participation in Regulation for Charities in England and Wales' (2014) 34(4) *Legal Studies* 660–81, p. 665.

169 Ibid., pp. 671–5.

over every charity. Further, the multiculturalists' primitive understanding of groups as mere extensions of 'Muslims' or 'Islamic culture' impedes clear-minded action against wrongdoing with a collective dimension. If a Muslim charity behaves unacceptably, for example, it is hard to see how that might be addressed without regulatory action being interpreted as a prejudicial attack on the 'Muslim community' as a whole. These limitations indicate that multiculturalism cannot supply the precise, systematic thought needed to find practical solutions to hard purposive questions. Fortunately, pluralism lights a better way forward.

5.5 A Pluralist Response to the Abuse of Charitable Religion

Throughout history, organised charity has been about applying wealth to accomplish good works. Regardless of legal form or religious affiliation, healthy charities are best understood as Gierkean fellowships – individual group units, with agency and aims of their own, arising naturally out of the human associational urge. As Adam Parachin has shown, 'charity is not a state phenomenon but rather a non-state phenomenon endorsed by the state through charity law. The state is present but it is not the central actor.'[170] Charities as such have intrinsic worth and require protection against external interference from the state or other actors. Yet, as with all organisms, charities are subject to entropy and may become corrupt, self-serving, subservient or dangerous. To guard against this, charity law must filter for improper purposes, structure the means of fundraising, establish the terms on which errors will be corrected, and define the powers of the regulator. If this is done well, charities will thrive in their own right as integrated components of the wider societal system to the benefit of individuals, civil society and the nation itself. This vision best explains the hybrid public–private character of charity law which balances individual initiative, organisational autonomy and the common good in conditions of diversity and disagreement.[171] It follows that British Muslim and Muslim-led charities each have intrinsic and instrumental worth as individual voluntary organisations, while their admirable and varied work at home and abroad is an indisputable national asset and legitimate source of pride.[172] It will not do to analyse them using the crude language of class – so far as the law is concerned, they are charitable organisations first and Muslim second. Doing them justice – in every sense of the word – means treating them on an individual basis whenever wrongdoing is suspected or

[170] 'A Charity Law Perspective on a Liberal Perspective on Charity Law' in Matthew Harding (ed.), *Research Handbook on Not-for-Profit Law* (Cheltenham: Edward Elgar, 2018), ch. 3 pp. 82–107 at p. 107.

[171] See generally Kathryn Chan, *The Public–Private Nature of Charity Law* (London: Bloomsbury, 2016).

[172] Baroness Barran, 'Applauding the Response of the Muslim Charity Sector during the Pandemic' (2021) 3 *The Forum: The Journal of the British Muslim Charity Sector* (Muslim Charities Forum) 6.

uncovered. Purposive abuses of charitable religion are the hardest of all to articulate and solve using conventional jurisprudence; they are much less so if one draws upon Gierkean insights and vocabulary.

From a pluralist perspective, it is intrinsically dangerous to permit foreign states to fund domestic charities. The Charity Commission has noted that decisions regarding the acceptance of funding sources are a matter for trustees and there is little it can do to intervene without a specific legal prohibition.[173] At the absolute minimum, therefore, direct and indirect foreign state funding for religious and educational charities should be made publicly known and then swiftly closed off altogether. This will expose the true scale of foreign interference in domestic affairs and promote home-grown religion with less susceptibility to foreign influence. It would be unlikely to cause too much disruption to everyday life as 'the vast majority of Britain's estimated 1,800 mosques were established and continue to operate thanks largely to the generous donations of the congregations they serve'.[174] Neither is it a partisan matter as Modood himself has spoken encouragingly of a national-oriented Islam and, as Jeremy Corbyn recently noted, it is high time that 'difficult conversations' are held with the Gulf States and others over their exportation of 'extremist ideology' and dirty money.[175] The point is to view charities as actors within a national context – to enjoy the benefits attendant on their status, they must benefit the nation and certainly not corrupt or endanger it. Foreign finance poses a threat to the health of true fellowships and, especially if the funding channels are opaque, risks replacing them with vassal institutions and self-serving privileged institutions. A charitable sector populated with such zombie entities will eventually lose all vitality and public confidence. What is more, charities and charitable works based around religious, ethno-national and kin-related causes do not promote inter-group contact or produce generalised trust across society, and are therefore 'less likely to build bridges across cultures'.[176] There is evidence to suggest that, despite their high levels of charitable giving, British South Asians tend to favour such causes over less insular ones.[177] In short, a reduction in easy foreign money is a small price to pay for the heart and soul of organised charity.

[173] CCE, 'Operating with Impunity – Hateful Extremism', p. 48.

[174] Hassan Joudi, 'Addressing Issues at Home: British Mosque Case Studies' (2020) 2 *The Forum: The Journal of the British Muslim Charity Sector* (Muslim Charities Forum) 10.

[175] Tariq Modood, *Multiculturalism: A Civic Idea* (2nd ed., Cambridge: Polity Press, 2013), pp. 78, 137–9; David Wearing, *AngloArabia: Why Gulf Wealth Matters to Britain* (Cambridge: Polity Press, 2018); Caroline Mortimer, 'Jeremy Corbyn Calls for "Difficult Conversations" with Saudi Arabia and Gulf States over Extremism Funding' (*The Independent*, 8 June 2017).

[176] Eric M. Uslaner, *The Moral Foundations of Trust* (Cambridge: Cambridge University Press, 2010), p. 134; Eric M. Uslaner, *Segregation and Mistrust: Diversity, Isolation, and Social Cohesion* (Cambridge: Cambridge University Press, 2012), p. 172.

[177] Uslaner, *Segregation and Mistrust*, pp. 189–91; Pnina Werbner, *The Migration Process: Capital, Gifts and Offerings among British Pakistanis* (New York: Berg, 2002), p. 305; Philip Wood, 'Marriage and Social Boundaries among British Pakistanis' (2018) 20(1) *Diaspora* 40–64, pp. 45, 49, 58.

Finally, the concept of extremism is superfluous to requirements as regards misconduct within or by charities. As noted earlier, officialdom has sought to define the nation in terms of 'British values' against 'extremism'. This is entirely unnecessary as well as being unnecessarily risky. It is unnecessary because the essence of the national tradition cannot be distilled into a trite set of liberal propositions. What makes it so distinct is precisely its ability to defy easy categorisation. It can be glimpsed in everything from manners to law to war, but there has never been a pressing need to try to pin it down.[178] The point is perhaps best put by Adrian Goldsworthy who, when asked about his personal philosophy, responded: 'I'm English, so obviously do not have a philosophy.'[179] This is precisely the problem with trying to define Englishness or Britishness in terms of a positive set of contingent values shorn of all the contradictions and complexity of history. These were not always British values, which might equally include 'queuing, drunkenness, nostalgia, loving pets, self-loathing, wit and eccentricity', and they are not necessarily virtues in every institution present in society.[180] Therein lies the danger. Disagreement with these values generally, or within a particular context, or interpreting them in an unusual way, risks incurring suspicion from public authorities. Conservative religious or social mores can easily be interpreted as an existential threat, and the application of the Prevent duty in universities has contributed to the growing climate of risk-aversion and censoriousness, not to mention the proliferation of pointless form-filling.[181] More generally, it has created confusion and an irresistible temptation for state authorities to issue political pronouncements upon theological affairs, as in *Begg*.[182] Further, the dearth of repercussions from that libel judgment in the charity sector is further proof that the regulatory system is unduly reliant upon a contentious label. Disputes over this only add an extra step to compliance proceedings which the Commission may not initiate in any event. All of this is the 'abstract noun problem' manifest, causing mundane mischief and legitimate advocacy for conservative positions to be mistaken for the real target: revolutionary activity.[183] Again, with reference to Gierkean theory it is possible to imagine a straightforward and depoliticised solution.

[178] See, for example, Kate Fox, *Watching the English: The Hidden Rules of English Behaviour* (2nd ed., London: Hodder & Stoughton, 2014) and R. V. Jones, *Most Secret War: British Scientific Intelligence 1939–1945* (London: Penguin, 2009).

[179] Undated interview with Orion Books.

[180] David Starkey quoted in Victoria Ward, 'Real British Values Are "Drunkenness and Self-Loathing", David Starkey Says' (*The Telegraph*, 29 January 2015).

[181] Tom Slater, 'Terrorism and Free Speech: An Unholy Alliance of State and Students' in Tom Slater (ed.), *Unsafe Space: The Crisis of Free Speech on Campus* (London: Palgrave Macmillan, 2016), ch. 9, pp. 106–17 at p. 109.

[182] Julian Hargreaves, 'What Does Extremism Mean? The British Public Aren't Sure' (*The Conversation*, 25 July 2019); Sean Coughlan, 'Is Extremism Really Getting Worse?' (*BBC News*, 9 May 2019).

[183] Julian Rivers, 'Counter-Extremism, Fundamental Values and the Betrayal of Liberal Democratic Constitutionalism' (2018) 2 *German Law Journal* 267–99.

Anything resembling the concept of extremism can be removed from regulations governing mundane misconduct altogether. In this aspect, the system could be remodelled along the lines of the professional standards of the Bar. Core Duty Five (CD5) of the Bar Standards Board (BSB) Code of Conduct requires that barristers 'must not behave in a way which is likely to diminish the trust and confidence which the public places in you or in the profession'.[184] This covers criminal conduct, seriously offensive or discreditable conduct, dishonesty, unlawful victimisation or harassment, and abusing one's professional position.[185] Breaching this duty may trigger a formal investigation and disciplinary proceedings resulting in a range of sanctions such as fines, suspensions or disbarment.[186] Charitable trustees are not regarded as professionals and therefore are not subject to a mandatory equivalent.[187] They owe a general duty of care to the charitable purposes of the charity (rather than to their charity as a distinct institution[188]) and must have regard to any relevant guidance published by the Commission.[189] As fiduciaries, they are required to, among other things, decide upon and act in the charity's best interests, manage risks and comply with its governing document and relevant laws.[190] This works well enough only if the trustees are honourable and possess a common-sense understanding of propriety. A heartening recent example can be seen in the mass resignation of the board of Islamic Relief Worldwide following an anti-Semitism scandal involving two successive trustees.[191] To their credit, the trustees issued a public apology and were replaced by an entirely new board as the charity initiated 'far-reaching governance reforms'.[192] Following the *Begg* judgment, however, the trustees of the Lewisham Islamic Centre denied outright that Shakeel Begg held the views attributed to him, rejected the characterisation of him as an extremist as 'fanciful and an impossible position for a personality like Imam Begg' and simply reaffirmed their 'unequivocal and unwavering

[184] BSB, *The BSB Handbook Version 4.6* (BSB, 31 December 2020), part 2(B): The Code of Conduct, The Core Duties, CD5.

[185] Ibid., gC25.

[186] BSB, 'How We Make Enforcement Decisions' (BSB, accessed 23 February 2021): www.barstandardsboard.org.uk/about-us/how-we-regulate/the-decisions-we-take/enforcement-decisions/how-we-make-enforcement-decisions.html.

[187] Sarah Atkinson, 'The New Charity Governance Code – Essential Reading for All Trustees' (Charity Commission, 13 July 2017).

[188] Recently confirmed in *Lehtimäki and others* v. *Cooper* [2020] UKSC 33 at para. 90.

[189] Trustees Act 2000, s. 1; Charities Act 2011, s. 17(5).

[190] For a general overview, see Peter Luxton, 'Conflicts of Interest in Charity Law' in Alison Dunn (ed.), *The Voluntary Sector, the State and the Law* (Oxford: Hart, 2000), ch. 15, pp. 226–40 and Charity Commission, 'Guidance: The Essential Trustee: What You Need to Know, What You Need to Do' (Charity Commission, 3 May 2018).

[191] Andrew Norfolk, 'Entire Board Resigns at Islamic Relief Worldwide' (*The Times*, 22 August 2020); Emma Graham-Harrison, 'Muslim Charity's Board Steps Down over Antisemitism Row' (*The Guardian*, 23 August 2020).

[192] Islamic Relief Worldwide, 'Islamic Relief Acts Swiftly and Creates New Board' (Islamic Relief Worldwide, 22 August 2020): www.islamic-relief.org/Islamic+Relief+acts+swiftly+and+creates+new+board.

continued support of our Head Imam'.[193] The Charity Commission seemingly took no notice. This variability suggests considerable interpretive leeway in the standards to which charitable trustees hold themselves.

Against this, importing BSB-style professional standards would achieve three things. First, it would clarify that trustees owe a duty to the public as well as to their organisation's charitable purposes. Second, it would provide a straightforward, less controversial and more objective standard to which trustees and charities could be held. This would enable the Commission to discipline them for behaving in a way that could reasonably be said to undermine public confidence in the sector, regardless of whether or not they can be described as extremist. The bar could be set slightly higher for charities themselves by requiring, for example, serious or repeated institutional misconduct before they are liable for serious sanctions such as being wound up. Third, it would highlight the mundane nature of much of the misconduct – regressive or offensive utterances, for example – and disassociate it entirely from state security concerns. Nuance as to findings of misconduct and any appropriate sanctions could be provided by paying due regard to the type of charity in question (e.g. religious or educational), the kind of activities it carries out (e.g. legitimate and heated controversy) and any common standards in the relevant field (e.g. what counts as anti-Semitism or good animal welfare practice). This would all make it simpler and more efficient to remove rogues without the need to prove extremism of any kind. It also befits both charities' and trustees' important status as trusted stewards of organised benevolence with the attendant benefits, prestige and public goodwill.

English law requires a much narrower and altogether more serious replacement for extremism to deal with more dangerous abuses with a political dimension. This can be done by reviving sedition and subversion.[194] Prior to its abolition, sedition was an offence committed by 'the speaking or writing of words that are likely to incite ordinary people to public disorder and insurrection' with the intention, through violence and disorder, of '(1) arousing hatred, contempt or disaffection against the sovereign, government, Parliament or administration of justice; (2) encouraging any change of the law by unlawful means; (3) raising discontent among Her Majesty's subjects or promoting ill-will and hostility between different classes of subjects'.[195] In essence, it was 'a crime against society, nearly allied to that of treason'.[196] Although never defined in

[193] Lewisham Islamic Centre Trustees, 'Imam Shakeel Begg vs the BBC' (Lewisham Islamic Centre, 29 October 2016): https://lewishamislamiccentre.com/2016/10/29/imam-shakeel-begg-vs-the-bbc/.

[194] Sedition was virtually abolished by the Coroners and Justice Act 2009, s. 73. MI5 states that, despite its importance throughout the twentieth century, 'the threat of subversion is now regarded as negligible and we do not currently carry out investigations in this area' (MI5, 'What We Do: Other Work', accessed 23 February 2021: www.mi5.gov.uk/what-we-do.).

[195] Elizabeth A. Martin, *Oxford Dictionary of Law* (7th ed., Oxford: Oxford University Press, 2008), pp. 498–9.

[196] *R* v. *Sullivan* (1868) 11 Cox CC 44, 45 per Fitzgerald J at p. 45.

English law, 'subversive activities are generally regarded as those which threaten the safety or well-being of the state, and which are intended to undermine or overthrow parliamentary democracy by political, industrial or violent means'.[197] This is analogous to the emerging phenomenon of 'lawfare' which is

> (1) the purposeful use of law taken toward a particular adversary with the goal of achieving a particular strategic, operational, or tactical objective; or
> (2) the purposeful use of law to bolster the legitimacy of one's own strategic, operational, or tactical objectives toward a particular adversary, or to weaken the legitimacy of a particular adversary's particular strategic, operational, or tactical objectives.[198]

Sedition can be proved directly; subversion may be inferred from a group's constitution, founding documents or mantras, then applied by extension to anyone or any other organisation affiliated to it. Having substituted sedition and subversion for extremism on these grounds, subject to the civil standard of proof, any charity established for seditious or subversive purposes, or any which maintains material links to any foreign state or group or person facilitating those ends, could then be justifiably dissolved. The rule against political propaganda masquerading as education should be extended to explicitly encompass religion so that, for example, an organisation working towards a pure ethno-national or religious state (such as a caliphate under which no distinction is drawn between religion and politics) is denied the benefits of public recognition. There would be three primary targets: (i) undeclared hostile state or terrorist activity; (ii) harmful activity by purported allies such as Saudi Arabia; and (iii) non-violent, non-terrorist revolutionary networks such as the Muslim Brotherhood, Hizb-ut-Tahrir and Jamaat-i-Islami.[199] Similar measures are being considered in France, which has already identified Muslim Brotherhood institutional capture as a serious threat and is preparing comprehensive countermeasures.[200]

In practice, this two-tier revamp would require two things. First, the Commission requires the impetus and powers to close down rogue charities as it remains too oriented towards rehabilitation and its current abilities are effectively limited to targeting trustees. However, as one senior (and seemingly

[197] Home Secretary Merlyn Rees quoted in R. J. Spjut, 'Defining Subversion' (1979) 6(2) *British Journal of Law and Society* 254–61, p. 254.

[198] Jill I. Goldenziel, 'Law as a Battlefield: The United States, China, and Global Escalation of Lawfare' (2020) 106(5) *Cornell Law Review* 1–76, p. 11. See also Orde F. Kittrie, *Lawfare: Law as a Weapon of War* (Oxford: Oxford University Press, 2016) and Charlie Dunlap, 'Guest Post: Andrés Munoz Mosquera's and Nikoleta Chalanouli's Essay: "China, an Active Practitioner of Legal Warfare"' (*Lawfire*, 2 February 2020).

[199] HMG, 'Muslim Brotherhood Review: Main Findings' (House of Commons, HC 679, 2015). However, see Mokhtar Awad, 'The Rise of the Violent Muslim Brotherhood' (Hudson Institute, 6 November 2017) and Foreign Affairs Select Committee, 'Written Evidence from Sujit Sen' (House of Commons, 25 May 2012).

[200] Damien McElroy, 'Ban on Qaradawi Urged by French Commission into Islamist Radicalisation' (*The National*, 21 July 2020).

Gierkean) practitioner notes, the public tends to 'think it's the charities that ought to be punished' rather than just the trustees in cases where the organisation has supported extremism.[201] Anglospheric precedent for this can be found in the more robust approach of Canada's Charities Directorate, which suspends or shuts down 'renegade' charities seen as 'harming the public and the system'.[202] Something similarly direct is required here so that the Commission can act efficiently to prevent the registration of, and deregister, fraudulent, seditious or subversive charities. The current provision for this is inadequate and ineffectual, resulting in extremely costly and protracted litigation even when it is used.[203]

Second, the Home Secretary would need powers to create and maintain a civil blacklist for the seditious and the subversive. Although it would not outlaw such groups or criminalise individuals, they would be precluded from charitable status or trusteeships, and would be unable to receive funds from domestic or overseas sources including other charities. Inclusion on the blacklist would also bar those on it from ever working in government and connect to the proposed BSB-style discipline regime so that involvement with blacklisted persons or organisations incurs appropriate sanctions. Given the serious consequences for those subject to these sanctions, the list and reasons for inclusion would have to made publicly available in the interests of accountability. This would ensure that charities are clear about which organisations – charitable or non-charitable – they can give money to.[204] The government would also have to publish clear 'criteria for engagement' with those on the blacklist so that the regime is 'informed by democratic principles and limited to identifiable behaviours as opposed to beliefs'.[205] Cumulatively, there will likely be a positive knock-on effect on banks by encouraging them to make their opaque and potentially counterproductive de-risking policies more transparent.[206] Driven by reputational, money laundering and terrorist financing concerns, major banks have started refusing services to, and closing the accounts of, individuals and organisations deemed 'high risk'.[207] Many Muslim charities have been affected.[208] Risk assessments are typically conducted with reference to the confidential World-Check database owned by Thomas Reuters and 'used by 49 out of the world's biggest 50

[201] Barrister Francesca Quint of Radcliffe Chambers quoted in Webb, 'Wolves in Sheep's Clothing', p. 142. See also Francesca Quint, 'Protection of Charities under the Charities (Protection and Social Investment) Act 2016: Too Little or Too Much?' (2016) 19(1) *Charity Law and Practice Review*.

[202] Webb, 'Wolves in Sheep's Clothing', p. 142. [203] Ibid., pp. 142–3.

[204] For an illustration of this problem, see *Cage Advocacy UK Ltd* v. *Charity Commission (with the Joseph Rowntree Charitable Trust [JRCT] participating as an interested party)* Case No: CO/2562/2015 and the resulting guidance: Charity Commission, 'Guidance for Charities with a Connection to a Non-charity' (Charity Commission, 29 March 2019).

[205] Stuart, 'Counter-Terrorism and Extremism in Great Britain Since 7/7', p. 2.

[206] See UKNRA 2015, p. 95; UKNRA 2017, p. 74; UKNRA 2020, pp. 127–8.

[207] Tracey Durner and Liat Shetret, 'Understanding De-risking and Its Effects on Financial Inclusion: An Exploratory Study' (Global Center on Cooperative Security, November 2015).

[208] Ibid., p. 9.

banks'.[209] Several claimants have won libel actions resulting from their inclusion under the 'terrorism' category on the database.[210] While scrupulous de-risking is an inevitable and necessary counter-measure against financial crime in the private sector, any comparable state measures such as the one proposed would need to tend more towards transparency and due process.[211]

There is considerable scope to improve upon the legal and regulatory infrastructure currently in place to deal with the abuse of charities. Once the problems identified in this chapter – from the mundane and the technical to the structural and the moral – have been adequately addressed, it is likely that religious charities will come to be seen as relatively uncontroversial. In some cases, namely Muslim charities operating humanitarian relief missions abroad, their public image will improve organically as they gain experience and reliable partners in the Middle East and beyond. Be that as it may, the main challenges require legislative action. As discussed, there are severe limits to what can be achieved if this is modelled on liberal individualism or multiculturalism. With the intellectual resources of pluralism, however, the issues can be clarified, the hard questions redefined and principled solutions laid out.

[209] Josh Halliday, 'London Mosque Chairman Demands Removal from Banks' Terrorism Blacklist' (*The Guardian*, 28 July 2015).

[210] Quilliam, 'Press Release – Maajid Nawaz Wins Legal Battle against Thomson Reuters World Check' (Quilliam, 18 October 2017); Harriet Sherwood, 'Finsbury Park Mosque Wins Apology and Damages from Thomson Reuters' (*The Guardian*, 1 February 2017).

[211] For a critical but jargon-heavy appraisal of this position, see Marieke de Goede and Gavin Sullivan, 'The Politics of Security Lists' (2016) 34(1) *Environment and Planning D: Society and Space* 67–88.

6

Schools

6.1 Introduction

This chapter is concerned with the abuse and regulation of schools. It begins with a brief history of religion and education law to highlight the governing principles and recurring themes. The centrepiece of the chapter is an examination of the Trojan Horse Affair which began in 2014 and reverberates down to the present. An extraordinary volume of disinformation encrusts this series of events, such that one BBC investigator recently warned that 'everyone who gets up close to the Trojan Horse becomes a conspiracy theorist'.[1] To avoid becoming one himself, the author relates a brisk outline of the salient facts as drawn from official reports and court cases; reliance upon newspaper articles and academic commentary is kept to a supplementary minimum. The related issues of illegal schools and unregulated madrassas are also raised in brief. The theoretical discussion illustrates that liberal individualism views education as a means to emancipate the individual into secularism, whereas multiculturalism treats it as a means to preserve and perpetuate minority cultures. It concludes that these perspectives fail to take schools seriously as institutions whose primary purpose is to provide as many British children as possible with a good education. The pluralist response points to what the Trojan Horse Affair and education law are really about: ensuring that every school, regardless of classification, is properly regulated, well governed and capable of rebuffing threats to its good functioning from any quarter.

6.2 A Brief History of Law, Religion and English Schools

The first English school was 'part and parcel of the first church' founded in 597 at Canterbury by Saint Augustine of Canterbury and endowed by King Ethelbert of Kent. Its purpose was to serve the Christian mission by educating native Anglo-Saxon recruits in Latin and liturgy. Before long, two distinct types of school emerged and spread across England: the Song School provided a specialised education for the 'sons of gentlefolk' to sing in cathedral choirs

[1] Jo Fidgen (presenter) and Emma Rippon (editor), 'Trojan Horse: The Anonymous Letter' (BBC Radio 4, The Corrections, Episode 1 of 3, 6 November 2020).

while the Grammar School provided a general education in the Classics and bureaucratic skills necessary for a career in government or the Church.[2] While these schools were successful on their own terms – preserving literacy, transmitting Christianity, fostering high culture in the north-east – they were branches of the Church or great households rather than free-standing institutions in their own right. It was not until the incorporation wave of the 'long twelfth century' that they took on a distinct and public character with sophisticated governing charters.[3] As the Middle Ages progressed, wealthy benefactors began founding public schools and the vocational nature of schooling shifted to cater for fee-paying laity and promising boys under scholarship.[4] The medieval curriculum was ostensibly modelled around the seven liberal arts (grammar, rhetoric, logic, arithmetic, geometry, music, astronomy), but in practice these were adapted for Church purposes and 'average attainments were limited to reading and writing'.[5] This gradually changed as the Renaissance introduced the Italian conception of soulcraft, the idea that nation and civilisation could be transformed by shaping the very character of citizens through humane education.[6] To this were added the demands of the Reformation during which schools 'got caught up in [Tudor] religious and financial policies'.[7] Schooling became 'a means of increasing religious fervour and enforcing [Protestant] orthodoxy' while harnessing the middle class to the bureaucratic state.[8] Grammar schools expanded along with vernacular teaching which 'contributed much towards developing the uniform speech of an educated class'.[9] These in turn precipitated a boom in legal education at the Inns of Court, although the proliferating students were notorious for their 'high degree of absenteeism' as well as 'fighting, theft and licentiousness'.[10] While the early modern era did see some experimentation with ideas such as universal free education, 'the state fell back on the traditional form of

2 Arthur Francis Leach, *The Schools of Medieval England* (2nd ed., London: Methuen and Co., 1915), pp. 1–7; Derek Gillard, Education in England: A History (unpublished and pages unnumbered, May 2018), ch. 1 ('Beginnings up to 1500'): www.educationengland.org.uk/history/chapter01.html.

3 Nicholas Orme, *Medieval Schools: Roman Britain to Renaissance England* (New Haven, CT: Yale University Press, 2006), p. 48; Charles Homer Haskins, *The Renaissance of the Twelfth Century* (Cambridge, MA: Harvard University Press, 1971).

4 Orme, ibid., p. 225; Raymond Williams, *The Long Revolution* (London: Chatto & Windus, 1961), pp. 129–30.

5 Leach, *The Schools of Medieval England*, p. 136; John Lawson and Harold Silver, *A Social History of Education in England* (London: Methuen and Co., 1973), p. 10.

6 See James Hankins, *Virtue Politics: Soulcraft and Statecraft in Renaissance Italy* (Cambridge, MA: Harvard University Press, 2019).

7 Orme, *Medieval Schools*, p. 334.

8 Nicholas Orme, *Education in the West of England, 1066–1548* (Exeter: Exeter University Press, 1976), p. 27; Gillard, *Education in England: A History*, ch. 2 ('Renaissance and Reformation 1500–1600').

9 Joan Simon, *Education and Society in Tudor England* (Cambridge: Cambridge University Press, 1966), pp. 364–5.

10 Kenneth Charlton, *Education in Renaissance England* (London: Routledge, 1965), pp. 177, 184.

participation in education, regulating practitioners and institutions according to political and religious tests'.[11] The general curriculum became more recognisable as it expanded, but still varied considerably among institutions.[12] All schools under the English common law fell under ecclesiastical oversight and education was regulated mainly through charitable trusts and contract law.[13] Provision for the poor remained meagre and, even after the Enlightenment, anyone looking to 'improve his condition' would be viewed as 'a disaffected person, who was not satisfied with the station in which God had placed him, but, forgetting the humility that belonged to his condition, was contriving how to raise himself out of his proper place'.[14] While there was no such thing as a coherent system of schools and education law in pre-modern England, many familiar tensions can be glimpsed down the centuries: religion versus state, innovation versus tradition, institutional autonomy versus uniformity, soulcraft versus vocation, breadth versus depth, quality versus quantity – it is all there in the early history.

In the nineteenth century, the population growth precipitated by the Industrial Revolution forced a national debate over the soul of education. Three rival factions emerged: the 'old humanists', the 'public educators' and the 'industrial trainers', with the last prevailing and shaping mass education 'in terms of training and disciplining the poor as workers and citizens'.[15] Starting with the Factory Act 1802 – which required employers to provide their young apprentices with four years of rudimentary education – that state became increasingly involved in the provision and regulation of education.[16] The Treasury issued its first grants in 1833 to assist efforts to establish schools for poor children and by 1840 an administrative committee and inspectorate had been established. The Education Department was established in 1856 and has continued to exist, with numerous name changes and reorganisations, up to the present day.[17] Towards the end of the nineteenth century, it had become apparent that the existing patchwork of charities and church schools could not meet the needs of a modern society, let alone any ideal of equality.[18] The

[11] Charles Webster, *The Great Instauration: Science, Medicine, and Reform, 1626–1660* (London: Duckworth, 1975), p. 114.

[12] Williams, *The Long Revolution*, p. 134; Gillard, *Education in England: A History*, chs. 4 ('Restoration 1660–1750') and 5 ('Towards Mass Education 1750–1860').

[13] Julian Rivers, *The Law of Organized Religions: Between Establishment and Secularism* (Oxford: Oxford University Press, 2010), pp. 234, 238; *Cox's Case* (1700) 1 P Wms 29, 24 ER 281.

[14] James Booth quoted in Lawson and Silver, *A Social History of Education in England*, pp. 227–8; Gillard, *Education in England: A History*, chs. 4 and 5.

[15] Williams, *The Long Revolution*, p. 142; Gillard, *Education in England: A History*, ch. 5.

[16] Gillard, ibid.

[17] Ann Ruff, *Education Law: Text, Cases and Materials* (Oxford: Oxford University Press, 2002), pp. 2–3.

[18] John Ford, Mary Hughes, Karen May, Marian Shaughnessy and Helen Gill, *Education Law and Practice* (4th ed., London: LexisNexis, 2016), p. 3; Stephen McKinney, 'Mapping the Debate on Faith Schooling in England' in Stephen McKinney (ed.), *Faith Schools in the Twenty-First Century* (Edinburgh: Dunedin, 2008), ch. 1, pp. 1–14 at p. 3.

Elementary Education Act 1870 did not make elementary education free or compulsory, but it did begin the process by establishing school boards in areas where provision was inadequate.[19] The trend towards universal education culminated in the 'landmark' Education Act 1944, which greatly expanded the provision of free compulsory schooling for all children aged five to fourteen and introduced the primary, secondary and further stages in education. Interestingly, the provision of mass and more equal education played a crucial role in the reduction of corruption by equipping greater numbers of citizens with the means and power to oppose it.[20] Many of the surviving voluntary and religious schools accepted state financial aid in exchange for their governors ceding some authority to local education authorities (LEAs). The Act was amended many times before its residual elements were incorporated into the Education Act 1996, but its basic ethos 'still forms the backdrop of much of the current legislative framework'.[21] Having established basic standards and welfare provision for disadvantaged pupils, successive governments have tried to improve the overall quality of schooling through further investment and regulation. The ever-changing national curriculum, for example, came into effect in 1989.[22] However, the School Standards and Framework Act (SSFA) 1998, with its attendant regulations, is 'the most significant piece of legislation' in this regard as, among other things, it limited class sizes and gave LEAs and the Secretary of State more powers to intervene in problem schools.[23] In short, the foundational statutes of education law are premised on basic equality and state oversight, designed to promote pupil welfare and attainment, and aspire to create a citizenry with the range of competencies necessary for success in the modern world.

The Education Act 1980 introduced a novel element of consumerism into the provision of education, with parents gaining increasing rights and with government becoming more accountable to them.[24] As part of this trend, the power of LEAs diminished as governors assumed greater responsibility for the running of schools and central government cut costs and promoted litigation as an error-correction mechanism.[25] New Labour's diversity agenda was very much an extension of this consumerist ethos writ large on to 'communities'. After 1997, the traditional understanding of the nature, culture and place of religious schools was displaced by the concept of 'faith schools'.[26] Whereas the old church schools were very much part of the establishment and supported

[19] Ford et al., *Education Law and Practice*, pp. 1–2.

[20] See generally Eric M. Uslaner, *The Historical Roots of Corruption: Mass Education, Economic Inequality, and State Capacity* (Cambridge: Cambridge University Press, 2017).

[21] Education became compulsory for all children aged five to ten from 1880. See Rivers, *Law of Organized Religions*, p. 237 and Ford et al., *Education Law and Practice*, p. 3.

[22] Education Reform Act 1988.

[23] Ford et al., *Education Law and Practice*, p. 6.

[24] Ruff, *Education Law*, p. 6.

[25] Gillard, Education in England: A History, ch. 15 ('Thatcher and the New Right 1979–1990') on the Education Act (No. 2) 1986; Ruff, *Education Law*, pp. 5–6.

[26] Rivers, *Law of Organized Religion*, p. 241.

the liberal consensus (not least because they depended on it for state funding), under Blair the mere fact of having more schools of non-Christian faiths to choose from was taken as a good in itself.[27] Although independent Muslim schools had existed for several decades, the *Parekh Report* noted that the first two state-maintained Muslim schools in Britain had opened in Birmingham and Brent by 2000; by 2011 there were twelve; and by 2019 there were thirty-one.[28] The negative press and widespread anxiety generated by these schools eventually prompted New Labour to 'pull in opposite directions' by stressing the need for social cohesion while advocating for their continued expansion.[29] The acme of consumerism in education, however, was the decade-long process of undercutting the local public interest in education through the creation of academy schools beginning with the Learning and Skills Act 2000 and culminating with the Academies Act 2010.[30] The majority of state-maintained schools now have 'academy status', meaning that they are free of LEA control and answerable to central government; they are structured as charitable trusts (which can encompass multiple academies) and may receive additional funding from non-state donors.[31] The basic point of academisation was to grant 'greater autonomy to individual schools' by freeing them, regardless of religious denomination, from 'the blob', a disparaging term for the vested interests in the educational sector including local authorities, unions and parasitic teacher-training providers.[32] In sum, the marketisation and partial deregulation of English schools over the past four decades is broadly liberal in character, affirming the importance of choice alongside attainment and citizenship.[33]

Alongside all this, there has been a growing realisation that educational institutions can be dangerous on multiple levels. As regards national security, after 9/11 the government developed the Prevent Strategy to stop children

[27] Ibid., pp. 234–8; Ruff, *Education Law*, p. 11.

[28] Richard Race, *Multiculturalism and Education* (London: Continuum, 2011), p. 64; Tariq Modood, *Multiculturalism: A Civic Idea* (2nd ed., Cambridge: Polity Press, 2013), p. 173; Suhraiya Jivraj, *The Religion of Law: Race, Citizenship and Children's Belonging* (London: Palgrave Macmillan, 2013), p. 131; Robert Berkeley and Savita Vij, *Right to Divide? Faith Schools and Community Cohesion* (London: Runnymede Trust, 2005), p. 9; Bhikhu Parekh et al., *The Future of Multi-Ethnic Britain: The Parekh Report* (London: Runnymede Trust and Profile Books, 2000), p. 241; Fran Abrams, 'Islamic Schools Flourish to Meet Demand' (*The Guardian*, 28 November 2011); Robert Long and Shadi Danechi, 'Faith Schools in England: FAQs' (House of Commons, Briefing Paper No. 06972, 20 December 2019), p. 21.

[29] Rumy Hasan, *Multiculturalism: Some Inconvenient Truths* (London: Politico Press, 2010), p. 201.

[30] See Neville Harris, 'Local Authorities and the Accountability Gap in a Fragmenting Schools System' (2012) 75(4) *Modern Law Review* 511–46.

[31] Ford et al., *Education Law and Practice*, pp. 38–9, 44–5.

[32] Gillard, *Education in England: A History*, ch. 19 ('Gove v The Blob 2010–2015').

[33] Rex Adhar and Ian Leigh, *Religious Freedom in the Liberal State* (2nd ed., Oxford: Oxford University Press, 2015), p. 243; William A. Galston, *Liberal Purposes: Goods, Virtues, and Diversity in the Liberal State* (Cambridge: Cambridge University Press, 1991).

being recruited for terrorist causes at school and in madrassas, noting the need for adequate safeguarding measures against radicalisation.[34] As for child protection, the Independent Inquiry into Child Sexual Abuse (IICSA) has been investigating child sexual abuse across a range of state and non-state institutions since 2014.[35] It found that abuse took place in every kind of school regardless of religious affiliation or academic success.[36] Indeed, as Diane Vaughan notes, there is often a dark side to institutions whereby deviance becomes routine as a result of individual decisions and organisational norms.[37] Law and policy also reflect concerns that religious schools – Muslim ones especially – are endangering the liberal framework of British society. As early as 1985, the Swann Report raised concerns about the negative impact that separate minority schooling could have upon attempts to reduce community segregation; similar sentiments were expressed in the Cantle Reports (2001, 2006) which raised concerns about 'parallel lives' and 'polarisation' developing in increasingly isolated faith communities.[38] In a 2005 speech, the Chief Inspector of Schools, David Bell, singled out Islamic schools as being a particularly dangerous 'threat to national identity': 'traditional Islamic education does not entirely fit pupils for their lives as Muslims in modern Britain'.[39] A BBC *Panorama* investigation in 2010 found that thousands of children in Muslim schools were being exposed to anti-Semitic and homophobic teachings, while, in 2012, concerns were raised in government about 118 independent schools (nearly all Muslim) which were being run by extreme Islamist groups and/or inculcating extremism in their pupils.[40] In the summer of 2014, the Al-Madinah Free School in Derby was closed down after just two years of operation as a result of damning inspections and oppressive and discriminatory Islamic practices being forced upon staff and pupils.[41]

Likewise, European Court of Human Rights (ECtHR) case law holds that the knowledge imparted through teaching must be delivered in an 'objective, critical and pluralistic manner' and cannot amount to 'indoctrination' as this is recognised as 'the most extreme departure from this standard and is

[34] HMG, 'Prevent Strategy' (London: HMG, Cm 8092, June 2011), pp. 65–71.

[35] IICSA, 'Terms of Reference' (IICSA, accessed 23 February 2021) www.iicsa.org.uk/terms-reference.

[36] See generally Sarah Brown, Theresa Redmond, Dafydd Rees, Stephanie Ford and Sophia King, 'Truth Project Thematic Report: Child Sexual Abuse in the Context of Schools' (IICSA, December 2020).

[37] Diane Vaughan, 'The Dark Side of Organisations: Mistake, Misconduct and Disaster' (1999) 25 *Annual Review of Sociology* 271–5.

[38] Hasan, *Multiculturalism*, p. 194.

[39] Tony Halpin, 'Islamic Schools Are Threat to National Identity, Says Ofsted' (*The Times*, 18 January 2005); David Bell, 'Speech on Faith Schools' (*The Guardian*, 17 January 2005).

[40] Haroon Siddique, 'BBC's Panorama Claims Islamic Schools Teach Antisemitism and Homophobia' (*The Guardian*, 22 November 2010); Duncan Gardham, 'Extremism Unchecked in Schools, Secret Briefing Reveals' (*The Telegraph*, 31 December 2012).

[41] Inderdeep Bains and Ben Spencer, 'Female Teachers at Islamic School "Made to Sign Contract Agreeing to Wear Headscarf Even if They're Not Muslim"' (*Daily Mail*, 20 September 2013).

absolutely prohibited'.[42] As regards the content of religious education, the state must not overstep the boundary between 'transmitting information' on a religion and 'providing instruction' in it.[43] In *R (Begum)* v. *Denbigh High School Governors* [2006] UKHL 15, Lady Hale recognised that restrictions on the right of pupils to manifest their religion are justified as 'schools are different ... [from the general free environment of everyday life and must] promote the ability of people of diverse races, religions and cultures to live together in harmony. Fostering a sense of community and cohesion within the school is an important part of that.'[44] In *HM Chief Inspector of Education, Children's Services and Skills (Appellant)* v. *The Interim Executive Board of Al-Hijrah School (Respondent)* [2017] EWCA Civ 1426, the Court of Appeal held that 'separate but equal' sex segregation in a co-ed maintained faith school amounted to unlawful discrimination regardless of whether or not boys or girls were treated worse than the other because both groups were being detrimentally prevented from interacting with the opposite sex purely on account of their own.[45] The upshot of all this is that schools are recognised as being critical to the reproduction of liberal national culture and the law will intervene if the balance of competing interests and freedoms is threatened.[46]

All schools must be registered and are subject to inspection.[47] Most independent schools are inspected by the approved Independent Schools Inspectorate (ISI) whereas the state-maintained sector is covered by the Office for Standards in Education, Children's Services and Skills (Ofsted). Although schools were inspected on an ad hoc basis for centuries, it was not until 1839 that the government instituted Her Majesty's Inspectors of Schools (HMI) to begin systematic national inspections.[48] The regulations and remit steadily expanded throughout the later nineteenth and twentieth centuries until the Major government modernised the system and introduced the new Office for Standards in Education (Ofsted).[49] It has been frequently modified ever since.[50] Much like the Charity Commission, Ofsted and its predecessors have been attacked from every angle for all kinds of reasons including a lack of

[42] See, respectively, *Kjeldsen, Busk Madsen and Pedersen* v. *Denmark* (1979–80) 1 EHRR 711, para. 53; *Campbell and Cosans* v. *UK* (1982) 4 EHRR 293, para. 31; Rivers, *Law of Organized Religion*, pp. 245–6.

[43] *Hasan and Eylem Zengin* v. *Turkey* (2008) 46 EHRR 44; Rivers, *Law of Organized Religion*, p. 249.

[44] Para. 97. [45] Paras. 48–56, 62–73, 80.

[46] See Neville Harris, *Education, Law and Diversity: Schooling for One and All?* (2nd ed., Oxford: Hart, 2020), ch. 6.

[47] Education Act 2002, ss. 158–159, 162A–162B.

[48] Patrick Michael Finucane, 'School Inspection in Canterbury and East Kent 1850–1870 and 1992–2000: A Comparative Study' (unpublished doctoral thesis for the Institute of Education, University of London, 2000), p. 7; Jenny Ozga and Martin Lawn, 'Inspectorates and Politics: The Trajectories of School Inspection in England and Scotland' (2014) 186 *Revue française de pédagogie* 11–21, p. 13.

[49] Education (Schools) Act 1992.

[50] See, for example, Education and Inspections Act 2006 and Ofsted, 'Guidance Education Inspection Framework (EIF)' (Ofsted, 2 September 2019).

independence, a narrow bureaucratic mindset, inconsistency, arbitrary and excessive interventionism, insufficient proactivity, undue progressivism, undue conservatism, and a lack of expertise and resources.[51] Two of the three major watchdogs of the independent sector, the Bridge Schools Inspectorate and the School Inspection Service, were closed in 2015 and 2019, respectively. These were the creation of several religious lobby groups and were responsible for inspecting many Christian and most Muslim independent schools.[52] Their inspectors were largely drawn from their parent organisations and were found by Ofsted to have been insufficiently rigorous on issues such as extremism and safeguarding.[53] Following a successful campaign by the British Humanist Association (BHA), all approved inspectorates must now maintain complete independence from both the schools they inspect and the body which established them.[54] In short, establishing and maintaining school standards is a seemingly mundane yet near-impossible and inevitably controversial endeavour. The issues are only ever amplified when religion is involved. There is no better demonstration of this than the most ferocious educational dispute in recent history.

6.3 The Trojan Horse Affair

The affair came to public attention thanks to the investigative reporting of Richard Kerbaj and Sian Griffiths at *The Sunday Times*. They ran a story on 23 February 2014 which reported that a former teacher at Park View Academy in Birmingham had been treating non-Muslim staff unfairly and placing undue emphasis on Islamic studies.[55] This was followed by their explosive article on 2 March 2014 which detailed '[a]n Islamist plot to take over schools' being investigated by Birmingham City Council (BCC).[56] Five days later, BCC announced that it was investigating a number of schools after receiving a copy

[51] R. F. Goodings and J. E. Dunford, 'Her Majesty's Inspectorate of Schools, 1839–1989: The Question of Independence' (1990) 22(1) *Journal of Educational Administration and History* 1–8; House of Commons Education Committee, 'The Role and Performance of Ofsted: Second Report of Session 2010–11' (House of Commons, HC 570 Vols. I and II, 17 April 2011); Harriet Waldegrave and Jonathan Simons, 'Watching the Watchmen: The Future of School Inspections in England' (London: Policy Exchange, 2014).

[52] The Association of Muslim Schools (AMS), the Christian Schools Trust (CST) and the Focus Learning Trust (FLT). See Jess Staufenberg, 'Ofsted Give Mixed Verdict on Independent School Inspectorates' (*Schools Week*, 23 December 2016).

[53] Andrew Gilligan, 'Schools Watchdog with Links to Extremists Shut Down' (*The Telegraph*, 14 June 2015); Charlotte Santry, 'Need to Know: Independent School Inspections under Scrutiny' (*TES*, 12 March 2018); Caroline Henshaw, 'Private School Watchdog School Inspection Service Closes' (*TES*, 31 January 2019).

[54] Department for Education (DfE), 'Independent Inspectorates: Regulations and Advice – Government Consultation Response' (DfE, August 2014).

[55] Richard Kerbaj and Sian Griffiths, 'Top Academy Investigated for "Sidelining" Non-Muslim Staff' (*The Times*, 23 February 2014).

[56] Richard Kerbaj and Sian Griffiths, 'Islamist Plot to Take Over Schools' (*The Times*, 2 March 2014).

of an anonymous letter detailing a plot to bring about an Islamist takeover of multiple schools and claiming responsibility for leadership changes at four schools while identifying another twelve that were vulnerable. Shortly after this announcement, Ofsted conducted a snap inspection of Park View Academy, which several years earlier had been graded 'outstanding'. The Trojan Horse letter set out a 'five-step' programme for taking over schools: (i) identify target schools in Muslim areas; (ii) identify hard-line Salafi parents in that school community because of their commitment and tenacity; (iii) install a governor to 'drip feed' Islamist ideals into the school; (iv) identify weak or disgruntled staff and get them to complain and spark an investigation; (v) establish an anonymous lettering campaign to local MPs, authorities and relevant groups.[57] The letter is thought to have been 'written by someone knowledgeable of Birmingham schools and of specific conflicts between governors and head teachers'.[58] Nevertheless, its authenticity has been hotly disputed. On one hand, the Education Commissioner for Birmingham appointed in September 2014, Sir Mike Tomlinson, stated that 'it was no hoax'.[59] On the other, various journalists have alleged that it was fake and then-Prime Minister David Cameron later stated in his memoirs: 'The letter itself was a fraud, but there was little doubt that there was a concerted effort to indoctrinate children with hard-line Islamist values.'[60] The provenance of the letter is the least important matter in the whole affair in light of the substance of the allegations against the individuals and organisations involved.[61]

Within a year of the scandal breaking, no fewer than nine overlapping reports commissioned by five different authorities were published. In chronological order, these were: (1) the first Education Funding Agency (EFA) Review of Park View Educational Trust (May 2014); (2) the second EFA Review of Oldknow Academy Trust (May 2014); (3) the Wilshaw Report for Ofsted (June 2014); (4) the Kershaw Report for BCC (14 July 2014); (5) the Trojan Horse Review Group Report for BCC (18 July 2014); (6) the Clarke Report for the Department for Education (DfE) (22 July 2014); (7) the Wormald Review for the DfE (January 2015); (8) the third EFA Review of Park View Educational

57 Phil Mackie, '"Islamic Takeover Plot" in Birmingham Schools Investigated' (*BBC News*, 7 March 2014).

58 John Holmwood and Therese O'Toole, *Countering Extremism in British Schools? The Truth about the Birmingham Trojan Horse Affair* (Bristol: Bristol University Press, 2017), p. 10.

59 BBC News, 'Birmingham Trojan Horse Letter "No Hoax"' (*BBC News*, 16 July 2015).

60 Dominic Kennedy, Greg Hurst and Ruth Gledhill, 'New Evidence Raises Doubts about Extremist Plot to Take Over School' (*The Times*, 11 March 2014); Richard Adams, 'Is the Trojan Horse Row Just a Witch Hunt Triggered by a Hoax?' (*The Guardian*, 8 June 2014); Richard Garner, 'Trojan Horse Row Q&A: What Is the "Muslim Plot" All about – and Why Is It so Important?' (*The Independent*, 9 June 2014); Samira Shackle, 'Trojan Horse: The Real Story behind the Fake "Islamic Plot" to Take Over Schools' (*The Guardian*, 1 September 2017); James Fergusson, *Al-Britannia, My Country: A Journey through Muslim Britain* (London: Corgi, 2018), ch. 5; David Cameron, *For the Record* (London: William Collins, 2020), p. 507.

61 Peter Clarke, 'Report into Allegations Concerning Birmingham Schools Arising from the "Trojan Horse" Letter' (House of Commons, HC 576, July 2014), p. 8.

Trust (February 2015); and (9) the House of Commons Education Committee (HCEC) Report (March 2015). Given differences in the terms of remit, focus and findings – plus the mass of news reports from the period – it is extremely difficult to reconstruct an entirely coherent picture of events. The truth has been obscured still further by the aggressively partisan nature of much (but not all) of the media reporting and academic literature.[62] What follows is a straightforward distillation of the reports and a condensed account of the legal proceedings that took place in the wake of the Trojan Horse Affair. This will provide a general picture of the allegations and issues, the bureaucratic failings that preceded and followed them, and a sense of weight as regards the confusing evidence.

6.3.1 Education Funding Agency (EFA) Reports

The first EFA report examined the practices, governance and oversight of Park View School, Nansen Primary School and Golden Hillock School within the Park View Educational Trust (PVET).[63] It found the Trust 'inadequate' as regards the coherence and clarity of governance responsibilities, funding arrangements, curriculum, record keeping, child safeguarding, opaque recruitment and appointment processes, and leadership decisions.[64] For example, the chair of the Trust had inappropriate and excessive involvement in the everyday running of the school and circumvented formal governance structures by holding undocumented meetings with the individual head teachers.[65] At Golden Hillock, governors were dismissive of female staff and governors.[66] At Park View, pupils were addressed by one Sheikh Shady al-Suleiman who among other things had previously declared: 'Give victory to Muslims in Afghanistan … Give victory to all the Mujahideen all over the world. Oh Allah, prepare us for the jihad.'[67] This led the EFA to conclude that PVET was not doing enough to promote community cohesion and had inadequate vetting procedures for external speakers.[68] Further, the school was not doing enough 'to make the school attractive to all faith denominations including pupils of no faith'.[69] This was because it had introduced 'a Madrassa curriculum in Personal Development' whereby loudspeakers broadcast the Islamic call to prayer while posters promoted its virtues and even declared: 'If you do not pray, you are worse than a kafir.'[70] Gender segregation took place in mixed lessons; the curriculum was narrow and unbalanced to reflect 'conservative Islamic teaching'; at Nansen School, the children complained about the lack of

62 Susan Divald, 'The Trojan Horse Controversy: Mapping the Construction of Justice in UK Media' (2019) Ethos Working Paper, p. 4.

63 Education Funding Agency (EFA), 'Review of Park View Educational Trust' (EFA, May 2014), p. 4.

64 Ibid., p. 3. 65 Ibid., p. 5. 66 Ibid., p. 6.

67 DfE and Michael Gove, 'Oral statement to Parliament on Birmingham Schools: Secretary of State for Education's Statement' (DfE, 9 June 2014).

68 EFA, 'Review of Park View Educational Trust', p. 7. 69 Ibid.

70 Ibid; Gary Marks, 'Christmas "Was Cancelled" at Trojan Horse Probe School – Claim' (*Birmingham Mail*, 28 April 2014).

clubs and extra-curricular activities while the chair of governors told an undercover reporter that 'white women have the least amount of morals';[71] GCSE students looking to sit the Christian studies paper were left to teach themselves as Islamic studies, sex education and biology were either banned outright or qualified with statements such as 'This is not what we believe.'[72] Staff turnover was high across the Trust.[73] A tabular schedule detailing the breaches of the Academy's Funding Agreement and relevant legislation runs to six pages.[74] A follow-up EFA report from February 2015 (referred to as 'the third' in Section 6.3) confirmed that PVET had 'a poor financial control environment' leaving it and its schools 'susceptible to the risk of fraud and error', although it 'did not find any evidence that the Trust had been subject to either internal or external fraud'. It did, however, find around £70,000 in 'irregular expenditure' misapplied on things such as 'legal and public relations (PR) fees'.[75] Save for the Sheikh Shady Al-Suleiman incident, these reports do not refer to extremism, radicalisation or terrorism.

The second EFA report conducted a similar investigation into Oldknow Academy Trust (OAT). It identifies 'many weaknesses' across the Trust relating to the coherence and clarity of governance responsibilities, funding arrangements, curriculum, record keeping, child safeguarding, opaque recruitment and appointment processes, and leadership decisions.[76] For example, the chair of the Trust told inspectors that he had selected one governor for his 'white face and Christian faith' and was found to have inappropriate involvement with the everyday running of the school via undeclared visits.[77] Various multicultural activities that had run in previous years – summer fairs, Diwali performances, Christmas festivities, inter-faith visits, art and music extra-curriculars – had been discontinued while Islamic celebrations continued, causing upset among the children and disappointment among parents.[78] Non-Muslim staff were excluded from Friday assemblies during which the children were subjected to inappropriate language such as 'white prostitute'.[79] The Arabic and maths teacher was complained about in particular for getting children to rehearse sectarian chants, instituting gender segregation in mixed classes, putting boys in a cupboard for showing their thighs while changing for PE, and various misogynistic behaviours towards women.[80] The school's annual trip to Saudi Arabia was available only to Muslim pupils and cost around £50,000 thanks to the 'extravagant' practice of staying only in five-star hotels.[81] A tabular schedule detailing the breaches of the Academy's Funding

[71] Nick Sommerlad. 'Trojan Horse School Chief Exposed as Bigot Who Wants Adulterers and Gays Sent into Exile' (*The Mirror*, 22 July 2014).
[72] EFA, 'Review of Park View Educational Trust', pp. 10–11. [73] Ibid., p. 12.
[74] Ibid., pp. 16–21.
[75] EFA, 'Park View Educational Trust Investigation Report' (EFA, February 2015), p. 3.
[76] EFA, 'Review of Oldknow Academy Trust' (EFA, May 2014), pp. 2–3. [77] Ibid., p. 4.
[78] Ibid., pp. 6–7, 13. [79] Ibid., p. 8. [80] Ibid., pp. 7, 12. [81] Ibid., p. 11.

Agreement and relevant legislation runs to nine pages.[82] The report does not refer to extremism, radicalisation or terrorism.

6.3.2 Wilshaw Report

The Wilshaw Report for Ofsted summarises the findings of the inspections of twenty-one non-faith academies and maintained schools in Birmingham between March and May 2014. Fifteen were inspected at the request of then-Education Secretary Michael Gove, and the other six on account of 'Ofsted's concerns about the effectiveness of safeguarding and leadership and management in these schools'.[83] It identifies numerous breaches of academy funding agreements; child safeguarding failures; discriminatory treatment based on gender and faith; the ineptitude of BCC in dealing with complaints and concerns or protecting children from 'the potential risks of radicalisation and extremism . . . specific to their community'; 'a culture of fear and intimidation' in some of the schools as governors sought to exert greater control; 'a rapid decline' in the overall effectiveness of previously good or outstanding schools; the introduction in one school by the chair of governors of 'madrasa programmes of study into the personal, health and social education curriculum'; and evidence of 'an organised campaign to target certain schools in Birmingham' to destabilise their leadership before bringing them into line with a 'narrow faith-based ideology in what are non-faith schools'. It notes:

> The evidence suggests three broad categories of school: in some schools, the inappropriate influence of governors is widespread and deep-rooted; in others, there are significant weaknesses in governance, but the level of undue influence exerted by individual governors is less established; in a few schools, leaders have successfully resisted the attempts of governors to change the nature and ethos of their school.

It also found that 'children are being badly prepared for life in modern Britain' because of faith or gender segregation, narrowing curriculums and the promotion of religious and cultural intolerance. The three PVET schools, Oldknow Academy and Saltley School were all deemed inadequate and placed in special measures by Ofsted.[84]

6.3.3 Kershaw Report

The Kershaw Report for BCC primarily sought to determine whether there was any substance in the Trojan Horse letter allegations with a view to designing an

[82] Ibid., pp. 19–27.
[83] Michael Wilshaw, 'Advice Note Provided on Academies and Maintained Schools in Birmingham to the Secretary of State for Education, Rt Hon Michael Gove MP, as Commissioned by Letter Dated 27 March 2014' (Ofsted, 9 June 2014).
[84] Ibid., Annex One: Inspection Outcomes.

appropriate response if required. In brief, the report found 'little express evidence' for a systematic, coordinated plot to take over Muslim-majority schools or any 'conspiracy to promote an anti-British agenda, violent extremism or radicalisation'. It did find that various aspects of the tactics outlined in the original letter 'were present in a large number of the schools' (it looks at sixteen schools[85]) and that there were 'clear patterns of behaviour amongst groups of individuals ... so common that it is reasonable to infer that there are links between these various individuals'. These groups of predominantly British Pakistani men seemed to have had a dual purpose: to improve the poor quality of education afforded to Muslim children while at the same time promoting their own Islamic nostrums and factional interests. These 'activist governors', who were deemed 'corruptive' rather than 'extremist', typically sought to achieve this through unethical or unlawful means by demanding that head teachers narrow the curriculum and harassing them for information, managing them aggressively, undermining them during Ofsted inspections, interfering in everyday operations and making inappropriate nepotistic appointments of friends and relatives. Aside from manifest incompetence and a raft of mundane systems failures, Kershaw found that BCC, rather than taking a stand on principle and supporting the beleaguered head teachers, facilitated their downfalls 'through the profligate use of compromise agreements'. All this was exacerbated by 'a culture within the BCC of not wanting to address difficult issues' out of fear of accusations of racism or Islamophobia.[86] The investigations into the schools, including those within PVET and OAT, produced findings that broadly correspond to (and occasionally reference) the earlier EFA reports.[87] Kershaw concluded that 'it is not possible to discern a relationship' among the various authorities – BCC, Ofsted, EFA, DfE – as regards the sharing of 'critical data and intelligence' leading to inconsistencies and confusion in the oversight process.[88]

6.3.4 Trojan Horse Review Group Report

The BCC Trojan Horse Review Group Report was tasked with explaining 'the authenticity or otherwise of the Trojan Horse allegations' and making any necessary remedial recommendations to BCC.[89] It opens by noting that the various authorities running separate investigations were living in 'parallel universes' and had not shared information to develop a coordinated response.[90] Its authors had access to the EFA, Ofsted and Kershaw reports but not the Clarke Report.[91] It broadly endorses Kershaw's findings (from which its own conclusions are largely derived) but notes that he did not

[85] Ian Kershaw, 'Investigation Report: Trojan Horse Letter' (Northern Education and Eversheds, 14 July 2014), pp. 7–8.
[86] Ibid., pp. 3–5. [87] Ibid., pp. 23–71. [88] Ibid., p. 14.
[89] Trojan Horse Review Group, 'Report to Leader of Birmingham City Council' (Birmingham City Council, 18 July 2014), p. 4.
[90] Ibid., p. 4. [91] Ibid., pp. 2, 6.

establish the authenticity of the original letter because this was both an impossible task and the wrong thing to focus on: 'too many people will continue to be distracted – or choose to be distracted – by the provenance of this letter itself. Nonetheless, we accept that – even if the letter was a hoax generated by malicious intent – what it has triggered by way of investigation has been important, substantial and needs urgently addressing.'[92] It concludes that the main 'issues relate to risks of small groups of activists seeking to subvert a small number of schools' and that in future BCC must be under 'no illusion of the importance of confronting any ideology in relation to schools governance in whatever shape or form it takes'.[93] Despite generally corroborating the findings of earlier reports, it does raise an additional point concerning the 'inevitably contentious . . . relationship between ideology, radicalisation, extremism and violence'.[94] It recommends that this 'should be addressed through mature, evidence-based debate, and with much greater precision in the use of terminology' instead of the existing 'lazy conflation' among various terms such as 'narrow faith-based ideology', 'cohesion, extremism and violent extremism' and 'questions of radicalisation, extremism or terrorism'.[95] Sir Albert Bore, the leader of BCC, responded defensively to the initial exposure of the scandal by claiming that the original letter was 'defamatory' and that there were 'no serious flaws in what we do'.[96] After the publication of the Kershaw and BCC reports, he was more contrite, offering an apology to the people of Birmingham for having 'previously shied away from tackling this problem out of a misguided fear of being accused of racism'.[97]

6.3.5 Clarke Report

The primary objective of the Clarke Report was straightforwardly to 'establish the facts of what had happened' against a backdrop of 'a great deal of rumour, speculation and un-evidenced assertion'.[98] It also looked at sixteen schools and was partially coordinated with Kershaw's investigation; however, although Clarke shared 'the vast majority of evidence' with Kershaw, the two 'did not discuss their conclusions with each other'.[99] As regards the original letter, Clarke did not seek to 'establish who wrote the letter or whether it was what it purported to be' as the 'important issue is not who wrote it or whether it is a genuine extract from a letter between co-conspirators, but whether the events

[92] Ibid., p. 6. [93] Ibid., pp. 6, 13. [94] Ibid., p. 7. [95] Ibid., pp. 7, 13.

[96] BBC News, 'Birmingham Schools "Islam Plot" Letter "Is Defamatory"' (*BBC News*, 19 March 2014).

[97] Neil Elkes, '"We're Sorry" Council Leader Admits Staff Ignored Trojan Horse Issue for "Fear of Being Accused of Racism"' (*Birmingham Mail*, 18 July 2014).

[98] Clarke, 'Report into Allegations Concerning Birmingham Schools Arising from the "Trojan Horse" Letter', pp. 7, 15.

[99] Ibid., pp. 16, 46–7 (a seventeenth is also noted in passing – p. 116); Kershaw Report, pp. 72–3; John Ware, 'The Plot to Islamise Birmingham's Schools' (*Standpoint Magazine*, 27 August 2014).

and behaviours described have actually happened . . . [and] that although there are some factual inaccuracies in the letter, there is also a great deal that is true'.[100] The report states that it neither looked for nor found 'evidence of terrorism, radicalisation or violent extremism', but did find, based on the definitions in the CONTEST Strategy and David Cameron's Munich speech from February 2011, 'clear evidence that there are a number of people, associated with each other and in positions of influence in schools and governing bodies, who espouse, sympathise with or fail to challenge extremist views'.[101] These were Tahir Alam, – the 'central figure', – Monzoor Hussain and Razwan Faraz, among various unnamed others.[102] There was a 'common ideological stance' which Clarke describes variously as 'a hardline and politicised strand of Sunni Islam', 'an intolerant and politicised form of extreme social conservatism that claims to represent, and ultimately seeks to control, all Muslims' and 'Islamism'.[103] In the Birmingham schools, this manifested as 'anti-Western rhetoric, particularly anti-US and anti-Jewish; segregationism: dividing the world into "us and them", with "them" to include all non-Muslims and any other Muslims who disagree; perception of a worldwide conspiracy against Muslims; attempts to impose its views and practices upon others; intolerance of difference, whether the secular, other religions or other Muslims'.[104] For example, Hussain established and administered the 'Park View Brotherhood' (PVB), an online discussion group to which Faraz often contributed.[105] It hosted links to 'hard-line Salafi, Deobandi and occasionally Islamist' speakers and conspiracy theories; a range of homophobic, misogynistic and sectarian opinions as well as disparaging comments about the British armed forces and 'Uncle Tom' Muslims who associated with, or helped fundraise for, them; and suggestions as to how to segregate and politicise the schoolchildren under their care.[106] Alam claimed that Hussain, and by extension the PVB, 'reflected the educational attitudes and aspirations of the community'.[107] Clarke further notes that their ideological agenda stems from an

> international movement to increase the role of Islam in education . . . supported by bodies such as the Association of Muslim Schools UK (AMS-UK), the International Board of Educational Research and Resources (IBERR), [and] the Muslim Council of Britain (MCB) . . . The movement provides practical advice and religious legitimisation to those who, in the words of the IBERR, seek to '*Islamise the provision of educational services*'. Some of the individuals who have featured in the investigation were associated with, or held positions in, these bodies.[108]

Otherwise, Clarke's findings are broadly consistent with the earlier reports as regards the recurring types of behaviour described, the institutional changes effected, the impact on affected children and their parents, and the failings of

[100] Clarke Report, pp. 8, 54. [101] Ibid., p. 95. [102] Ibid., pp. 50, 51, 53.
[103] Ibid., pp. 95, 48. [104] Ibid., p. 49. [105] Ibid., p. 56. [106] Ibid., pp. 56–74.
[107] Ibid., pp. 72, 74. [108] Ibid., p. 48.

BCC as regards its policy of 'appeasement' towards the governors stemming from a misguided fear of stoking 'community tensions' or harming 'community cohesion' by taking appropriate action.[109]

6.3.6 Wormald Review

The Wormald Review was commissioned following a high-profile row between then-Education Secretary Michael Gove and then-Home Secretary Theresa May over revelations that several former school governors had alerted the government directly about extremist infiltration as far back as 1994 and again in 2008 and 2010.[110] May claimed that these were ignored by the DfE.[111] David Cameron himself intervened to settle the dispute, forcing Gove (who soon lost his position as Education Secretary in a Cabinet reshuffle) to issue an apology and May to fire her closest adviser.[112] The Wormald Review sought to establish what warnings were received between 1994 and 2013, the nature of these warnings and whether any appropriate action had been taken.[113] It adopted 'a wide definition of extremism', but found no evidence of concerns raised about 'violent extremism'.[114] It did confirm that, since 1994, multiple warnings had been received about 'Islamic radicalism' and issues similar to those described in the earlier reports, the earliest relating to 'the extremist group Hizb-ut-Tahrir gaining an influence over schools in [Birmingham]'.[115] The report essentially cleared the DfE of wrongdoing via inaction, although it did find that the Department 'lacked inquisitiveness about this issue' as well as a 'robust' system for dealing with such issues and that it should address these shortcomings in future.[116]

6.3.7 House of Commons Education Committee (HCEC) Reports

The HCEC report 'covers the response of the DfE, Ofsted and BCC to the situation and wider lessons for the school system'.[117] The Committee acknowledged that it had 'benefitted from' the Kershaw and Clarke reports in

[109] Ibid., pp. 95–7, 9, 12, 82.

[110] Afua Hirsch, '"Muslim School Plot" Fears Were Raised in 1994' (*Sky News*, 2 June 2014); Lizzie Edmonds, 'Fears of Islamic Trojan Horse Plot to Takeover Birmingham Schools "First Raised to Then Prime Minister John Major 20 Years Ago"' (*Daily Mail*, 3 June 2014); Sky News, 'May's Anger At Gove over "Muslim School Plot"' (*Sky News*, 4 June 2014); BBC News, 'May and Gove in Row over Extremism in Schools' (*BBC News*, 4 June 2014).

[111] Richard Adams, 'Theresa May Calls on Michael Gove to Act on Extremism in Schools' (*The Guardian*, 4 June 2014).

[112] Toby Helm, Daniel Boffey and Warwick Mansell, 'Furious Cameron Slaps Down Gove and May over "Islamic Extremism" Row' (*The Guardian*, 7 June 2014).

[113] Chris Wormald, 'Review into Possible Warnings to DfE Relating to Extremism in Birmingham Schools' (DfE, January 2015), p. 4.

[114] Ibid., pp. 4, 6. [115] Ibid., pp. 6–7. [116] Ibid., p. 6.

[117] House of Commons Education Committee (HCEC), 'Extremism in Schools: The Trojan Horse Affair – Seventh Report of Session 2014–15' (House of Commons, HC 473, March 2015), p. 7.

particular.[118] It found 'no evidence of extremism in schools', 'no evidence to support claims of an organised plot to take over English schools' and 'no evidence of direct radicalisation or violent extremism'.[119] It did note one 'unacceptable' instance of 'a film promoting violent jihadist extremism' shown to children in one classroom at Park View, although this later turned out to have been a BBC *Panorama* programme 'made at the request of West Midlands Police to use as illustrative material in a session for pupils at the school on the risks of radicalisation'.[120] The most important findings are relatively mundane: 'The number of overlapping inquiries contributed to the sense of crisis and confusion, and the number of reports, coming out at different times and often leaked in advance, was far from helpful.'[121] It also noted that information sharing among agencies was a problem, that 'more coordination could and should have been achieved' and that Ofsted's inability to identify the issues in its earlier reports 'raises questions about the appropriateness of the framework and the reliability and robustness of Ofsted's judgements and how they are reached'.[122] It concludes that the Trojan Horse Affair was ultimately 'less about extremism than about governance' and lauded the introduction in November 2014 of the mandatory active promotion of, and inspection for, British values in all schools.[123]

6.3.8 Aftermath

The aftermath of the year of the nine reports was just as messy. Conspiracy theories soon spread, with 'people not wanting to believe such practices were taking place, calling the episode the "Trojan hoax" and accusing Government and Ofsted of being anti-Muslim'.[124] The Counter-Terrorism and Security Act 2015 placed 'unprecedented responsibility' on schools by introducing a duty to have 'due regard to the need to prevent people from being drawn into terrorism' (the Prevent duty) and the DfE published extensive guidance for school governors.[125] In September 2015, the Education Secretary issued a prohibition direction against Tahir Alam for 'conduct aimed at undermining fundamental British values' and 'conduct so inappropriate' that it made him 'unsuitable to take part in the management of independent schools' or act as a governor in any maintained school.[126] His attempt to overturn the ban failed and the ban

[118] Ibid., p. 6. [119] Ibid., pp. 6–7.

[120] Ibid., pp. 6–7; Clarke Report, p. 52; Holmwood and O'Toole, *Countering Extremism in British Schools?*, pp. 196–7.

[121] Ibid., HCEC Report, p. 3. [122] Ibid., p. 3.

[123] Ibid., pp. 4, 29; DfE and Lord Nash, 'Guidance on Promoting British Values in Schools Published' (DfE, 27 November 2014).

[124] Dame Louise Casey, 'The Casey Review: A Review into Opportunity and Integration' (HMG, December 2016), p. 116.

[125] S. 26; DfE, 'The Prevent Duty: Departmental Advice for Schools and Childcare Providers' (HMG, June 2015); Harris, *Education, Law and Diversity*, p. 351.

[126] DfE, 'Regulation of School Managers and Governors: Prohibition Direction against Tahir Alam' (DfE, September 2015).

was upheld on appeal in 2018, although the proceedings cost £387,444 and the final decision was not made public because it 'makes reference to those witnesses and sets out the evidence they gave, which the tribunal considers could lead to their being identified locally'.[127] Alam was seemingly able to crowdfund £19,761 of his own legal expenses.[128] Other professional misconduct proceedings were initiated by the National College of Teaching and Leadership (NCTL), the regulator of the teaching profession which has since been replaced by the Teaching Regulation Agency. These were outsourced, ended up costing £884,055 and did not go well.[129] It was initially reported in April 2015 that 'up to 100 Islamist teachers' faced a ban by the NCTL.[130] In the event, charges of professional misconduct were brought against twelve to fifteen teachers (reports differ as to the actual number) and the hearings began in late 2015.[131] Over the next several years, all but one of these cases were discontinued or successfully overturned on appeal.[132] None of the reported cases involved allegations of extremism.[133] The only teacher to be sanctioned, Jahangir Akbar of Oldknow Academy, was found to have engaged in 'misconduct of a serious nature' including agreeing to 'the inclusion of an undue amount of religious influence in the education of pupils' and undermining 'fundamental British values, including mutual respect and tolerance of those with different faiths and beliefs'.[134] He was prohibited from teaching indefinitely, although he received permission to apply for the ban to be lifted after five years.[135]

The highest profile case to collapse was against five senior PVET teachers; it fell apart on account of incorrect and misleading document disclosure submissions by NCTL lawyers.[136] The case was framed in terms of 'a failure to respect diversity' via 'an agreement to the inclusion of an undue amount of

127 Alex Homer, '"Trojan Horse" Hearings against Teachers and Governor Cost £1.27m' (*BBC News*, 17 August 2018); BBC News, '"Trojan Horse" School Ruling Hush "Exceptional"' (*BBC News*, 2 January 2018); TES, 'Ruling on Ex-chair of Governors at "Trojan Horse" School Kept under Wraps' (*TES*, 2 January 2018).

128 Tahir Alam, 'Justice for Tahir' (*Crowd Justice*, 21 February 2017): www.crowdjustice.com/case/justice-for-tahir/.

129 Homer, '"Trojan Horse" Hearings against Teachers and Governor Cost £1.27m'.

130 Richard Kerbaj and Sian Griffiths, '100 Islamist Teachers Face Ban' (*The Times*, 5 April 2015).

131 Holmwood and O'Toole, *Countering Extremism in British Schools?*, p. 199; Karamat Iqbal, *British Pakistani Boys, Education and the Role of Religion: In the Land of the Trojan Horse* (London: Routledge, 2020), p. 38.

132 Iqbal, ibid.

133 Holmwood and O'Toole, *Countering Extremism in British Schools?*, pp. 210–11.

134 NCTL, 'Mr Jahangir Akbar: Professional Conduct Panel Outcome – Panel Decision and Reasons on Behalf of the Secretary of State for Education' (NCTL, September 2015), pp. 25, 33, 35.

135 Ibid., pp. 35–7.

136 NCTL, 'Monzoor Hussain, Hardeep Saini, Arshad Hussain, Razwan Faraz, Lyndsey Clark: Professional Conduct Panel Outcome – Panel Decision and Reasons on Behalf of the Secretary of State for Education in Respect of Applications for the Proceedings to Be Discontinued' (NCTL, May 2017), para. 104.

religious influence in the education of pupils' rather than 'an evil plot to indoctrinate young people in extremist ideologies'.[137] Regardless, the abuse of process was 'of such seriousness that it [offended] the Panel's sense of justice and propriety', bringing 'the integrity of the process into disrepute' so that it would be 'fair and appropriate' to discontinue the proceedings.[138] All through the proceedings, there had been 'a lack of candour and openness with regard to the underlying reasons for those failures and a lack of cooperation in assisting the Panel to get to the bottom of what has happened'.[139] However, this was attributed to 'a significant breakdown in communication between those responsible for the conduct of this case' and 'an extraordinarily serious error of judgement as opposed to bad faith'.[140] Even the NCTL pleadings were 'far from ideal' as they were drafted in such a way that for just one particular it was 'necessary to reach 64 separate decisions'.[141] This all constituted a serious procedural miscarriage of justice which is unlikely ever to be remedied. This cuts two ways. First, the accused have effectively been denied their right to be heard before an independent adjudicator and will never have the opportunity to publicly and definitively answer the accusations and evidence against them. Second, it means that the public will never know whether the serious charges brought were valid or unfounded. What it is not is an exoneration on substance and fact. In a related case which collapsed for similar reasons, the judge noted that it was 'inappropriate for me to express a view as to the underlying merits of the allegations'.[142] As much seems to have been understood by Razwan Fawaz as regards his own case; he himself accepts that '[w]e weren't [really] exonerated in the public court'.[143]A substantial body of evidence and allegations, disputed or otherwise, remains on record in the multitude of official and media reports. Satellite litigation has confirmed that at least some of it is accurate. Faraz, who had been dismissed as deputy head teacher of PVET Nansen Primary School for gross misconduct in February 2015, subsequently brought an employment claim for unfair dismissal amounting to religious discrimination. He lost. It was found that he had been lawfully dismissed for making 'demonstrably homophobic' comments in the PVB group chat which had 'clear links to his work' and 'nothing to do with the expression of any religious belief'. What is more, 'both the disciplinary and appeal [*sic*] panels (each differently constituted and including Muslim members) all [*sic*] concluded unanimously after a full consideration of the case that the Claimant's explanations were not credible'.[144] Dr Karamat Iqbal – an academic, educationalist and school governor from Birmingham – provides a scrupulously neutral assessment of the allegations and concludes that

137 Ibid., paras. 46, 164. 138 Ibid., para. 174. 139 Ibid., para. 173. 140 Ibid., para. 169.

141 Ibid., para. 46.

142 *Anwar* v. *National College for Teaching & Leadership & Anor* [2016] EWHC 2507 (Admin) at para. 46.

143 Aina J. Khan, '"Big Bad Muslim": The Play That Allowed Trojan Horse Teachers to Start Healing' (*Middle East Eye*, 21 February 2020).

144 *Mr R Faraz* v. *Core Education Trust* 1303060/2015 (ET) 23 March 2018 at paras. 156–65.

many of the concerns were well-founded and may even recur based on testimonies from within the affected community.[145] Likewise, affected staff and pupils subsequently described how the schools and their education had improved in the years since the complained-of governors departed.[146] A striking feature of the reports, news stories and legal proceedings is just how consistent and pervasive the atmosphere of intimidation against witnesses seems to have been, with many requiring special measures to conceal their identities.[147]

Various oddities have taken place since the collapse of the NCTL hearings. The affair itself has been dramatised as a play, *Trojan Horse*, which toured for a time before being staged 'in a secret, gorilla [*sic*] performance' on the premises of Park View School for the enjoyment of Tahir Alam, Razwan Fawaz and others.[148] Alam himself has taken to 'holding sex education seminars' while Fawaz 'has now rebranded as a parenting coach'.[149] The former resurfaced again during the 2019 'No Outsiders' controversy over the teaching of LGBT diversity in Birmingham schools, claiming that the curriculum was 'indoctrinating' children and that 'in Islam, it's not OK to be in a gay relationship'.[150] These activist-led parent protests became so menacing and oppressive that BCC obtained a High Court injunction to restrain the abuse and establish an exclusion zone around the affected school, Anderton Park Primary.[151] Its head teacher noted 'numerous similarities between the protests and the Trojan Horse affair':

> It's only ever a handful of people. It's never everybody. But it's coercive, controlling behaviour by mainly men, making demands ... Back in Trojan Horse times, they were saying things like 'she's fixed the SATs results' or 'she spent money where she shouldn't spend money'. Now it's 'she's a vile Islamophobe' and 'she's a paedophile' ... It's one of these situations, a bit like Trojan Horse, where actually nobody knows what to do.[152]

145 Iqbal, *British Pakistani Boys, Education and the Role of Religion*, pp. 39–40; Karamat Iqbal, 'Birmingham: A Land of Trojan Horses?' (*BERA*, 22 October 2019).

146 Hannah Stuart and John David Blake, 'Trojan Horse: "If Anyone Is Still in Any Doubt That the Practices Uncovered Were Inappropriate, Just Listen to the Pupils"' (*TES*, 16 June 2017).

147 Martin Robinson, 'Dozens of Anonymous Whistleblowers Whose Evidence Helped Expose the Trojan Horse Plot in Birmingham Schools Have Been Told Their Identities Will Be Revealed to the Ringleaders' (*Daily Mail*, 4 January 2017); Rachel Williams, 'Warnings of Trojan Horse Complacency Risk' (*The Guardian*, 12 May 2015).

148 Traverse Theatre, 'Meet Those Closest to the Trojan Horse Enquiry' (YouTube, 4 February 2020): www.youtube.com/watch?v=JbpCKsDZ9bw; Khan, 'Big Bad Muslim'.

149 Neil Johnston, 'Banned "Trojan Horse" School Governor Holding Sex Education Seminars' (*The Times*, 8 July 2019); Lara Keay, 'Deputy Head, 39, Who Lost His Job at Trojan Horse School after Branding Gay People "Animals" in WhatsApp Chat Is Back in the Classroom Giving Advice to Teachers' (*Daily Mail*, 2 January 2020).

150 Neil Johnston, 'Banned School Governor Tahir Alam Fights Gay Equality Lessons' (*The Times*, 13 February 2019); The Economist, 'Muslim Parents Protesting against LGBT Primary School Lessons Is Only One of Birmingham's Many Culture Wars' (*i. by The Economist*, 17 April 2019).

151 *Birmingham CC* v. *Afsar* (No 3) [2019] EWHC 3217 (QB).

152 Freddie Whittaker, 'Feature on Sarah Hewitt-Clarkson at Anderton Park' (*Schools Week*, 7 June 2019).

Professor of Education Leadership at the University of Birmingham Colin Diamond similarly observed:

> [T]here have been worrying signs that the Trojan-type behaviours are being driven from outside the school gates. In recent years there have been two other Birmingham schools where parents sought to discredit the leadership via subversive letter-writing campaigns. They led to Ofsted inspections, the outcomes of which were influenced by organised unruly student behaviour. There are signs that activists from Trojan days are behind some of the campaigns.[153]

6.3.9 Illegal Schools

It was observed in the wake of the Trojan Horse Affair that numerous pupils were vanishing from the school register system altogether.[154] Their fates are unknown, but in 2016, amid intensifying concerns over religious extremism in schools, a special task force was established to investigate the 'huge nationwide problem' of illegal schools.[155] Between January 2016 and August 2020, Ofsted investigated 740 suspect educational settings serving around 6,000 pupils nationwide; 15 per cent of these existed primarily to provide religious instruction, of which the largest number with a known denomination were Muslim (46 compared to 20 Jewish and 19 Christian).[156] Unless or until schools are detected, and regardless of whether they are faith-based or not, there is no way to determine what the attending children are being taught and by whom, what condition the premises are in and what child safeguarding issues are involved. It is an offence to conduct an unregistered independent school.[157] The first successful conviction occurred in 2018 after the director and the head teacher of the 'Al-Istiqamah Learning Centre' in Ealing were prosecuted for running an illegal school which presented itself as offering part-time tuition.[158] However, another couple of convicts have simply carried on teaching at what they argue is not a full-time school.[159] Ofsted and the government have acknowledged that the former's powers are inadequate – it cannot search for or seize evidence and has 'no powers to close [schools] down' even after

153 Colin Diamond, 'Parkfield School and No Outsiders: We Must Learn from Trojan Horse History in Birmingham' (*Schools Week*, 20 March 2019).

154 Sean Coughlan, 'Ofsted Trojan Horse Warning on Pupils Taken out of School' (*BBC News*, 14 July 2015).

155 Ofsted, 'New Data Shows Illegal Schools Are a Huge Nationwide Problem' (Ofsted, 12 April 2019); DfE, 'Policy Statement: Prosecuting Unregistered Independent Schools' (DfE, August 2019).

156 Ofsted and Anita Patel, 'Unregistered Schools Management Information – 1 January 2016 to 31 August 2020', Tables 2a–c (Ofsted, 18 November 2020).

157 Education and Skills Act 2008, s. 96(2).

158 Sean Harford, 'Schools in the Shadows: Investigating and Prosecuting Unregistered Schools' (Ofsted, 25 October 2018).

159 Tom Pyman, 'Muslim Head and Her Father Carried On Teaching Despite Being Convicted of Running an Illegal £2,500-a-Year Islamic School That Failed to Promote Core British Values, Court Hears' (*Daily Mail*, 13 January 2021).

a successful prosecution has been brought – but no reforms have yet been introduced.[160] In its most recent annual report, Ofsted reiterated that 'there is no room for complacency or inaction' and that it 'must again emphasise how urgent it is for government to make this a priority'.[161]

6.3.10 Unregulated Madrassas

Unregulated madrassas attached to unregistered mosques which instruct pupils in Islam in an out-of-school setting raise similar concerns.[162] In 2006, a major report by a Muslim group raised concerns over widespread and significant sexual and physical child abuse within Britain's estimated 700 unregulated madrassas.[163] It was noted that 'all these schools are outside the law; nobody actually knows what is happening. It's not good for these institutions; it's not good for the children.' Recommendations were that a national register be set up and that accountability and regulatory oversight be drastically improved.[164] Similar concerns were raised in 2009 and 2011, by which point the number of official madrassas had reached 2,000.[165] Despite more than 400 allegations of abuse, only 2 successful prosecutions were brought, which indicates that this was merely the 'tip of the iceberg'.[166] The rising number of cases has been described by one prominent cleric as 'very, very alarming and shocking'.[167] One publicised example occurred in September 2015 when two teachers in a Birmingham madrassa were jailed

[160] Amanda Spielman, 'The Annual Report of Her Majesty's Chief Inspector of Education, Children's Services and Skills 2018/19' (Ofsted, HC 28, January 2020), p. 23; HMG, 'Integrated Communities Strategy Green Paper: Summary of Consultation Responses and Government Response' (HMG, February 2019), p. 15.

[161] Amanda Spielman, 'The Annual Report of Her Majesty's Chief Inspector of Education, Children's Services and Skills 2019/20' (Ofsted, HC 972, December 2020), pp. 20–1.

[162] Charity Commission, 'Parliamentary Briefing: Survey of Mosques in England and Wales' (Charity Commission, 1 February 2009); Anna Bawden, 'Thinktank Issues New Report on Madrasas' (*The Guardian*, 28 November 2011).

[163] Yasmin Valli, 'From Madrassa to Mainstream – The Role of the Madrassa in Shaping the Core Islamic Values and Practice among Young British Muslims' in Max Farrar, Simon Robinson, Yasmin Valli and Paul Wetherly (eds.), *Islam in the West: Key Issues in Multiculturalism* (London: Palgrave Macmillan, 2012), ch. 13, pp. 187–200 at p. 190.

[164] Alexandra Smith, 'Call for National Register of Mosque Schools' (*The Guardian*, 22 March 2006).

[165] Valli, 'From Madrassa to Mainstream', p. 187; Bawden, 'Thinktank Issues New Report on Madrasas'; Sukhi Hayer, 'Call for More Checks on Madrassas' (*BBC News*, 14 October 2009); Tazeen Ahmad, 'Shame of Britain's Muslim Schools: Secret Filming Shows Pupils Being Beaten and "Taught Hindus Drink Cow P***"' (*Daily Mail*, 13 February 2011).

[166] Murray Wardrop, 'More Than 400 Claims of Physical Abuse on Children Attending British Madrassas' (*The Telegraph*, 18 October 2011); Kate Loveys, 'Hundreds of Children "Abused in UK Madrassas" . . . but Only TWO Have Been Convicted' (*Daily Mail*, 19 October 2011); Fran Abrams, 'Child Abuse Claims at UK Madrassas "Tip of Iceberg"' (*BBC News*, 18 October 2011).

[167] Myriam Cherti and Laura Bradley, 'Inside Madrassas: Understanding and Engaging with British Muslim Faith Supplementary Schools' (Institute for Public Policy Research, November 2011), p. 14.

for beating and abusing a ten-year-old boy for failing to recite the Koran properly (among other things) and are likely to be barred from ever teaching children again.[168] At the time of writing, the IICSA is conducting a broad inquiry into child sexual abuse within religious organisations including madrassas.[169] The government response has been inconsistent at best: in 2012, it refused to propose registration regulations; in May 2014, it announced that it would draw some up; in October 2014, it shelved them again; in 2015, it revived plans for a registration and inspection regime, but these have not been acted upon either, after encountering stiff opposition from 'faith leaders'.[170]

6.4 Interpreting the Trojan Horse Affair

The Trojan Horse Affair would be difficult enough to interpret without the disjointed evidence and disinformation surrounding it given the inherently contentious nature of education and schools policy. Nevertheless, there are better and worse ways to do this depending on the theoretical approach adopted. For the interpretation to be convincing, it must offer some account of what schools are for and how education and religion should relate to one another, explain what went wrong in this instance and point towards a coherent legal response.

6.4.1 Via Liberal Individualism

Many aspects of the official reaction can be explained with reference to liberal individualism. For Ronald Dworkin, a 'liberal public education' was about two things. On a societal level, its purpose was to fashion 'a culture of independence' as a bulwark against 'a culture of conformity' and 'totalitarian epistemology'; for the individual, it was about imparting 'the importance and depth of an allegiance to personal rather than collective truth' as a prerequisite for 'a life of personal conviction'.[171] Schools are at risk of becoming 'engines of conformity' if they are poorly

[168] Steven Morris, 'Islamic Centre Teachers Jailed for a Year for Beating 10-Year-Old' (*The Guardian*, 10 September 2015).

[169] Harriet Sherwood, 'Child Sexual Abuse Inquiry to Be Held into Religious Organisations' (*The Guardian*, 2 May 2019).

[170] National Secular Society (NSS), 'Government Resists Calls to Regulate Madrassas' (NSS, 26 January 2012); Patrick Wintour, 'Code of Conduct Drawn Up for UK Madrasas' (*The Guardian*, 18 May 2014); BBC News, 'Code of Practice for Religious Schools Shelved' (*BBC News*, 23 October 2014); Sally Weale, 'Muslim Leaders Voice Concerns about Tory Crackdown on Madrasas' (*The Guardian*, 7 October 2015); HMG, 'Counter-Extremism Strategy' (HMG, Cm 9148, October 2015), pp. 14, 26–7; DfE, 'Out-of-School Education Settings: Call for Evidence for Government Consultation' (DfE, November 2015); John Bingham, 'Sunday Schools and Bell Ringing Groups Could Face "Radicalisation" Inspections' (*The Telegraph*, 11 December 2015); Sean Coughlan, 'Mosques Oppose Madrassa Registration' (*BBC News*, 7 January 2016); Jess Staufenberg, 'Out-of-School Settings Won't Be Forced to Register – for Now' (*Schools Week*, 10 April 2018).

[171] Ronald Dworkin, *Freedom's Law: The Moral Reading of the American Constitution* (Oxford: Oxford University Press, 1996), p. 252.

run or regulated.[172] The curriculum should confront students with 'the most contentious political controversies', while teachers must 'steer between anodyne banality and indoctrination' as they impart a sense of the complexity of the issues, an ethic of 'conscientious and respectful argument' and, critically, 'some understanding of positions different from those the students are likely to find at home or among friends'.[173] If all of this is done properly, it will create and sustain a tolerant secular society populated by individuals capable of making informed democratic decisions; if done badly or not at all, the callow citizenry will be at the mercy of 'the fiats of priesthood or junta or majority vote' from which dissent is regarded as treason.[174] A good education is therefore emancipatory and a good school fosters tolerance towards others as much as towards new ideas.

The government's response to the Trojan Horse Affair can well be described as 'muscularly liberal'.[175] It framed the issues in terms of 'conservative Islamic teaching', 'a failure to respect diversity' and an 'undue amount of religious influence'; preserved the consumeristic ethos of the academies programme with piecemeal amendments promoting greater transparency and accountability of governing bodies; and concentrated legislative efforts upon enshrining liberal values and instituting counter-extremism training for teachers.[176] On one hand, this was relatively permissive in that the government settled for a controlling stake in the political balance of power under which faith-based education is tolerated until its purveyors sought to rewrite the terms of the social contract.[177] On the other, it entailed considerable scope for intervention, with religious educational institutions tolerated on the basis of autonomy and choice but only so long as they moderated themselves and still produced good liberal citizens.[178] As regards illegal schools and madrassas, the government stressed that there 'should be no "ungoverned spaces" in which extremism is allowed to flourish without firm challenge and, where appropriate, by legal intervention'.[179] Regardless, the focus was ultimately upon liberal values and the individual rather than groups and institutions in their own right. This is certainly understandable

[172] Ibid.

[173] Ronald Dworkin, *Is Democracy Possible Here? Principles for a New Political Debate* (Princeton, NJ: Princeton University Press, 2006), pp. 148–9.

[174] Dworkin, *Freedom's Law*, pp. 252–3.

[175] David Cameron, 'PM's Speech at Munich Security Conference' (HMG, 5 February 2011).

[176] Harris, *Education, Law and Diversity*, pp. 168–72; John Dickens, 'Ofsted Starts Talks over More Anti-extremism Teacher Training' (*Schools Week*, 14 November 2015); Richard Pring, 'Faith Schools: Can They Be Justified?' in Roy Gardner, Jo Cairns and Denis Lawton (eds.), *Faith Schools: Consensus or Conflict?* (London: Routledge, 2005), ch. 4, pp. 51–60 at pp. 54–6.

[177] Alan Dagovitz, 'When Choice Does Not Matter: Political Liberalism, Religion and the Faith School Debate' (2004) 38(2) *Journal of Philosophy of Education* 165–80; Neil Burtonwood, 'Social Cohesion, Autonomy and the Liberal Defence of Faith Schools' (2003) 37(3) *Journal of Philosophy of Education* 415–25.

[178] Johan De Jong and Ger Snik, 'Why Should States Fund Denominational Schools?' (2002) 36(4) *Journal of Philosophy of Education* 573–87.

[179] HMG, 'Prevent Strategy' (London: HMG, Cm 8092, June 2011), p. 9.

given that the implicated governors and teachers flouted all manner of liberal values, purposes and regulations underpinning the education system.[180] It is also true that Muslim schools tend to be 'more religiously stringent' and that, long before the Trojan Horse Affair, many non-religious state schools with a large proportion of Muslim pupils underwent 'adjustments to their fundamental character and a gradual transformation of every aspect of education provision'.[181] Further, while 'faith schools in general do not promote social division on racial and ethnic lines', Muslim schools 'counter the dominant model' by prioritising the 'development of a collective identity' over 'the development of connections between people who are different'.[182] Nevertheless, this is all somewhat beside the point. Education does not need to be secular and liberal to be good.[183] Muslim-led or Muslim-majority schools are neither inherently problematic nor a threat to the state – one has recently launched an Army Cadet Force.[184] The problems at the heart of the Trojan Horse Affair are difficult to articulate with the limited vocabulary of liberal individualism, as the confusion and messy aftermath showed.

6.4.2 Via Multiculturalism

Unusually, there is a dedicated multicultural literature on education law and the Trojan Horse Affair. Unfortunately, it is of exceptionally poor quality even by the standards of the multiculturalists. The only book-length treatment of the topic purports to be 'The Truth about the Birmingham Trojan Horse Affair', but concludes, as one reviewer understood it, that 'there were no egregious practices in the Trojan Horse affair'.[185] Incredibly, it is dedicated to Tahir Alam, the PVET teachers and their lawyers.[186] The authors repeatedly liken the 'accepted narrative' to the Hillsborough Disaster, yet derive their own 'radically different' account from a 'long association with the city of Birmingham'.[187] Much is made of 'fake news' and 'the disparagement of experts', yet the publication is unironically endorsed as an 'alternative analysis'.[188] Among its many ridiculous and trite assertions are things like 'multiculturalism works', 'local governance of schools works', 'it is hard to avoid the conclusion that [the success of Park View]

[180] Dickens, 'Ofsted Starts Talks over More Anti-extremism Teacher Training'; Pring, 'Faith Schools: Can They Be Justified?', pp. 54–6.

[181] John Flint, 'Faith-Based Schools: Institutionalising Parallel Lives?' in Adam Dinham, Robert Furbey and Vivien Lowndes (eds.), *Faith in the Public Realm: Controversies, Policies and Practices* (Bristol: Policy Press, 2009), ch. 9, pp. 163–82 at pp. 169–73.

[182] Elizabeth Oldfield, Liane Hartnett and Emma Bailey, 'More Than an Educated Guess: Assessing the Evidence on Faith Schools' (London: Theos, 2013), pp. 23–6.

[183] Nicolas Tate, *The Conservative Case for Education: Against the Current* (London: Routledge, 2018).

[184] Armed Forces Muslim Association (AFMA), 'Tauheedul Islam Boys' High School Becomes First Islamic School in Britain to Launch Army Cadet Force (AFMA, 6 December 2018).

[185] Iqbal, *British Pakistani Boys, Education and the Role of Religion*, p. 39.

[186] Holmwood and O'Toole, *Countering Extremism in British Schools?*, p. viii.

[187] Ibid., pp. vii, 15, 138, blurb. [188] Ibid., pp. 229, 245–6, back cover.

made the school a target' and the 'high-salaried ... charismatic leadership' of Michael Gove and Michael Wilshaw 'helps to create the conditions for authoritarianism'.[189] The lead author has stated elsewhere, 'I certainly don't argue that there's a sort of conspiracy around manufactured [evidence] so I think it's a series of tragic contingencies.'[190] However, he has consistently made even kookier claims alongside serious accusations of foul play:[191]

(i) 'there is no evidence in the Clarke Report', 'it is not simply that Clarke rigged the evidence' and 'everything I say about Clarke applies to Kershaw';[192]
(ii) 'I think there is corrupt and dishonest behaviour' among the investigating authorities;[193]
(iii) 'the positive thing you can take from this is that you should, at the end of this process, wish that every school in Britain was like Park View Academy, and if it were like Park View Academy we wouldn't be talking about any problems of integration';[194]
(iv) 'whiteness is part of the problem' because white parents will not enrol their children in Muslim or Muslim-majority schools;[195]
(v) 'populist "othering" of minorities is the wind that keeps the ship of state on its neo-liberal course';[196]
(vi) 'I don't think anything went wrong other than a sort of everyday prejudice against Muslims, I'll put it as bluntly as that. That, at every moment when you could have said there's an alternative explanation for what people believed they were seeing here, people wanted to believe the worst';[197]
(vii) the Trojan Horse Affair 'was a story of journalists manipulated by politicians and willing to collude in the destruction of the livelihoods of teachers and the reputations of governors and the local community of British Muslims'.[198]

[189] Ibid., pp. 227–52.
[190] John Holmwood, 'The Trojan Horse Affair Exposed' (PREVENT Watch, 6 January 2021): www.youtube.com/watch?v=aXmWodsx5Gw&feature=youtu.be (accessed 24 February 2021) from 42.15.
[191] See 'IHRC Author Evening: Countering Extremism in British Schools? by John Holmwood, 18 April 2018' (Islamic Human Rights Commission TV, 12 March 2018): www.youtube.com/watch?v=yAq3hnQQZBo (accessed 22 July 2020).
[192] Ibid. at 15.02/1.18.20/17.45. [193] Ibid. at 39.00. [194] Ibid. at 1.14.47.
[195] Ibid. at 1.12.17. [N.B. When a white pupil did enrol at Anderton Park school, a Muslim parent told staff: 'Get a white chair and a white desk and put the white kid in a white corner with a white teacher and keep him away from the others. If that fails, get rid of the white kid. It's what the community want you to do' (Clarke Report, p. 44).]
[196] John Holmwood, 'Markets, Publics and Education: A Tale of Trojan Horses' (*Discover Society*, 1 July 2014).
[197] Holmwood, 'The Trojan Horse Affair Exposed' from 12.24.
[198] Quoted in Peter Oborne and Mahdi Mustafa, 'BBC Trojan Horse Report: Failing to Put Right Shocking Falsehoods' (*Middle East Eye*, 5 February 2021).

With respect, this is not scholarship but polemical activism at its most unhinged, undignified and incompetent.[199] Everyone concerned deserves much better from senior sociologists. To that end, it is possible to interpret the Trojan Horse Affair according to multiculturalism in a more dispassionate and constructive way. One might proceed from Parekh and Modood's rejection of the 'hegemonic power' and discriminatory tendencies of secular liberalism.[200] On this view, Muslim demands for religious schools and special educational provisions are understood as another facet of 'Muslim struggles for dignity and equality in Western Europe[, against Western domination, which] are inseparable from those in the global *umma*'.[201] Once granted, the resulting institutions form an integral part of 'Muslim consciousness' and are welcome expressions of group self-identity regardless of their assertiveness, values or ends. Indeed, Muslims are 'not a homogeneous group' but a 'social category', yet should nevertheless 'be treated as a legitimate group in their own right'. Accordingly, the state must compromise on secularism and liberal individualism to ensure equality among minority groups by designing 'sensitive policies' in consultation with religious 'representatives' such as the MCB and funding Muslim or Muslim-majority schools on an equal basis to those of other denominations. In the interests of coexistence and social peace, it would be 'foolish to disparage and dismantle the cohesiveness of Muslim communities'. Accusing them of practising 'extremist politics, religious obscurantism and an unwillingness to integrate' is both morally and factually wrong.[202] Muslims do not need emancipating from themselves. Thus, any regulatory focus on Muslim schools is tantamount to orientalist 'othering' and the 'racialising' of Islam.[203] On this philosophical basis, the Trojan Horse Affair is interpreted as either a manufactured or a misguided attempt by the liberal state to impose itself on and in the Muslim community. This necessitates a defensive stance which may tip into suggestions that the Affair was little more than a 'moral panic' which relegated Muslim governors and teachers to 'second-class citizenship'.[204] In short, the government response was an unacceptable infringement on the

[199] For similar examples, see Miriam Francois-Cerrah, 'In the So-Called "Trojan Horse" Debacle, Birmingham Schools Have Become Gove's Sacrificial Lamb' (*New Statesman*, 17 July 2014) and Patrick Wintour, 'Muslim Council of Britain Rejects Findings of Trojan Horse Report' (*The Guardian*, 23 July 2014). Similar responses were provoked by the discovery of problems in madrassas: Sajda Khan, 'It's Wrong to Blame Madrassas for Extremism – I Went to One and It Didn't Make Me an Intolerant Muslim' (*The Independent*, 11 October 2015).

[200] Tariq Modood, 'Muslims and the Politics of Difference' (2003) 74(1) *Political Quarterly* 100–15, p. 110.

[201] Bhikhu Parekh, 'Feeling at Home: Some Reflections on Muslims in Europe' (2009) 8 *Harvard Middle Eastern and Islamic Review* 51–85, p. 81.

[202] Modood, 'Muslims and the Politics of Difference', pp. 100, 103, 108–14; Tariq Modood, 'Landmark Interview' (Goldsmiths, University of London, undated): www.gold.ac.uk/faithsunit/current-projects/reimaginingreligion/landmark-interviews/tariq-modood/.

[203] Jivraj, *The Religion of Law*, pp. 136–40, 157.

[204] John R. Bowen, *British Islam: Religion, Law, and Everyday Practice in Sharia Councils* (Princeton, NJ: Princeton University Press, 2016), pp. 203–5.

integrity of the Birmingham Muslim community which had, upon its own initiative, shaped the schools to reflect its identity and cater to the demands of local parents.

As regards policy, the academisation of the school system is a welcome development regardless of any wrongdoing that it may or may not have facilitated. This is because it allows minority groups considerable autonomy to establish and run their own schools with state aid. An example of what this might entail can be seen in the MCB's seventy-two-page guidance document (co-authored by Tahir Alam himself in 2007) entitled *Toward Greater Understanding: Meeting the Needs of Muslim Pupils in State Schools.* It sets out a programme for the Islamisation of state schools in the name of responding 'positively to issues related to cultural diversity and . . . meeting the needs of Muslim pupils' through gender segregation, the avoidance of 'idolatrous' art classes, a ban on dance 'and much more'.[205] Far from encouraging separatism and segregation, these are merely manifestations of a multicultural citizenship which celebrates diversity among communities and, in doing so, brings them together under a remade national identity. While it met with anxiety from the press and was dismissed by the government, similar officially endorsed policies are still operating in other local educational authorities with high proportions of Muslim pupils, such as Wandsworth.[206] The need for similar initiatives will only become more pressing over time given that around one in twelve pupils across Britain are Muslim and schools in some urban wards in Birmingham and Tower Hamlets in London have Muslim intakes of up to 80 per cent and 60 per cent, respectively.[207] Going forward, central government would be well advised to invest more in Muslim schools which can play a decisive role in improving outcomes for disadvantaged children.[208] Rather than criminalising those who run illegal Muslim schools, it would be less inflammatory to bring these institutions within the system and properly fund them to improve child safety and educational standards. As regards regulation, a co-regulatory model akin to that used for charitable fundraising would likely be preferable to oversight by Ofsted. That way, British Muslims can have more input into the supervisory process and thereby develop a more reciprocal relationship with government. Whatever form this takes, state authorities must not panic and attempt to impose majority values on minority institutions including schools

[205] Press Association, 'Government Dismisses Muslim School Guidance Document' (*The Guardian*, 21 February 2007); Rivers, *The Law of Organized Religions*, p. 259.

[206] Ibid.; Holmwood and O'Toole, *Countering Extremism in British Schools?*, pp. 129–30.

[207] Lucy Crossley, 'Number of Muslim Children in England and Wales Doubles in a Decade with One in 12 School Pupils Now Brought Up in Islamic Faith' (*Daily Mail*, 12 February 2015); Abrams, 'Islamic Schools Flourish to Meet Demand'; Dominic McGoldrick, 'The Compatibility of an Islamic/Sharia Law System or Sharia Rules with the European Convention on Human Rights' in Robin Griffith-Jones (ed.), *Islam and English Law* (Cambridge: Cambridge University Press, 2013), ch. 4, pp. 42–71 at p. 66.

[208] See generally, but with special reference to British Pakistani boys, Iqbal, *British Pakistani Boys, Education and the Role of Religion.*

and madrassas. In sum, a multicultural education policy would likely represent a continuation of consumerism with even greater emphasis on parental choice. Once again, however, the main problems with this perspective are to do with its simplistic understanding of groups. To begin with, thinking in class terms of 'Muslim/Muslim-led/Muslim-majority schools' confuses the basic object of study, which is simply 'schools'. There is no homogeneous desire among Muslim parents en bloc to send their children to Muslim schools – opinions and wishes naturally vary across the Muslim population.[209] This is yet more proof that the 'Muslim community' is not a meaningful entity possessed of collective rights. However, in interpreting the inspection and restructuring of local schools as an attack on the community itself, multiculturalism cannot provide clear answers as to when the state can legitimately intervene.

6.5 A Pluralist Response to the Trojan Horse Affair

The Trojan Horse Affair is best understood in historical perspective. 'Education has always been a pious duty for Muslims' and has always taken place within a variety of informal and formalised settings ranging from salons and study circles to colleges and specialised madrassas attached to mosques.[210] While devotional exercises, scriptural recitation and the study of religious law remain central to traditional Islamic education, they do not necessarily conflict with secular learning.[211] However, over the past century, the democratisation of knowledge through print and the Internet has precipitated a crisis in religious authority, so much so that now 'any Ahmad, Mahmud or Muhammad' can 'make what they will' of important religious texts and then 'claim to speak for Islam'.[212] While Islamic scholars have been able to greatly extend their influence over public affairs and still command respect, the roots of their power as transmitters and guardians of the faith have withered away and they may eventually 'end up like teachers in the universities of the West'. The practical result has been 'a rapid florescence of sectarianism. Group after group sprang up: Deobandis, Barelvis, Ahmadis, Necharis, Ahl-i Hadiths, Ahl-i Quran, Jamaatis, etc. – almost all of which . . . have been translated to Britain'.[213] From these have emerged faith leaders who 'often fail to provide the kind of religious leadership required in modern society' because of their hostility towards innovation and what they claim are un-Islamic ideas.[214] As a consequence, Islamic education has bifurcated as Muslims grapple with the

209 McKinney, 'Mapping the Debate on Faith Schooling in England', p. 10; Sean Coughlan, 'Should There Be More Muslim State Schools?' (*BBC News*, 6 October 2016).

210 Malise Ruthven, *Islam in the World* (3rd ed., Oxford: Oxford University Press, 2006), p. 145.

211 Mehdi K. Nakosteen and Joseph S. Szyliowicz, 'Aims and Purposes of Muslim Education' (Encyclopaedia Britannica, accessed 28 February 2021).

212 Francis Robinson, 'Technology and Religious Change: Islam and the Impact of Print' (1993) 27(1) *Modern Asian Studies* 229–51, p. 245.

213 Ibid., p. 246.

214 John L. Esposito, *Islam: The Straight Path* (Oxford: Oxford University Press, 1988), pp. 197–8.

sometimes competing demands of tradition and the study of non-religious disciplines such as the natural sciences, political science, engineering and secular law.[215] This has in turn created an opening for radicals who have been able to exploit the wishes of Muslim parents who want to 'give their children some grounding in their own inherited religious and cultural tradition'.[216] In the West, this is often available only through 'private schools, religious seminars, mosque schools, holiday camps and, increasingly, prisons', even though many are little more than Jamaat-i-Islami, Muslim Brotherhood or Gulf-funded 'indoctrination centres'.[217]

The Trojan Horse Affair itself requires careful interpretation in light of these trends and the limitations of the evidence. The first routine matter is to strip away the conspiratorial accretions. This cuts both ways. The original plot looks a lot more like opportunistic clannism than an Islamist masterstroke. Clannism will be discussed in detail in Chapter 8, but for now it suffices that it combines, and is characterised by, elements of religious and social conservatism, nepotism and out-group hostility. This seems to be how Baroness Sayeeda Warsi viewed the goings-on in Birmingham: 'a bunch of blokes with pretty misogynistic, conservative and intolerant views had decided that they were right and everyone else was wrong, that their vision of the world was going to trump others and through the brown boys network had managed to keep power in the hands of themselves and their mates'.[218] Shabana Mahmood MP came to a similar conclusion: 'There is no doubt that a small group of people in our city went on a massive power trip and behaved completely inappropriately – going way beyond the remit and the parameter for governors.'[219] The problem, in other words, was not conservative Islam as such but rather a particular mode of practising politics and arranging social affairs. At the same time, it is stretching all credibility to argue that the government response was somehow part of a determined neoconservative agenda to attack Muslims as such, or that any sort of discernible narrative or discourse was promulgated by 'the media'.[220] The unheeded warnings dating back to the early 1990s, the chronic bureaucratic failures, the need for investigative reporting to prompt any kind of response, the sheer number of uncoordinated reports hastily commissioned and reaching broadly similar conclusions, the inept and inarticulate legal proceedings, the recurrence of similar rogue behaviour in subsequent events, the furious culture warring among different journalists and between academic sociologists and

[215] Ibid.; Fazlur Rahman, 'Revival and Reform in Islam' in P. M. Holt, Ann K. S. Lambton and Bernard Lewis (eds.), *The Cambridge History of Islam* (Cambridge: Cambridge University Press, Vol. 2B, 1977), part 8, ch. 7, pp. 632–56 at pp. 654–6.

[216] Bernard Lewis, *The Crisis of Islam: Holy War and Unholy Terror* (London: Phoenix, 2004), p. 110.

[217] Ibid.; Esposito, *Islam*, pp. 197–8; Ruthven, *Islam in the World*, p. 333.

[218] Sayeeda Warsi, *The Enemy Within: A Tale of Muslim Britain* (London: Penguin, 2018), p. 150.

[219] Quoted in Shackle, 'Trojan Horse: The Real Story behind the Fake "Islamic Plot" to Take Over Schools'.

[220] Holmwood and O'Toole, *Countering Extremism in British Schools?*, pp. v, 229.

everyone else – none of this is suggestive of anything other than chaos and the characteristic massed incompetence of a sector sometimes referred to as 'the blob'.[221] As ever, Barbara Tuchman proves the best inoculation against 'voodoo history': 'Mankind, it seems, makes a poorer performance of government than of almost any other human activity. In this sphere, wisdom, which may be defined as the exercise of judgment acting on experience, common sense and available information, is less operative and more frustrated than it should be.'[222]

To sum up the Trojan Horse Affair: there really were unacceptable practices going on in Birmingham schools; these required a coherent, principled and decisive response from regulators; this was not forthcoming; and a fever-swamp of loose ends, exaggeration, denialism, wild speculation and daft academic theorising has formed over the mundane truth. Or, in a line, '[i]ncompetence runs riot in the halls of education'.[223]

Good education – moral and practical – is vital both to children as individuals and to the continuing success of the nation as a whole. The former rely upon it for positive character development, the basic skills and competencies required for modern life, and a passport to success in higher education. The nation depends on it for the preservation of its best traditions, continuing engagement with its own past and place in the world, and to realise a vision for the future. These are all particularly important in areas with high levels of deprivation like Birmingham. None of this can happen without a thriving and well-regulated ecosystem of schools, one which is not averse to experimentation so long as it is capable of self-correction. This requires vigilance against threats from any direction, whether from parents, teachers, governors, poor regulation, underfunding, excessive bureaucracy, corruption or any number of other sources. The state will inevitably need to play a significant role in the provision of universal education to a large population, but this does not necessitate cloying uniformity. It is entirely natural for local communities to colour their local schools and for parents to combine to create new ones. To some extent, these institutions must be assessed instrumentally and objectively by an external regulator to ensure high standards, adequate safeguarding measures, and dedication to soulcraft in the national interest. Even so, their intrinsic worth as group persons must be respected so long as they remain genuine fellowships dedicated to their primary educational purpose. Put in Gierkean terms, the Trojan Horse Affair was an instance of fellowships being turned into vassal institutions of a particular group with a view to replicating its ideology and entrenching the personal privileges of its leading members.

[221] Richard Garner, 'What Is "the Blob" and Why Is Michael Gove Comparing His Enemies to an Unbeatable Sci-fi Mound of Goo Which Once Battled Steve McQueen?' (*The Independent*, 7 February 2014).

[222] *The March of Folly: From Troy to Vietnam* (London: Abacus, 1990), p. 2. On the allure and malign impact of conspiratorial thinking, see David Aaronovich, *Voodoo Histories: How Conspiracy Theory Has Shaped Modern History* (London: Vintage, 2010).

[223] Raymond Hull, 'Introduction' in Laurence J. Peter, *The Peter Principle: Why Things Always Go Wrong* (new ed., London: Souvenir Press, 1994), pp. 9, 13.

The vision they were bringing into being was a nightmare of balkanisation. Whether or not theirs was 'good Islam' is immaterial and not something that any state or non-Muslim can or should pronounce upon. Any amount of public scandal, professional embarrassment and temporary disruption was a price worth paying to arrest it. The stakes could not have been higher for the children, their parents, the schools, the cities, the state and the nation. Going forward, it is crucial that the problems are cleanly differentiated, diagnosed and dispatched.

The wrongdoing of the implicated teachers and governors should have been articulated and dealt with solely in terms of routine professional misconduct. As regards the former, the means to do this have long been available through the professional misconduct procedure and in the *Teachers' Standards* which stipulate that '[t]eachers uphold public trust in the profession and maintain high standards of ethics and behaviour, within and outside school'.[224] As regards the latter, the Education Committee Report noted that 'the greater autonomy of academies makes it easier for a group of similar-minded people to control a school' and that 'the DfE needs to be alert to the risks of abuse of academy freedoms of all kinds and be able to respond quickly'.[225] To this end, new regulations and guidance for academies were issued in the years following the Trojan Horse Affair which provide for checking, monitoring and disciplining rogue governors.[226] Again, expectations and allegiances would be further clarified with the introduction of a BSB-CD5-style professional standard so that governors could be sanctioned appropriately for misconduct of the sort seen during the Affair.[227] To avoid a repeat of the disastrous NCTL hearings, the government would need to improve its procurement processes to ensure that legal services are outsourced, if at all, to capable law firms. The current conception of extremism, widely invoked in the press and cursorily discussed in the official reports, simply confused matters when it could not be proved, became tied up with non-existent issues of radicalisation and terrorism, and ended up playing no role in the final disciplinary proceedings against the teachers. In the interests of depoliticisation, simplification and efficacy, extremism should be removed altogether from the vocabulary of educational regulation.

[224] NCTL and TRA, 'Guidance for School Leaders, School Staff and Governing Bodies' (DfE, July 2011), part 2: Personal and Professional Conduct, p. 14.

[225] HCEC, 'Extremism in Schools: The Trojan Horse Affair', p. 3.

[226] DfE, (1) *Governance Handbook: Academy Trusts and Maintained Schools* (DfE, October 2020), pp. 38–40, 102; (2) *A Competency Framework for Governance: The Knowledge, Skills and Behaviours Needed for Effective Governance in Maintained Schools, Academies and Multi-academy Trusts* (DfE, January 2017); (3) *Schools Causing Concern: Guidance for Local Authorities and Regional Schools Commissioners on How to Work with Schools to Support Improvements to Educational Performance, and on Using Their Intervention Powers* (DfE, September 2020).

[227] See Chapter 5.

There are also two distinct collective aspects of the Trojan Horse Affair which need to be addressed discretely. First, the Clarke Report noted that the ideological agenda being pushed in the Birmingham schools 'appears to stem from an international movement to increase the role of Islam in education'.[228] As discussed in Chapter 5, this could easily be curtailed or prevented as part of a general drive to restrict the foreign funding of charities (including schools and madrassas) and a civil blacklist of specified groups deemed seditious or subversive. There is an ongoing and systemic vulnerability in this regard as many academies have significant financial deficits which, when coupled with limited transparency as regards funding agreements, sponsors and academy chains, present a tempting target for anyone seeking to acquire influence over educational institutions.[229] Increased state investment would go some way to countering this, but if similar problems recur and the rogues responsible are found to have some kind of material connection to malign organisations, then the state should have the power to dissolve their financial and organisational capabilities. The point is to stress that certain groups, not conservative values or entire religions, are the real target. The same holds for the second issue, clannism. The nepotistic and intolerant network identified by Baroness Warsi is a classic manifestation of this. These group units revolve around extended family ties and are the subject of Chapter 8 where the appropriate countermeasures are discussed. For now, it suffices to say that the danger they present to schools, though severe, is more to do with corruption than anything related to radicalisation or terror. On the available evidence, it is difficult to determine whether subversion or clannism was central to the Trojan Horse Affair, but both should be guarded against, regardless.

Specifics aside, there are wider problems with the schools system which can be solved only with political vision. First, the Affair revealed thoroughgoing incompetence throughout the British state. From central government downwards, there were catastrophic failures in terms of understanding, articulation, coordination, outsourcing and proactivity, culminating in an unresolved mess. This has been compounded by persistent 'ungoverned spaces' like illegal schools and unregistered madrassas as well as the failure of co-regulation in the private sector with the regulators' capture by the very schools they were created to supervise. The authorities look ridiculous and have handed ample ammunition to cranks. Although the civil service has been threatened with a 'hard rain', it remains to be seen whether the state can be revitalised to the extent that it could deal competently with

[228] Clarke Report, p. 48. For a similar interpretation and discussion, see Sean Oliver-Dee, *Courting Islam: US–British Engagement with Islam since the European Colonial Period* (Lanham, MD: Lexington Books, 2020), pp. 51, 128–31.

[229] See HCEC, (1) '*Academies and Free Schools*, Fourth Report of Session 2014–15' (House of Commons, HC 258, March 2015), pp. 3–4 and (2) '*A Ten-Year Plan for School and College Funding*, Tenth Report of Session 2017–19' (House of Commons, HC 969, July 2019), pp. 14–20.

challenges of this complexity in future.[230] To their credit, Ofsted and its current Chief Inspector, Amanda Spielman, have made commendable efforts to pressure the government to address these issues.[231] Second, the unnecessary complexity and piecemeal character of education law make it expensive to navigate and, in all likelihood, an impediment to the creation of new institutions and the good governance of existing ones. For example, John Bowen raises a valid point when he writes that, at the very least, 'the matter showed that the boundaries between legitimate and illegitimate introduction of religious elements into a school were unclear'.[232] There would be great value in a consolidation and simplification programme that managed to avoid levelling all difference based on the view that any divergence in quality or substance threatens children's autonomy and rights.[233] Finally, and most importantly, it is vital that Muslim or Muslim-majority schools (or indeed those of any other religion) are neither attacked nor defended on a class basis as expressions or extensions of a faith. Rather, they should be viewed in Gierkean terms and treated as individual institutions whose primary purpose is education. New Labour's promotion of faith schools with a diversity of ethoses led to a warped understanding of their nature and purpose as well as official timidity in the face of serious problems. This must be reversed and the original position, of schools with a religious character complementary both to their *raison d'être* and to the common good, restored. Regulating education is an inescapably moral enterprise and making a success of it requires a level of conviction and lucidity that only pluralism can provide.

[230] Francis Elliot, 'Hard Rain Is Going to Fall on Civil Service, Says Dominic Cummings' (*The Times*, 25 June 2020).

[231] See Spielman, 'Annual Reports'. [232] *On British Islam*, p. 204.

[233] Roger Marples, 'Against Faith Schools: A Philosophical Argument for Children's Rights' (2005) 10(2) *International Journal of Children's Spirituality* 133–47.

7

Elections

7.1 Introduction

This chapter examines the link between election fraud and British Muslim populations. It begins with a brief history of electoral fraud from the earliest times to draw out the recurring challenges and past attempts to meet them. This is followed by an overview of the workings of modern election fraud encompassing systemic vulnerabilities, opportunities and mechanisms as well as the attendant statistical difficulties. This sets the phenomenon in context and explains the nature of its association with South Asian Muslims. The chapter proceeds with a theoretical discussion on the ways in which election fraud can be interpreted and addressed through law. It notes that a liberal individualistic approach can justify strong safeguards against individual wrongdoing but struggles to account for the collective dimensions of elections, while multiculturalism pays greater heed to the importance of groups but suffers from an indiscriminate understanding of the various types. The chapter concludes with a pluralist response which systematises the individual and group elements of the democratic process before developing an historically informed programme for practical reform. For convenience, the four leading judgments will be referred to, following their introduction, as '[year] [City] case' in both the main text and the footnotes.

7.2 A Brief History of Corruption

English election law grew out of the medieval canonical system which recognised something 'very like a modern right' to vote. This provided safeguards to ensure that it had substance as well as form, such as a requirement to give adequate notice prior to the gathering of eligible participants to enable them all to participate.[1] Then, as now, the point was to select a suitable candidate for a particular office, duty or obligation; then, as now, sophisticated measures were devised to ensure transparency,

1 See Richard H. Helmholz, '*Fundamental Human Rights in Medieval Law*' (Chicago: University of Chicago Fulton Lectures, 2001), pp. 1–20 at pp. 6–9.

non-manipulability, honesty, strategy-proofness and accountability.[2] Nevertheless, pre-modern elections were vulnerable to mob violence, royal interference, financial corruption and litigation.

Medieval elections were often 'chaotic and sometimes violent'.[3] Ordinary people were politically conscious, civic-minded and collectively self-assured. They might take direct action if the 'wrong' person got elected, if the process was thought unfair, if a general sense of disenfranchisement took hold, if subversion was deemed necessary to check corruption, or even if talk from the elite rang hollow. York, for example, was in 'an almost constant state of turmoil' between 1462 and 1536, suffering through countless popular petitions, civic disobedience, procedural wrangling, town hall scuffles, at least six election riots, seven enclosure riots and two general uprisings.[4] Well into the nineteenth century, elections were characterised by 'an unusual amount of drunkenness' and 'much colourful employment' in the form of brass bands and drummers (to drown out the opposition), kidnapping operations (to decommission hostile voters) and armed gangs of intimidators with a proclivity for clubbing opponents.[5] Hustings were equally raucous:

> The candidates were proposed and seconded in face of each other . . . in the presence of a vast tumultuous crowd, three-quarters of whom were generally drunk, and all of whom were inflamed by the passion of furious partisanship . . . Brickbats, dead cats and rotten eggs came flying like bewildering meteors across the eyes of rival politicians on the hustings. The crowds generally enlivened the time by a series of faction fights among themselves.[6]

Intimidation could come from above as well as below. When the canons of Winchester set about electing a new bishop in 1173, Henry II wrote to spare them the trouble: 'I command you to hold a free election, but I do not want you to accept anyone but my clerk Richard, archdeacon of Poitiers.'[7] Centuries later, the Tudor Crown took an equally pragmatic view of elections and stacked the Commons with obsequious servants often elected unopposed following surreptitious backroom deals.[8] In 1514, the Commons was also granted, at the expense

[2] Sara and Joel Uckelman, 'Strategy and Manipulation in Medieval Elections' (University of Amsterdam COMSOC Seminar, 2010) 1–12, pp. 1–2; Iain McLean, 'The Borda and Condorcet Principles: Three Medieval Applications' (1990) 7(2) *Social Choice and Welfare* 99–108; Iain McLean, Haidee Lorrey and Josep M. Colomer, 'Social Choice in Medieval Europe' (2008) 4 (1) *Electronic Journal for History of Probability and Statistics* 1–23.

[3] Caroline Morris, *Parliamentary Elections, Representation and the Law* (Oxford: Hart, 2012), p. 71.

[4] Christian D. Liddy and Jelle Haemers, 'Popular Politics in the Late Medieval City: York and Bruges' (2013) 128(533) *English Historical Review* 771–805, pp. 771, 777, 789, 792.

[5] Robert Pearce and Roger Stern, *Government and Reform: Britain 1815–1918* (2nd ed., London: Hodder & Stoughton, 2000), p. 15.

[6] Contemporary journalistic account quoted in ibid., p. 16. See also Charles Dickens, *The Pickwick Papers* (London: Penguin Classics, 2003).

[7] Björn Weiler, '8 Things You (Probably) Didn't Know about Medieval Elections' (*History Extra*, 30 October 2019), thing 7.

[8] Simon Payling, 'Electoral Independence in Tudor England' (*The History of Parliament: British Political, Social and Local History*, 27 April 2015).

of the courts, the privilege of regulating its own composition and determining the outcome of disputed elections; this jurisdiction would eventually become exclusive and lasted until 1868 when it was ceded back to the judiciary.[9] Likewise, Charles I sought to abolish balloting boxes because secret voting caused him 'manifold inconveniences', namely a spirit of independence and reduced scope for intimidation, as he strove to retain control over the boroughs and corporations of England.[10]

Elections could also be swung with cold hard cash. Although anti-corruption legislation was passed periodically from 1695, the 'unreformed system' became a byword for vice.[11] As early as the 1750s, for example, William Hogarth painted *Four Prints of an Election* satirising Georgian elections in all their grotesque splendour.[12] By 1770, the Earl of Chatham was railing against the influx of foreign-won money:

> The riches of Asia have been poured in upon us, and have brought with them not only Asiatic luxury, but, I fear, Asiatic principles of government. Without connections, without any natural interest in the soil, the importers of foreign gold have forced their way into Parliament by such a torrent of private corruption as no private hereditary fortune could resist ... The corruption of the people is the great original cause of the discontents of the people themselves, of the enterprises of the Crown, and the notorious decay of the internal vigour of the constitution.[13]

Thomas Cochrane – the inspiration for C. S. Forester's Horatio Hornblower and Patrick O'Brian's Jack Aubrey – became embroiled in the Great Stock Exchange Fraud of 1814, but subsequently distinguished himself in the Commons by delivering a speech 'so abusive that the record had to be filled with asterisks to cover the swear words'.[14] County seats were overwhelmingly dominated by the established gentry, but 'pocket boroughs' (sometimes containing few or no residents while returning two MPs) could be purchased by virtually anyone with enough wealth to ensure that he had, as the 'celebrated auctioneer' of the Gatton constituency put it,

> no hurricanes to dread, no passions to allay, no tormenting claims of insolent electors to evade, no tinkers' wives to kiss, no impossible promises to make, none

[9] Morris, *Parliamentary Elections, Representation and the Law*, pp. 76–86.

[10] Charles Gross, 'The Early History of the Ballot in England' (1898) 3(3) *American Historical Review* 456–63, p. 458.

[11] Corrupt Practices Act 1695; Parliamentary Elections Act 1770.

[12] Eveline Cruikshanks, *Hogarth's England* (London: Folio Society, 1957), pp. 32–6.

[13] William Pitt the Elder, Earl of Chatham, 'The State of the Nation' (1770) extracted in Francis Thackeray (ed.), *A History of the Right Honourable William Pitt, Earl of Chatham* (London: C. & J. Rivington, Vol. 2 of 2, 1877), p. 161. See also Philip Lawson and Jim Phillips, '"Our Execrable Banditti": Perceptions of Nabobs in Mid-Eighteenth Century Britain' (1984) 16 (3) *Albion: A Quarterly Journal Concerned with British Studies* 225–41, p. 238.

[14] Brian Vale, 'Introduction' to *Admiral Lord Cochrane: Memoirs of a Fighting Captain* (London: Folio Society, 2005), pp. xiv–xvi.

> of the toilsome and not very clean paths of canvassing to drudge through; but, with his mind at ease and his conscience clear, with this elegant constituency in his pocket, the honours of the state will await his plucking and with its emoluments his purse will overflow.[15]

Yet, even before the advent of mass democracy, 'there were a few people, vindictive, litigious, or touchy enough to take their cases to court', some of whom were perhaps driven by a sense of natural justice, and all of whom together left a lasting imprint on the law.[16] The small size of electorates and the ability of elite families to dominate them were constants over many centuries of legal experimentation. From the first (successful) recorded challenge to a county election in 1318 for a false return 'against the will of the community', the means of contestation evolved with the times – from direct appeals to the monarch, petitions to various courts, counter-suits using the prerogative writ of mandamus, Parliamentary committee hearings – before settling into the current petitions system overseen by an ad hoc bench of the High Court.[17] This took shape throughout the nineteenth century as the franchise expanded and modern ideals of fairness and propriety became entrenched via mass education and in successive anti-corruption statutes.[18] The three pillars of modern election law were erected in this period of 'quiet progress':[19] voter registration, a formalised controversion mechanism and defined electoral offences.

First, the Great Reform Act 1832 introduced 'an elaborate system of registration' to standardise and reduce the costs of verification and to allay fears that the newly widened franchise would open the floodgates to personation.[20] The resulting system provided for annually updated registers overseen by 'revising barristers' who would hear objections and strike off the recently deceased and anyone found guilty of corruption. Nevertheless, it failed in its objects on account of being too ponderous, too off-putting for apathetic voters and too open to abuse by fraudsters, party agents and incompetent bureaucrats.[21] Despite piecemeal adjustments, the registration process remained 'exceptionally slow, inefficient and politicised', and made no accommodations for servicemen posted abroad, until it was greatly simplified and extended by the

15 From the memoirs of Thomas Holcroft quoted in Pearce and Stern, *Government and Reform*, p. 15.

16 J. E. Neale quoted in Morris, *Parliamentary Elections, Representation and the Law*, p. 68.

17 Morris, ibid., pp. 68–73; John Baker, *An Introduction to English Legal History* (5th ed., Oxford: Oxford University Press, 2019), pp. 158–9; Ludwig Riess, *The History of the English Electoral Law in the Middle Ages*, K. L. Wood-Legh (transl.) (Cambridge: Cambridge University Press, 2011), pp. 4–7.

18 See generally Eric M. Uslaner, *The Historical Roots of Corruption: Mass Education, Economic Inequality, and State Capacity* (Cambridge: Cambridge University Press, 2017).

19 G. M. Trevelyan quoted in David Loades (ed.), *Reader's Guide to British History* (London: Fitzroy Dearborn, Vol. 1, A-L, 2003), p. 586.

20 Charles Seymour, *Electoral Reform in England and Wales: The Development and Operation of the Parliamentary Franchise, 1832–1885* (New Haven, CT: Yale University Press, 1915), pp. 106–8, 113–16.

21 Ibid., pp. 112–16.

Representation of the People Act 1918.[22] Thereafter, it was periodically improved and personation seemingly remains uncommon, although cases of child voters – one *in utero* – persisted into the mid-twentieth century.[23] The initial stringency and prolonged relaxation of registration law reflected Victorian anxieties about mass democracy and revolution.[24] With hindsight, it would be easy to overstate the level of contemporary dissatisfaction as 'rising prosperity was carrying successive layers of working men up to the [retreating franchise] boundary' and the procedures themselves 'did very broadly produce an electorate which enjoyed some social cohesion'.[25]

Second, the accepted mode of disputing elections completed the long transition from 'arms, malice, and menacing' to formalised election petitions.[26] For centuries prior to the Election Petitions and Corrupt Practices (or Parliamentary Elections) Act 1868, election disputes were heard by the House of Commons itself. The inevitable skulduggery, aversion to scandal, and reluctance to stigmatise the respectable had long been resented. After the failure of various compromise measures, a rare bout of cross-partisan radicalism transferred jurisdiction outright to the courts.[27] This proved effective and popular as the number of failed election petitions began to fall and incremental refinements were introduced in subsequent decades.[28] Despite an increase since the 1940s, the number of petitions has never again reached pre-reform Victorian levels.[29] Very little of substance has changed since then excepting the creation of the Electoral Commission in 2001 to investigate and regulate financing and standards.[30] As with the Charity Commission, Ofsted and the old Commons committee system, it has been criticised for incompetence and political bias.[31]

22 Peter Keeling, 'The Armed Forces and Parliamentary Elections in the United Kingdom, 1885–1914' (2019) 134(569) *English Historical Review* 881–913, pp. 889, 912.

23 Peter Keeling, 'Child Voters' (2020) 70(7) *History Today* 42–51; Electoral Commission, 'Electoral Fraud Data' (accessed 2 March 2021): www.electoralcommission.org.uk/who-we-are-and-what-we-do/our-views-and-research/our-research/electoral-fraud-data.

24 Seymour, *Electoral Reform in England and Wales*, p. 116.

25 K. Theodore Hoppen, 'The Franchise and Electoral Politics in England and Ireland 1832–1885' (1985) 70(229) *History* 202–17, pp. 204–5.

26 Freedom of Election Act 1275 quoted in Caroline Morris, 'From "Arms, Malice, and Menacing" to the Courts: Disputed Elections and the Reform of the Election Petitions System' (2012) 32(2) *Legal Studies* 226–54, p. 229.

27 Ibid., pp. 238–41; Seymour, *Electoral Reform in England and Wales*, pp. 422–4.

28 Ibid., pp. 241–3; Ibid., pp. 425–7.

29 See Caroline Morris and Stuart Wilks-Heeg, '"Reports of My Death Have Been Greatly Exaggerated": The Continuing Role and Relevance of Election Petitions in Challenging Election Results in the UK' (2019) 18(1) *Election Law Journal* 31–46.

30 Political Parties, Elections and Referendums Act (PPERA) 2000; Political Parties and Elections Act 2009.

31 Among many examples, see Nigel Vinson, 'The Electoral Commission Needs Reforming. Will Anyone Dare Try?' (*The Spectator*, 5 June 2015); BBC News, 'Darren Grimes: Brexit Campaigner Wins Appeal against £20,000 Fine' (*BBC News*, 19 July 2019); BBC News, 'PMQs: Peter Bone Calls for Abolition of Electoral Commission' (*BBC News*, 13 May 2020); Harry Yorke, 'Electoral Commission Should Be Overhauled or Abolished, Say Conservative Party' (*The Telegraph*, 29 August 2020).

Indeed, the Commission's relationship with the parties it regulates has been characterised as an 'ongoing contest' over compliance, loophole exploitation and regulatory capture.[32] Taken in isolation, however, the 'new' election courts have had 'but slight effect upon electoral morality' as they embody a 'rather haphazard inquisitorial method' and rely upon individuals to bring petitions who may themselves be frustrated by extra-legal means.[33]

The final and perhaps most crucial strand of the Victorian anti-corruption drive was thus the passage of several acts designed to define and penalise corrupt practices. In the decades after the Great Reform Act, it became clear that intimidation and bribery were as rife as ever.[34] The general election of 1852 was so blighted by successful petitions that within two years Parliament had passed the first major Corrupt Practices Prevention Act (1854) which 'gave the first exact and complete definition of bribery'.[35] Even this had a 'negligible deterrent effect' and two more decades elapsed before the 'final attack' on corruption began.[36] The Ballot Act 1872 effected 'great institutional change' by mandating secret voting, but, according to one contemporary, it was passed 'in spite of the all but unanimous hostility of the House of Lords, the secret disapproval of the House of Commons, and the indifference of the general community'.[37] Its effects were 'marked and salutary' as mob violence, mass drunkenness and intimidation gave way to orderliness and the almost regrettable mundanity of the modern polling day.[38] Yet it was not enough. The general election of 1880 'achieved the dubious honour of producing more successful petitions than any other election after 1832'; the sheer extent of the corruption and Heliogabalian expenditure shocked even the most inured Victorians who strongly suspected that 'the evils revealed by petitions represented only the tip of the iceberg'.[39] The resulting Corrupt and Illegal Practices Prevention Act 1883 was an 'enormous advance' in the purity of elections for it set stringent campaign spending limits, refined and criminalised bribery, introduced serious sanctions for breaches and subsequently led to significant reductions in petitions.[40] The increasingly fractious situation in Ireland throughout this period prompted the creation of the offence of undue spiritual influence, expanded upon in subsequent case law, to counter the perceived influence of the Roman Catholic Church over elections.[41] The leading

32 Alastair Clark, 'The Relationship between Political Parties and Their Regulators' (2017) 23(6) *Party Politics* 646–56, p. 655.

33 Seymour, *Electoral Reform in England and Wales*, p. 427.

34 See generally Norman Gash, *Politics in the Age of Peel: A Study in the Technique of Parliamentary Representation, 1830–1850* (London: Faber Finds, 2013).

35 Seymour, *Electoral Reform in England and Wales*, p. 227; Kathryn Rix, '"The Elimination of Corrupt Practices in British Elections"? Reassessing the Impact of the 1883 Corrupt Practices Act' (2008) 123(500) *English Historical Review* 65–97, p. 67.

36 Rix, ibid., p. 68; Seymour, ibid., p. 418. 37 Seymour, ibid., pp. 431–2. 38 Ibid., pp. 432–3.

39 Rix, 'The Elimination of Corrupt Practices in British Elections', p. 67.

40 Seymour, *Electoral Reform in England and Wales*, pp. 442–51.

41 See Corrupt Practices Prevention Act 1854, s. 5; Corrupt and Illegal Practices Prevention Act 1883, s. 2. For commentary on the statutes and case law, see Aileen McColgan, 'Undue Spiritual

authority on these reforms is laudatory: 'Parliament managed within one generation to sweep away traditions that were centuries old.'[42] Likewise the pre-eminent scholar of modern election law: 'After the First World War, the twentieth century saw very few election petitions, so few that it could have confidently been said that an election petition was a rare event, to be seen perhaps once every decade or so. It was assumed that the problem of corruption, which had so plagued elections, had been eradicated.'[43]

Again, little of substance has changed in the intervening century and the anti-corruption offences are now consolidated within the Representation of the People Act 1983. Other major legislation has been either consolidatory or concerned with administrative reorganisation, restrictions based on age or other status, and updating voting methods in line with advancing technology and new lifestyles.[44] Yet corruption never died out completely. Of all public wrongs, it has a singular quality: 'there was no crime where the number of offences proved and punished bore so small a proportion to the number of offences discovered'.[45] Flawed registration requirements, the inefficiencies of the petitions system, unsatisfactory definitions, and official complacency all survived the Victorian purification process. This fact alone must qualify overly sanguine views as to the endurance and scale of electoral malpractice down to the present.[46] What is more, the cosy twentieth-century consensus that 'by the end of the nineteenth century controverted elections law was ... settled ... no longer holds'.[47] The reasons for this must now be considered in detail.

7.3 Understanding Modern Electoral Fraud

Electoral fraud is a direct threat to the integrity of any democratic process. It is a distinguishing feature of undemocratic elections in developing countries and, though less common, takes place in mature democracies such as the UK where it is often but not exclusively associated with Pakistani and Bangladeshi communities.[48] English law is concerned primarily with defining, detecting and countering electoral fraud wheresoever it originates and in whatever guise. The

Influence: A Historical Analysis' (2017) 28(2) *King's Law Journal* 279–308, pp. 282–3 and Megan Pearson, 'Undue Spiritual Influence and the Permissible Interaction of Religion and Politics' (2017) *Public Law* 562–70, pp. 562–3.

42 Cornelius O'Leary, *The Elimination of Corrupt Practices in British Elections, 1868–1911* (Oxford: Clarendon Press, 1962), p. 233.

43 Morris, 'From "Arms, Malice, and Menacing" to the Courts', pp. 241–2.

44 See, for example, Representation of the People Act 1918; Representation of the People Act 1949; PPERA 2000; Electoral Administration Act (EAA) 2006.

45 Seymour, *Electoral Reform in England and Wales*, p. 194.

46 Rix, 'The Elimination of Corrupt Practices in British Elections', pp. 65–6.

47 Morris, 'From "Arms, Malice, and Menacing" to the Courts', pp. 241–2.

48 Eleanor Hill, Maria Sobolewska, Stuart Wilks-Heeg and Magda Borkowska, 'Explaining Electoral Fraud in an Advanced Democracy: Fraud Vulnerabilities, Opportunities and Facilitating Mechanisms in British Elections' (2017) 19(4) *British Journal of Politics and International Relations* 772–89, p. 772. See also the major case law cited below.

range of offences designed to tackle its various manifestations include voting more than once, exercising undue influence, bribery, treating, personation, making false postal or proxy vote applications, and making false statements about a candidate's character or conduct.[49] An election will be avoided (nullified) by such practices and/or by general corruption when these have so extensively prevailed that they may be reasonably supposed to have affected the result.[50] Electoral fraud has a tendency to spread across multiple authorities and activities and thus is often intertwined with other forms of corruption concerning public procurement, financial crime and illegal immigration.[51] In practice, the commission of such offences is facilitated by a 'causal chain' of systemic vulnerabilities, opportunities and mechanisms.[52]

7.3.1 Vulnerabilities

Any democracy will have inherent vulnerabilities that make fraud possible to begin with. In the British context, some of these are structural and ineradicable whereas others are generated by potentially ameliorable social problems. As regards the former, majoritarian first-past-the-post systems of national and local elections involve higher, winner-takes-all stakes which create greater incentives for competing parties to strategise compared with systems based on proportionate representation.[53] As regards the latter, inequality creates propitious conditions for electoral fraud. For example, patronage and bribery are more effective in poorer communities where financial rewards or improved status have higher value; patriarchal family structures, language and knowledge barriers among new immigrants and women, and the influence of 'homeland' political culture and organisations all increase the scope for manipulation in terms of postal voter fraud, personation and undue influence; and racial discrimination may generate a perception that ethnicity is an obstacle to genuine political engagement which

49 Representation of the People Act 1983, ss. 61(2), 115, 113, 114, 60, 62A, 106. For a detailed overview of these and other relevant offences, see Bob Posner and Louise Footner (eds.), *Schofield's Election Law* (3rd ed., London: Sweet and Maxwell, updated to December 2019), Vol. 1, part 6: 'Election Offences', chs. 13–16. Although corrupt practices are punished more severely than illegal ones, the somewhat academic distinction between them is reviewed at paras. 13-001 and 14-001.

50 Ss. 159(1) and 164(1).

51 Eric Pickles, 'Securing the Ballot: Report of Sir Eric Pickles' Review into Electoral Fraud' (Cabinet Office, August 2016), p. 2; John Stewart, 'A Banana Republic? The Investigation into Electoral Fraud by the Birmingham Election Court' (2006) 59(4) *Parliamentary Affairs* 654–67, p. 667.

52 Hill et al., 'Explaining Electoral Fraud in an Advanced Democracy', p. 773 footnote 64. For a useful tabular summary, see Maria Sobolewska, Stuart Wilks-Heeg, Eleanor Hill and Magda Borkowska, 'Understanding Electoral Fraud Vulnerability in Pakistani and Bangladeshi Origin Communities in England: A View of Local Political Activists' (Electoral Commission, January 2015), p. 23.

53 Hill et al., 'Explaining Electoral Fraud in an Advanced Democracy', p. 774; Fabrice Lehoucq and Kiril Kolev, 'Electoral Fraud Is Less Common in Proportional Representation Systems than It Is in Plurality Systems' (Democratic Audit UK, 19 May 2015).

can only be overcome by other means.[54] Most of the highest risk areas in the UK have above-average rates of deprivation.[55] These are undoubtedly vast and difficult problems for any government to solve, although they can be mitigated through greater investment in deprived areas, appropriate anti-discrimination measures, public education and immigration law reforms. In short, systemic vulnerability to electoral fraud can be reduced by addressing various kinds of inequality.

7.3.2 Opportunities

Weaknesses in the regulatory regime create opportunities for rogues to exploit. Since the turn of the twenty-first century, the number of controverted elections has surged while electoral fraud has been effected by post, personation and intimidation.[56] Each shall be taken in turn.

7.3.2.1 Postal Voting

Postal voting on demand allows for electors to apply for, fill out and return a ballot paper by post.[57] It is the best-studied and most common type of electoral fraud and accounts for the majority of allegations and convictions over the past two decades.[58] Despite the introduction of postal voting in 2001, voter turnout at the general election that year fell to its lowest since near-universal franchise was established in 1918.[59] While several localised trials of all-postal elections recorded drastic increases in turnout, with the sole exception of the Brexit referendum in 2016, it has never again come close to the levels seen in and before 1997.[60] Turnout in local and devolved elections has been lower still.[61] Perhaps the most notable impact of the innovation was to trigger justified fears over widespread fraud and New Labour's party-political motivations behind the move, both of which have undermined public confidence in the democratic process.[62] Voting by post lacks the usual secrecy and security of the polling station and means that the elector – who may have poor English and even poorer knowledge of the relevant forms and law – can be subjected to intimidation, undue influence and vote-buying by family

[54] Ibid., pp. 775, 778–9. [55] Ibid., p. 776.

[56] Ibid., p. 780; Morris, *Parliamentary Elections, Representation and the Law*, pp. 86–7.

[57] Representation of the People (England and Wales) Regulations 2001/341, Schedule 4, Regulation 51.

[58] Hill et al., 'Explaining Electoral Fraud in an Advanced Democracy', p. 780.

[59] Toby S. James, 'Fewer Costs, More Votes? United Kingdom Innovations in Election Administration 2000–2007 and the Effect on Voter Turnout' (2011) 10(1) *Election Law Journal: Rules, Politics, and Policy* 37–52, p. 38.

[60] Ibid., pp. 42–3; D. Clark, 'Voter Turnout in General Elections and in the Brexit Referendum in the United Kingdom from 1918 to 2019' (*Statista*, 3 February 2021).

[61] Daniel Wainwright, 'Council Elections: Why Don't People Vote?' (*BBC News*, 9 April 2019); Oliver Hawkins, 'Scottish Parliament Elections: 2016' (House of Commons, CBP7599, 20 May 2016), pp. 21–2.

[62] James, 'Fewer Costs, More Votes?', pp. 37, 39–41.

members or community activists within their own home.[63] In some instances, thc rightful recipients never received their ballot papers at all, these apparently having being completed and returned by somebody else entirely.[64] In other cases, electors would bring their entire family's signed but incomplete ballots before their preferred candidate to demonstrate loyalty with a view to securing future claims on the candidate's services.[65] The watershed 2005 Birmingham case, *Akhtar and others* v. *Jahan and others Iqbal and others* v. *Islam and others* [2005] All ER (D), concerned postal voting in the local elections in the Birmingham wards of Bordesley Green and Aston. The Commissioner uncovered postal electoral fraud so severe that it would 'disgrace a banana republic' and avoided the elections.[66] In Bordesley Green, at least 1,500 and potentially over 2,000 bogus votes had been cast; in Aston, it was around 1,000.[67] The Aston Labour respondents had been working in a warehouse to fill out blank ballot papers while altering or destroying those that went against them. The Bordesley Green respondents had used multiple methods of personation. All this had been compounded by bureaucratic failures: first, because the returning officer had been overwhelmed by an unexpected number of postal votes and, second, because the returning officer had also breached regulations by allowing votes to be transported informally and insecurely. Further, Muslim community leaders had abused the respect and trust they enjoyed by persuading voters to hand over unused or completed ballots to party canvassers.[68] Likewise, the Labour Party had lost a significant number of Muslim voters after the Iraq War and had sought to shore up their formerly secure wards by large-scale fraud.[69] Commissioner Richard Mawrey QC also noted that it was 'inescapable' that corrupt and illegal practices were going on across Birmingham and not just within these wards.[70] He outlined his concerns that the electoral system did not provide for adequate identity checks, did not ensure the secure delivery of ballot envelopes to their intended recipients and lacked the necessary resources and powers to detect fraud.[71] He ended his judgment with a damning indictment of the legal safeguards against fraud and the government's complacent approach to reform: 'The systems to deal with fraud are not working well. They are not working badly. The fact is that there are no systems to deal realistically with fraud and there never have been. Until there are, fraud will continue unabated.'[72] A prescient article following the 2005 Birmingham case concluded that 'the danger of electoral corruption and fraud is that it is presently hidden. The Birmingham election court exposed its presence in one major British city. It is possible it would be found elsewhere if the same degree of scrutiny were applied.'[73]

[63] Hill et al., 'Explaining Electoral Fraud in an Advanced Democracy', p. 780.
[64] Ibid., pp. 779, 782. [65] Ibid., p. 784.
[66] *Akhtar and others* v. *Jahan and others Iqbal and others* v. *Islam and others* [2005] All ER (D) 15 per Commissioner Richard Mawrey, QC at paras. 712, 716.
[67] Paras. 419, 525–6. [68] Para. 696. [69] Para. 697. [70] Para. 691.
[71] Paras. 72–96; Stewart, 'A Banana Republic?', pp. 661–2. [72] Para. 717.
[73] Stewart, 'A Banana Republic?', p. 667.

Another case arose from the 2007 Aston elections involving one of the original respondents from the 2005 litigation, a Mr Muhammed Afzal. By this time, the initial finding of guilt against him had been overturned by the Court of Appeal and he had been successfully elected to the council. This second case concerned allegations of a 'smear campaign' of false statements by the respondent against his defeated Liberal Democrat rival (the petitioner) via leaflets and vehicular loudspeakers parading about the neighbourhood on polling day. The Election Court dismissed the petition, although, in his judgment, Commissioner Timothy Straker QC noted that neither the petitioner nor his agent had behaved 'creditably or honourably' during the campaign.[74] Indeed, one of their own supporters' cars had been recorded blaring 'Kick out Labour. Labour means corruption, the party of [the unbelievers].'[75]

7.3.2.2 Personation

Personation occurs where somebody unlawfully casts the vote of another person who may be living, deceased or fictitious. In the 2005 Birmingham case, Commissioner Mawrey QC identified a non-exhaustive list of fourteen methods by which to commit personation, including roll-stuffing and vote appropriation.[76] The former involves registering the dead, the fictitious or the ineligible to inflate the electoral roll so the personator can vote by post or in person on behalf of the bogus elector. The latter involves voting on behalf of a real person who has either had their postal ballot stolen or has voluntarily given their voting card to another who then votes in person.[77] In some cases, multiple people are temporarily moved into an address shortly before an election and moved out again shortly thereafter.[78] By these means and others, entire 'armies of ghost voters' can be conjured on to the electoral roll.[79] There are several illustrative examples from the case law.

In *Simmons* v. *Khan* [2008] EWHC B4 (QB), a Conservative candidate for Slough Borough Council, one Eshaq Khan, and his agents had been inflating the electoral roll with an abnormally high number of new voters with Asian names shortly before the election, many of whom turned out to be fictitious or at least not residents of the relevant ward. One of the properties investigated contained a Polish couple but 'no Asians and certainly not nineteen Asians'.[80] Bogus registrations and postal votes were uncovered at many other addresses alongside the 'virtual migration' of voters from a ward with no Conservative candidate to the ward in question.[81] In short, extensive personation via roll-stuffing had in this case been committed blatantly and with appalling ease.[82]

[74] *Aehmed* v. *Afzal & Anor* [2008] EWHC B5 (QB) at para. 195. [75] Para. 196.
[76] Paras. 386–413.
[77] For more detail on these methods, see James Slater and Bob Watt, 'In Defence of Democracy: The Criminalisation of Impersonation' (2015) 14(2) *Election Law Journal* 165–85.
[78] See *Erlam & Ors* v. *Rahman & Anor* [2015] EWHC 1215 (QB) per Mawrey QC at paras. 74–81.
[79] *Ali* v. *Bashir & Anor* [2013] EWHC 2572 (QB) per Mawrey QC at para. 281.
[80] Paras. 190, 251. [81] Para. 301. [82] Paras. 324–8, 345.

Khan and five associates were subsequently convicted and imprisoned.[83] Similarly, in *Ali* v. *Bashir & Anor* [2013] EWHC 2572 (QB), which arose from the election for Woking Borough Council the previous year, a significant number of fictitious voters were entered on to the electoral roll in respect of addresses controlled by the respondent, a Mr Mohammed Bashir of the Liberal Democrat Party. Commissioner Mawrey QC again identified all the hallmarks of widespread fraud: an abnormally high number of late registrations, multiple registrations at the same property, a high proportion of postal to personal votes and an abnormally high turnout.[84] In total, twenty-two in-person ballots and sixty-four postal ballots were identified as products of personation or registration fraud.[85] The accused, his agents and his extended family had also sought to cover their tracks by lying about their involvement and the extent of their activities.[86] Five members of the extended family, but not the candidate himself, were subsequently convicted.[87] It should also be noted that personation can be committed inadvertently as occurred when the violinist Nigel Kennedy admitted to asking a friend to vote in person on behalf of his absent wife (he was not charged as the police did not commence an investigation within the required twelve months).[88] Similar behaviour occurs on a larger scale in Northern Ireland and in South Asian communities where asking people informally to cast a ballot without an official proxy vote is seen as a matter of convenience.[89] In other cases, people using informal names different from their birth name simply forget which was entered on the voting forms.[90]

7.3.2.3 Intimidation

Intimidation outside polling stations and elsewhere is also being reported in some areas. In the 2005 Birmingham case, it was noted that one Somali postman (an illegal immigrant) delivering ballot packs was threatened or blackmailed into handing them over to the fraudsters and that the same could easily have happened to others.[91] In *Erlam & Ors* v. *Rahman & Anor* [2015] EWHC 1215 (QB), one voter was recorded crying outside the polling station having been told that it was 'un-Islamic' and the mark of a bad Muslim not to vote for Lutfur Rahman in the 2014 Tower Hamlets mayoral election.[92] In other cases, competing gangs of activists have surrounded voters and even a returning officer on their way into the polling station to influence or intimidate them.[93] In 2010, Jerome Taylor, a reporter for *The Independent*, was physically attacked in Tower

[83] Dominic Kennedy, 'Six Jailed for Postal Vote Fraud over Rigged Election in Slough' (*The Times*, 2 May 2009).

[84] Paras. 115–31. [85] Paras. 6, 97. [86] Paras. 106, 135–6, 167.

[87] BBC News, 'Five Sentenced for Maybury and Sheerwater Ballot Fraud' (*BBC News*, 9 June 2015).

[88] Slater and Watt, 'In Defence of Democracy' [draft version], pp. 11–12.

[89] Hill et al., 'Explaining Electoral Fraud in an Advanced Democracy', pp. 780–1. [90] Ibid.

[91] Paras. 90, 406. [92] Pickles Report, p. 45. For more detail, see Mawrey, QC at paras. 575–624.

[93] Pickles Report, p. 8.

Hamlets for investigating allegations of registration fraud.[94] Abuse has also been directed towards campaigners and candidates themselves.[95] Convictions for such 'thuggish behaviour' are exceptionally rare, however, as the law 'requires a high degree of physical intimidation to be applied to the voter'.[96] Indeed, many victims of threatening or intimidating conduct at the polls would be 'disappointed, even horrified' that the law can do little to protect them.[97]

Undue spiritual influence is a related phenomenon practically unheard of since Victorian times. The Tower Hamlets case became infamous largely on account of this novel dimension, although it also found bribery, personation, postal vote fraud, illegal provision of false information, illegal voting, making false statements about candidates, and the illegal employment of paid canvassers.[98] Part of the wider s. 115 offence of undue influence, 'the mischief at which [spiritual injury] is directed is the misuse of religion for political purposes'.[99] It means that clergy cannot use their religious office to convince the faithful that it is their religious duty to vote in a certain way.[100] It is applicable to any religion, but must be aimed at those from a 'community which is traditional, respectful of authority and, possibly, not fully integrated with the other communities living in the same area'.[101] Controversially, Mr Rahman had been currying favour with Islamic religious figures for some time before the controverted 2014 election in a community where Bangladeshi Muslims are the largest racial and religious group.[102] As campaigning began, however, he made increasing use of the 'religious card'.[103] His core message was that Islam was under threat and it was the religious duty of any true Muslim to vote for Rahman.[104] A letter signed by 101 Muslim clerics, arranged by the influential Chairman of the Council of Mosques, was also placed in the local Bengali newspaper exhorting the faithful to 'make Lutfur Rahman victorious' by showing their 'unlimited support' as a matter of religious duty.[105] This contributed to a finding of undue spiritual influence as well as the decision to avoid the election.[106] Despite this ruling in the election court, no concurrent criminal prosecutions were brought nor any convictions secured because 'the policing of the election and the subsequent investigation were deficient in too many areas'.[107] In 2017, Rahman lost an appeal against his disqualification, but this expired in 2020 and he is reportedly 'on manoeuvres' to run again in 2022.[108]

[94] Jerome Taylor, 'The First Punch Came, Landing on My Nose, Sending Blood Down My Face' (*The Independent*, 22 October 2011).

[95] See Neil Johnston and Noel Dempsey, 'Abuse and Intimidation of Candidates and the Public in UK Elections' (House of Commons, CDP0151, July 2017); Sarah Priddy and Noel Dempsey, 'Intimidation in Public Life' (House of Commons, CDP0124, May 2019).

[96] 2015 Tower Hamlets case, paras. 168, 624. [97] Ibid., para. 624. [98] Pickles Report, p. 65.

[99] Para. 158. [100] Ibid. [101] Paras. 151, 152, 159. [102] Paras. 179, 530. [103] Para. 529.

[104] Ibid. [105] Paras. 158, 532, 546–66. [106] Paras. 672, 680.

[107] Her Majesty's Inspectorate of Constabulary and Fire & Rescue Services (HMICFRS), *Operation Lynemouth: Final Report* (HMICFRS, March 2019), p. 3.

[108] *R (On the Application of Rahman)* v. *The Local Government Election Court* [2017] EWHC 1413 (Admin); Dave Hill, 'Tower Hamlets: Return of Lutfur Rahman?' (OnLondon, 12 November

Nevertheless, Mawrey QC urged Parliament to reconsider undue spiritual influence and restate it clearly in a form suitable for the twenty-first century.[109]

7.3.2.4 Typology of Problems with the Electoral System

7.3.2.4.1 Regulatory Problems

There are essentially three types of problem with the electoral system: regulatory, bureaucratic and structural. The first concerns defects in the rules governing elections. The 2005 Birmingham case revealed that 'cheating the system would scarcely require the talents of Professor Moriarty'.[110] The voter registration and identification requirements include the following weaknesses:[111] the address to which the ballot package can be sent need not be the same as the elector's address; signature requirements are effectively useless in the absence of stringent witness requirements and checks by the Elections Office; the elector need not return the ballot to the Elections Office themselves, meaning that candidates or canvassers can handle them; and it is relatively easy to harvest both unused and completed ballot packages by theft or deception.[112] Personation, although potentially risky at the polling station, can also be perpetrated on a small scale in the absence of identity checks.[113] The government's position at the time was: 'There are no proposals to change the rules governing election procedures for the next election, including those for postal voting. The systems already in place to deal with the allegations of electoral fraud are clearly working.'[114] Mawrey QC lamented that concerns were being dismissed as mere 'scaremongering' by an establishment in 'a state not simply of complacency but of denial'.[115] However, the scandal ensuing from the 2005 case prompted the government to pass the Electoral Administration Act (EAA) 2006, which contained a mere two sections introducing a few new anti-fraud offences and a personal identifier system based on signature and date of birth comparisons.[116] This dealt with only one of the fourteen or so ways in which fraud can easily be committed and, in any event, was effectively useless given that election officers lack the time, training or resources to carry out stringent handwriting checks.[117] It did little to assuage concerns about the system's failing integrity or the security of postal voting, and similar cases followed.[118] Registering to vote remains 'simplicity itself' and '[a]mazingly, the applicant is not even obliged to provide his personal identifier. The registration of the elector is purely mechanical. Provided the form seems to be in order, the Electoral Registration Officer must add the name to

2020): www.onlondon.co.uk/tower-hamlets-return-of-lutfur-rahman/; Steerpike, 'The return of Lutfur Rahman' (*The Spectator*, 11 March 2021).

[109] 2015 Tower Hamlets case, para. 669. [110] Para. 71.

[111] Leading to at least fifteen types of fraud (para. 385). [112] Paras. 39–41, 48, 87.

[113] Para. 101. [114] 2005 Birmingham case, para. 715. [115] Ibid., paras. 714, 716.

[116] Ss. 15, 23, 40; 2008 Slough case, paras. 103–9; James, 'Fewer Costs, More Votes?', p. 41.

[117] Paras. 110–22. [118] Morris, *Parliamentary Elections, Representation and the Law*, pp. 86–7.

the Register. No form of verification is required: no enquiries are or can be made: the name is added.'[119]

The Coalition government eventually passed the Electoral Registration and Administration Act 2013, which replaced multiple registration by the head of the household with individual registration, although, given the other problems with the system, it is unlikely to have had much impact. Mawrey QC's position is that 'the correct solution would have been to re-consider and, preferably, to abandon the system of postal voting on demand. It was (and is) doubtful whether such a system could ever be made to work without the risk of widespread fraud'.[120] He acknowledges that this would likely be opposed because

> [f]ar too much political capital had been invested in postal voting on demand for it to be scrapped. There remained a strong, though wholly unsubstantiated, belief that postal voting on demand had increased voter turnout. The reason why the belief was unsubstantiated was that, even when there appeared to be a modest increase in turnout, there was absolutely no way of knowing whether this was a result of increased voter participation or of electoral fraud (or a combination of both). Similarly there persists a belief in some political circles, notwithstanding serious academic research indicating the contrary, that postal voting on demand favours one political party at the expense of the others.[121]

Each of his judgments contains an afterword reiterating the problems and berating successive governments for their reluctance to reform the law in any meaningful way.[122]

Election offences 'cannot fairly be described as well drafted' and are a 'disorganised bag' rather than 'a coherent body of rules'.[123] For example, to establish general corruption, it must be proved that corrupt and illegal practices 'prevailed so extensively that they may be reasonably supposed to have affected the result of the election'.[124] This stringent requirement is 'unsatisfactory' and 'obsolete' in that it places an unrealistic evidential burden on petitioners and means that corruption can be shown to be widespread but legally inconsequential if it cannot be shown to have swung the outcome of the election.[125] Another problem concerns the offence of undue influence which 'sets the bar much too high for dealing with intimidatory behaviour during the conduct of the poll' because it 'demands quite a serious level of violence' or duress and requires proof that voters were actually induced to change their vote. This means that 'unacceptable intimidation' and general thuggery can take place, as they did in the Tower Hamlets case, without affecting the validity of the election.[126]

[119] 2008 Slough case, para. 139. [120] Ibid., para. 99.

[121] Ibid., paras. 100–1. See also paras. 143–4.

[122] 2005 Birmingham case, paras. 714–17; 2008 Slough case, paras. 343–52; 2013 Woking case, paras. 279–86; 2015 Tower Hamlets case, paras. 681–6.

[123] 2008 Slough case, para. 15. [124] S. 164(1). [125] 2008 Slough case, paras. 36–41.

[126] 2015 Tower Hamlets case, paras. 614–24.

7.3.2.4.2 Bureaucratic Problems

The bureaucratic problems are mostly to do with policing, resources and election officials' powers. In many cases, 'the attitude of the police leaves a lot to be desired'.[127] In the 2005 Birmingham case, Mawrey QC criticised them for not being 'remotely proactive'[128] and more than a decade later Sir Eric Pickles noted that 'state institutions had turned a blind eye to such behaviour because of "politically correct" over-sensitivities about ethnicity and religion'.[129] These echo complaints made elsewhere.[130] The police are, however, typically under-resourced and poorly trained when it comes to investigating large-scale election fraud, a commitment comparable to cases of serious financial crime.[131] As regards postal voting, local election offices do not have the resources to monitor for fraud and, in any case, returning officers have no duty to investigate nor any standing to bring election petitions.[132] Further, the bulk of postal votes often arrive at the last minute so there would be little time to carry out labour-intensive checks.[133] In some instances, significant administrative errors have occurred in the setting up of polling stations, the secure handling of ballots and the counting of votes.[134] Again, most of these issues are ameliorable and could be addressed through adequate investment in staffing and training.

7.3.2.4.3 Structural Problems

As to structure, the election petitions process 'is both inadequate and inappropriate as a method of controlling fraud. For electoral probity to be policed by what are, in effect, private civil law actions brought at the expense of the litigant, cannot be acceptable.'[135] The law, which dates from 1868, is archaic and uneven. To challenge a parliamentary election, for example, only one elector is required to bring a petition, but in local elections a minimum of four is needed.[136] Political parties are unable to bring election petitions in their own right, which places the burden, cost and risk solely upon candidates and party members as individuals.[137] In all cases, tight, inflexible limitation periods apply, regardless of complexity.[138] Morris has shown that, aside from such procedural irregularities, the central issue is that the current system was designed in Victorian times when corruption was on the way out of British democracy, but it is now being overwhelmed by corruption's resurgence. The system still treats public interest issues, many with a criminal dimension, as private disputes and ensures that 'the policing of electoral fraud by anyone is minimal'.[139] She suggests that, at the very least, access to justice should be improved via reduced costs and legal aid provision, although ideally the system

[127] 2005 Birmingham case, para. 23. [128] Paras. 145–7, 157. [129] Pickles Report, p. 22.
[130] Ss. 14–15. [131] 2005 Birmingham case, paras. 152–4. [132] Ibid., paras. 77, 139, 22.
[133] 2008 Slough case, para. 112. [134] Pickles Report, pp. 30, 35.
[135] 2005 Birmingham case, paras. 159–60, p. 106. [136] Pickles Report, p. 35.
[137] Pickles Report, pp. 35–6; on the financial risks, see *Greene* v. *Forbes* [2020] EWHC 676 (QB).
[138] Pickles Report, pp. 38–9. [139] 2005 Birmingham case, para. 161.

itself should be reoriented towards public law with the Electoral Commission assuming an additional monitoring and investigatory role while being granted standing to bring petitions itself.[140] There is now a broad consensus that major reform is necessary to ensure the integrity of elections by addressing these regulatory, bureaucratic and structural problems which generate such abundant opportunities for fraud.[141]

7.3.2.5 Statistical Difficulties

Even so, '[s]ystematic and reliable evidence about the quality of elections is essential for scholars and practitioners'.[142] Such a body of evidence does not exist for the UK and it is hard to obtain an accurate picture of the scale of electoral fraud. Broadly speaking, expert opinion divides into two camps which might be termed, respectively, the minimalists and the revisionists. The former argue that electoral fraud is neither widespread nor something that routinely proves decisive in important elections.[143] Professor Toby James notes that, while allegations of fraud are common and a useful tactic for defeated candidates, proven cases are few and attempted personation at polling stations is exceptionally rare even in the most at-risk areas.[144] In support of this, he cites the Electoral Commission's conclusion (2014) that '[e]lectoral fraud is not widespread across the UK and reports of significant fraud are focused in specific places in England, concentrated in a small number of local authority areas. We do not believe it is likely that fraud has been attempted in more than a handful of wards in any particular local authority area.'[145] The Electoral Commission itself has consistently subscribed to this view. For example, it has variously suggested that electoral fraud is 'on the decrease and continues to be relatively rare' (2009), that it is 'unthinkable' on any large scale (2011), that there is 'no evidence to suggest that there have been widespread, systematic attempts to undermine or interfere with recent elections' (2014) and that there 'remains no evidence of large-scale electoral fraud' (2020).[146] Similarly, Hill et al. have claimed that it has become 'more politically salient, even if it remains

[140] See generally Morris, *Parliamentary Elections, Representation and the Law*, pp. 91–100; Morris and Wilks-Heeg, 'Reports of My Death Have Been Greatly Exaggerated'.

[141] See, for example, Electoral Commission, 'Electoral Fraud in the UK: Final Report and Recommendations' (Electoral Commission, January 2014); Cabinet Office, 'A Democracy That Works for Everyone: A Clear and Secure Democracy – Government Response to Sir Eric Pickles' Review of Electoral Fraud' (HMG, December 2016); Law Commission, 'Electoral Law: A Joint Final Report' (Law Commission, March 2020).

[142] Pippa Norris, *Why Elections Fail* (Cambridge: Cambridge University Press, 2015), p. 26.

[143] Toby S. James, 'Postal Voting and Electoral Fraud: A Reply to Richard Mawrey, QC' (Democratic Audit UK, 12 March 2014).

[144] Hill et al., 'Explaining Electoral Fraud in an Advanced Democracy', p. 774.

[145] Electoral Commission, 'Electoral Fraud in the UK', p. 3.

[146] See Michael Pinto-Duschinsky, 'Electoral Omission' (Policy Exchange, October 2014), p. 28; Stuart Wilks-Heeg, Andrew Blick and Stephen Crone, 'What Is the Extent of Electoral Fraud at English Elections?' (Democratic Audit UK, 26 November 2013); Electoral Commission, 'Electoral Fraud Data: 2019 Electoral Fraud Data' (Electoral Commission, September 2020).

infrequent',[147] while the Electoral Reform Society (the oldest electoral reform campaign group in the world) declares: 'Thankfully[,] electoral fraud is very rare in the UK. Where voter fraud has occurred, it has been isolated and therefore is best tackled locally.'[148] The available statistics certainly lend credibility to this camp. Local elections are likely more vulnerable, although parliamentary elections can also be affected.[149] Geographically, electoral fraud is concentrated in eighteen high-risk areas which include Birmingham, Bradford, Peterborough, Tower Hamlets and Woking.[150] There has been a marked upswing in controverted elections in the twenty-first century, although the number of allegations fluctuates considerably each year (for example: 262 in 2010, 148 in 2013, 518 in 2015, 336 in 2017, 592 in 2019).[151] The same is true for the number of convictions, which remains, by and large, very low (for example: one in 2001, twenty-two in 2004, seven in 2007, one in 2010, three in 2013, one in 2018, three in 2019).[152] The Electoral Commission's annual reports over the past decade show that the vast majority of all reported allegations result in no further action being taken by the police. As regards the type of allegations, most relate to campaigning malpractice, whereas those concerning voting and registration offences typically make up fewer than half of all annual cases when combined. Several consolidatory reports confirm this general statistical picture.[153]

By contrast, the revisionists think that these statistics are misleading and serve to conceal the true massive scale of electoral fraud; claims that corruption remains relatively insignificant are 'beginning to sound hollow from over-use'.[154] Chief among them is the UK's foremost election lawyer, Richard Mawrey QC, who has used every available opportunity and forum to condemn the current legal regime. His learned judgments exude exasperation. Each starts and ends with a denunciation of weak safeguards and government inaction. Every time he has correctly predicted that a near-identical case will follow. His view is that the UK operates a poorly regulated, 'shambolic electoral

[147] Hill et al., 'Explaining Electoral Fraud in an Advanced Democracy', p. 785.

[148] Electoral Reform Society (ERS), 'Voter ID: An Expensive Distraction' (ERS, accessed February 2020): www.electoral-reform.org.uk/campaigns/upgrading-our-democracy/voter-id/.

[149] See *Watkins* v. *Woolas* [2010] EWHC 2702 and Morris, *Parliamentary Elections, Representation and the Law*, p. 87.

[150] Cabinet Office, 'A Democracy That Works for Everyone', pp. 29–30.

[151] Morris, *Parliamentary Elections, Representation and the Law*, p. 86; Electoral Commission, 'Analysis of Cases of Alleged Electoral Fraud in the UK in 2017: Summary of Data Recorded by Police Forces' (Electoral Commission, 2018), p. 6.

[152] Ibid.; Electoral Commission, 'Electoral Fraud Data' (Electoral Commission, September 2020).

[153] See Stuart Wilks-Heeg, 'Purity of Elections in the UK: Causes for Concern' (Joseph Rowntree Trust, 2008); Isobel White, 'Postal Voting and Electoral Fraud 2001–09' (House of Commons, March 2012); Electoral Commission, 'Electoral Fraud in the UK: Final Report and Recommendations'; Pickles Report; Isobel White and Neil Johnston, 'Electoral Fraud since 2010' (House of Commons, No. 6255, January 2017).

[154] K. D. Ewing, *The Cost of Democracy: Party Funding in Modern British Politics* (Oxford: Hart, 2007), p. 26.

system'.[155] Provisions for the registration of voters are 'chaotic' and have been 'carefully constructed so as to ensure that no checks are ever made as to the veracity or the existence of the person applying to be placed on the register'.[156] This has created ample opportunities for 'massive and well-organised fraud' on an 'industrial scale', with each new case merely another instance of 'déjà vu'.[157] This assessment is supported for the most part by Bob Watt and Caroline Morris. The former takes something of a law and order approach to electoral integrity, arguing that personation is a serious and increasingly prevalent threat to British democracy, which much be countered with reinforced civil and criminal penalties. He takes the minimalist camp's view on the scale of election fraud to be 'unjustifiably optimistic' in light of the case law which highlights the ways in which weak safeguards have provided opportunities to hijack elections for family, business and sectarian interests.[158] Similarly, Morris is concerned that debates over electoral integrity have taken place within a 'near-vacuum of information' created by unreliable statistics and the blunt fact that 'many instances of maladministration and malpractice never reach the stage of triggering an election petition'.[159] Reports from external election monitors also lend weight to this view. Special Rapporteurs for the Parliamentary Assembly of the Council of Europe observed in 2008 that 'it is clear that the electoral system in Great Britain is open to electoral fraud. This vulnerability is mainly the result of the, rather arcane, system of voter registration without personal identifiers. It was exacerbated by the introduction of postal voting on demand.'[160] Likewise, Commonwealth Election Observers noted in 2010:

> [T]he system itself contains vulnerabilities that make the system corruptible and open to fraud. The UK electoral system operates under trust; it is assumed and understood that both voters and officials are honest and do not have plans to defraud the electorate. Because of this, vulnerabilities have not been addressed and may not be recognised as weaknesses in the system. Trust may have been a sufficient anchor for the system in the past, but while trust is good, caution and deterrent controls are better.[161]

The revisionist stance is thus that the statistics supporting the rival camp are in fact being distorted by several factors. The first concerns the problem of deficient data.[162] This is a consensus among criminologists that compilations of statistics, official or otherwise, are inherently limited and will mislead if used

[155] 2013 Woking case, para. 11. [156] Ibid., para. 25. [157] Ibid., para. 12.

[158] Slater and Watt, 'In Defence of Democracy' [draft version], pp. 35, 45.

[159] Morris and Wilks-Heeg, 'Reports of My Death Have Been Greatly Exaggerated', pp. 44–6; Morris, *Parliamentary Elections, Representation and the Law*, pp. 86–7, 100.

[160] Council of Europe Parliamentary Assembly Monitoring Committee, 'Application to Initiate a Monitoring Procedure to Investigate Electoral Fraud in the United Kingdom' (Council of Europe, January 2008), p. 1, para. 3.

[161] Commonwealth Observer Team to the UK General Election 2010, 'Final Report' (Royal Commonwealth Society and Commonwealth Parliamentary Association UK Branch, 2010), p. 1.

[162] Noah Carl, 'Ethnicity and Electoral Fraud in Britain' (2017) 50 *Electoral Studies* 128–36, p. 129.

incautiously. In terms of reported criminal activity, a lot depends on what is policed, prioritised, detected, recorded, counted and published.[163] In the present context, the police are given little training in the field and appear to take a passive approach to investigations.[164] The obvious consequence is that at least some actual fraud never makes it into the records. What is more, no authoritative resource on electoral fraud exists and one can only hope to piece together impressionistic estimates pulled from disparate cases, articles and reports (the Electoral Commission's website is woefully disorganised and many of its resources have to be located indirectly via Google). Second, there is a zemiological (from the Greek for harm, *zemia*) point to be made against the current system: there are many harmful electoral practices which are either beyond the scope of the existing law altogether or else categorised as mundane fraud or forgery offences.[165] This serves to deflate the reported figures even further. Examples of this might include the requirement that physical intimidation reach a serious level before it is criminalised and the very nature of election petitions themselves, which hinders access to justice. In brief, the statistics relied upon by the minimalist camp may not be worthless, but they are not much good either. There is an implicit final strand to revisionist thinking about the prevalence of electoral fraud. Even if the current statistics somehow turn out to be substantially accurate, it is important not to frame the problem too narrowly in numerical terms. The point here is that incidence and gravity are separable: electoral fraud is so corrosive of democratic integrity and public trust that even infrequent occurrences must be guarded against with utmost vigilance and strict regulation.

7.3.3 Mechanisms

Caroline Morris has observed that 'modern corruption, like its historical counterpart, appears to know no geographical or political boundaries'.[166] It knows no racial, religious or cultural boundaries either as cases occur in virtually every segment of society. Nevertheless, all but one of the areas at high risk of electoral fraud have sizeable Pakistani or Bangladeshi populations and nearly all of the significant litigation implicates members of these populations.[167] Indeed, 'percentage Pakistani and Bangladeshi is a moderate-to-strong predictor of electoral fraud allegations' in any given area.[168] The

[163] See Stephen Jones, *Criminology* (6th ed., Oxford: Oxford University Press, 2017), p. 51; Katherine Williams, *Textbook on Criminology* (7th ed., Oxford: Oxford University Press, 2012), pp. 98–9.

[164] 2005 Birmingham case, paras. 145–7.

[165] See generally Paddy Hillyard, Christina Pantazis, Steve Tombs and Dave Gordon (eds.), *Beyond Criminology: Taking Harm Seriously* (London: Pluto Press, 2004).

[166] *Parliamentary Elections, Representation and the Law*, p. 87.

[167] Pickles Report, pp. 64–5; Owen Bowcott, 'Judge Who Disqualified Tower Hamlets Mayor Leads Drive to Reform Election Law' (*The Guardian*, 24 April 2015).

[168] Carl, 'Ethnicity and Electoral Fraud in Britain', p. 135.

most convincing reasons for this are anthropological and relate to South Asian family structures rather than race or (for the most part) religion.

Pakistani and Bangladeshi communities tend to be organised around kinship networks called, respectively, *biraderi* (male kin) and *brath-thitho* (brotherly relationships). In essence, these are clans of extended families, held together by ancestral ties and consanguineous marriages, which operate as strict patriarchal hierarchies. They consolidate identities and provide social support for new migrants and the existing diasporas while being tightly controlled by self-proclaimed male leaders who reward obedience and punish deviancy. Clan structures are discussed in greater depth in Chapter 8, but for now it suffices that their power draws upon clan loyalties reinforced by a reciprocal patronage system to deliver bloc votes. They are often more trusted than the justice system and the police.[169] This means that votes can be either exchanged for guarantees of all-hours full-spectrum support on a range of business and personal issues or, in some cases, coerced out of vulnerable and low-status individuals who are then intimidated to cover up the fraud.[170] Successful candidates are thus understood to have 'earned' their votes from supporters, and anyone who voted for the opposition will have no claim on his time.[171] This serves to personalise election contests and raises the stakes for rival factions far beyond the usual win/lose binary in the first-past-the-post system. As such, the incentive to mobilise one's kin and fight dirty becomes even harder to resist. In his successful 2005 campaign to become MP for Bethnal Green and Bow, George Galloway even visited Bangladesh to meet village dignitaries and political party leaders who were encouraged to call relatives and affiliates in London and persuade them to vote in his favour.[172] Regular religious attendance and hearing political messages in places of worship can significantly increase political participation and mobilisation among minority groups.[173] Endorsements from religious leaders are therefore highly sought after and provide additional legitimacy, whereas non-Muslim candidates, however diverse, often fare badly.[174] This is regarded with particular distrust by the general population, which typically takes a dim view of religious involvement in politics.[175] *Biraderi*-politicking is likely responsible for

[169] Parveen Akhtar, 'The Paradox of Patronage Politics: Biraderi, Representation and Political Participation amongst British Pakistanis' in Timothy Peace (ed.), *Muslims and Political Participation in Britain* (London: Routledge, 2015), ch. 1, pp. 15–31 at p. 21.

[170] Hill et al., 'Explaining Electoral Fraud in an Advanced Democracy', p. 776.

[171] Ibid., p. 783.

[172] Timothy Peace and Parveen Akhtar, 'Biraderi, Bloc Votes and Bradford: Investigating the Respect Party's Campaign Strategy' (2015) 17 *British Journal of Politics and International Relations* 224–43, p. 232.

[173] Maria Sobolewska, Stephen D. Fisher, Anthony F. Heath and David Sanders, 'Understanding the Effects of Religious Attendance on Political Participation among Ethnic Minorities of Different Religions' (2015) 54 *European Journal of Political Research* 271–87, pp. 271, 283, 284–5.

[174] Peace and Akhtar, 'Biraderi, Bloc Votes and Bradford', pp. 231, 233.

[175] Sobolewska et al., 'Understanding the Effects of Religious Attendance on Political Participation among Ethnic Minorities of Different Religions', p. 272.

higher rates of political participation among South Asian communities despite their newer members' poorer performance across a range of other integration measures.[176] However, it 'ultimately has quite a corrupting influence on politics because the determining factor in exercising such influence becomes less about political conviction and more about which candidate will be indebted to you'.[177] Richard Mawrey QC has specifically and repeatedly criticised *biraderi* leaders for abusing their position within their families and communities during elections.[178]

Command of *biraderi* support is now a promising, even essential, component of election campaign strategy. Political parties have been quick to capitalise and frequently court clan elders as power brokers to compensate for a dearth of local activists and their consistent failure to maintain meaningful contact with Black, Asian and minority ethnic (BAME) voters.[179] The typical *biraderi* candidate will not usually need or receive support from the central party but will adopt its brand to signal his prestige and seriousness.[180] While canvassing door to door, he will normally speak only to the male head of the household on the assumption that they will be deciding how their family and residents vote.[181] In some cases, however, young electors have rebelled against their disenfranchisement within their *biraderi* and voted for anti-establishment parties like George Galloway's Respect.[182] For the most part, however, engagement with these kinship networks serves to consolidate their hierarchical power over the community, limiting opportunities for selection (especially for women and the young) and tarnishing the legitimacy of candidates actually selected by the party.[183] Eleanor Hill has argued that political parties bear much of the responsibility for pandering to this 'shady politicking' which is 'particularly worrying for the quality of our democracy'.[184] Although it pays dividends in the short term, the *biraderi* system is dangerously subversive of democratic candidate selection, protections for vulnerable voters and safeguards against massive electoral fraud. She

176 Ibid., p. 274; Hill et al., 'Explaining Electoral Fraud in an Advanced Democracy', p. 781; Hiranthi Jayaweera, 'Migration, Integration and Transnational Involvement: Muslim Family Migrants in Urban Areas in Britain' in Katharine Charsley (ed.), *Transnational Marriage: New Perspectives from Europe and Beyond* (London: Routledge, 2012), ch. 5, pp. 81–104 at pp. 88–90, 94–5.

177 Salma Yaqoob quoted in Peace and Akhtar, 'Biraderi, Bloc Votes and Bradford', p. 228.

178 2005 Birmingham case, para. 696; 2013 Woking case, paras. 106–17; 2015 Tower Hamlets case, para. 563.

179 Hill et al., pp. 784, 786.

180 Ibid., pp. 784–5; Akhtar and Peace, 'Biraderi, Bloc Votes and Bradford', p. 227.

181 Akhtar and Peace, ibid.

182 Ibid., p. 235; Hill et al., 'Explaining Electoral Fraud in an Advanced Democracy', p. 783.

183 Sobolewska et al., 'Understanding Electoral Fraud Vulnerability in Pakistani and Bangladeshi Origin Communities in England', p. 33; Parveen Akhtar and Timothy Peace, 'Ethnic Minorities in British Politics: Candidate Selection and Clan Politics in the Labour Party' (2018) 45(11) *Journal of Ethnic and Migration Studies* 1902–18, p. 1914.

184 Eleanor Hill, 'Political Parties Need to Take Greater Responsibility for Pakistani and Bangladeshi Clan Politicking in Order to Protect Our Democracy' (Democratic Audit UK, 28 May 2015).

recommends that parties start treating voters as individuals by canvassing for each individual vote, implementing selection processes that counter *biraderi*-based discrimination, and providing training in election law to ensure that their campaigners follow the rules.[185]

Hill further notes that, despite some basic similarities, *biraderi* are considerably more problematic than other types of political network such as trade unions, which have occasionally been implicated in electoral fraud. This is because, compared with the unions, it is impossible to trace or track the revenue streams being channelled through them, their use of coercion to restrict electoral choice and candidate selection, their ability to manipulate vulnerable voters with limited English or procedural understanding, their active efforts to consolidate elders' power at the expense of under-represented members of their community, and their tendency to serve as instrumental vehicles for personal and clan – as opposed to party or ideological – advancement.[186] It would be reasonable to assume that *hawala* plays an important role in the financing of *biraderi* campaigns.[187] What is more, the structure of the *biraderi* networks is fundamentally different from that of the trade unions.[188] Whereas the latter are relatively open and accountable, the former are closed and resistant to scrutiny, which makes it much harder to discover and punish any wrongdoing by or within them. Whereas trade unions' fortunes are tied to their party's success and good reputation, *biraderis* are unconcerned with this unless it directly affects their own interests and will be comparatively less concerned with allegations that they have broken the law. Whereas trade unions share party connections, information and resources among their diverse membership, *biraderis* remain relatively homogeneous and their membership is less likely to be exposed to the new ideas, information and skills which promote legitimate practices around candidate selection and electoral conduct. In brief, *biraderi* activity is especially dangerous because it tends towards electoral misconduct, restricts electoral choice and remains unaccountable as a consequence of the opaque, unidentifiable and exclusive nature of these clan networks.[189]

7.3.4 Summing Up

Electoral fraud in the UK is ultimately rooted in the incentives created by the first-past-the-post system and socio-economic deprivation. The legal regime currently in place to ensure the integrity of elections is compromised by

[185] Sobolewska et al., 'Understanding Electoral Fraud Vulnerability in Pakistani and Bangladeshi Origin Communities in England', p. 45; Eleanor Hill, 'It's Not What You Know, It's Who You Know: What Are the Implications of Networks in UK Politics for Electoral Choice?' (unpublished PhD thesis, University of Manchester, 2018), pp. 225–7, 231–3.

[186] Hill, 'It's Not What You Know, It's Who You Know', pp. 207–15, 218.

[187] See Chapter 4 and Roger Ballard, '*Hawala* and *Hundi*: Vehicles for the Long-Distance Transmission of Value' in Joya Chatterji and David Washbrook (eds.), *Routledge Handbook of the South Asian Diaspora* (London: Routledge, 2013), ch. 5, pp. 53–66 at pp. 54–6.

[188] Hill, 'It's Not What You Know, It's Who You Know', pp. 219–22.

[189] Ibid., pp. 222–4.

a variety of regulatory, structural and bureaucratic weaknesses. These defects have created ample opportunities for localised and large-scale fraud, a fraction of which has resulted in serious litigation. While the available statistics would suggest that it is uncommon, the data has severe limitations and it is plausible that corruption is far more extensive than is often assumed. Pakistani and Bangladeshi communities are at greater risk because their kinship networks make it easier to manipulate voters, a fact which has not escaped political parties who have taken full advantage of these ready-made campaigning machines. All but the first of these problems can at least be ameliorated and are potentially solvable. Clearly electoral fraud has no single cause or cure.[190] Yet, by juridifying it, sensitive issues around ethnicity and religion appear less as mere fodder for the culture wars and more like a portfolio of interconnected problems with technical solutions. Arranging the evidence into a three-tiered causal chain grants a reasonably clear view of what these are, their relative importance and what might be done to remedy them. That *biraderi*-politicking is a major problem has been recognised both by British Muslim groups and by the government as a major barrier to participation and integration.[191]

7.4 Interpreting Modern Electoral Fraud

7.4.1 Via Liberal Individualism

Ronald Dworkin regarded democratic integrity as 'a prerequisite of civilization'.[192] Liberal political morality was, to his mind, a coherent composition of fair political structures, the just distribution of resources and opportunities, and procedural due process.[193] The state's legitimacy rests upon principle rather than raw majoritarian power. As such, there can be no conflict between true democracy and individual rights: the former is a partnership of equal individuals acting collectively in the enterprise of self-government. Electoral minorities and their individual constituents, as well as individual members of majorities, are no less participants in self-government than the majority qua majority. Democracy is inseparable from the individual rights, procedures and judicial interventions that constrain the majority's power and place conditions on its legitimacy. This contrasts with crude majoritarianism – in society as a whole or within any given minority – which equates democracy with a statistically aggregated general will. On this view, only the majority

[190] Valdeep Gill, Natalie Jago and Fatima Husain, 'Elections, Voting and Electoral Fraud: An Exploratory Study Focusing on British Pakistanis and Bangladeshis' (NatCen, January 2015), pp. 53, 58.

[191] Citizens' Commission on Islam, Participation and Public Life, 'The Missing Muslims: Unlocking British Muslim Potential for the Benefit of All' (Citizens UK, 2017), pp. 11, 46–8; Dame Louise Casey, 'The Casey Review: A Review into Opportunity and Integration' (HMG, December 2016), pp. 163–4.

[192] Ronald Dworkin, *Law's Empire* (Oxford: Hart-Bloomsbury, 1998, reprint of Fontana Press original, 1986), p. 166.

[193] Ibid., pp. 164–7.

group possesses agency and, so long as electoral procedures are capable of making it out as a majority, its wishes are to be regarded as the true voice of the people. Democracy and justice are considered separable and may conflict where the majority's will clashes with internal dissent or external judicial review.[194] In rejecting this, Dworkinian democracy ultimately rests upon the ethical independence of the individual and rejects outright any pretentions by any community to dictate the fundamental ethical convictions of its members. The right to equal participation in the making of laws is 'the right of rights' for it is constitutive of formal democratic procedure and guarantees the social conditions for the state's legitimacy.[195] Put simply, democracy is about political standing rather than political power. It

> confirms in the most dramatic way the equal concern and respect that the community together, as the custodian of coercive power, has for each of its members . . . If any citizen is assigned less electoral impact than others, either because he is denied the vote or they are given extra votes . . . or for any other reason, then the difference signals a lesser political standing.[196]

The liberal individualistic case for eradicating electoral fraud is therefore unambiguous and uncompromising. Fraud may or may not swing a particular result or seat, which may or may not in itself be consequential in the grand scheme of things like a general election, which may or may not have desirable consequences for the nation, its minorities or any particular individuals. The actual impact is irrelevant; the harm is not contingent and strikes at the roots of human dignity and the state's duty to hold free and fair elections.[197] Intimidation or violence on polling day violates individual choice; postal fraud violates equality by stripping some citizens of their vote and granting others outsized importance; undue spiritual influence and clannism are clear instances of communities dictating the ethical choices of their members and quashing their personal responsibility; all these things together corrode the democratic partnership of equals that holds modern British society together. There is little to quibble with here so far as concerns reforming the law to better guarantee formal equality between individual citizens. However, Dworkin's interpretation of democracy is 'incomplete' and 'vote-centric' – he paid little attention to political parties and treated the internal norms of criminal

[194] See Ronald Dworkin, *Justice for Hedgehogs* (Cambridge, MA: Harvard University Press), pp. 382–4 and 'Equality, Democracy and Constitution: We the People in Court' (1990) 28(2) *Alberta Law Review* 324–46.

[195] Jeremy Waldron, *Law and Disagreement* (Oxford: Oxford University Press, 1999), ch. 11. For an extension of Dworkin's thesis, see Alexander Latham, 'Dworkin's Incomplete Interpretation of Democracy' (2018) 10(2) *Washington University Jurisprudence Review* 155–81.

[196] Dworkin, *Justice for Hedgehogs*, p. 390.

[197] Protocol to the European Convention for the Protection of Human Rights and Fundamental Freedoms, Article 1, Protocol 3.

organisations as legally irrelevant.[198] Yet the democratic process is replete with group actors – some legitimate, some not; some regulated, some not – which play a greater part than any individual and it is impossible to devise effective solutions to election fraud without a well-developed theory of collective entities.

7.4.2 Via Multiculturalism

One might attempt to surmount this problem using multiculturalism. Its starting point is the worldly power, or lack thereof, of disadvantaged minorities. Although Dworkin conceded that this issue 'is not academic', he argued that significant disparities in the political impact of different citizens' votes are not necessarily anti-democratic so long as two conditions are met. The first is that there can be no 'aristocracy of birth' in terms of wealth, race, gender, caste, religion, etc. and will be satisfied so long as there is universal suffrage and safeguards against 'thinly disguised attempts to disenfranchise some despised and feared race or the poor'. The second is that the constitutional arrangements that created the disparity improve the legitimacy of the democratic community by serving 'some purpose in promoting equal concern for all . . . [so that any] disadvantage would be merely an incidental side effect of a justified arrangement and would be acceptable for that reason'. Representative democracy is a good example of this: it partially disenfranchises 'all unelected groups and persons equally' in comparison to direct democracy by lowering 'the political impact of all citizens across the board' at the cost of making certain 'swing constituencies' disproportionately important in real terms. By contrast, multiculturalism considers any disparity in political clout as inherently unacceptable and seeks what Dworkin called 'a new constitutional settlement' whereby the powerful agree to cede their advantages to the disempowered.[199] It posits that British Muslims are in some sense a group with political agency and united by 'common interests', even though there is 'a risk of reductionism' as its diverse members 'follow distinct grammars'.[200] They are a 'securitised' community subject to state attacks via the Prevent programme.[201] Muslims use their agency to take part in British democracy by making themselves visible and heard with a view to acquiring a greater share of resources and having their distinctiveness recognised. Their successes in this regard are automatically considered to be encouraging signs of integration and

198 Will Kymlicka quoted in Latham, 'Dworkin's Incomplete Interpretation of Democracy', p. 174; Dworkin, *Justice for Hedgehogs*, pp. 315, 321.

199 Dworkin, ibid., pp. 392–5.

200 Jan Dobbernack, Nasar Meer and Tariq Modood, 'Misrecognition and Political Agency: The Case of Muslim Organisations in a General Election' (2015) 17(2) *British Journal of Politics and International Relations* 189–206, p. 195; Therese O'Toole, Daniel Nilsson DeHanas, Tariq Modood, Nasar Meer and Stephen H. Jones, 'Taking Part: Muslim Participation in Contemporary Governance' (Centre for the Study of Ethnicity and Citizenship, University of Bristol, 31 January 2013), p. 6.

201 O'Toole et al., ibid., pp. 55–6.

equalisation as their position vis-à-vis other subgroups improves. Activist organisations are both expressions of Muslim culture and the vehicles by which Muslims participate in democratic life.[202] Even if no particular group or leader represents Muslims as such, they are nevertheless vital 'supplements' to individual agency and constitute a 'democratic constellation' of legitimate advocates for particular causes or claims representative of Muslim interests.[203] As regards clans, one could point to evidence that 'social connections in some crony relationships and apparently nepotic ones' can enrich and make family organisations more effective without necessarily leading to unethical behaviour, and that these advantages can be threatened by aggressive counter-measures which may themselves amount to prejudice or 'unfair discrimination on the basis of group memberships'.[204] The political mobilisation of the *biraderi* networks, while 'perhaps open to critique', should therefore not be 'selectively used to marginalise and silence some groups'.[205] Like other Muslim institutions, it might be better to somehow accommodate them in the interests of mutual dialogue and an inclusive national identity.[206] In short: 'Groups can speak for Muslims – or Muslim women, Muslim converts and so on – on some issues and not on others, at some times and not others.'[207]

The danger here, of course, is that Muslims are treated as an entity with rights and defined interests. The Runnymede Trust, for example, recently published an article claiming:

> Ethnic minority cabinet ministers continue to uphold institutional racism today, using their identities to give us the illusion of progress when in reality they maintain and uphold systems of oppression. Such tokenism is deeply insidious and allows the government off the hook . . . Priti Patel may well be the daughter of immigrants, but this does not mean she has the interests of immigrant communities at heart.[208]

202 Ibid., p. 9.

203 Ibid., p. 6; Stephen H. Jones, Therese O'Toole, Daniel Nilsson DeHanas, Tariq Modood and Nasar Meer, 'A "System of Self-Appointed Leaders"? Examining Modes of Muslim Representation in Governance in Britain' (2015) 17(2) *British Journal of Politics and International Relations* 207–23, pp. 207, 213, 220.

204 Robert G. Jones and Tracy Stout, 'Policing Nepotism and Cronyism Without Losing the Value of Social Connection' (2015) 8(1) *Industrial and Organizational Psychology* 2–12. Against this, however, see Omar K. Burhan, Esther van Leeuwen and Daan Scheepers, 'On the Hiring of Kin in Organizations: Perceived Nepotism and Its Implications for Fairness Perceptions and the Willingness to Join an Organization' (2020) 161 *Organizational Behavior and Human Decision Processes* 34–48.

205 Dobbernack et al., 'Misrecognition and Political Agency', p. 194.

206 Tariq Modood, 'Multicultural Citizenship & the Sharia Controversy in Britain' in Rex Ahdar and Nicholas Aroney (eds.), *Sharia in the West* (Oxford: Oxford University Press, 2010), ch. 2, pp. 33–42.

207 Jones et al., 'A System of Self-Appointed Leaders?', p. 214.

208 Taj Ali, 'Race Matters: The Government Is Using Its "Diverse" Cabinet to Deflect from Racial Inequality' (Runnymede Trust, 29 January 2021): www.runnymedetrust.org/blog/the-government-is-using-its-diverse-cabinet-to-deflect-from-racial-inequality.

Aside from being difficult to substantiate, accusations of bad faith such as this are disingenuous. The implication is that successful minority politicians have somehow betrayed 'their communities' by working for the 'wrong' party or having the 'wrong' convictions for someone with their background or characteristics. For example, while it is true that the Labour Party has traditionally been the main beneficiary of Muslim participation and voting, not least because of its adept exploitation of racialised patronage politics, its hegemony over ethnic minorities has been decreasing as a result of disillusionment and other parties responding in kind.[209] Interestingly, as regards Brexit, around 31 per cent of all ethnic minorities and one-third of all British Asians voted to leave the EU.[210] In Luton and Bradford, for instance, areas with South Asian populations of more than 25 per cent, the Leave vote was 56.5 per cent and 54.2 per cent, respectively, results which 'could not have been delivered without a significant number of Asian voters opting for Brexit'. Many appear not to have felt European and were 'left unoffended' by 'the supposedly xenophobic and racist elements of the Leave campaign'.[211] Thus, Muslim voting patterns should not be seen as a sign of a community having any necessary connection to a particular party or cause – the picture is far more complex, reflecting the diversity of local populations and the shifting economic and political realities of the day. At the same time, this line of thinking induces a characteristically defensive attitude towards evidence of minority-perpetrated electoral fraud. In 2015, for example, the barrister and judge Peter Herbert OBE spoke at a 'Defend Democracy' rally in support of Lutfur Rahman and apparently against Commissioner Mawrey QC:

> There can sometimes be justice but you have to fight for it. Lutfur Rahman and the people of Tower Hamlets are fighting for it, do not stop that fight . . . Racism is alive and well and living in Tower Hamlets, in Westminster, and sometimes, yes, in the judiciary . . . So don't let anybody fool you that just because you have a judgment in a court that it is somehow sacrosanct. It is not. But do not put your faith in a system that is not designed for you. You are not regarded as British. You are not regarded as part of here and now otherwise this decision would not be made . . . Sometimes you have to take direct and peaceful action to get redress outside of the system. And while we're here, the press and the media you know is laid against you . . . So if you want change you have to fight for change and stand

[209] See Eren Tatari and Renat Shaykhutdinov, 'Muslims and Minority Politics in Great Britain' (2014) 34(1) *Journal of Muslim Minority Affairs* 22–44, p. 39; Eren Tatari, *Muslims in British Local Government: Representing Minority Interests in Hackney, Newham, and Tower Hamlets* (Leiden: Brill, 2014), pp. 44–5; Humayun Ansari, *The Infidel Within: Muslims in Britain Since 1800* (2nd ed., London: Hurst, 2018), pp. 251–6; Timothy Peace, 'Muslim Political Participation in Britain: The Case of the Respect Party' (Madrid: 22nd World Congress of Political Science, July 2012).

[210] Ipsos Mori, 'How Britain Voted in the 2016 EU Referendum' (Ipsos Mori, 5 September 2016); Lord Ashcroft, 'How the UK Voted on Brexit, and Why – A Refresher' (Lord Ashcroft Polls, 4 February 2019).

[211] Rakib Ehsan, 'The British Asian Vote for Brexit Contains a Few Surprises' (LSE Blog, 20 February 2017).

> on principle. We are with you Lutfur Rahman. We are with the people of Tower Hamlets.[212]

One academic sympathised, calling Mawrey QC's judgment 'highly problematic' because of what she perceived as 'a rush to judgment of religious influences whose apparent impropriety appears to have owed much to the "otherness" of those involved'.[213] The Judicial Conduct Investigations Office (JCIO) did not agree, however, finding that Herbert's comments were 'inappropriate and put the reputation of the judiciary at risk, which amounted to misconduct'.[214] Herbert objected in turn, appealing against the finding but agreeing 'not to make any more controversial comments' while simultaneously receiving an apology from the JCIO (for making a disproportionate recommendation for his suspension); he has since sued the Ministry of Justice for 'race discrimination and victimisation'.[215]

Relatedly, successive instances of Rahman's impropriety were exposed long before the 2015 Tower Hamlets case, following a March 2010 *Dispatches* documentary. He was removed as a Labour candidate for mustering ineligible electors who did not live at their purported addresses,[216] spending £115,000 of public money on a 'vanity office'[217] and spending £72 per day of public money on a chauffeur-driven Mercedes.[218] Despite this, he was treated uncritically as a good faith actor in two subsequent academic reports. The first of these, published in November 2010, attacked the investigative journalists and local politicians it claimed had created 'a narrative of "Islamist" infiltration' in Tower Hamlets to 'lend weight to criticism of Rahman and his supporters' who had 'suffered prejudice in the literal sense of the word'.[219] This was later partially retracted with an apology and the Gulf-funded centre responsible for

212 Uploaded by Fourman Films, 'Peter Herbert Barrister at Law Defend Democracy in Tower Hamlets 30 04 15' (YouTube, accessed 2 May 2015): www.youtube.com/watch?v=Fgpxi4CI5og.

213 McColgan, 'Undue Spiritual Influence: A Historical Analysis', pp. 280, 308.

214 Judicial Conduct Investigations Office (JCIO), 'Statement on Recorder Donald Peter Herbert OBE' (JCIO 13/17, 6 April 2017).

215 See Diane Taylor, 'Black Judge Claims He Was Discriminated Against by Disciplinary Panel' (*The Guardian*, 8 January 2017); Josh Halliday, 'Peter Herbert Becomes First Judge to Sue MoJ over Race Discrimination' (*The Guardian*, 12 September 2019); Melanie Newman, 'Ruling Elite' (*Law Society Gazette*, 17 February 2020); Izin Akhabau, 'Peter Herbert: A Black Judge Said Racism Existed in the Judiciary, and Was Almost Dismissed – His Legal Battle against "Racism and Bullying" in Judicial Institutions Continues' (*The Voice*, 13 January 2021).

216 Dave Hill, 'Tower Hamlets: Lutfur, Labour and Beyond' (*The Guardian*, 11 February 2011).

217 Nadia Sam-Daliri, 'Mayor of Poorest Borough Spends £115,000 on New "Vanity" Offices' (*Evening Standard*, 17 June 2011).

218 Nadia Sam-Daliri, 'Council Forks Out £72 a Day to drive mayor Around in Top-Class Mercedes' (*East London Advertiser*, 13 July 2011).

219 Unredacted version of Jonathan Githens-Mazer and Robert Lambert, 'Islamophobia and Anti-Muslim Hate Crime: A London Case Study' (EMRC, 2010; amended 2011) quoted in Trevor Phillips, John Jenkins and Martyn Frampton, 'On Islamophobia: The Problem of Definition' (Policy Exchange, May 2019), pp. 27–8; see also Martin Bright, 'New Questions on Exeter's Middle East Funding' (*Jewish Chronicle*, 14 April 2011).

commissioning it, the 'European Muslim Research Centre' (EMRC) at the University of Exeter, was shut down.[220] The second report, co-authored by Modood, was published in January 2013 and claims:

> Muslim organisations and individual actors [in Tower Hamlets] have become integral parts of local representative bodies and faith sector networks . . . and have contributed in important ways to equality advocacy and to service delivery. Attempts to dislodge such actors from their roles in the faith sector (e.g. due to their alleged connection with Islamism) would be not only difficult but also counter-productive.[221]

Satellite litigation and academic standards aside, this obfuscation precludes an effective response to corruption beyond the humdrum rationalisation of outdated election laws. The uncomfortable fact is that there is a collective dimension to electoral fraud and that participation in democracy via group activism is not an unqualified good in itself. As Mawrey QC noted back in 2005, 'there are those on the fringes of politics who may seek to use this judgment for racist ends. There is no warrant for anyone to do so and I hope they will not.'[222] Even if they did, there is still the need to decipher collective wrongdoing and introduce clear-minded reforms to prevent it. The worst has happened 'when those in authority are afraid to confront wrongdoing for fear of allegations of racism and Islamophobia. Even in the multicultural society which is 21st-century Britain, the law must be applied fairly and equally to everyone. Otherwise we are lost.'[223] Again, what multiculturalism lacks is a vocabulary capable of distinguishing between individual and collective interests as well as between legitimate and illegitimate groups.

7.5 A Pluralist Response to Modern Election Fraud

It is more fruitful to start by setting election fraud in historical context. The British political system emerged during the early modern period as government became more centralised and powerful, with local agendas being aggregated and coordinated by political parties then rearticulated as national interests.[224] That political parties enjoyed no special legal recognition whatever – 'a social body unknown to the state organism and without binding force or authority' – was 'something to be proud of'.[225] Even now they are treated as unincorporated associations governed by private 'club law', with no existence separate from that

220 Phillips et al., ibid., pp. 27–8.

221 O'Toole et al., 'Taking Part', pp. 44–5 – Rahman's participation in the study is acknowledged at p. 69.

222 2005 Birmingham case, para. 694. 223 2015 Tower Hamlets case, para. 686.

224 See generally Pradeep K. Chhibber and Ken Kollman, *The Formation of National Party Systems: Federalism and Party Competition in Canada, Great Britain, India, and the United States* (Princeton, NJ: Princeton University Press, 2004); Gash, *Politics in the Age of Peel*, pp. xviii, 394.

225 Heinrich Triepel quoted in Morris, *Parliamentary Elections, Representation and the Law*, p. 106.

of their members; 'there is little direct regulation of the internal affairs of the parties by legislation' and 'the courts have expressed reluctance about being drawn into rule-book disputes, preferring the parties themselves to resolve internal conflicts'.[226] The regulatory regime was 'most primitive' and for decades scandals involving donations, favours and appointments rocked the establishment until New Labour itself established the Committee on Standards in Public Life (the Neill Committee) in 1997.[227] Reporting back the following year, it set out seven principles for public life including integrity, accountability, openness and honesty, which inspired a raft of legislation.[228] Prior to the Political Parties, Elections and Referendums Act 2000, British political parties were among the least regulated in Europe; they are now required to be registered and their financial activities are among the most highly regulated.[229] (It should be noted, however, that even the most dubious applications and financial structures are merely rubber-stamped by the Electoral Commission.[230]) Yet while political parties remain the centre of attention, in key respects they have entered long-term decline and the law has not kept pace with new modes of campaigning. For example, membership has been dropping for decades and the devolution of power has diluted the relevance and appeal of two-party national government.[231] At the same time, informal networks of interest groups have grown in power and importance.[232] Concerns about the influence of 'dark money' – via corporate lobbyists to think tanks through trade unions and big tech – have proliferated over the past decade.[233] Election law is still poorly equipped to govern online campaigning and third-party activities which go largely unsupervised.[234] Thus, regardless of any 'Asian

[226] Ewing, *The Cost of Democracy*, p. 67; Morris, *Parliamentary Elections, Representation and the Law*, pp. 105–6.

[227] See Keith Ewing, 'The Funding of Political Parties in Britain: Prospects for Reform' (1998) 7(2) *Griffith Law Review* 185–208, p. 185; Lisa Klein, 'On the Brink of Reform: Political Party Funding in Britain' (1999) 31(1) *Case Western Reserve Journal of International Law* 1–46; Michael Pinto-Duschinsky and Lynne Middleton, *Reforming Public Appointments* (Policy Exchange, December 2013).

[228] Committee on Standards in Public Life, 'Fifth Report: The Funding of Political Parties in the United Kingdom' (HMG, Vol. 1, October 1998), p. ii.

[229] Keith Ewing, 'Transparency, Accountability and Equality: The Political Parties, Elections and Referendums Act 2000' (2001) *Public Law* 542–70, p. 542; Paul Webb, 'Parties and Party Systems: Modernisation, Regulation and Diversity' (2001) 54(2) *Parliamentary Affairs* 308–21; Ewing, *The Cost of Democracy*, p. 63; Morris, *Parliamentary Elections, Representation and the Law*, pp. 105–6.

[230] 2015 Tower Hamlets case, paras. 263–78.

[231] Niall Ferguson, *The Great Degeneration: How Institutions Decay and Economies Die* (London: Penguin, 2014), pp. 119–22; Chhibber and Kollmann, *The Formation of National Party Systems*, pp. 222–3.

[232] Niall Ferguson, *The Square and the Tower: Networks, Hierarchies and the Struggle for Global Power* (London: Allen Lane, 2017), p. 349.

[233] See generally Peter Geoghegan, *Democracy for Sale: Dark Money and Dirty Politics* (2nd ed., London: Head of Zeus, 2021) and Jane Mayer, *Dark Money* (London: Scribe, 2016).

[234] See generally Lord Hodgson, 'Third Party Election Campaigning – Getting the Balance Right: Review of the Operation of the Third Party Campaigning Rules at the 2015 General Election'

factor'[235] in certain types of corruption, there is a pressing need to bring the general regulatory apparatus up to date so that it can cope with this changed landscape.

Malign social media activity – ranging from foreign propaganda through fake news to dirty memes via shitposting – is another matter entirely.[236] Even if Western legislatures somehow summon the courage to regulate big tech companies as publishers, that is still no solution to human nature. To give just one telling example, shortly before the 2019 general election the then-leader of the Liberal Democrats, Jo Swinson, was the subject of a bogus but 'believable' *Daily Mirror* article by one 'Wurrance Telephene'. It purported to contain evidence that she liked to assassinate both varieties of squirrel, or 'pleb bunnies', with a pebble-loaded slingshot while exclaiming, 'I don't go for the head because that's too clean a death.'[237] The story was so widely shared online that Swinson had to publicly disavow this proclivity and reaffirm that 'I . . . like squirrels.'[238] She lost her seat regardless. The only workable long-term response to this sort of thing is to build up dispassionate educational and media institutions with the will, resources and cross-partisan credibility to push back against it. That and historical perspective. For example, Professor Martin Jehne notes that modern trolling pales in comparison to normal behaviour across all social classes in classical Rome, the cosmopolitan epicentre of the ancient world. In a society without libel laws, 'the best of arguments was personal abuse' and the best of this concerned 'disgusting immorality, degrading pursuits and ignoble origin'.[239] Accusations of incest were de rigueur, being called a rent boy par for the course, and arriving well endowed at the baths pretext for 'a round of nervous applause'.[240] Moreover, those on the receiving end 'did not always suffer discredit or damage. On the contrary. The Romans possessed a feeling for humour and a strong sense of the dramatic . . . It was a point of honour in a liberal society to take these things gracefully.'[241] Researching this led Jehne to 'considerably reduce [his] level of

(HMG, Cm 9205, March 2016); ERS, 'Fair Elections under Threat? The Loophole List' (ERS, September 2019), pp. 1–5; Jacob Rowbottom, 'The Regulation of Third Party Campaigning in UK Elections' (2020) 91(4) *Political Quarterly* 722–30; Bethany Shiner, 'General Election 2019: Unregulated Digital Political Advertisements Are Damaging Our Democracy' (Democratic Audit UK, 8 November 2019).

235 2005 Birmingham case, paras. 693–9.

236 See BBC News, 'Fake News a Democratic Crisis for UK, MPs Warn' (*BBC News*, 28 July 2018); Digital, Culture, Media and Sport Committee, 'Disinformation and "Fake News": Final Report – Eighth Report of Session 2017–19' (House of Commons, HC1791, February 2019).

237 Dan Bloom, 'Jo Swinson Gives Fake News Warning after Hoax Story She Stoned Squirrels Goes Viral' (*Daily Mirror*, 19 November 2019); Joel Golby, 'This Week's Biggest Twitter Controversy? Jo Swinson's Squirrel Problem' (*The Guardian*, 21 November 2019).

238 Chris Smyth, 'I Don't Torture Squirrels, Says Jo Swinson after Fake News Story' (*The Times*, 19 November 2019).

239 Ronald Syme, *The Roman Revolution* (Oxford: Oxford University Press, 1960), p. 149.

240 Tom Holland, 'The Romans Took Their Graffiti Seriously – Especially the Phalluses' (*The Guardian*, 28 February 2019).

241 Syme, *The Roman Revolution*, pp. 151–2.

excitement at new abuses in the present'.[242] Recent studies into online abuse indicate that if it does not originate from marketing strategists or cyberwarfare programmes, it is often motivated by a desire to offend for the sheer pleasure of triggering hysteria.[243] The consistent target is the 'normie' (read bourgeois) cult of sensibility built around the affectations and hypocrisies of college-educated millennials and their dingy professorial mentors.[244] This holds across the political spectrum and no particular 'side' comes out of it well; even the Bar Standards Board felt the need to issue professional guidance reminding barristers that '[i]t is also advisable to avoid getting drawn into heated debates or arguments'.[245] Once all this is understood then 'there is nothing unexpected or surprising about even the strangest online behaviour'.[246] Indeed, much of it is redolent of the viral taunts – 'applicable to every circumstance, and the universal answer to every question' – that swept Victorian London during Charles Mackay's day.[247] The job is one for everyone and it requires black humour, better civic education and a greater willingness to simply switch off from online feuding.

As to the Asian factor itself, it would be a mistake to frame it in religious or cultural terms. Despite claims that what constitutes corruption is culture-specific, something like a general international jurisprudence has developed in recent decades. The concept now 'travel[s] reasonably well in respect of the modern public sector of nation-states, especially state bureaucracies'.[248] Again, religions and cultures are not meaningful entities and it would be inaccurate – not to mention insulting – to suggest that there is 'any community disposition to fraud or misconduct'.[249] South Asian Muslims have been enthusiastic and valuable contributors to British democracy at least since *Maulvi* (religious scholar) Sir Rafiuddin Ahmed stood as a Conservative parliamentary

[242] Phoebe Weston, 'Today's Online Insults Are NOTHING Compared to Public Slander in Ancient Rome and People Need Be More Thick-Skinned, Says Top Historian' (*Daily Mail*, 27 August 2018).

[243] See Ryan Holiday, *Trust Me I'm Lying: Confessions of a Media Manipulator* (2nd ed., New York/London: Portfolio/Penguin, 2013); Peter Pomerantsev, *This Is Not Propaganda: Adventures in the War Against Reality* (London: Faber & Faber, 2019), pp. 13–46; Angela Nagle, *Kill All Normies: Online Culture Wars from 4CHAN and TUMBLR to Trump and the Alt-Right* (Alresford: Zero Books, 2017); Wil Crisp and Suadad al-Salhy, 'Inside Hizbollah's Fake News Training Camps Sowing Instability across the Middle East' (*The Telegraph*, 2 August 2020); Internet Historian, 'Main Channel: Videos' (YouTube, accessed 1 January 2017): www.youtube.com/c/InternetHistorian/videos.

[244] For striking parallels with the eighteenth-century satirists, see Karen Halttunen, 'Humanitarianism and the Pornography of Pain in Anglo-American Culture' (1995) 100(2) *American Historical Review* 303–34.

[245] BSB, 'BSB Handbook: Social Media Guidance' (BSB, October 2019), para. 3.

[246] Whitney Phillips and Ryan M. Miller, *The Ambivalent Internet: Mischief, Oddity, and Antagonism Online* (Cambridge: Polity, 2017), blurb.

[247] See Charles Mackay, 'Popular Follies of Great Cities' in his *Extraordinary Popular Delusions and the Madness of Crowds* (Ware: Wordsworth Editions, 1995), pp. 619–31.

[248] William Twining, 'Have Concepts, Will Travel: Analytical Jurisprudence in a Global Context' (2005) 1(1) *International Journal of Law in Context* 5–40, pp. 25–34.

[249] 2005 Birmingham case, para. 694.

candidate in the 1895 general election.[250] It would be equally mistaken, however, to view *biraderis* as vehicles for minority empowerment and participation. That is the proper domain of legitimate political parties and campaign groups of which there is a great variety from almost every section of society for almost any conceivable aim.[251] These clans are entirely unconcerned with the common good and, as one British Pakistani reporter explained, neither party loyalty nor political idealism features in their deliberations:

> Some people are supporting a candidate from one constituency and a second candidate from a different party in a different constituency . . . not because they were the same party but [because they are from the same *biraderi* or caste] . . . They have no values, no respect [for the British system] and do not know or do not want to know about [British] party politics and policies.[252]

In other words, the pattern of corruption in election fraud cases results from the functioning of a specific group unit, not an ethnic characteristic or religious injunction or cultural trait. Unlike other third-party campaign organisations, clans have no legal existence or structure whatever and, in exchange for influence, they offer political parties bloc votes over mere cash. This renders conventional regulations and offences useless against the collective element of the problem. That any party would court them evokes Robert Michels' 'iron law of oligarchy' which holds that the natural functioning of any organisation – state or non-state, left or right – will concentrate power in the hands of a self-interested elite.[253] Democracy has 'rough and slatternly foundations'[254] and local politics are reliably vituperative.[255] Yet even these will collapse if the organisations responsible for sustaining them turn inwards away from their ideals and lose sight of their ultimate purpose: to legitimately acquire legitimate power to govern the whole of society for the good of all.[256] Dealing with all of these problems – from general regulatory dilapidation to the specific threat of *biraderi* politicking – therefore requires an unconventional approach to law reform. This is first and foremost a matter for pluralism.

[250] Miles Taylor, 'The Indian Muslim Who Greatly Influenced Queen Victoria and Her India Policies' (*Scroll.in Magazine*, 19 July 2018).

[251] See Allen Potter, *Organized Groups in British National Politics* (London: Faber & Faber, 1961) and David Boothroyd, *Politico's Guide to the History of British Political Parties* (London: Politico, 2001).

[252] Quoted in Philip Lewis, *Young, British and Muslim* (London: Continuum, 2007), p. 52.

[253] Seymour Martin Lipset, 'Introduction' to Robert Michels, *Political Parties: A Sociological Study of the Oligarchical Tendencies of Modern Democracy*, Eden and Cedar Paul (transl.) (New York: Free Press, 1962; original published in German in 1915), p. 15.

[254] Winston S. Churchill quoted in Edmund Fawcett, *Liberalism: The Life of an Idea* (2nd ed., Princeton, NJ: Princeton University Press, 2018), p. 158.

[255] For a classic example, see Sky News, 'You Have No Authority Here, Jackie Weaver: Parish Meeting Descends into Chaos' (*Sky News*, 5 February 2021).

[256] Lipset, 'Introduction', pp. 15–39; Morris, *Parliamentary Elections, Representation and the Law*, p. 124.

The contours and defects of modern election law stem from its individualistic Victorian roots. It has been left to develop with insufficient attention paid to its public rationale as the 'fundament of power' in a democratic society. It has still not 'come wholly to terms with the political subject matter it regulates', namely political parties and campaign groups as entities acting as 'conduits of public power'.[257] Even today, 'there exists no general theory of parties' and jurisprudential thinking on the subject remains underdeveloped, largely descriptive and focused only upon on their bare legal existence as mere clubs or employers.[258] These are failures of the imagination with huge ramifications at every level of society and the cure must begin with theory. This is where Gierke can assist. On this view, elections are the deliberative organ of the nation which enable it to remain as one despite internal disagreement. Voting is the right and responsibility of the individual alone, although the insignificance of a single equal vote can be counteracted through association. Legitimate collective action occurs through political parties, Gierkean fellowships whose purpose is to compete to control the larger unit of the state in a lawful and ethical manner, with assistance on particular issues from more specialised campaign organisations. Political parties – not identities or classes – are the means by which individuals acquire true collective agency for the sole purpose of right governance; campaign groups are the means by which individuals acquire true collective agency for the sole and more limited purpose of influencing public opinion, political parties and government on issue-specific matters. Neither can be considered a true fellowship if it deviates from its purpose by, for example, discriminating on the basis of ethnicity or religion or non-membership of a particular family. Their sphere of competence extends only to those who purport to share their particular vision of the common good and it is on this basis alone that they are permitted to exclude from their ranks non-members and non-conformists. It is entirely natural and healthy for political fellowships to arise all across society for myriad reasons. While these groups can redress the disenfranchisement of the disadvantaged, they can also decay into privileged institutions or even vassals of other privileged institutions. At the theoretical level, corruption should therefore be understood in suitably organic terms: 'to make putrid, to taint, to debase, to spoil, to destroy the purity of, to pervert, to bribe'.[259] The job of election law is to regulate these interlocking relationships, define the spheres of group jurisdictions (i.e. what is a matter for state regulation and what should be properly left to the party organisation) and stymie or reverse any corruption of these entities and processes.

British Muslims seem to have little trouble navigating and participating in this system – there are countless campaign groups adapted to life under the liberal state and an increasing number of increasingly prominent Muslim or

[257] Morris, ibid., pp. 151–2. [258] Maurice Duverger quoted in ibid., pp. 22–3 footnote 112.
[259] *Chambers' Dictionary* quoted in Ewing, *The Cost of Democracy*, p. 88.

Muslim-heritage politicians.[260] Muslim-led groups, whether liberal or conservative, have intrinsic value as fellowships and instrumental value in so far as they allow individuals to cohere and take collective action. They are first and foremost expressions of the associational urge in humanity coloured by the communities in which they arose, not an extension of 'Muslims' or representative embodiments of a culture. As such, they should be treated as representatives for their own and their members' interests, not as spokesmen for a population or its 'mainstream' views. Election fraud long predates the growth of large South Asian populations and is not confined to them. Nevertheless, the endurance of clan structures in this portion of the general public is disordering the body politic. There are individual and collective dimensions to the harm inflicted: internal minority dissenters, non-minority minorities within the affected constituency, reputational damage to implicated populations and the nation as a whole, and diminished public trust in their representatives and their state. When litigation involving South Asian Muslims arises, it is not a slight on all within that category but simply justice meted out to offending individuals and specific organisations. Electoral fraud perpetrated by Muslims is not an expression of their culture, nor are counter-measures an attack on the faith or the faithful en bloc. As ever, crude class-based analyses serve nobody well. *Biraderis* are an ideal illustration of the privileged institution: their primary purpose is to protect and enhance the position of the kinship group and its patriarchal elite within British society and in the country of origin. The democratic process is either an instrument to this end or an obstacle to be subverted, just as political parties are treated as vassal institutions to be commandeered for family or factional interests. A perfect illustration of this is Tower Hamlets First, described by Mawrey QC as 'never really a party but the alter ego of Lutfur Rahman'.[261] Given the stakes, it might be thought surprising that this type of corruption goes unchecked and election law is allowed to fall into such a poor state of repair. This is probably the result of a combination of prosaic factors: the available statistics deflate the scale of the problem, academic activism obscures the real issues, and the regulations themselves are arcane and convoluted. While complacency and pessimism have prevailed thus far, doing nothing will further deflate domestic and international confidence in British democracy and may eventually lead to political instability and even violence.[262] The growing number of official

[260] See generally Stephen H. Jones, *Islam and the Liberal State: National Identity and the Future of Muslim Britain* (London: I.B. Tauris, 2021); Hamed Chapman, 'Record Number of Muslim MPs Elected' (*Muslim News*, 23 June 2017); Narjas Zatat, 'A Record Number of British-Muslim MPs Were Elected to Parliament in 2019' (*The New Arab*, 18 December 2019).

[261] Quoted in Sebastian Payne, 'Lutfur Rahman Removed as Mayor of Tower Hamlets' (*The Spectator*, 23 April 2015).

[262] See generally Pippa Norris, *Strengthening Electoral Integrity* (Cambridge: Cambridge University Press, 2017) and *Why Electoral Integrity Matters* (Cambridge: Cambridge University Press, 2014).

reports suggests that there is gathering momentum for reform.[263] From a pluralist perspective, depoliticisation, joined-up thinking and a coherent package are what is required. A general programme of consolidation and simplification would be a good start because, as one leading practitioner concedes, '[t]here are bits hanging off it everywhere' and '[a]lmost no one knows how it all works'.[264] More specifically, electoral corruption was historically curtailed by improvements to voter registration, the petitions process and the clarity of offences. Each shall be taken briefly in turn.

First, postal voting on demand is all but unsalvageable, as Mawrey QC notes, and there is 'no evidence to show that people are exercising their votes because they have a postal vote rather than going to a polling station in order to cast their votes'.[265] He is almost certainly correct to recommend jettisoning it entirely unless a secure hi-tech alternative can be found and made to work. Introducing voter ID requirements at the polling station would be another valuable safeguard against personation. Concerns about its effect on voter turnout are likely misconceived, the more so given the statistical problems around electoral fraud.[266] For some years after the introduction of compulsory registration in 1832, many apathetic voters 'failed to appreciate the advisability of registration . . . and did not see why they should have anything of the kind to do'.[267] Yet, in time, civic education, the incremental refinement of the system, and campaign group mobilisation turned registration into standard practice. There is every reason to believe that bringing ID to the polling station – now standard practice across the Continent – can be similarly encouraged and made to work, especially in the internet age.[268] Second, and least controversially, the Victorian petitions system must be rationalised and opened up to collective action by political parties to take the burden off private citizens and improve access to justice. This being done, a much better statistical picture of the scale of election fraud will emerge. Third, the relevant criminal offences need to be simplified and the penalties increased to improve deterrence and prevent repeat offending. Likewise, the Law Commission has recommended abolishing the concept of 'undue spiritual influence' and replacing it with a catch-all 'improper pressure' offence to cover every type of malpractice in this regard.[269] Given that

[263] Committee in Standards on Public Life, 'Committee on Standards in Public Life Announces Review of Electoral Regulation' (HMG, 8 June 2020).

[264] Gavin Millar, QC quoted in Geoghegan, *Democracy for Sale*, p. 25.

[265] Select Committee on the Electoral Registration and Administration Act 2013, 'An Electoral System Fit for Today? More to Be Done – Report of Session 2019–21' (House of Lords, HL83, July 2020), p. 60.

[266] See, for example, Heather Green, 'The Voter ID Pilots: An Unlawful Electoral Experiment' (2019) *Public Law* 242–50; Ben Stanford, 'The 2018 English Local Elections ID Pilots and the Right to Vote: A Vote of (No) Confidence?' (2018) 6 *European Human Rights Law Review* 600–13.

[267] Seymour, *Electoral Reform in England and Wales*, p. 116.

[268] For an overview of the arguments and trials, see Select Committee on the Electoral Registration and Administration Act 2013, 'An Electoral System Fit for Today?', pp. 67–75.

[269] Law Commission, *Electoral Law: A Final Joint Report*, pp. 138–40.

clannism and religion are often inseparable (and learning the lessons from the Trojan Horse litigation), this is eminently sensible for it reduces the scope for public misunderstanding, depoliticises the issue whenever minorities are involved and makes prosecutions and particularisation more straightforward. It would also be advisable to regulate the relationship between political parties and the *biraderi*, perhaps by creating a corporate offence of improper pressure or undue influence by proxy.

In combination, these amendments would better secure Dahl's five criteria for a pluralist democracy: effective participation, voting equality, enlightened or informed understanding, control of the political agenda, and inclusion.[270] Nevertheless, 'it is important to emphasise that corruption will not be prevented by regulating political parties alone'.[271] These practical steps are all necessary but insufficient as they leave the most important threats unaddressed at source. Foreign states and revolutionary groups such as the Muslim Brotherhood should be allowed nowhere near the nation's democratic infrastructure or the educational establishments that purport to study them. Once again, there is a need for the concepts of sedition and subversion to isolate these movements and prevent any of their affiliates from standing or participating in elections. Clannism presents a distinct and probably graver challenge to British democracy. How this can best be dealt with is the subject of the final chapter (Chapter 8) of this book.

270 Robert A. Dahl, *Democracy and Its Critics* (New Haven, CT: Yale University Press, 1989), p. 222.

271 Ewing, *The Cost of Democracy*, p. 26.

8

Clans

8.1 Introduction

This chapter analyses the nature, functioning and regulation of Muslim clans. It begins with a history of the regulation of endogamy in England. This is because clans are held together through consanguineous marriage and the prohibited degrees of relationship are the most relevant branch of law. There follows an analysis of the clan as a group unit with negative implications for public health as well as the social and political fabric of the nation. The point is to demonstrate that clannish behaviours, which present most prominently among British Muslim populations, are the product of a set of institutional norms rather than manifestations of any supposedly inherent ethnic, cultural or religious characteristics. The chapter proceeds with a theoretical discussion of clans and clannism. It observes that liberal individualistic approaches tend to focus on rights and demographic statistics while ignoring the clan phenomenon itself, while multiculturalism tends to insist on the integrity of minority cultural forms, over-emphasising the positives and evading difficult questions about the place of clans in the UK. The pluralist response focuses squarely on clans as group entities and constructs the legal argument for their dissolution through marriage law reform. For convenience, the term 'clan' serves as an ideal type to encompass the general features of multiple regional varieties.

8.2 A Brief History of Endogamy and English Law

The incest taboo is, almost, a human universal.[1] Although its conceptual core (i.e. parent–child, etc.) is relatively stable the world over, the ways in which it is regulated and its penumbra defined vary considerably across time and cultures. Despite the prevalence of endogamy throughout the Islamic world, for example, some medieval Muslim scholars were aware that marrying 'foreign

[1] Donald Brown, *Human Universals* (New York: McGraw-Hill, 1991) ch. 5, p. 118. The Ptolemies and other royal dynasties being the exceptions that prove the general rule: Sheila L. Ager, 'The Power of Excess: Royal Incest and the Ptolemaic Dynasty' (2006) 48 (2) *Anthropologica* 165–86.

women' outside their pure-blooded Arab kin 'could bring benefits in terms of the physical and mental attributes of any offspring'.[2] The West, by contrast, has typically taken a broad, dim view of its myriad forms which have, since classical times, been considered 'immoral and vile'.[3] Under early Germanic law, consanguineous couples were liable to have their marriages dissolved, their children declared illegitimate, and face heavy fines; by the sixth century, such relationships were vanishingly rare.[4] Following Roman law, the early medieval Church forbade relationships between lineal and collateral relatives within 'four degrees' (including first cousins); in the early ninth century this was expanded to the 'seven forbidden degrees' which remained as standard until the thirteenth century when it was reduced back to four.[5] These prohibitions were taken very seriously. The Pope himself would intervene in important cases to grant rare dispensations or forbid consanguineous unions while lawmakers, canonists and administrators worked vigorously at all levels of society to suppress them.[6] There were theological and pragmatic reasons for doing so. Incest was a criminal breach of divine law and the Church was expanding its authority over every aspect of family life, disrupting the succession of concentrated landholdings on which the rival power of feudal nobility rested.[7] In practice, the results were mixed but produced unintended consequences of monumental importance.[8] On one hand, the forbidden degrees were so expansive that they would have prevented virtually every match in small immobile communities had they not been violated on a huge scale.[9] As for the bottom, more so for the top. As Maurice Druon remarked of the Capetian dynasty in his *Accursed Kings* series:

> These cousins were all destined to marry each other to serve the political strategy of their parents, who had themselves all been married in a similar fashion: in the

[2] Simon Barton, *Conquerors, Brides and Concubines: Interfaith Relations and Social Power in Medieval Iberia* (Philadelphia: University of Pennsylvania Press, 2015), p. 43.

[3] Jonathan H. Turner and Alexandra Maryanski, *Incest: Origins of the Taboo* (Boulder, CO: Paradigm, 2005), p. 5.

[4] James A. Brundage, *Law, Sex, and Christian Society in Medieval Europe* (Chicago: Chicago University Press, 1987), pp. 130–1.

[5] Constance B. Bouchard, 'Consanguinity and Noble Marriages in the Tenth and Eleventh Centuries' (1981) 56(2) *Speculum* 268–87, pp. 269–70; Antonio García y García, 'The Fourth Lateran Council and the Canonists' in Wilfried Hartmann and Kenneth Pennington (eds.), *The History of Medieval Canon Law in the Classical Period, 1140–1234* (Washington, DC: Catholic University of America Press, 2008), ch. 11, pp. 367–78, at p. 377.

[6] Brundage, *Law, Sex, and Christian Society in Medieval Europe*, pp. 191–2.

[7] Ibid., pp. 191–3; Bouchard, 'Consanguinity and Noble Marriages in the Tenth and Eleventh Centuries', p. 271; Turner and Maryanski, *Incest*, p. 6.

[8] Joseph Henrich, *The Weirdest People in the World: How the West Became Psychologically Peculiar and Particularly Prosperous* (London: Allen Lane, 2020), chs. 5–8.

[9] Turner and Maryanski, *Incest*, pp. 6–7. See also Christof Rolker, 'Two Models of Incest: Conflict and Confusion in High Medieval Discourse on Kinship and Marriage' in Per Andersen, Kirsi Salonen, Helle Moller Sigh and Helle Vogt (eds.), *Law and Marriage in Medieval and Early Modern Times: Proceedings of the Eighth Carlsberg Academy Conference on Medieval Legal History* (Copenhagen: Djoef, 2012), pp. 139–59.

> closest consanguinity. How many dispensations must be asked of the Pope that territorial interests might take precedence of the laws of religion and the most elementary considerations of health! How many cripples and madmen were there in prospect! The only difference between Adam's descendants and Capet's was that that the latter had so far avoided incest between brothers and sisters.[10]

On the other, European Christendom was permanently imbued with a revulsion towards consanguineous marriages. Tales of incest were wildly popular among the laity who found them shocking, entertaining and educational in equal measure.[11] Even the nobility were usually careful to abide by the law – first cousin marriages were unknown in the tenth and eleventh centuries and many lords declined strategic matches by 'marrying down' to avoid opprobrium.[12] This attitude was a defining feature of medieval Christianity and the cumulative effect was the effective destruction of the extended kinship group.[13] In so doing, it broadened networks of trust; reduced nepotism and corruption, hierarchical obedience and ethnic conflict; permitted romantic love based on individual choice; reattached loyalty to impersonal, rule-based national institutions; all of which are necessary for the large-scale cooperation and coordination upon which the formation of modern democracy depended.[14] Low levels of consanguinity even precipitated the emergence of a distinctive 'Western, Educated, Industrialized, Rich and Democratic (WEIRD)' psychology characterised by greater analytical-mindedness, individualism, independence and extra-familial trust, and less conformity, obedience, in-group loyalty and nepotism.[15] These conditions were not replicated elsewhere in Eurasia, where religious prohibitions differed and harsher environments with labour-intensive irrigation systems incentivised lower marriage ages, greater intra-familial interdependency, and endogamy to keep scarce resources within the kin group.[16] To this day, the prevalence of consanguinity between second cousins or closer remains 'a major predictor of levels of democracy' and an 'important determinant' of corruption and social fractionalisation.[17]

10 *The Royal Succession* (London: Harper, Vol. 4 of 7, 2014), pp. 125–6.

11 Turner and Maryanski, *Incest*, pp. 7–11.

12 Bouchard, 'Consanguinity and Noble Marriages in the Tenth and Eleventh Centuries', p. 272; Megan McLaughlin, *Sex, Gender, and Episcopal Authority in an Age of Reform, 1000–1122* (Cambridge: Cambridge University Press, 2010), pp. 28–31.

13 Jonathan F. Schultz, 'The Churches' Bans on Consanguineous Marriages, Kin-Networks and Democracy' (Nottingham: University of Nottingham CEDEX Discussion Paper No. 2016–16/ ISSN 1749-3293, November 2016), pp. 14–17.

14 Ibid., pp. 7–9; see also Eric M. Uslaner, *Corruption, Inequality and the Rule of Law* (Cambridge: Cambridge University Press, 2008).

15 Jonathan Schulz, Duman Bahrami-Rad, Jonathan Beauchamp and Joseph Henrich, 'The Church, Intensive Kinship, and Global Psychological Variation' (2019) 366(6466) *Science* 1–12, p. 1.

16 Philip Wood, 'Marriage and Social Boundaries among British Pakistanis' (2018) 20(1) *Diaspora* 40–64, p. 42; Jack Goody, 'Comparing Family Systems in Europe and Asia: Are There Different Sets of Rules?' (1996) 22(1) *Population and Development Review* 1–20.

17 Michael Woodley and Edward Bell, 'Consanguinity as a Major Predictor of Levels of Democracy: A Study of 70 Nations' (2012) 44(2) *Journal of Cross-Cultural Psychology* 263–80;

With the coming of the Reformation under Henry VIII, the forbidden degrees retreated within the bounds set by *Leviticus* 18:6–18, which does not mention cousins.[18] This followed the zeitgeist for pruning man-made accretions and hewing as closely as possible to scripture.[19] The common law affirmed the legality of cousin marriage during the Restoration era and thereafter it became accepted practice among landed and wealthy Georgians.[20] Indeed, both George I and George IV married their first cousins and 'cousins in love, &c.' featured prominently in the literature of Jane Austen.[21] The Victorian era was at once the high watermark and the turning point as regards the social acceptability of cousin marriage. Queen Victoria herself married her first cousin, Prince Albert, and acted as matchmaker behind 'the European cousinhood' with a view to dominating the continent through endogamous marriage alliances.[22] Many of her descendants were to die prematurely of 'the Royal disease', haemophilia.[23] Similarly, three of Charles Darwin's children from his marriage to his first cousin, Emma (née Wedgwood), died young from diseases associated with inbreeding.[24] Darwin himself feared this to be the case and his pioneering ideas on biology would do much to discredit cousin marriage, which began to decline in popularity from around 1860.[25]

Mahsa Akbari, Duman Bahrami-Rad and Erik O. Kimbrough, 'Kinship, Fractionalization and Corruption' (2019) 166 *Journal of Economic Behavior and Organization* 493–528.

18 Marriage Act 1540. See also Martha Bailey, 'The Marriage Law of Jane Austen's World' (2015) 36(1) *Persuasions* and Adam Kuper, *Incest and Influence: The Private Life of Bourgeois England* (Cambridge, MA: Harvard University Press, 2009), pp. 61–3.

19 Saskia Lettmaier, 'Marriage Law and the Reformation' (2017) 35(2) *Law and History Review* 461–510, p. 499.

20 Nancy Fix Anderson, 'Cousin Marriage in Victorian England' (1986) 11(3) *Journal of Family History* 285–301, pp. 285–6.

21 Mary Jean Corbett, '"Cousins in Love, &c." in Jane Austen' (2004) 23(2) *Tulsa Studies in Women's Literature* 237–59.

22 Tony Rennell, 'Game of Thrones! How Queen Victoria Sat at the Centre of a Spider's Web of European Royal Connections – and Used Them to Find a Match for Her "Foolish" Grandson Prince Albert Victor' (*Daily Mail*, 17 May 2019).

23 Yelena Aronova-Tiuntseva and Clyde Freeman Herreid, 'Haemophilia: "The Royal Disease"' (2003) *SUNY Science Cases* 1–5. Recent research has indicated that inbreeding among another famous royal lineage, the Habsburgs, was the cause of their mandibular prognathism, or distinctive deformed chin: Román Vilas et al., 'Is the "Habsburg Jaw" Related to Inbreeding?' (2019) *Annals of Human Biology* (2019) 553–61. Perhaps unsurprisingly, greater inbreeding worsened state performance: Sebastian Ottinger and Nico Voigtländer, 'History's Masters: The Effect of European Monarchs on State Performance' (Cambridge, MA: National Bureau of Economic Research Working Paper, December 2020).

24 Tim M. Berra, Gonzalo Alvarez and Francisco C. Ceballos, 'Was the Darwin/Wedgwood Dynasty Adversely Affected by Consanguinity?' (2010) 60(5) *BioScience* 376–83. See also Katherine Harmon, 'Charles Darwin's Family Tree Tangled with Inbreeding, Early Death' (*Scientific American*, 3 May 2010).

25 Martin Ottenheimer, *Forbidden Relatives: The American Myth of Cousin Marriage* (Champaign: University of Illinois Press, 1996), pp. 85–90; Mary Jean Corbett, *Family Likeness: Sex, Marriage, and Incest from Jane Austen to Virginia Woolf* (Ithaca, NY: Cornell University Press, 2008), p. 221; Adrian Desmond and James Moore, *Darwin* (London: Penguin, 1990), p. 447; Adam Kuper, 'Commentary: A Darwin Family Concern' (2009) 38(6) *International Journal of Epidemiology* 1439–42.

Thereafter, or thereabouts, the tenor of debate might best be summed up by Anthony Trollope's Dr Crofts in *The Small House at Allington* (1862–4): 'I'm not quite sure that it's a good thing for cousins to marry.' Darwin's fifth child, the barrister and polymath Sir George Howard Darwin, produced some of the most accurate and important contemporary studies on cousin marriage in Britain.[26] He discovered considerable variation according to social class in that, respectively, 4.5 per cent of aristocratic, 3.5 per cent of bourgeois, 2.25 per cent of rural and 1.15 per cent of urban (London) marriages were between first cousins.[27] By the late nineteenth century, 7.5 per cent of Jewish marriages were between first cousins, a rate twice that of the same occurring between English aristocrats, five times higher than those of Londoners and roughly three times greater than those of the general non-Jewish population.[28] The principal families of the Anglo-Jewish gentry, like their non-Jewish counterparts of the period, favoured consanguineous marriages and were known as 'the Cousinhood'.[29] It also formed the basis for the Victorian intellectual aristocracy, with Oxbridge and magic circle law firms dominated by the relatively closed ranks of a few prominent families.[30]

During this period, the United States diverged sharply from Europe in its approach to cousin marriage. Once widespread, it came to be popularly reviled and was prohibited by civil law in the majority of states.[31] While there was certainly a growing awareness of the health implications, the primary motivation in America for confronting it this forcefully appears to have been a desire to ensure that immigrants integrated properly into society.[32] In England, a greater awareness of the biological risks, increasing social mobility, female emancipation, disproportionately high casualty rates among the upper classes during World War I, and growing popular disapproval resulted in a precipitous drop of cousin marriages rates during the early twentieth century.[33] Before the Great War, such unions were already stigmatised and unusual enough not to be

26 George H. Darwin, 'Marriages between First Cousins in England and Their Effects' (1875) 38(2) *Journal of the Statistical Society* 153–84.

27 Kuper, *Incest and Influence*, p. 97. This rate seems to have remained steady throughout the nineteenth century (p. 251).

28 Joseph Jacobs, *Studies in Jewish Statistics: Social, Vital and Anthropometric* (London: D. Nutt, 1891), p. 3; Cyrus Adler and Joseph Jacobs, 'Consanguinity among Jews' in *Jewish Encyclopaedia* (New York: Funk and Wagnalls, 1906), pp. 229–30.

29 For a general history, see Chaim Bermant, *The Cousinhood* (New York: Macmillan, 1972).

30 Noel Annan, 'The Intellectual Aristocracy' (1955 reprint) and 'The Dons Create and Intellectual Aristocracy' in *The Dons: Mentors, Eccentrics and Geniuses* (London: Macmillan, 2000), respectively, (*Annexe*) pp. 304–41 and pp. 5–23; Marc Galanter and Simon Roberts 'From Kinship to Magic Circle: The London Commercial Law Firm in the Twentieth Century' (2008) 15:3 *International Journal of the Legal Profession* 143–78; Mary Jean Corbett, 'Cousin Marriage, Then and Now' (2013) 39(2) *Victorian Review* 74–8.

31 Martin Ottenheimer, 'Lewis Henry Morgan and the Prohibition of Cousin Marriage in the United States' (1990) 15(3) *Journal of Family History* 325–34; Kuper, *Incest and Influence*, pp. 246–9.

32 See generally Ottenheimer, *Forbidden Relatives.*

33 Kuper, *Incest and Influence*, pp. 249–53.

considered for a statutory ban, but after it, they became 'almost unthinkable' and 'extremely rare'.[34] Thus, by the 1930s only 1 in 6,000 marriages was to a first cousin, while a later study of middle-class Londoners from the 1960s found that this had dropped even further to 1 in 25,000.[35] It was under these conditions that the Marriage Act 1949 – which does not include cousins in the prohibited degrees – was passed, prior to the post-British Nationality Act 1948 influx of immigrants among whom cousin marriage was still popular. This omission created an 'immigration superhighway' for certain Commonwealth populations to 'transpose the kin group' back into the UK.[36]

Approximately 20 per cent of the world population lives in societies which prefer consanguineous marriage (typically defined as a relationship between second cousins or even closer relatives).[37] Globally, first cousin marriages are the most common form and they predominate in the Muslim world, with a prevalence of around 68 per cent in Kuwait and 60 per cent in Pakistan.[38] There are no reliable or comprehensive statistics for Britain, although a recent estimate suggests that it has risen from less than 1 per cent in the late twentieth century to somewhere between 1 and 4 per cent by 2015.[39] The available data on specific subgroups is fragmentary at best, with some populations – namely British Pakistanis – being better studied than others. It has been claimed, although on what basis is unclear, that around 25 per cent of cousin marriages in the UK are between white Britons.[40] Most British Pakistanis marry foreign spouses (71 per cent) and, with regional variances, the proportion of marriages within the extended family ranges from 59 to 87 per cent, with 38 to 59 per cent between first cousins.[41] These rates are

[34] Ibid., p. 250; Nancy Anderson, p. 297.

[35] Ibid., pp. 250–1; Adam Kuper, 'Kissing Cousins' (*New Humanist*, 9 September 2009).

[36] The Economist, 'The Immigration Superhighway' (*The Economist*, 16 April 2009); see also John Bowen, *On British Islam: Religion, Law, and Everyday Practice in Sharia Councils* (Princeton, NJ: Princeton University Press, 2016), p. 22.

[37] See A. H. Bittles and M. L. Black, 'Consanguinity, Human Evolution, and Complex Diseases' (2010) 107(1) *PNAS* 1779–86; Munir Ahmad Bhinder, Haleema Sadia, Nasir Mahmood, Muhammad Qasim, Zawar Hussain, Muhammad Mudassar Rashid, Muhammad Yasir Zahoor, Rashid Bhatti, Wasim Shehzad, Ali Muhammad Waryah and Shah Jahan, 'Consanguinity: A Blessing or Menace at Population Level?' (2019) 83(4) *Annals of Human Genetics* 214–19.

[38] Oniya Olumbunyi, Karen Neves, Ahmed Badreldeen and Justin C. Konje, 'A Review of the Reproductive Consequences of Consanguinity' (2019) 232 *European Journal of Obstetrics & Gynaecology and Reproductive Biology* 87–96, p. 89.

[39] M.T. Smith, 'Estimates of Cousin Marriage and Mean Inbreeding in the United Kingdom from "Birth Briefs"' (2001) 33(1) *Journal of Biosocial Science* 55–66, p. 59; A. H. Bittles, 'The Global Prevalence of Consanguinity' (Consang.net, undated, accessed summer 2019).

[40] Mohammed Zaheer, 'Cousin Marriages Could Die Out for British Muslim Pakistanis' (VICE, 10 September 2019); Aamra Darr, 'HGSG Briefing Paper: Consanguineous Marriage and Inherited Disorders' (University of Bradford, October 2010), p. 2.

[41] Noah Carl, 'Ethnicity and Electoral Fraud in Britain' (2017) 50 *Electoral Studies* 128–36, pp. 132–3; Katharine Charsley, 'Vulnerable Brides and Transnational *Ghar Damads*: Gender, Risk and "Adjustment" among Pakistani Marriage Migrants to Britain' (2005) 12(2–3) *Indian Journal of Gender Studies* 381–406, p. 384; Katharine Charsley, *Transnational Pakistani Connections: Marrying 'Back Home'* (London: Routledge, 2013), p. 89; Ammara Maqsood,

probably higher than in Pakistan itself – 'Pakistanis become more likely to marry their cousins when they move to Britain'[42] – where rates have steadily increased from 39 per cent in 1980 (Lahore) to 61 per cent by 2010 (entire country).[43] Numerous studies have shown a comparable increase in the UK, from 33 to 55 per cent in West Yorkshire and 37 to 59 per cent in Oxford, over a single generation.[44] Although 90 per cent of first cousin marriages are transnational, fewer than half of marriages to spouses in the UK were to relatives.[45] Despite some suggestions that younger British Pakistanis are starting to question the practice, 'there appear to be no such clear indications of a decline in cousin marriage'.[46] What is more, such 'reformist' trends tend to be over-represented in ethnographic literature because of biases in the techniques and interpretations used.[47] The data is much more limited for British Bangladeshis, although cousin marriage is also known to be common in this demographic: provincial estimates from within Bangladesh range from 7 to 18 per cent, but in that part of Asia the general prevalence tends to be between 20 and 30 per cent.[48] The prevalence of cousin marriage matters because it is 'the cornerstone of the perpetuation of the *biraderi*', the *brath-thitho* and other varieties of clan.[49]

8.3 Clans, Public Health, Clannism and Geopolitics

8.3.1 The Clan as a Group Unit

As a group unit, clans must be taken on their own terms and as such it is important to avoid 'sticking to the language and terms that fit Western

'From Pakistan with Love: Islam, Intimacy and Transnational Marriages' (UK Research and Innovation, ES/L009757/1, 2014–17): https://gtr.ukri.org/projects?ref=ES%2FL009757%2F1.

42 Bowen, *On British Islam*, p. 20.

43 M. Bildirici, M. Kökdener and Ö. Ersin, 'An Empirical Analysis of the Effects of Consanguineous Marriages on Economic Development' (2010) 35(4) *Journal of Family History* 368–94, p. 377; Charsley, *Transnational Pakistani Connections*, p. 89.

44 Alison Shaw, 'British Pakistani Cousin Marriages and the Negotiation of Reproductive Risk' in Alison Shaw and Aviad E. Raz (eds.), *Cousin Marriages: Between Tradition, Genetic Risk and Cultural Change* (Oxford: Berghahn, 2015), ch. 5, pp. 113–29 at pp. 116–17.

45 Charsley, *Transnational Pakistani Connections*, p. 89; Charsley, 'Vulnerable Brides and Transnational *Ghar Damads*', p. 384; Alison Shaw, 'Drivers of Cousin Marriage among British Pakistanis' (2014) 77(1–4) *Human Heredity* 26–36; Maqsood, 'From Pakistan with Love'.

46 Zaheer, 'Cousin Marriages Could Die Out for British Muslim Pakistanis'; Shaw, 'British Pakistani Cousin Marriages and the Negotiation of Reproductive Risk', p. 117; Katharine Charsley, Marta Bolognani, Evelyn Ersanilli and Sarah Spencer, *Marriage, Migration and Integration* (London: Macmillan, 2020), p. 107.

47 See Marta Bolognani and Jody Mellor, 'British Pakistani Women's Use of the "Religion vs. Culture" Contrast: A Critical Analysis' (2012) 13(2) *Culture and Religion: An Interdisciplinary Journal* 211–26.

48 Carl, 'Ethnicity and Electoral Fraud in Britain', p. 132; A. H. Bittles and M. L. Black, 'The Impact of Consanguinity on Neonatal and Infant Health' (2010) 86(11) *Early Human Development* 737–41, p. 740.

49 Alison Shaw, *Kinship and Continuity: Pakistani Families in Britain* (London: Routledge, 2000), p. 4.

academic sensibilities'.[50] To properly understand them, 'we must put our preconceptions to one side. We must imagine ourselves into a world where action [is] governed by norms reflecting exclusively the claims of the family, its memories, rituals and roles, rather than the claims of individual conscience.'[51] The clan is the most enduring form of human organisation and our species' default social setting; in historical terms, clans were 'the world until yesterday' and allow 'all societies a glimpse of their origins'.[52] Their ultimate purpose is to secure family assets – material, human, reputational – and identities across time and space.[53] They are highly effective at this, acting as guarantors of solidarity and hence survival in inhospitable conditions. In so doing, they simultaneously fulfil every function and exercise every power the Western mind now compartmentalises: familial, political, cultural, economic, defensive, diplomatic, educational, religious, ethical, etiquette, lifestyle, disciplinary, adjudicational, administrative, executive. They are each and all of these things at once, an entity in which individual and collective are undifferentiated and inseverable. Kin, ethnicity, caste, sect and regional identity blur and blend into one another, although the clan is the idiom typically used to define relatedness and demarcate difference.[54] To give a sense of their importance relative to one another, one tribal elder's self-description is revealing: 'I have been a Pashtun for six thousand years, a Muslim for thirteen hundred years, and a Pakistani for twenty-five.'[55] The normative codes of honour and hospitality binding clan members together, such as the *Pashtunwali* of the Pashtuns or the *xeer* of the Somalis and many others, are rigorously applied and enforced regardless of territorial jurisdiction.[56] Men are expected to be virile and women sexually prudent.[57] Individual and collective reputation are inalienable: a person's conduct reflects not just upon them but also upon their clan's integrity and standing.[58] Justice therefore requires the careful balancing of both individual and group interests with a view to reaching a tolerable settlement and averting a blood feud.[59] The treatment one receives ultimately depends upon one's status within the kin group.[60] Any shameful behaviour or scandal is taken as

[50] Matthew Engelke, *Think Like an Anthropologist* (London: Pelican, 2017), p. 109.

[51] Larry Siedentop, *Inventing the Individual: The Origins of Western Liberalism* (London: Penguin, 2015), p. 7.

[52] Jared Diamond, *The World until Yesterday* (London: Penguin, 2013), pp. 12–19; Akbar Ahmed, *The Thistle and the Drone: How America's War on Terror Became a Global War on Tribal Islam* (Washington, DC: Brookings Institution Press, 2013), p. 4.

[53] Ikhlaq Din, *The New British: The Impact of Culture and Community on Young Pakistanis* (Farnham: Ashgate, 2006), p. 143; Bowen, *On British Islam*, pp. 18–22.

[54] Shaw, *Kinship and Continuity*, pp. 157–8; Shaw, 'British Pakistani Cousin Marriages and the Negotiation of Reproductive Risk', p. 115.

[55] Ahmed, *The Thistle and the Drone*, pp. 21–2.

[56] Ibid.; Henry Srebrnik, 'The Traditional Systems of Justice of Pashtuns and Somalis' (*Journal Pioneer*, 29 September 2017).

[57] Charsley, *Transnational Pakistani Connections*, pp. 146–7. [58] Ibid., pp. 148–9.

[59] Ahmed, *The Thistle and the Drone*, pp. 21–7.

[60] Mark S. Weiner, *Rule of the Clan: What an Ancient Form of Social Organization Reveals about the Future of Individual Freedom* (New York: Picador, 2013), p. 9.

a sign of disunity, itself signalling weakness and a loss of control, in turn a blight on the clan's prestige and honour.[61] Advancement within the clan requires respect accrued from being male and married, lifelong obedience, and age enough to count as an elder.[62] All this makes clans extraordinarily resilient and resistant to control by even the most powerful nation or empire.[63] The Roman Empire manipulated the competitive honour culture of local aristocracies to govern for centuries; one of Muhammad's main worldly achievements was to fashion the first Islamic polity from stateless Arabian tribes with promises of heaven and booty.[64] Throughout recorded history, then, clans often appear as antagonists to the state (and vice versa), useful instruments of it, or as a means for elites to capture it.[65]

Clans originating in environments requiring labour-intensive irrigation systems are incentivised to retain especially strict control over scarce property and human resources compared with those in more temperate regions which permit easier relocation and the scattering of households with each generation.[66] Their cohesion has typically been achieved, as with modern British Pakistanis and Bangladeshis, through endogamous marriage preferences. These are expressed through a descending preference hierarchy from *khandan* (extended family), *biraderi* (clan) and *zat* (caste) through sect and religion, to ethnicity and nationality.[67] Matches between relatives are typically arranged for strategic purposes to maximise personal and family advantages while reinforcing existing clan bonds.[68] Informal and intergenerational *kameti* financing schemes as well as multinational property enterprises are

[61] Wood, 'Marriage and Social Boundaries among British Pakistanis', p. 42; Charsley, *Transnational Pakistani Connections*, p. 146; Din, *The New British*, p. 141.

[62] Din, ibid., p. 144.

[63] Jakub J. Grygiel, *The Return of the Barbarians: Confronting Non-state Actors from Ancient Rome to the Present* (Cambridge: Cambridge University Press, 2018), pp. 39–42; James C. Scott, *The Art of Not Being Governed: An Anarchist History of Upland Southeast Asia* (New Haven, CT: Yale University Press, 2009).

[64] J. E. Lendon, *Empire of Honour* (Oxford: Oxford University Press, 2001); Deepak Lal, *Unintended Consequences: The Impact of Factor Endowments, Culture and Politics on Long-Run Economic Performance* (Cambridge, MA: MIT Press, 2001), pp. 50–2.

[65] On the former, see generally Adrian Goldsworthy, *The Fall of the West: The Death of the Roman Superpower* (London: W&N, 2010) and Frank Holt, *Into the Land of Bones: Alexander the Great in Afghanistan* (Berkeley: University of California Press, 2012); on the next, see G. W. Bowersock, *The Throne of Adulis: Red Sea Wars on the Eve of Islam* (Oxford: Oxford University Press, 2013), George McDonald Fraser, *The Steel Bonnets: The Story of the Anglo-Scottish Border Reivers* (London: HarperCollins, 1989) and Giles Milton, *Russian Roulette: How British Spies Defeated Lenin* (London: Hodder, 2013); on the latter, see Tom Holland, *Dynasty* (London: Abacus, 2016) and Bamber Gascoigne, *The Dynasties of China* (London: Folio Society, 2014).

[66] See Goody, 'Comparing Family Systems in Europe and Asia', p. 4; Wood, 'Marriage and Social Boundaries among British Pakistanis', p. 42; Per G. Fredriksson and Satyendra Kumar Gupta, 'Irrigation and Culture: Gender Roles and Women's Rights' (GLO Discussion Paper No. 681, October 2020).

[67] Wood, 'Marriage and Social Boundaries among British Pakistanis', p. 42.

[68] Charsley, *Transnational Pakistani Connections*, p. 83.

underpinned by this 'set of shared cultural premises'; they are administered by the *biraderi* who decide on everything down to 'where to buy land in Pakistan, what kind of house to build', who to marry, where to settle, and so on.[69] In many cases, the dictates of the *biraderi* 'override the wishes of the parents' and the prospective spouses alike, from whom unquestioned loyalty is expected.[70] Yet, however much these pressures may influence individuals' decisions to marry their cousins, they are not necessarily determinative. Some are 'actually happy' to marry someone from Pakistan of the same sect and cast; some are 'totally against' cousin marriage and find it 'weird'; others do it reluctantly out of a sense of familial duty; a few have parents willing to risk dishonour by supporting their daughters' choices.[71] One study found that 83 per cent of young British Pakistanis (of both sexes) would prefer to select a partner themselves as opposed to a mere 8 per cent who thought that their parents should do this.[72] Most wanted a well-qualified British partner who could speak English and were wary of marrying uncool 'freshies' from Pakistan who were comparably less well educated and culturally incompatible.[73] In short, endogamy consolidates clan assets and remains a powerful driver of transnational marriage trends among British Pakistanis; it does not go uncontested and neither is it practised by everyone for identical reasons or with the same degree of enthusiasm. There are two types of problem associated with its growth in the UK.

8.3.2 Clans and Public Health

The first set of issues is to do with public health and arises from the fact that endogamous reproduction leads to higher rates of inherited disorders and other medical conditions. In clinical terms, consanguineous relationships are typically defined as those between relations up to and including second cousins (beyond this, genetic relatedness differs only slightly from that of the general population).[74] On average, double first cousins share 25 per cent of their DNA (share both sets of grandparents and are as genetically similar as half siblings), first cousins 12.5 per cent (share one set of grandparents) and second cousins 3.125 per cent (share one set of great-grandparents). Cousin marriages are associated with higher-than-average fertility rates and the risk of having an

[69] Ibid., p. 102; Din, *The New British*, p. 144; Bowen, *On British Islam*, p. 24.

[70] Din, *The New British*, p. 143.

[71] Ibid.; Charsley et al., *Marriage, Migration and Integration*, p. 107; Charsley, *Transnational Pakistani Connections*, pp. 149–51; Zaheer, 'Cousin Marriages Could Die Out for British Muslim Pakistanis'.

[72] Din, *The New British*, p. 142.

[73] Ibid., p. 143; Katharine Charsley and Marta Bolognani, 'Being a Freshie Is (Not) Cool: Stigma, Capital and Disgust in British Pakistani Stereotypes of New Subcontinental Migrants' (2017) 40 (1) *Ethnic and Racial Studies* 43–62.

[74] A. H. Bittles, 'Consanguinity and Its Relevance to Clinical Genetics' (2001) 60(2) *Clinical Genetics* 89–98.

affected child doubles from 2 to 3 per cent to 4 to 6 per cent.[75] These risks intensify, and otherwise rare diseases cluster, with each generation of the endogamous group because of their greater number of shared ancestors.[76] The relevant disorders – such as Tay-Sachs, cerebral palsy, cystic fibrosis, beta thalassaemia – require lifelong intensive treatment and often result in premature death.[77] For example, research conducted in 2005 by BBC2's *Newsnight* found that while British Pakistanis accounted for 3.4 per cent of all births nationwide, their children accounted for 30 per cent of recessive gene disorders.[78] Diseases inherited from consanguineous relationships have led to excessive child death rates in Bradford and are the cause of one in five child deaths in the East London borough of Redbridge.[79] Beyond these, there are other negative health implications of varying seriousness: increased susceptibility to various cancers and infectious pathogens such as hepatitis; greater frequencies of birth defects including facial clefts and cardiovascular conditions; increased risks of various psychoses such as mood disorders, schizophrenia and Alzheimer's; and higher infant mortality rates.[80] If one puts stock in IQ as a measure of human intelligence, higher consanguinity rates correlate with lower national IQ scores.[81] As regards the attitude of British Pakistanis and Bangladeshis towards these risks, some were dismissive and uninformed adherents of bogus folkloric biology, some were dimly or largely aware of the dangers but willing to take their chances in light of the perceived social benefits, others fatalistic and resigned to 'Allah's will', yet others sought to manage or avoid the risks altogether.[82] Whenever these risks materialize,

75 Shaw, 'British Pakistani Cousin Marriages and the Negotiation of Reproductive Risk', p. 119.

76 Mohammed Amin, 'Playing Russian Roulette with My Baby's Health: The Health Risks of Marrying One's First Cousin' (author's blog, 21 May 2019): www.mohammedamin.com /Community_issues/Russian-roulette-with-baby.html.

77 Baroness Ruth Deech, 'Cousin Marriage' (Gresham College Lectures, 23 March 2010); Martina Merten, 'Keeping It in the Family: Consanguineous Marriage and Genetic Disorders, from Islamabad to Bradford' (2019) *British Medical Journal* 365.

78 See Justin Rowlatt, 'The Risks of Cousin Marriage' (*BBC Newsnight*, 16 November 2005); BBC News, 'Birth Defects Warning Sparks Row' (*BBC News*, 10 February 2008).

79 Nazia Parveen, 'Cousin Marriages Cited as Significant Factor in Bradford Child Deaths' (*The Guardian*, 15 February 2019); Sue Mitchell, 'Did My Children Die Because I Married My Cousin?' (*BBC News*, 14 December 2018).

80 Emily J. Lyons, Angela J. Frodsham, Lyna Zhang, Adrian V. S. Hill and William Amos, 'Consanguinity and Susceptibility to Infectious Diseases in Humans' (2009) 5(4) *Biology Letters* 574–6; Ruth McQuillan et al., 'Evidence of Inbreeding Depression on Human Height' (2012) 8 (7) *PLOS Genetics* 1–14; Olubunmi Oniya, Karen Neves, Badreldeen Ahmed and Justin C. Konje, 'A Review of the Reproductive Consequences of Consanguinity' (2019) 232 *European Journal of Obstetrics & Gynecology and Reproductive Biology* 87–96; Aideen Maguire, Foteini Tseliou and Dermot O'Reilly, 'Consanguineous Marriage and the Psychopathology of Progeny: A Population-Wide Data Linkage Study' (2018) 75(5) *JAMA Psychiatry* 438–46.

81 M. Sadaat, 'Consanguinity and National IQ Scores' (2006) 62(6) *Journal of Epidemiology & Community Health* 566–7.

82 Shaw, 'British Pakistani Cousin Marriages and the Negotiation of Reproductive Risk', pp. 113–27; Deech, 'Cousin Marriage'; Santi Rozario and Sophie Gilliat-Ray, 'Genetics, Religion and Identity: A Study of British Bangladeshis 2004-7' (ESRC Working Paper, 2007), pp. 37, 91;

tragedy results on every level: the blight of illness for each individual child, the heartbreak and stress for the child's carers, the burden on already stretched local NHS services. The problems are not confined to the medical sphere.

8.3.3 Manifestations of Clannism

8.3.3.1 Harms to Members

The second set of issues has to do with clannism. This term denotes the social and political problems arising from the functioning of clans. The spectrum of behaviours described ranges from antisocial to criminal; these behaviours are best viewed as mechanisms by which the clan, as a group unit, demarcates its own boundaries against other out-groups, including the host society.[83] This is best achieved through increasingly ostentatious displays of belief (religious or otherwise) which become ritualised to secure in-group cooperation and signal affiliation, commitment and status to outsiders.[84] Life within the clan is thus conditioned by a distinctive set of institutional norms. Clan members' lives, and those of women especially, are tightly controlled by relatives. *Biraderi* life is typically concentrated in small geographical areas spread across a few streets or nearby neighbourhoods where there is little need or opportunity to have much to do with wider society or practise the English language.[85] In this microcosm, the greatest collective fear is 'renegadism', or behaviour by members which contravenes shared norms and jeopardises the integrity or image of the in-group.[86] Sustained interaction with non-relatives, immodest dress, experimentation with drink and drugs, inappropriate education, marital infidelity, female promiscuity, homosexuality, apostasy, generic disobedience or eccentricity – these are not just individual choices to be disapproved of but grave threats to the entire group akin to treason. The punishments and pre-emptive measures can be correspondingly severe: domestic violence, confinement, abductions, female genital mutilation (FGM), forced marriage, honour murders. Evidence of their infliction must also be concealed wherever possible. Otherwise, deviance is deterred by financial threats, constant unannounced visits by in-laws and fear of merciless gossip, with ostracism being particularly effective where urban cosmopolitanism is weak.[87] Men are also manipulated,

Santi Rozario, 'Genetics, Religion and Identity among British Bangladeshis: Some Initial Findings' (2005) 2 *Diversity in Health and Social Care* 187–96.

83 Wood, 'Marriage and Social Boundaries among British Pakistanis', pp. 40, 58.

84 Eric Funkhouser, 'A Tribal Mind: Beliefs That Signal Group Identity or Commitment' (2020) *Mind & Language* 1–21, pp. 5–7.

85 Bowen, *On British Islam*, pp. 18–19, 24; Shaw, *Kinship and Continuity*, pp. 69–109; Wood, 'Marriage and Social Boundaries among British Pakistanis'.

86 Simon Cottee, *The Apostates: When Muslims Leave Islam* (London: Hurst, 2015), p. 13.

87 Stephen H. Jones, *Islam and the Liberal State: National Identity and the Future of Muslim Britain* (London: I.B. Tauris, 2021), p. 90; Weiner, *Rule of the Clan*, pp. 113–15; Wood, 'Marriage and Social Boundaries among British Pakistanis', p. 56; Mark S. Granovetter, 'The Strength of Weak Ties' (1973) 78(6) *American Journal of Sociology* 1360–80.

neglected and abused under this system – one-fifth of reported victims of honour abuse are male.[88] They can be forced to abandon education and ambitions for menial work 'to keep the family happy', for example, or might be goaded by covetous relatives (claiming he has a *gori*, or 'white woman on the side') into 'losing it' and winding up in jail so that their wife will revert to someone else. In other cases, young people are unwittingly dispatched to Pakistan or Bangladesh to marry cousins at the behest of their elders, sometimes remaining for long periods at great cost to their progress at school.[89] If men develop addictions, they will often be spirited away to villages in Pakistan so that this weakness may be concealed and the clan's reputation protected. However, 'village rehab seldom works' as proper medical treatment is absent and, in any event, Afghan drug barons have moved in to capitalise on a captive market protected by a 'wall of silence'.[90] It bears repetition that clannism is not simply traditionalism or conservativism; it is the unwritten code propping up an exclusive and tangible social institution.

8.3.3.2 Harms to Non-members

Outsiders are also affected because clans treat them as inferiors on regional, religious or racial grounds. It is not accurate to portray this as 'British Pakistanis' or 'British Bangladeshis' refusing en bloc to have anything to do with outsiders. Rather, specific clans are jostling for position against other clans from different villages, regions and castes with different traditions and so on.[91] The rest of British society is simply collateral damage as petty rivalries and pointless feuds are prosecuted on a transnational scale.[92] At times, this takes on comical proportions: *biraderi* competition over who could put on the most lavish and best-attended wedding 'got so out of hand' that Pakistan had to legislate against 'Ostentatious Displays and Wasteful Expenses'.[93] The dark side to this is that British spouses end up having to foot enormous bills for their relatives' ceremonies; one British Pakistani woman even broke off her engagement to a Pakistani fiancé when she learned of his plans to pay for each of his four sisters' weddings.[94] Many inter-clan disputes involve local squabbles combined with marriage issues, such as the struggle for control over Aston mosque in Birmingham in 2013 when police were called because one *biraderi* wanted to take the microphone from another and each mobilised their kin for a fight.[95]

[88] Katie Razzall and Yasminara Khan, 'Charities Sound the Alarm on Male "Honour Abuse"' (*BBC News*, 11 April 2017).

[89] Philip Lewis, *Young, British and Muslim* (London: Continuum, 2007), p. 47.

[90] Ibid., p. 50.

[91] Alison Shaw, 'Kinship, Cultural Preference and Immigration: Consanguineous Marriage among British Pakistanis' (2001) 7(2) *Journal of the Royal Anthropological Institute* 315–34.

[92] Lewis, *Young, British and Muslim*, p. 48.

[93] Ibid., p. 50; Charsley, *Transnational Pakistani Connections*, pp. 36–7, 40; Shaw, Kinship and Continuity, pp. 242–5; Law and Justice Commission of Pakistan, 'Prohibiting Excessive Expenditure on Marriage Ceremony and Dowry Report No. 59' (LJCP, 2003).

[94] Charsley et al., *Marriage, Migration and Integration*, p. 236.

[95] Bowen, *On British Islam*, pp. 23–4.

Another violent assault occurred in Oxford because a British Pakistani girl had eloped with her boyfriend, prompting her brothers and their friends to attack his. They justified their actions in this way: 'she could have been my sister – it's my duty to take revenge on him for his insulting us like this'. The attackers did not accept that their English girlfriends warranted the same type and degree of concern: 'That's different. The difference is, English people don't care . . . If their brothers or fathers got angry, we would understand, but they don't bother . . . How can you respect men like that? They just say it's the girl's choice, it's her life, and that's what the girls say too.'[96] The same researcher was told of all kinds of disputes – ranging from insults, elopements, divorces, late payments and so on – being settled by vengeful 'women putting ground glass into samosas . . . brothers using hockey sticks to beat up a lodger not paying rent . . . an enraged husband attacking an adulterous wife with an axe'.[97] There is no lack of self-awareness of this kind of behaviour: 'This was a kin thing, a fucking *biraderi* thing, an OUR mother-fucking thing that I wanted no part of. We were worse than the fucking Mafia when it came to those troublesome family matters.'[98]

To avert such violence, clan mediation is trusted and preferred to the involvement of state authorities.[99] In Oxford, for example, a convicted British Pakistani shoplifter, who had relied unsuccessfully on a local 'big man' patron to get the charges dropped, simply thought himself unlucky in his choice of community representative, 'protested his innocence in the eyes of God and seemed quite unconcerned about how the English court viewed him'.[100] In Woolwich and elsewhere, British Somali *gars* (de facto tribunals convened by elders in informal settings such as cafés) are known to deal with serious criminal violence within 'their community' – a skull-crushing attack with a metal bar, the stabbing of a teenager by a gang of youths – through inter-family arbitration resulting in financial recompense and apologies.[101] In one instance, 'the victim's family told officers the matter would be settled out of court and the suspects were released on bail'.[102] Sharia councils operate much the same way in the shadow of English family law; applying Islamic norms to resolve marital disputes through mediation, adapting services in response to

[96] Shaw, *Kinship and Continuity*, p. 173. [97] Ibid., p. 295.

[98] Yunis Alam quoted in Marta Bolognani, *Crime and Muslim Britain: Race, Culture and the Politics of Criminology among British Pakistanis* (London: Tauris, 2009), p. 59.

[99] Parveen Akhtar, 'The Paradox of Patronage Politics: Biraderi, Representation and Political Participation amongst British Pakistanis' in Timothy Peace (ed.), *Muslims and Political Participation in Britain* (London: Routledge, 2015), ch. 1, pp. 15–31 at p. 21; Shaw, *Kinship and Continuity*, p. 262.

[100] Shaw, ibid., pp. 259–60.

[101] Joshua Rozenberg, 'Sharia Law Is Spreading as Authority Wanes' (*The Telegraph*, 29 November 2006); Fiona Barton and Alex McBride, 'A Brutal Beating and Justice Meted Out in a Humble Back Street Cafe: How Sharia Law Already Operates in Britain' (*Daily Mail*, 10 February 2008); Edna Fernandes, 'Sharia Law UK: Mail on Sunday Gets Exclusive Access to a British Muslim Court' (*Daily Mail*, 4 July 2009).

[102] Martin Bentham, 'Sharia Court Frees London Knife Youths' (*Evening Standard*, 12 April 2012).

local conditions and South Asian customs, and generally helping to create 'a home away from home' for new migrants and/or the devout.[103]

The competitive nature of honour, hospitality and status-flaunting may extend into organised criminal activity and strengthen participation in gangs, with in-built familial solidarity, an omerta-like code and well-established international networks through which drugs and fleeing suspects can move to lie low or undergo 'village rehab'.[104] In Bradford, British Pakistanis have taken over the drug trade from Afro-Caribbeans who 'have sort of moved on', or rather been forcibly 'kicked out'. Despite widespread acknowledgement that drug-dealing is *haram*, exploiting infidel addicts and enjoying the resultant 'war booty' is sometimes employed as a justification for dominating the criminal economy in that area.[105] What is more, the profits from the drug trade greatly enhance the wealth and prestige of prominent families, the source of which will not be looked at too closely for fear of sparking scandal.[106] In other cases, feuding behaviour exacerbates racial tensions and results in murder and the obstruction of justice. In Somers Town, London, in 1994, for example, Richard Everitt was fatally stabbed in an unprovoked attack by a gang of Bangladeshi youths 'willing to have a go at any isolated white boys' following an earlier, minor and unconnected dispute between teenagers.[107] The murderer was never identified for the investigation was 'hampered by the silence of Bangladeshi families [while] several of the suspects were dispatched to relatives in Bangladesh ... The Everitts were targeted with hate mail and moved to a safe house under the witness protection scheme, eventually relocating to the north of England.'[108]

In addition to demarcating themselves from one another, clans instil members with various prejudices to distinguish them from non-members. For example, the racial attitudes of British Pakistanis are complex and contradictory. On one hand, fair skin is coveted in Pakistan and confers a higher status. White converts are treated as special and in some ways deserving of greater respect than those from other ethnic minorities, although they are sometimes told by Muslim friends, 'You're turning into a Paki now.'[109] Darker skin is

[103] See Bowen, *On British Islam*, chs. 2–3; Ihsan Yilmaz, *Muslim Laws, Politics and Society in Modern Nation States: Dynamic Legal Pluralisms in England, Turkey and Pakistan* (Farnham: Ashgate, 2005), pp. 65–6; Sebastian Poulter, *Ethnicity, Law and Human Rights: The English Experience* (Oxford: Clarendon Press, 1998), pp. 201–2, 210–12; Machteld Zee, 'Five Options for the Relationship between the State and Sharia Councils: Untangling the Debate on Sharia Councils and Women's Rights in the United Kingdom' (2014) 16 *Journal of Religion and Society* 1–18, p. 14.

[104] Bolognani, *Crime and Muslim Britain*, p. 33; Lewis, *Young, British and Muslim*, p. 49.

[105] Bolognani, ibid., pp. 80–1, 90. [106] Lewis, *Young, British and Muslim*, pp. 48–9.

[107] Rosemary Harris, 'Interpreting Teenage Inter-ethnic Violence' (1996–7) 4(3–4) *International Journal on Minority and Group Rights* 301–21, p. 316.

[108] Michael Collins, 'The Wrong Kind of Race Murder' (*The Critic*, September 2020); John McKie, 'Gang Leader Gets Life for Killing Boy' (*The Independent*, 22 October 2011); Rosemary Harris, 'A Death in the Ghetto' (*Prospect*, 20 July 1997).

[109] Leon Moosavi, 'The Racialization of Muslim Converts in Britain and Their Experiences of Islamophobia' (2015) 41(1) *Critical Sociology* 41–56, p. 43.

typically associated with lower caste status and inferior racial origins, with Afro-Caribbeans ranking lowest beneath Bangladeshis.[110] One migrant spouse who married her cousin even complained that her British relatives treated her as an inferior 'Paki'; another reported that the only racial prejudice she had suffered since arriving was at the hands of other British Pakistanis.[111] 'Jungle-dweller' and 'village-dweller' are common insults for new arrivals.[112] At the same time, however, white English people are regarded with ambivalence or disdain, the term 'white' being bound up with loose sexual mores and the sin of unbelief.[113] Alison Shaw notes that English women are generally regarded as 'promiscuous and unfaithful'; even when they marry a Pakistani man, he may be taunted with comments about her sexual history.[114] A common racialised slur is *desi gori*, or 'homemade white/English woman'.[115] Such women are 'simultaneously exciting and despised'; if they are raped, it is 'always the woman's fault because it is the "natural" result of [her] dressing provocatively and being out alone'.[116] Shaw relates that some of her long-time research participants in Oxford remained convinced that she would 'burn in hell' for her lack of belief and use of contraception.[117] Charsley relates how one marriage collapsed upon the husband's arrival in the airport because his young wife greeted a male university friend she happened across, which the husband deemed intolerably 'corrupt'.[118] Similar views are recorded among young children in Cardiff who had little time to interact with non-Muslims owing to the demands of religious instruction and feared that mixing with immoral 'Christians' would mean that 'Allah will punish you and you'll go to hellfire and you burn'.[119] One long-time resident of Savile Town, Dewsbury reported that, from the 1980s, white sportswomen began to be subjected to abuse from Muslim youths – the police told them their presence was 'provocative' – and the premises were repeatedly burnt and glassed before being abandoned altogether and sold to a mosque for £1 'in the interest of community relations'.[120] Thus, white, Western or Westernised women are treated with particular suspicion and contempt, although they are simultaneously regarded as being sexually available to Pakistani men, some of whom see no contradiction between upholding Islamic values and taking advantage of those who do not share them.[121] These carefully inculcated attitudes are standard clan norms and can have catastrophic consequences.

Debates over group-based child sexual exploitation (CSE) have tended to concentrate on statistics and terminology as regards the prevalence of

[110] Shaw, *Kinship and Continuity*, pp. 265–6.
[111] Charsley and Bolognani, 'Being a Freshie Is (Not) Cool', p. 59. [112] Ibid., p. 55.
[113] Shaw, *Kinship and Continuity*, p. 266. [114] Ibid., pp. 58, 162. [115] Ibid., p. 170.
[116] Ibid., p. 167. [117] Ibid., p. 266.
[118] Charsley, *Transnational Pakistani Connections*, p. 68.
[119] Jonathan Scourfield, Sophie Gilliat-Ray, Asma Khan and Sameh Otri, *Muslim Childhood: Religious Nurture in a European Context* (Oxford: Oxford University Press, 2013), p. 135.
[120] James Fergusson, *Al-Britannia: My Country* (London: Corgi, 2018), pp. 30–1.
[121] Shaw, *Kinship and Continuity*, p. 170.

offenders from particular ethnic/cultural/religious backgrounds.[122] The main focus has fallen upon British Pakistani perpetrators and the arguments have become as ill-tempered as they are unproductive.[123] A long-anticipated Home Office review concluded that while 'community and cultural factors are clearly relevant to understanding and tackling offending, ... it is difficult to draw conclusions about the ethnicity of offenders as existing research is limited and data collection is poor'.[124] Criminology has generally neglected the group dimensions of CSE despite the importance of context-specific networks in this field.[125] While there is no common structure to offender networks at the general level, they 'tend to be based on pre-existing social connections including work and family ... [or belonging to] a relatively small ethnic community'. This group dynamic can exacerbate disregard for victims by encouraging offenders to dehumanise them, 'either in relation to the fact that they are from a different community or in relation to their gender'.[126] This can be seen in many high-profile cases involving British Pakistani offenders in Rotherham, Rochdale, Derby, Bristol, Telford, Huddersfield, Oxford, Newcastle and possibly Barrow-in-Furness.[127] The abuse was grotesque: victims being branded as sex slaves, having their tongues nailed to tables, being passed around the extended families of their abusers, undergoing forced abortions, being forced into drug addiction and dependency on their captors.[128] The harm was often compounded by the reluctance of state authorities to investigate out of a fear of being thought racist. For example, council staff in Rotherham recalled 'clear direction from their managers' not to identify the ethnicity of perpetrators, while Greater Manchester Police detectives were 'told to try and get other ethnicities'.[129] Another detective superintendent claimed that 'concerns about creating further community tensions did not influence any of his investigative

[122] See Haras Rafiq and Muna Adil, 'Group Based Child Sexual Exploitation – Dissecting Grooming Gangs' (Quilliam, December 2017) and Ella Cockbain and Waqas Tufail, 'Failing Victims, Fuelling Hate: Challenging the Harms of the "Muslim Grooming Gangs" Narrative' (2020) 61(3) *Race & Class* 3–32.

[123] See Kenan Malik, 'We're Told 84% of Grooming Gangs Are Asian. But Where's the Evidence?' (*The Guardian*, 11 November 2018) and John Pitts, 'Street Grooming, Criminality and Culture' (*Youth & Policy*, 6 April 2018).

[124] Priti Patel, 'Foreword' to Home Office, 'Group-Based Child Sexual Exploitation: Characteristics of Offending' (HMG, December 2020), p. 3.

[125] Ella Cockbain, Helen Brayley and Joe Sullivan, 'Towards a Common Framework for Assessing the Activity and Associations of Groups Who Sexually Abuse Children' (2014) 20(2) *Journal of Sexual Aggression* 156–71, p. 157.

[126] Home Office, 'Group-Based Child Sexual Exploitation', pp. 8–9, 33.

[127] Gerry Lynch, 'The Blind Eye Turned to Barrow' (*The Critic*, 12 June 2020).

[128] See Michael Race, 'How the Net Closed on Oxford's Grooming Gang' (*BBC News*, 13 March 2020) and for a helpful collection of many relevant links to newspaper reports, see generally Peter McLoughlin's *Easy Meat: Inside Britain's Grooming Gang Scandal* (New English Review, 2016). The book itself should be treated with some caution as it is rather polemical and the author's credentials are uncertain.

[129] Alexis Jay, 'Independent Inquiry into Child Sexual Exploitation in Rotherham 1997–2013' (Rotherham Council, August 2014), p. 2; Malcolm Newsam and Gary Ridgway, 'Independent Assurance Review of the Effectiveness of Multi-agency Responses to Child Sexual Exploitation

decisions', but then admitted that 'the impact clearly had to be considered by the ... command group'.[130] Similarly, many politicians who have spoken – articulately or otherwise – about this type of CSE over the last decade have been met with accusations of racism or worse.[131] One such is Sarah Champion, Labour MP for Rotherham, who has been variously denounced as 'incendiary and irresponsible', 'unwise' and a 'useful idiot' for 'insidious' forces.[132] Under pressure from fellow Labour politicians, she resigned from the Corbyn shadow cabinet in 2017 and received additional police protection upon receipt of death threats.[133] In her own words: 'I have been vilified, smeared and threatened, by the far right and the far left, who use this crime for their own political agenda.'[134]

All of this has an institutional quality. The CSE itself bears the hallmarks of clannism and, with the usual caveat that 'the available evidence is weak and robust data is scarce', is merely the pinnacle of 'a wider spectrum of antisocial behaviour' encouraged by clan norms.[135] Although the government recently published the first 'Tackling Child Sexual Abuse Strategy',[136] it will be hard to design 'specific responses to specific threats' so long as the problem as regards British Pakistanis is framed in categorical terms of ethnicity or religion.[137] Targeting law reform at group entities has paid dividends in the struggle against CSE within the Roman Catholic Church, which, like the clan, has a distinct set of internal norms and processes which facilitate wrongdoing.[138] The point is not to terminate all CSE, which as a general phenomenon is too various and multifaceted, but to eliminate risks and practices in specific group

in Greater Manchester: Part One, An Assurance Review of Operation Augusta' (Greater Manchester Combined Authority, January 2020), p. 101.

130 Newsam and Ridgway, ibid., p. 47.

131 BBC News, 'Jack Straw Criticised for "Easy Meat" Comments on Abuse' (*BBC News*, 8 January 2011).

132 Naz Shah, 'We Need to Dispel the Dangerous Myth That It's Only Asian Men Who Sexually Assault Young Women' (*The Independent*, 12 August 2017); Sean O'Grady, 'Let's Not Feel Sorry for Sarah Champion – She Knew Exactly What She Was Doing' (*The Independent*, 17 August 2017).

133 Jessica Elgot and Graham Ruddick, 'Sarah Champion Distances Herself from Sun Article on British Pakistani Men' (*The Guardian*, 16 August 2017); Jessica Elgot, 'Sarah Champion Resigns as Shadow Equalities Minister' (*The Guardian*, 16 August 2017); Helen Pidd, 'Labour MP Given Added Police Security after Death Threats' (*The Guardian*, 25 July 2018).

134 Sarah Champion, *Hansard*, HC, Vol. 688, 6.43 p.m. 3 February 2021, Debate on Grooming Gangs: https://hansard.parliament.uk/commons/2021-02-03/debates/65D3BAF4-00FF-42B3-8430-AAF2CCD8826E/GroomingGangs.

135 Home Office, 'Group-Based Child Sexual Exploitation', p. 6; Wood, 'Marriage and Social Boundaries among British Pakistanis', p. 58.

136 HMG, 'Tackling Child Sexual Abuse Strategy' (HMG, January 2021).

137 Home Office, Home Office, 'Group-Based Child Sexual Exploitation', p. 6.

138 See Timothy D. Lytton, *Holding Bishops Accountable: How Lawsuits Helped the Catholic Church Confront Clergy Sexual Abuse* (Cambridge, MA: Harvard University Press, 2008) and Patrick Nash, 'The Never-Ending Story? Or, Does the Roman Catholic Church Remain Vulnerable to Charges of Improper Handling of Clergy Child Sex Abuse?' (2019) 8(2) *Oxford Journal of Law and Religion* 270–99.

contexts. Thus, while addressing the clan problem will not stop CSE generally or offending among British Pakistanis, it will remove a recurring collective dynamic upstream of frontline policing and social work. As for the disastrous response to CSE, a contributing factor looks to be what Professor Mary Anne Case terms 'the stumbling block of scandal'. This is common in institutional contexts and occurs when an organisation calculates that any public acknowledgement or admission of wrongs committed by its staff, members or supporters is worse than the wrongs themselves. Inconvenient truths are ignored and difficult questions stop being asked. Disclosure becomes unthinkable as it would create a stumbling block to the faith and trust placed in the organisation by its supporters and the general public. Thus, 'secrecy to the point of cover-up' comes to be seen 'not as a problem but as an imperative, a contribution to the greater good' so that reputations, personal and institutional, can be managed effectively.[139] In other words, a confused and very multicultural-looking understanding of racism seems to have taken root in policing and politics during the New Labour era, sometimes leading to reputational concerns for British Pakistanis en bloc and the veneer of social peace being prioritised over safeguarding and natural justice.

8.3.3.3 Harms to British Democracy

Clannism is also corrupting both the process and the substance of British democracy, which is 'routinely subverted'.[140] The corrupting effect on elections was discussed at length in Chapter 7, but it is also important to note that the *biraderis* transplant the turbulent religious politics of Pakistan into the UK.[141] This is evident from the Rushdie Affair, the persecution of Asia Bibi and Ahmadiyya Muslims, and the vicious style of campaigning that is coming to blight campaigns in Bradford and elsewhere. Each shall be taken briefly in turn. As regards the Rushdie Affair, Modood himself describes it as 'not so much a Muslim as a South Asian Muslim response'[142] driven by those who were 'only one generation away from rural peasantry' and who retain strong links to 'the peasant world' to this day.[143] Following protests against Rushdie's knighthood in 2007, the late Christopher Hitchens, referencing the view of Tariq Ramadan, observed that 'the protests against it in Pakistan are purely a matter of violent, vicious internal politics there, it's part of a jostling for position'.[144] In Britain, the

[139] Mary Anne Case, 'Institutional Responses to #MeToo Claims: #VaticanToo, #KavanaughToo, and the Stumbling Block of Scandal' (2019) 2 *University of Chicago Legal Forum* 1–35, p. 2.

[140] Fergusson, *Al-Britannia*, p. 29.

[141] Philip Wood, 'This Is a Mirpur Problem Not a Muslim One' (Policy Exchange Integration Hub, 6 December 2016).

[142] Tariq Modood, *Multicultural Politics: Racism, Ethnicity, and Muslims in Britain* (Edinburgh: Edinburgh University Press, 2005), p. 106.

[143] Tariq Modood, *Not Easy Being British: Colour, Culture and Citizenship* (Stoke: Trentham Books, 1992), p. 261; Shaw, *Kinship and Continuity*, p. 291.

[144] Uploaded by CaNANDian, 'Christopher Hitchens – On Question Time [2007]' (YouTube, 2 August 2012) at 2.40: www.youtube.com/watch?v=Hmv2sL2qkIM.

MCB called the knighthood a 'deliberate provocation' and its general secretary stated that it 'can only do harm to the image of our country in the eyes of hundreds of millions of Muslims across the world'.[145] Lord Ahmed of Rotherham protested: 'This man – as you can see – not only provoked violence around the world because of his writings, but there were many people that were killed around the world and honouring the man who has blood on his hands . . . is going a bit too far.'[146] The same is true for the Muslim constituents in Tower Hamlets, where 'the politics of Bangladesh have also been transported to Britain' as religious groups with transnational ties to Islamist parties vie for influence with more secular activists.[147] It is notable that these Muslim-majority countries and their populations have remained silent about China's Uighur Muslim concentration camps, and even blocked a motion calling for the Chinese Communist Party to allow monitoring by independent observers, which suggests that power and national confidence speak more than principle on such matters.[148]

Over the course of the last decade, Asia Bibi, a Christian farm labourer from rural Pakistan, was denounced by Muslim villagers, convicted of blasphemy, imprisoned and condemned to death. Although her conviction was eventually overturned by the Supreme Court in 2018, she was unable to flee the country until 2019 because of hostile protests and appeals against her acquittal.[149] She sought and was offered asylum by a range of Western countries and finally settled with her family in Canada, although she lives under continual threat.[150] The UK government reportedly declined to offer her asylum in part because 'her moving to the UK would cause security concerns and unrest among certain sections of the community'.[151] Similarly, Ahmadiyya Muslims are widely persecuted in Pakistan and Britain as, variously, heretics, blasphemers or apostates.[152] In 2016, Glaswegian shopkeeper Asad Shah, himself born in Pakistan, was

145 MCB, 'MCB Urges Muslims to Face Provocation with Dignity and Wisdom' (Wayback Machine, 22 June 2007): https://web.archive.org/web/20070704052542/http://www.mcb.org.uk/media/presstext.php?ann_id=259.

146 Prasun Sonwalkar, 'Britain in a Tizzy as "Sir" Rushdie Turns 60' (*Hindustan Times*, 20 June 2007).

147 Timothy Peace, 'Muslim Political Participation in Britain: The Case of the Respect Party' (Madrid: 22nd World Congress of Political Science, July 2012), p. 11.

148 Nick Cohen, 'Why Do Muslim States Stay Silent over China's Abuse of the Uighurs?' (*The Guardian*, 4 July 2020).

149 Shumaila Jaffery, 'Asia Bibi: Pakistan's Notorious Blasphemy Case' (*BBC News*, 1 February 2019).

150 Harriet Sherwood, 'Asia Bibi Begins New Life in Canada – but Her Ordeal May Not Be Over' (*The Guardian*, 8 May 2019).

151 Amardeep Bassey, 'UK "Won't Offer Asylum to Asia Bibi Amid Security Concerns"' (*Huffington Post*, 9 November 2018).

152 See generally Jon Lunn and Timothy Robinson, 'Persecution of Ahmadiyya Muslims and Other Religious Minorities in Pakistan' (House of Commons, CDP0039, 8 February 2016); Nigel Walker and Ben Smith, 'Persecution of the Ahmadiyya Muslim Community' (House of Commons, CDP0129, 22 May 2018).

murdered by one Tanveer Ahmed for religious reasons including 'disrespecting the Prophet' and supporting the abolition of Pakistan's blasphemy laws.[153] Following his incarceration, Ahmed reportedly earns money from the sale of signed photographs and conducts meet-and-greets with admirers.[154] It is notable that the Muslim Council of Britain, while condemning the act of Shah's murder, reiterated its position that Ahmadis are not true Muslims and was unwilling to disaffiliate with a charity accused of calling for the killing of Ahmadis as apostates.[155] In Scotland, prominent Muslim groups failed to participate in an Ahmadiyya-led campaign against violent persecution.[156] Fiyaz Mughal, a prominent inter-faith activist, summed up the Shah murder in the following blunt terms: 'We have a violent extremism problem exported from Pakistan. It's providing the toxic perfect storm for this violent rhetoric so people like Ahmed are seen as warriors rather than murderers.'[157]

In Bradford, recent elections have been marred by abuse. Covering the 2015 election contest between George Galloway and Naz Shah, the journalist Ben Judah was punched in the head and told, 'Get out, you fucking Jew!' A 'close aide' of Galloway explained to Judah, as a campaign bus flying Pakistan flags sped around:

> It's been a brutal, a brutal election campaign, and no doubt it will get worse. It's different, Bradford ... It would take me much longer than I've got to explain *biraderi* politics in Bradford, clan-based politics, and people actually do deliver 20, 30, 50 votes. Through their extended families, what tends to happen is, the kind of head of the household, or the kind of head of the clan, makes a decision how they'll vote. So if somebody in, I don't know, Penge (South London) said I could deliver you 50 votes you would laugh. But here it's true. They deliver bundles of votes.[158]

Naz Shah MP (who won) later encountered anti-Semitic chanting ('Jew! Jew! Jew!') and had her 'pedigree compared to that of a dog' during an internal Labour election contest against the activist Salma Yaqoob for the West Midlands mayoralty. As she explained, it involved:

153 Secunder Kermani, 'Why Was Shopkeeper Asad Shah Murdered?' (*BBC News*, 7 July 2016).

154 Matt Coyle and Gordon Blackstock, 'CELL-EBRITY MONSTER: Extremist Tanveer Ahmed Who Murdered Glasgow Shopkeeper Asad Shah Held Jail Meet-and-Greets with Fanatics Who Hail Him as a Hero' (*Scottish Sun*, 2 December 2018).

155 MCB, 'Position Statement: The Muslim Council of Britain and Ahmadis' (MCB, 6 April 2016); Tahir Nasser, 'The Muslim Council of Britain Is Failing Ahmadis Like Asad Shah' (*The Guardian*, 25 April 2016); Tom Porter, 'Muslim Council of Britain Anti-terror Campaign Criticised after "Unwillingness" to Blacklist "Kill Ahmadis" Group' (*International Business Times*, 28 October 2016).

156 Libby Brooks, 'Scottish Muslim Groups Fail to Attend Ahmadi Anti-extremism Event' (*The Guardian*, 18 April 2016).

157 Quoted in Coyle and Blackstock, 'CELL-EBRITY MONSTER'.

158 Ben Judah, 'A Jew in Bradford' (Politico, 6 May 2015).

> a certain, specific group, a small minority of men who are very much steeped deeply in the concept of *biraderi* politics. *Biraderi* politics, clan politics, family politics, [are] a type of mafia of [*sic*] political control within Bradford West [which] damages democracy ... Some of that is misogyny, some of that is patriarchy ... It was the same kind of politics of division, politics of a narrative of conspiracy theories[;] it was a politics which was suggesting that I was libelling my whole community. When an imam stood there and said: 'Who is the better Muslim?', [Yaqoob] did not challenge that and say this is not about being Muslim ... My genuine fear, and it is coming true, is that [it] is creating a toxic politics within the West Midlands and that is exactly what happened in Bradford West, and my fear is for my party, my fear is for democracy, my fear is for real socialism ... This was honour abuse.[159]

Putting an end to all this will be noisy and difficult because it has been left unchecked for so long. The large size of the Pakistani diaspora and the political clout of *biraderi* lobbyists will complicate attempts at meaningful reform.[160]

Biraderis often have control over mosque committees and Muslim campaign organisations.[161] For example, the Foreign Affairs Committee noted: 'The UK policy-making process (as well as our "establishment") with respect to Pakistan is strongly influenced by a skilful and far-reaching Pakistani lobby ... many of whom are wealthy and some of whom constitute an important – perhaps even decisive – political constituency in some marginals.'[162] Nevertheless, many younger British Pakistanis recognise the need to push back against the clans. Navid Akhter, a documentary maker, describes the *biraderi* as

> the heart of the problem ... Invisible to the outside world, a battle is taking place between *biraderi* diehards and those who believe it has no place in modern British society. The youth are the casualties ... This void continues to grow and is a cause of unrest with the young ... Open debate, the exchange of ideas and

159 Naz Shah MP, 'A Thread of Ten Tweets' (Twitter, 22 October 2019): https://twitter.com/NazShahBfd/status/1186744246096879619; see also BBC News, '"Anti-Semitic" Comments at Bradford Hustings Probed by Police' (*BBC News*, 3 June 2017); Nazia Parveen and Rajeev Syal, 'Labour Mayoral Candidate Calls for Truce in Row with Naz Shah' (*The Guardian*, 2 October 2019); Jonathan Walker, 'How a Bad-Tempered Election in Bradford in 2017 Is Affecting the Battle to Become West Midlands Mayor' (*Birmingham Mail*, 6 October 2019); Sonia Sodha, 'This Battle to Become West Midlands Mayor Reminds Us Women of Colour Face a Double Oppression' (*The Guardian*, 27 October 2019).

160 Katharine Charsley, 'Marriage Migration and Transnational Social Spaces: A View from the UK' in Katharine Charsley (ed.), *Transnational Marriage: New Perspectives from Europe and Beyond* (London: Routledge, 2012), ch. 11, pp. 189–208 at p. 204; The Economist, 'Pakistani Politics: East of Edgeware' (*The Economist*, 7 June 2014).

161 Philip Lewis, *Islamic Britain: Religion, Politics and Identity Among British Muslims* (London: I. B. Tauris, 2002), p. 86.

162 House of Commons Foreign Affairs Committee, 'The UK's Foreign Policy Approach to Afghanistan and Pakistan: Fourth Report of Session 2010–11' (House of Commons, HC514, Vol. 1, March 2011), p. 20, para. 13 [Evidence 84 submitted by Professor Shaun Gregory, University of Durham].

> the promotion of merit, not clan loyalty, should be embraced. Forty years after arriving in Britain we are in danger of going backwards, divided by outdated and discriminatory practices.[163]

Others have variously described *biraderi* clannism as a 'constraint', 'detrimental to the community as a whole', 'a baleful influence' and a method of political mobilisation which 'habitually ends in a cul-de-sac'.[164] Most ominously of all, radical Islamic groups promising a life of excitement, egalitarianism and empowerment start to seem progressive and attractive by comparison.[165] The 2017 *Missing Muslims* report acknowledged that '*biraderi* (kinship) and clan politics within some of the UK's Muslim communities stifles progress, and are keenly felt by women and young people as a barrier to participation'.[166] Several respondents described its impact: 'the political mainstream needs to address this'; 'it is not just the Pakistani women and young people who are marginalised, but anybody who is not part of that *biraderi* system. Their voice is taken away from them and they feel alienated'; 'I received a few threats from Asian males and had to launch a police inquiry, as it was believed that being a single mother was casting aspersions on my character.'[167] In short, the negative effects of domestic clannism are well understood by British Muslims, but have received scant attention from government.

8.3.4 Geopolitical Significance of Clans

On the world stage, Anglo-American geopolitical strategy since 9/11 has similarly failed to pay due regard to clannism. In *The Thistle and the Drone*, Akbar Ahmed posits a fascinating reinterpretation of the War on Terror. Often misunderstood by all parties as somehow a clash of civilisations or war against Islam itself, it is in fact, Ahmed argues, rooted in the traumatic encounter between peripheral tribal society (represented by the thistle) and the forces of globalisation and state centralisation (the drone).[168] In a sense, it is a far more violent version of the divisions currently playing out in the West between wealthier liberal urban centres and poorer conservative provinces.[169] The resulting disruption has induced a mutation of tribal ethics centred upon honour, blood feuds, retribution, lineage, patriarchy, dignity, hospitality and radical egalitarianism, through which Islam is interwoven as a common

163 Quoted in Lewis, *Young, British and Muslim*, pp. 46, 53.

164 Ibid., pp. 48–53; Fergusson, *Al-Britannia*, p. 239; Tahir Abbas, 'Implementing "Prevent" in Countering Violent Extremism in the UK: A Left-Realist Critique' (2019) 39(3) *Critical Social Policy* 396–412, p. 406.

165 Lewis, ibid., p. 122.

166 Citizens' Commission on Islam, Participation and Public Life, 'The Missing Muslims: Unlocking British Muslim Potential for the Benefit of All' (Citizens UK, 2017), p. 44.

167 Ibid., pp. 47–8.

168 Ahmed, *The Thistle and the Drone*, pp. 4–5.

169 See generally David Goodhart, *The Road to Somewhere: The Populist Revolt and the Future of Politics* (London: Penguin, 2017).

reference point.[170] Whereas this package of values was once a necessary guarantor of survival, stability and autonomy in remote impoverished regions, it has found itself at loggerheads with the very precepts of modernity (such as individualism, consumerism and gender equality) and appears 'out of touch, unsure, dazed and antiquated'.[171] With 'the breakdown of the tribal universe and everything which it stood for' have come displaced feelings of fractured identity, emasculation and rage.[172] Across the predominantly Islamic tribal world, this has taken on a nihilistic momentum of its own, with escalating violence, couched in terms of honour and justified by religion, directed at anything Western and often at anyone at all, be they fellow elders, imams or co-religionists.[173] This interpretation is broadly reflected in Professor Amy Chua's work in which she notes that the Taliban 'is not only an Islamist movement but also an ethnic movement ... led by Pashtuns', a fact missed by the American leadership with 'calamitous results'.[174]

Ahmed may also have a point when he describes the War on Terror as 'the mediocre leading the confused in pursuit of the dubious',[175] although several commentators were certainly aware of the relevant anthropology both before and during it. As early as 1989, David Pryce-Jones predicted that nation-building would be next to impossible in the Middle East, not because the Arab peoples are somehow inferior or unworthy of democracy but because the clan loyalties of tribal society militate against close out-group cooperation and hence the survival of institutions based upon impersonal common consent.[176] In 2003, Steve Sailer warned that 'we are almost utterly innocent of how much the high degree of inbreeding in Iraq could interfere with our nation-building ambitions'.[177] Stanley Kurtz, writing in 2007, noted that 'Islamic society has found a way to turn a uniquely intense form of in-marriage to its advantage (if advantage is defined strictly in terms of cultural survival, rather than adaptive change).'[178] While Western kinship bonds are 'thin and watery things', cousin marriage is the Velcro which 'acts as a social "sealing mechanism" to block cultural interchange'. Hence, 'if we want to change any of this, it will be impossible to restrict ourselves to the study of religious Islam'.[179] In the event, abstruse anthropology went unheeded in Washington and the War on Terror proceeded as it has.

[170] Ahmed, *The Thistle and the Drone*, pp. 8–34. [171] Ibid., p. 343. [172] Ibid., pp. 345–6.
[173] Ibid., p. 346.
[174] *Political Tribes: Group Instinct and the Fate of Nations* (London: Penguin, 2019), p. 60.
[175] Ahmed, *The Thistle and the Drone*, p. 327.
[176] *The Closed Circle: An Interpretation of the Arabs* (rev. ed., Chicago: Ivan R Dee, 2009).
[177] Steve Sailer, 'Cousin Marriage Conundrum' (*American Conservative*, 13 January 2013).
[178] Stanley Kurtz, 'Marriage and the Terror War: Part I' (*National Review*, 15 February 2007).
[179] Stanley Kurtz, 'Marriage and the Terror War: Part II' (*National Review*, 16 February 2007).

8.4 Interpreting Clans

8.4.1 Via Liberal Individualism

For Ronald Dworkin, the family was analogous to the state as an association of individuals capable of generating certain obligations under certain conditions. These 'obligations of role' are 'the special responsibilities social practice attaches to membership in some biological or social group, like the responsibilities of families or friends or neighbors'.[180] These might be incurred involuntarily, through birth, or voluntarily, through marriage and parenthood, but become genuine only if the group is a 'true community' and not just a 'bare' one.[181] This requires reciprocity among members who treat their bond as special to that group, personal between its constituent individuals and based upon heartfelt equal concern for the welfare of each of these persons.[182] As with one's political obligations to the national community, family responsibilities therefore 'run directly from each member to each other member, not just to the whole in some collective sense'.[183] The family may be legitimately hierarchical and even patriarchal, but if its cultural practices endanger egalitarian justice then its members either will cease to be bound altogether in the most serious cases (i.e. the Mafia) or else may invoke rights to trump particular collective demands.[184] The point is to account for the idiosyncrasies of diverse families while protecting individuals both within and outside of the family group. However, it is of limited practical utility as regards clans.

Dworkin's emphasis on individual family members rather than the family group itself presents several difficulties. At a general theoretical level, his analogy between family and state is another symptom of a poor vocabulary for very different sorts of group unalike in size, scope and purpose.[185] More specifically, he argues that these groups 'will rarely meet or long sustain [the conditions that generate genuine obligations] unless [their] members by and large actually feel some emotional bond with one another'.[186] In other words, nations and families will not endure unless their members regard each other with equal, deep and abiding concern.[187] Aside from being unrealistic and unnecessary, this claim is anthropologically inaccurate: clan members may despise one another to the point of murder, but the clan itself endures. Indeed, it has done since prehistory, despite lacking any substantive notion of egalitarianism or individual worth, because members are primarily attached to it

[180] Ronald Dworkin, *Law's Empire* (Oxford: Hart-Bloomsbury, 1998, reprint of Fontana Press original, 1986), pp. 195–6.

[181] Ibid., p. 201. [182] Ibid., pp. 198–9, 201. [183] Ibid., p. 199.

[184] See Ronald Dworkin, ibid., pp. 202–6; *Justice for Hedgehogs* (Cambridge, MA: Harvard University Press, 2011), pp. 315, 321; 'Rights as Trumps' in Jeremy Waldron (ed.), *Theories of Rights* (Oxford: Oxford University Press, 1984), pp. 153–67.

[185] Lucan Gregory, 'Ronald Dworkin, T.H. Green, and the Communal Theory of Political Obligation' (2006) 32(2) *Social Theory and Practice* 191–212, pp. 193–4.

[186] Dworkin, *Law's Empire*, p. 201.

[187] A. John Simmons, 'Associative Political Obligations' (1996) 106(2) *Ethics* 247–73, pp. 259–60.

rather than their fellows as equals. Dworkin's treatment of the relationship between family and culture is also sloppy. He tends to talk about culture as though it were an actor: 'We may have to concede that unjust dominion lies at the heart of some culture's practices of family, or that indefensible discrimination is at the heart of its practices of racial or religious cohesion.'[188] In denying the existence of groups as entities in their own right, however, this effectively means that 'a culture' is an aggregate of the beliefs and practices of a given population of autonomous individuals. Collective prejudice and discrimination reflect upon each person making up that culture – it is they who are the subject of any moral condemnation and it is they who bear ultimate responsibility for perpetuating, fighting or escaping injustice. There are three important problems with this approach.

First, while clannism is often presented as a problem of Muslim or South Asian culture, it is more accurate to think of it the other way around: as a manifestation of a particular institution's norms. Second, in neglecting the clan as a group in its own right, Dworkin makes too much of, and places too much faith in, individual agency. In his discussion of honour culture, for example, he maintains that a daughter who disobediently marries for love still owes her father an apologetic explanation. She 'has something to regret' and 'should in other ways strive to continue her standing as a member of the community she otherwise has a duty to honor' – if she still faces coercion, it is on her to seek protection and enforce her rights.[189] This betrays a very dated understanding of domestic violence. In effect, he is saying that 'the onus for challenging an unjust practice rests squarely upon the individual affected' when, 'all too often, the victims lack the capacity and ultimately the will to break the chains of their own oppression'.[190] Third, treating collective injustice as the product of an aggregate of individuals is not an effective way to resolve it. There is ample proof of this in public debate over Muslims and South Asians, much of which boils down to declamatory moralising and misdirected policy. This is integral to the methodology of many major studies of 'integration' which proceed from an individualistic premise regardless of their eventual conclusions. For example, they typically take a population sample and quantify the success of individuals over time across a range of social, economic, cultural and civic measures such as employment status, qualifications gained, residential trends, social networks, voting patterns, English language proficiency, and so on.[191] Yet, for all this, as David Goodhart concedes,

[188] Dworkin, *Law's Empire*, pp. 203–5. [189] Ibid., p. 205.

[190] S. S. Berns, 'Dworkin's Account of Associative Obligations: New Clothes for an Old Theory?' (1991) 21(1) *Western Australian Law Review* 89–121, pp. 107, 105.

[191] See generally Hiranthi Jayaweera, 'Migration, Integration and Transnational Involvement: Muslim Family Migrants in Urban Areas in Britain' in Charsley, *Transnational Marriage*, ch. 5, pp. 81–104; David Goodhart, *The British Dream: Successes and Failures of Post-War Immigration* (London: Atlantic Books, 2014), pp. 47–112; Charsley et al., *Marriage, Migration and Integration*.

integration remains 'hard to both [*sic*] define and to measure'.[192] This has led senior policy-makers to misidentify the target as being 'transnational marriages' and frame clannism in terms of an 'unabsorbed diaspora', the 'self-inflicted cultural wound' of segregation and the 'withdrawal into behaviours and practices that should have been left behind centuries ago as society progressed'.[193] In other words, large numbers of the immigrant population must be emancipated from their own illiberalism and ignorance so that they may take their place in the prevailing liberal order as self-authoring individuals.

Further, Dworkin's threshold for the dissolution of group bonds is as unclear as it is impractical.[194] Requiring families to be so thoroughly criminal in all aspects that they resemble the Mafia – composed of criminals and directed towards criminality – before they qualify for liquidation precludes an effective response to clans. This is because they have no legal existence; combine legitimate structures, activities and ends with unlawful, merely destructive and completely unrecognised ones; engage in or promote criminality only as incidental to their self-interested concerns; produce an emergent effect on individual members' behaviour; and are held together by the mechanism of cousin marriage which remains legal and easily defensible as a matter of individual autonomy. Liberal individualistic responses have accordingly been characterised by either paralytic equivocation or circumlocution. For example, a little-known aspect of John Rawls' work is that he supported negative eugenics: 'over time a society is to take steps to preserve the general level of natural abilities and to prevent the diffusion of serious defects. These measures are to be guided by principles that the parties would be willing to consent to for the sake of their successors.'[195] Dworkin was even less decisive and regarded the ethics of eugenics as 'a challenge we must take up' with reason, responsibility and seriousness.[196] Thus, while there may be a general public health argument to be had over cousin marriage, there is no clear-cut case on the social and institutional consequences of this practice.

Moreover, Baroness Deech has claimed: 'There can be no question of banning cousin marriage here, despite the genetic pitfalls, because it is a practice undertaken by half the world and a ban would no doubt offend human rights law.'[197] Educate and debate with gusto, 'work with voluntary organisations on issues around first-cousin marriages', enforce the laws against

[192] Goodhart, *The British Dream*, p. 68.

[193] Dame Louise Casey, 'The Casey Review: A Review into Opportunity and Integration' (HMG, December 2016), p. 32; Paul Collier, David Goodhart and Dame Louise Casey quoted in Charsley et al., *Marriage, Migration and Integration*, pp. 3, 12.

[194] Berns, 'Dworkin's Account of Associative Obligations', pp. 108–9.

[195] John Rawls, *A Theory of Justice: Revised Edition* (Cambridge, MA: Belknap Press, 1999), p. 92; David Shaw, *Genetic Morality* (Bern: Peter Lang, 2006), p. 147.

[196] Ronald Dworkin, 'Playing God' (*Prospect Magazine*, 20 May 1999).

[197] Baroness Ruth Deech, 'Reflections on 40 years of IVF and Its Impact on the Family' (2018) *Family Law* 1296–1303, p. 1302.

forced marriage and FGM.[198] Do all of these things, but do not ban endogamy. Clannism is simply the by-product of personal lifestyle choices about who to marry, what genetic risks to take and how to live their lives. That people make problematic choices is regrettable and must result from a dearth of information, but ultimately the state cannot restrict their freedom to make bad decisions. Some policy-makers have tried to get around this with contorted reasoning. For example, Danish immigration law presumes that consanguineous marriages are forced and sets the minimum age for spouses and sponsors at twenty-four;[199] similarly, in the 'Rights and Freedoms' section of the UK's *Integrated Communities Strategy*, such marriages are deemed 'detrimental where they restrict individuals' right to choose, as well as potentially having harmful health consequences for children born to [them]'.[200] The majority of cousin marriages are not forced.[201] Alternatively, in *The Rule of the Clan*, the American constitutional scholar Mark S. Weiner argues that 'the question liberals face is not how to eliminate [the clan as a "jural unit"] entirely, but rather how to manage the impulses underlying it'.[202] This can be accomplished only by a 'robust state' dedicated to the common interest and underpinned by a shared public identity built around the rule of law, universalism, democracy, egalitarianism, social welfare and permissiveness, material prosperity, the valorisation of the self, and mass education.[203] To sustain itself, the state must cultivate a population of individuals who each 'recognise themselves implicitly as a blank slate, and thus in abstract individual terms, as in some meaningful sense presocial and prepolitical, an understanding of the self necessary for imagining the existence of a common public interest'.[204] The state, in other words, must be authoritative and centralised, vigilant and visible, interventionist and internationalist. Only then will it be capable of protecting itself and its citizens from factionalism, the tyranny of inherited status and the all-consuming claims of clan membership at home and abroad.[205] In short, soft power and statism are all that liberal individualism has to offer.

8.4.2 Via Multiculturalism

While there is another dearth of explicitly multicultural literature on clans, several major studies of transnational consanguineous marriage appear

[198] Deech, 'Cousin Marriage'; HMG, 'Integrated Communities Strategy Green Paper' (HMG, March 2018), p. 58.

[199] Charsley et al., *Marriage, Migration and Integration*, pp. 94–5; Shaw, 'British Pakistani Cousin Marriages and the Negotiation of Reproductive Risk', p. 119; Martin Bak Jørgensen, 'Danish Regulations on Marriage Migration: Policy Understandings of Transnational Marriages' in Charsley, *Transnational Marriage*, ch. 4, pp. 60–79 at pp. 60–1.

[200] Casey Review, p. 32; HMG, 'Integrated Communities Strategy Green Paper', p. 56.

[201] Katharine Charsley, '"A First Generation in Every Generation"? Spousal Immigration in the Casey Review and Integrated Communities Strategy Green Paper' (*Discover Society*, 1 May 2018).

[202] Weiner, *The Rule of the Clan*, pp. 3, 169. [203] Ibid., pp. 3–15. [204] Ibid., p. 193.

[205] Ibid., pp. 45–7.

broadly sympathetic to this theoretical perspective.[206] Nevertheless, it does not take much of an imaginative leap to construct a multicultural account of clans in outline. Clans can be interpreted as expressions of South Asian culture and/or, if one accepts the mixed evidence suggesting that they are responsible for increasing religiosity among British Pakistanis, as manifestations of British Muslim culture, too.[207] This is simply to say that clans are the way in which families from South Asian Muslim backgrounds tend to be structured and are the means by which this disadvantaged minority participates in British national life. As such, these groups have a right to integrity and the elders in charge should be regarded as legitimate representatives both of their own extended family and of South Asians / Muslims more generally. They have made historic contributions both to their own minorities and to the nation as a whole. For example, the *biraderi* and the *brath-thitho* have played a vital role in establishing South Asian Muslim communities in the UK: encouraging relatives to migrate, providing financial support for early communities, preserving cultural and religious identities, connecting British South Asians with culturally compatible marriage matches in their ancestral homelands, empowering disadvantaged communities to participate in and win elections. Such are the benefits they provide that many British Pakistanis, in full knowledge of the genetic risks of cousin marriage, opt freely to practise endogamy. Popular assumptions about the negative impact of transnational marriages on integration are typically based on a statistical snapshot of a particular domain (economic, education, social, etc.) at a particular time in someone's life (upon or soon after arrival, etc.), which means that they are often simplistic and inaccurate. Integration is a dynamic process affected by the interrelationship of factors and the onward march of time – there can be no endpoint upon which to base a definitive conclusion about a particular population and, in any event, it is entirely possible for transnational marriages to positively assist the process in a variety of ways: British-born women can gain more domestic power and better-educated matches than are available locally while migrant spouses can receive important employment opportunities from their in-laws (despite their often formidable qualifications not being recognised in the UK).[208] Further, *biraderis* engage in a range of legitimate and valuable activities such as transcontinental economic transactions which have 'nothing to do with segregation [and] everything to do with creating worldwide social capital'.[209] All this has served to make the UK a more diverse and therefore better place to live. It also speaks to the point that every culture and cultural expression has its advantages and should not be generalised about or judged by outsiders.

[206] See Charsley et al., *Marriage, Migration and Integration*; Shaw and Raz (eds.), *Cousin Marriages*.

[207] See Wood, 'Marriage and Social Boundaries among British Pakistanis', pp. 47–8; Charsley et al., *Marriage, Migration and Integration*, pp. 241–2.

[208] Charsley, 'A First Generation in Every Generation?'.

[209] Bowen, *On British Islam*, p. 24.

If there are any problems with clans, it is important not to panic or overstate them for they are being contested internally by Muslim / South Asian communities. Some of the most vigorous campaigners against honour violence are Muslim women; the power of the *biraderi* elders is now being challenged by the British Pakistani youth.[210] These reformers must be careful about challenging abuses too vigorously or with the wrong tone, however, else they risk betraying their communities and becoming 'coconuts'. At any rate, issues that might collectively be termed 'clannism' – violence against women, racial or religious stereotyping, political corruption, genetic illness – affect all communities and cultures so there is nothing unique or especially troubling when South Asians engage in them. Minorities have their own resources and mechanisms for resolving problems – such as sharia councils or Somali *gars* – which should generally be recognised and regulated by English law.[211] It is possible to support both established and reformist groups so that all such cultural expressions are validated by British society. This might result in a compromise solution such as tolerating non-fatal honour violence under certain conditions or permitting clitorectomies but not the full removal of the female genitalia. Western culture bears the lion's share of the burden for accommodating new arrivals from elsewhere to redress historical injustices. Thus, artists such as Salman Rushdie should think very carefully about producing work that provokes minorities into criminality, and perhaps British women should also understand that dressing immodestly in the Western fashion drives some men to abuse them. CSE scandals may have contained 'an element of racial empowerment' as the perpetrators – 'perhaps subconsciously seeking revenge for colonialism, the oppression of their ancestors' and slavery – may have derived 'satisfaction from symbolically turning the tables on the white society that lorded it over them by raping their daughters'.[212] Yet it may be that, in relation to the worst excesses, even 'the doctrine of multiculturalism in modern Britain has its limits'.[213] In such cases, invoking the law must be a last resort which 'needs to be enforced with compassion and sensitivity and to be accompanied by a reformist campaign within the communities involved by their own leaders'.[214] Unpleasant public scandals sow discord between communities and it is imperative that they be avoided or minimised at all costs. Regardless, outsiders must tread very carefully around internal minority affairs. To suggest that a particular community has a particular problem courts bigotry and risks stigmatising all Muslims or South Asians. Any attack on a common or recurring or cherished practice is tantamount to an

210 Fauzia Ahmad and Tariq Modood, 'Muslims in Bristol and Britain' (Bristol City Council, 2008), p. 17; Parveen Akhtar, *British Muslim Politics: Examining Pakistani Biraderi Networks* (London: Palgrave, 2013), p. 177.

211 Tariq Modood, 'Multicultural Citizenship & the Sharia Controversy in Britain' in Rex Ahdar and Nicholas Aroney (eds.), *Sharia in the West* (Oxford: Oxford University Press, 2010), ch. 2, pp. 33–42 at pp. 39–42.

212 Fergusson, *Al-Britannia*, pp. 217–18.

213 Shaw, *Kinship and Continuity*, p. 295.

214 Bhikhu Parekh, 'Minority Practices and Principles of Toleration' (1996) 30(1) *International Migration Review* 251–84, p. 270.

attack on the entire group.[215] Likewise, trying to 'engender concern over the issue' will feed murky 'social and political agendas … popular prejudice and powerful media constructions'; worse still, one might cross a line into Islamophobia or cultural racism and become 'controversial', 'conservative' or 'right-wing'.[216] Introducing additional immigration restrictions to counter so-called problems like transnational cousin marriage should be off the table entirely. The existing regime is already too unfeeling and serves to keep extended families apart, a great injustice given the emotional trauma incurred.[217] What is more, many barriers to integration and belonging may come instead from restrictive immigration regimes, inadequate state support, domestic prejudices and ham-fisted integration policies.[218] Indeed, as one practitioner puts it, 'there is surely a special place in hell for the drafters of the immigration rules which govern family migration and private life applications in the UK … [because] the people with the least are given the most arduous and costly road to follow'.[219] In the end, migrants are most likely to identify with Britain when they can migrate unhindered with their families and afterwards live according to their culture.[220]

If the foregoing is a fair representation of the strongest multicultural account of this issue put at its best, problems remain. The first concerns unanswered – perhaps unanswerable – questions over conflicted identities when membership of a clan interferes with obligations attendant on membership of other groups. For example, perpetrating election fraud or honour violence in accordance with clan norms certainly conflicts with one's duties as a citizen of the UK and could just as easily violate cultural and religious precepts derived from one's background as a South Asian Muslim. If one disobeys one's clan, or mounts a vocal challenge to its activities, does that constitute cultural treason? Should national identity be remade such that clannism is accepted as the price of diversity? Does *biraderi*-politicking really improve the situation and public perception of British Muslims? What if the functioning of clans undermines specialised institutions such as Muslim banks, charities or schools? Are these not better and legitimate means for minorities to participate? Even if clans create a net benefit for their members and communities, what of any net loss to non-members and society as a whole? No clear answers are forthcoming with the intellectual resources of multiculturalism. Second, much of what is attacked as unacceptable foreign culture is

215 Charsley et al., *Marriage, Migration and Integration*, pp. 274–5; Shaw, 'British Pakistani Cousin Marriages and the Negotiation of Reproductive Risk', pp. 118–19.

216 Shaw, ibid., pp. 15–16; Charsley, 'Marriage Migration and Transnational Social Spaces', p. 193; Charsley, 'A First Generation in Every Generation?'.

217 See Katharine Charsley, Rissa Mohabir, Caroline Coombs, Paige Ballmi, Emma Agusita and Helena Wray, 'Kept Apart: Couples and Families Separated by the Immigration System' (UK: Reunite Families UK, 2020).

218 Charsley et al., *Marriage, Migration and Integration*, pp. 261–78.

219 Ruth Mullen, 'Family Migration and the Highway through Hell' (*Family Law*, 29 August 2019).

220 Charsley et al., *Marriage, Migration and Integration*, pp. 273, 278.

a product of the clan rather than vice versa. Without a refined vocabulary for group entities that goes beyond classes with agency, there is no way to identify the source of the problem and mount an effective critique without either smearing whole categories of people or backing off altogether. This is antithetical to an exact diagnosis and coordinated policy-making. Third, as with Dworkin on individual rights, a policy of non-interference and community self-help looks unsustainable. The available data on cousin marriage rates indicates that, if anything, clans are getting stronger while the sheer range of criminal, threatening and antisocial activity gives every reason for growing alarm. There is no convincing evidence to suggest that these institutions can be reformed from within or that a policy of mere damage limitation from without will suffice. From clannism, under multiculturalism, there is no way forward and no way out. Yet, as Brian Barry presciently put it as regards law reform, 'How could anybody seriously imagine that citing the mere fact of a tradition or custom could ever function as a self-contained justificatory move?'[221] In short, prevarication and peace at almost any price are all that multiculturalism can offer.

8.5 A Pluralist Response to Clans

As ever, historical experience is the best guide to confronting the clan. Any society that abuts or contains functioning clans is plagued by them. In the former case, endemic raiding and unruliness are the norm; in the latter, serious and widespread corruption prevails. There are only two proven ways of dismantling them. The first is medieval and peaceful. As discussed in Section 8.2 of this chapter, modernity became possible precisely because the medieval Church legislated away consanguineous marriage. With it went tribal society and the worst of clannism.[222] The second is timeless and brutal. Violence and mass deportations were how Caesar conquered Gaul, Tiberius and Germanicus quashed the Great Illyrian Revolt, and Paulinus and Agricola subdued Britannia.[223] Hadrian's Wall was constructed in large part to deter tribal depredation and the last Roman attempt to overrun what is now Scotland in the early third century ended with huge loss of life on both sides.[224] Much the same goes for Charlemagne's founding of Germany and the winning of the American West.[225] Against all this, the success of modern

221 Brian Barry, *Culture and Equality: An Egalitarian Critique of Multiculturalism* (Cambridge: Polity Press, 2001), p. 253.

222 See generally Henrich, *The Weirdest People in the World.*

223 See Adrian Goldsworthy, *Pax Romana: War, Peace and Conquest in the Roman World* (London: W&N, 2017).

224 See Adrian Goldsworthy, *Hadrian's Wall* (London: Head of Zeus, 2018) and Simon Elliott, *Septimius Severus in Scotland: The Northern Campaigns of the First Hammer of the Scots* (Barnsley: Greenhill Books, 2018).

225 See Hywell Williams, *Emperor of the West: Charlemagne and the Carolingian Empire* (London: Quercus, 2011) and Peter Cozzens, *The Earth Is Weeping: The Epic Story of the Indian Wars for the American West* (London: Atlantic Books, 2018).

Scottish clans is sometimes offered up as a bloodless counter-example. Weiner suggests that 'repeated acts of the imagination' by Scottish writers and artists over the last two centuries have transformed these once-brutal organisations into harmless clubs and 'objects of positive romantic memory'.[226] Likewise, Akbar Ahmed notes that contemporary Scots with clan heritage are thriving in the global economy. They have developed high-tech industry, an enviable artistic scene and bustling commerce, all while celebrating their clans by, for instance, holding clan-chief conventions to discuss their role in the twenty-first century.[227] 'The first time such a gathering had been held in recorded history' occurred at the behest of the Scottish Parliament in July 2009.[228] In truth, however, authentic clan life was dismembered forever with the collaboration of its own chieftains during the post-Culloden Highland Clearances in the mid-eighteenth century.[229] Any surviving 'traditions' are little more than Victorian kitsch – today's twee tartanry is at once a pale reflection of a vanished world and a far cry from the grim reality of life in a tribal belt.[230] In short, history is clear that the liquidation of extended kinship loyalties is a prerequisite for nation-state formation, and this is forgotten at great peril.[231]

The presenting issues identified throughout this book – from *hawala* corruption and the Trojan Horse Affair through election fraud to toxic political campaigning – are all manifestations of clannism. Rather than fight a losing battle against these symptoms, or attempt in vain to define kinship networks with enough legal precision to enable them to be regulated directly, the obvious and correct solution is to simply dissolve the clans themselves through marriage law reform. This can be achieved in two straightforward steps. First, cousin marriage up to and including the second degree must be added to the prohibited degrees currently found in the Marriage Act 1949.[232] This will render them void in domestic law and trigger the dual domicile doctrine which will operate to ensure that any marriage conducted abroad between someone domiciled in England and his/her cousin would also be void.[233] It would also be necessary to add to the immigration rules a stringent requirement for non-European Economic Area (EEA) applicant spouses to prove that they are not within the new prohibited degrees of relationship.[234] This is to

[226] *The Rule of the Clan*, p. 27. [227] *The Thistle and the Drone*, p. 347. [228] Ibid.

[229] See John Prebble, *The Highland Clearances* (new ed., London: Penguin, 1982).

[230] See Eric Hobsbawm and Terence Ranger (eds.), *The Invention of Tradition* (Cambridge: Canto Classics, 2012).

[231] See also Ed West, 'The Church v. The Family' (*Catholic Herald*, 15 August 2014).

[232] Part I of the First Schedule.

[233] Marriage Act 1949, s. 1; see Jonathan Hill and Máire Ní Shúilleabháin, *Clarkson & Hill's Conflict of Laws* (5th ed., Oxford: Oxford University Press, 2016), pp. 365–6.

[234] This does not require legislation and can be achieved using the statutory powers of the Secretary of State under the Immigration Act 1971, s. 4(1); see Gina Clayton and Georgina Firth, *Immigration & Asylum Law* (Oxford: Oxford University Press, 2018), pp. 30–2.

cover the whole of the UK and overcome the considerable human ingenuity routinely deployed to 'overcome barriers to the movement of people'.[235] For example, the former British High Commissioner to Pakistan, Sir Adam Thomson KCMG, warned that 'fraud and forgery were very strong industries in Pakistan', such that it is 'a world leader in the visa fraud business which is why we have to check very scrupulously every single application, every single passport, every single document'.[236] Other embassies and Pakistani law firms have confirmed as much.[237] Second, the minimum age of marriage should be set without exception at eighteen years and any form of child marriage – formal or informal – conducted in the UK or abroad criminalised.[238] UNICEF considers marriage below eighteen 'a fundamental violation of human rights' and international obligations.[239] Despite several Private Members' Bills, English law currently allows child marriages to take place at sixteen years of age with parental consent; marriages beneath this age are void, but not criminalised.[240] This creates opportunities for *biraderi* elders and parents to force or pressure minors into marriages, often arranged to much older relatives.[241] Statistics are limited; girls are at greater risk – 59 per cent of Bangladeshi girls are married before they turn eighteen – but boys are affected too and can be tricked into leaving school and travelling abroad or worse.[242] Given that the average age of marriage has been rising and is now well over thirty, prohibiting marriage before eighteen is unlikely to prove burdensome to the general population.[243] Taken as one, this package will preclude future domestic and transnational consanguineous marriages and outlaw child marriage. The result, over a generation or so, will be a steady reduction in clannism

[235] Geoffrey Care, *Migrants and the Courts: A Century of Trial and Error?* (London: Routledge, 2013), p. 48.

[236] Quoted in 'Pakistan Is World Leader in Visa Fraud Business: British High Commissioner' (*Express Tribune*, 27 July 2012); Rob Crilly, 'British Ambassador Says Pakistan Is "World Leader" in Visa Application Fraud' (*The Telegraph*, 27 July 2012).

[237] Immigration and Refugee Board of Canada, 'Response to Information Request PAK105021.E' (IRBC, 14 January 2015), p. 1: www.justice.gov/sites/default/files/eoir/pages/attachments/2015/04/28/canada_coi_pak105021.e.pdf.

[238] Charlotte Proudman, Sara Browne and Natasha Rattu, 'Ban Child Marriage: Safeguard Futures' (*Counsel Magazine*, 21 October 2019).

[239] Catherine Fairbairn, Maria Lalic, Sue Holland and Philip Loft, 'Minimum Age for Marriage and Civil Partnership' (House of Commons, CDP0119, 14 May 2019), pp. 3–4.

[240] Marriage Act 1949, ss. 2–3; see Fairbairn et al., 'Minimum Age for Marriage and Civil Partnership'.

[241] Proudman et al., 'Ban Child Marriage: Safeguard Futures'.

[242] Lewis, *Young, British and Muslim*, p. 47; *KC & Anor* v. *City of Westminster Social & Community Services Department & Anor* [2008] EWCA Civ 198; Girls Not Brides, 'Child Marriage in the United Kingdom' (accessed 6 February 2021): www.girlsnotbrides.org/child-marriage/united-kingdom/; Hannah Summers, '"So Old He Was Losing His Hair": Survivors Urge MPs to End Scandal of UK's Child Brides' (*The Guardian*, 3 October 2020); Hannah Summers, 'Back Bill to Ban Marriage for Under-18s in England and Wales, MPs Urged' (*The Guardian*, 6 October 2020).

[243] Office for National Statistics (ONS), 'Marriages in England and Wales: 2017' (ONS, 14 April 2020).

and honour abuse as well as improved health outcomes for British South Asians.

It is likely, as Baroness Deech predicts, that a cousin marriage ban will be challenged under the European Convention on Human Rights (ECHR). She is unduly pessimistic about its prospects.[244] The attack is likely to be brought under Articles 12 (right to marry) and 8 (right to respect for private and family life). The former simply provides that '[m]en and women of marriageable age have the right to marry and to found a family, according to the national laws governing the exercise of this right'. Although European Court of Human Rights (ECtHR) case law on prohibited degrees tends towards liberalisation as regards affinity, consanguinity remains unaffected.[245] A recent judgment confirmed that 'as a general rule the limitations that affect the ability to enter into marriage [because of issues to do with] consent, consanguinity or prevention of bigamy are likely to be compatible with Article 12'.[246] States enjoy 'a wide margin of appreciation' on contentious issues such as this and the ban is likely to be upheld so long as it is not 'based simply on tradition' and can be 'justified on any logical, rational or practical ground'.[247] Further, Article 8(2) contains significant qualifications:

> There shall be no interference by a public authority with the exercise of this right except such as is in accordance with the law and is necessary in a democratic society in the interests of national security, public safety or the economic well-being of the country, for the prevention of disorder or crime, for the protection of health or morals, or for the protection of the rights and freedoms of others.

Even if fully consensual and informed, consanguineous relationships between cousins have knock-on effects which are detrimental to the family and society as a whole.[248] A ban would protect public health by halting the importation of a practice which doubles the risk of inherited disease. A defence of this on public health grounds alone may or may not be decisive. It could be argued, for example, that pregnancy in women over thirty-four entails a similar increase in risk and that discouraging this would never be regarded as socially and ethically acceptable.[249]

[244] Patrick Nash, 'Sharia in England: The Marriage Law Solution' (2017) 6(3) *Oxford Journal of Law and Religion* 523–43, pp. 538–9.

[245] See *B and L* v. *UK* (Application No 36536/02) [2006] 1 FLR 35; *Theodorou and Tsotsorou* v. *Greece* (Application No 57854/15) [2019] ECHR 611; Katie Weston, 'Man Marries His Own Mother-in-Law after Divorcing His Wife of Eight Years and Getting 500-Year-Old Law Overturned' (*Daily Mail*, 17 September 2020).

[246] *Theodorou and Tsotsorou* v. *Greece*, para. 28; see also Frank Cranmer, 'Marrying a Non-deceased Wife's Sister? *Theodorou and Tsotsorou*' (*Law & Religion UK*, 5 September 2019).

[247] *B and L* v. *UK*, paras. 17, 33.

[248] A relevant comparison, albeit involving sibling incest, can be found in *Stübing* v. *Germany* (Application Number 43547/08) [2012], para. 47. See also Linda Hart, 'Anthropology of Kinship Meets Human Rights Rationality: Limits of Marriage and Family Life in the European Court of Human Rights' (2018) 20(5) *European Societies* 816–34.

[249] Alison Shaw and Aviad Raz, 'Introduction' in Shaw and Raz, *Cousin Marriages*, p. 25.

Legally, this is a poor comparison, however. A ban on cousin marriage is a proportionate measure to halt a largely imported problem, whereas there would be no conceivable way of preventing women over thirty-four from having children even if that were somehow justifiable. The two phenomena are completely unalike. Regardless, a ban could also be defended as a matter of social policy even without reference to public health. There is precedent for doing so in the long-standing prohibition on polygamous marriages which carry no inherent genetic health risks.[250] Contrary to those who portray polygamous (usually polygynous) relationships simply as a matter of individual choice, they are in fact an emergent threat to any society.[251] Systematic literature reviews have found that polygamy was associated with 'more mental health problems, social problems and lower academic achievement for children and adolescents' as well as 'marital conflict, marital distress, father absence and financial stress'.[252] More broadly, polygamy is linked to severe educational, economic and gender inequality;[253] domestic violence and FGM;[254] violent intra-sex competition over sparse marriage partners;[255] and, ultimately, state fragility, organised group violence, social unrest and civil war.[256]

Similarly, a ban on cousin marriage would improve national security by reducing the scope for foreign interference in domestic politics; ensure public safety by protecting the public from the out-group hostility and criminality of clans; and promote the economic well-being of the country by terminating a practice linked to the poor economic performance of British Pakistanis. It would help to prevent crime and disorder, especially around elections and supposedly blasphemous art. It would also protect public morals by bolstering the historic and widespread taboo against consanguineous marriage and closing

[250] Catherine Fairbairn, Hannah Wilkins, Steven Kennedy and Djuna Thurley, 'Polygamy Briefing Paper' (House of Commons, No.05051, 20 November 2018), p. 10; this has been held to be compatible with Article 12 ECHR in *Khan* v. *UK* (1986) 48 DR 253.

[251] See, for example, Law Commission, *Getting Married: A Consultation Paper on Weddings Law* (Law Commission, No. 247, September 2020), para. 10.90.

[252] Mohammad Al-Sharfi, Karen Pfeffer and Kirsty A. Miller, 'The Effects of Polygamy on Children and Adolescents: A Systematic Review' (2016) 22(3) *Journal of Family Studies* 272–86; Salman Elbedour, Anthony J. Onwuegbuzie, Corin Caridine and Hasan Abu-Saad, 'The Effect of Polygamous Marital Structure on Behavioural, Emotional, and Academic Adjustment in Children: A Comprehensive Review of the Literature' (2002) 5(4) *Clinical Child and Family Psychology Review* 255–71.

[253] Aslıhan Okan İbiloğlu et al., 'Negative Effects of Polygamy on Family Members in the Province of Diyarbakir, Turkey' (2018) 43(4) *Cukurova Medical Journal* 982–8.

[254] Naomi Riley, 'The Problems with Polygamy' (Institute for Family Studies, 8 July 2015).

[255] Carlo Koos and Clara Neupert-Wentz, 'Polygynous Neighbours, Excess Men, and Intergroup Conflict in Rural Africa' (2020) 64(2–3) *Journal of Conflict Resolution* 402–31; University of British Columbia, 'Monogamy Reduces Major Social Problems of Polygamist Cultures' (*ScienceDaily*, 24 January 2012).

[256] The Economist, 'The Link between Polygamy and War' (*The Economist*, 19 December 2017); Cody T. Ross et al., 'Greater Wealth Inequality, Less Polygyny: Rethinking the Polygyny Threshold Model' (2018) 15(144) *Journal of the Royal Society* 1–15; Conor Friedersdorf, 'The Case Against Encouraging Polygamy' (*The Atlantic*, 9 July 2015); Jonathan Rauch, 'No, Polygamy Isn't the Next Gay Marriage' (*Politico*, 30 June 2015).

off a major source of racist and religious hatred emanating from clans.[257] It would also protect the rights and freedoms of clan members at risk of forced marriage as well as girls vulnerable to CSE. In the malleable language of ECtHR precedents, there are plenty of 'relevant and sufficient reasons' to institute a ban which is a 'proportionate' measure to address a 'pressing social need': cousin marriage is growing in popularity despite awareness that the risks and its emergent effects are only likely to worsen with time.[258] It bodes well that 'domestic authorities enjoy a wide margin of appreciation in determining how to confront incestuous relationships between consenting adults, notwithstanding the fact that this decision concerns an intimate aspect of an individual's private life'.[259] Likewise, that the relevant case law is 'so deferential to state powers of immigration control that the ECtHR often seems to be at pains not to upset states in the migration-related rulings it delivers'.[260] In short, the case for a ban is very arguable.

Legal arguments aside, it is important to address the best moral case against these proposals. This is likely to revolve around two issues. The first is that banning cousin marriage will inflict emotional trauma by keeping families apart.[261] There is no disguising the fact that a significant number of spouses will no longer be able to settle in the UK, a distressing outcome to all concerned. This is a serious and legitimate charge; it deserves a mature response shorn of pious posturing. To begin, anything short of an open borders policy will have unpleasant consequences for someone. Yet, for all practical purposes, it is inconceivable that any government would surrender its sovereignty and legitimate right to control the movement of people.[262] To do so would be a form of neoconservatism in reverse: importing the world's problems to solve at home with caution thrown to the wind. There is certainly a place for charity in the immigration and asylum system, but that can never be its sole or dominant purpose.[263] As Lord Hope notes: 'The world has become larger and more volatile. There is an ever-increasing need to exercise a strict

257 On the latter, see Roberto Perrone, 'Public Morals and the European Convention on Human Rights' (2014) 47(3) *Israel Law Review* 361–78.

258 Janneke Gerards, 'How to Improve the Necessity Test of the European Court of Human Rights' (2013) 11(2) *International Journal of Constitutional Law* 466–90; James Roffee, 'No Consensus on Incest? Criminalisation and Compatibility with the European Convention on Human Rights' (2014) 14 *Human Rights Law Review* 541–72.

259 *Stübing* v. *Germany*, para. 61.

260 Alan Desmond, 'The Private Life of Family Matters: Curtailing Human Rights Protection for Migrants under Article 8 of the ECHR?' (2018) 29(1) *European Journal of International Law* 261–79, p. 263.

261 See Charsley et al., 'Kept Apart: Couples and Families Separated by the Immigration System'.

262 For an interesting debate on this point, see, respectively, Joseph H. Carens, *The Ethics of Immigration* (Oxford: Oxford University Press, 2015); Liav Orgad, *The Cultural Defence of Nations: A Liberal Theory of Majority Rights* (Oxford: Oxford University Press, 2017); David Miller, *Strangers in Our Midst: The Political Philosophy of Immigration* (Cambridge, MA: Harvard University Press, 2018).

263 For an historical overview, see W. Mark Ormrod, Bart Lambert and Jonathan Mackman, *Immigrant England, 1300–1550* (Manchester: Manchester University Press, 2018).

control over the number of people who can be allowed to enter and remain in this country. The UK is simply not big enough to accommodate all those who, for a variety of reasons, would wish to live and work here.'[264] This requires regulation, and that means keeping some families apart. Too often, however, this is done arbitrarily as part of an unending 'numbers game' whereby successive governments have sought to reduce the inflow for the sake of it.[265] For example, the immigration rules run to thousands of pages seemingly designed to be hard and expensive to navigate.[266] To some extent this is understandable and forgivable: immigration policy is a branch of international relations wherein policy objectives must sometimes be pursued undeclared to avoid repercussions from foreign powers. Yet, as a general rule, it is far better to base restrictions on rational grounds and make it clear to potential applicants whether or not they will be eligible to settle. As discussed at length, there are many good reasons to prohibit cousin marriage and doing so would be an unambiguous statement as to what type of marriage the UK will not recognise and why. In the digital age where international communications, travel and financial transfers are rapid and accessible, there is no reason that extended families cannot maintain links once the ban is in place. What is more, in diasporas numbering in the millions – the total British Muslim population now stands at well over 3.3 million[267] – within a general population of more than 66 million, there is no convincing reason why British Pakistanis, Bangladeshis or indeed anyone else cannot search for partners beyond their own families. As the transnational clans slowly dissolve and clannism gradually evaporates, conspiracy theories around Muslims and mass migration are likely to disintegrate as well.[268] In short, the emotive argument against a ban is a species of moralism, that peculiar vice to which idealistic intellectuals seem most susceptible.[269]

The second accusation to answer is that the ban will disproportionately affect some groups more than others and is therefore racist. Given that this term is now cast so widely and thrown about so freely, there is only so much that any serious attempt at refutation can achieve. Regardless, there are several points to stress. The target of these proposals is indeed a group, the clan, which is a tangible and specific unit rather than a general category or class of people. Historically, clans are a universal phenomenon, but those now being transplanted into the UK happen to come from societies with strong tribal elements,

[264] Lord Hope of Craighead, 'Foreword' to Eric Fripp, Rowena Moffatt and Ellis Wilford (eds.), *The Law and Practice of Expulsion and Exclusion from the United Kingdom* (Oxford: Hart, 2015), p. v.
[265] Will Somerville, *Immigration under New Labour* (Bristol: Policy Press, 2007), pp. 65–6.
[266] Margaret Phelan, James Gillespie, Francis Allen, Julia Gasparro and Jo Swaney, *The Immigration Law Handbook* (10th ed., Oxford: Oxford University Press, 2018).
[267] ONS, 'Muslim Population in the UK' (ONS, 2 August 2018).
[268] See, for example, Renaud Camus, *Le Grand Remplacement* (Neuilly-sur-Seine: David Reinhard, 2011).
[269] Craig Taylor, *Moralism: A Study of A Vice* (London: Routledge, 2012), pp. 148–51.

namely Pakistan, Bangladesh and Somalia, among others. Likewise in Sweden and Germany where Middle Eastern and North African clans are spreading serious violent crime which state authorities, finding it politically uncomfortable, have 'deliberately ignored'.[270] Put in Gierkean terms, these groups are privileged institutions par excellence. The problems they create are emergent. This does not mean that every clan member is a bigot or a criminal, or that each consanguineous couple is somehow regressive or dangerous in and of themselves. What it does mean is that when consanguineous marriage becomes widespread in a population, it gives life to the clan as a group unit with its own internal norms, which then requires or incentivises individuals to engage in antisocial or illegal behaviours. The ethnicity or nationality of these clans is entirely irrelevant as they are dangerous regardless of their origins. While the majority of marriages in some categories of migrant are to cousins, there are sizeable minorities in each who do not practise endogamy. This suggests that it is not integral to 'their culture' or 'their religion' even if those were viable group units, which they are not.

There is no reason whatsoever that the legitimate financial activities of clans cannot be carried on by differentiated institutions once this is done to the benefit of all. For example, unregulated *kameti* are redundant now that international Islamic banking is flourishing under the law. The same goes for their legitimate family components. Gierke insisted that the nuclear family formed by consent, with its bounded size and defined responsibilities over family finances and child-rearing, was the fellowship that underpinned all others. Within that sphere of competence, family-generated norms reigned supreme and immune from interference unless they facilitated neglect or endangered life. Outside the immediate household, however, the family's norms had neither authority nor legitimacy. Clans are fundamentally different institutions: they are indifferent to consensual marriage, are of indefinite size, have unclear but extremely restrictive membership criteria, present myriad dangers to members and non-members, harbour ambitions far beyond the confines of the home, and expropriate the functions of other institutions. As such, they cannot be considered true fellowships with a right to integrity, and a clear pluralist policy objective emerges: the strengthening of the Muslim family against the transnational clan. This will be relatively easy to achieve and is already starting to gather momentum. While overly complex formalities remain a major deterrent for Muslim couples seeking a valid marriage, the issues are by now very well understood and marriage law is on the 'cusp of change'.[271] Despite myriad proposals for reform, there is at

[270] DW, 'German State Vows Crackdown on Criminal Clans' (DW, 16 May 2019); Matthias von Hein and Richard Connor, 'Berlin's Clans Are the Focus of Germany's Nationwide Fight against the Mounting Threat of Organized Crime' (DW, 22 September 2020); Paulina Neuding, 'Sweden's New Epidemic: Clan-Based Crime' (*The Spectator*, 19 September 2020); Jake Wallis Simons, 'How Sweden Became a Gangsters' Paradise' (*Daily Mail*, 12 October 2020).

[271] Rajnaara C. Akhtar, Patrick Nash and Rebecca Probert (eds.), 'Conclusion' to *Cohabitation and Religious Marriage: Status, Similarities and Solutions* (Bristol: Bristol University Press, 2020), ch. 12, pp. 155–60 at p. 159.

least a broad scholarly consensus that any new formalities system must maximise certainty, simplicity, fairness, equality and choice.[272] Once the expected reforms are introduced, entry into marriage will become more accessible, de facto polygamy will be discouraged as more cases become subject to the offence of bigamy, and sharia councils will be confined to their proper sphere of competence: the issuing of religious divorce certificates subject to the oversight of domestic courts.[273] Straightforward marriage regulations will, if joined with a ban on cousin marriage, fundamentally reorder English family life along pluralist lines.

To sum up, the historic achievement of the *biraderis* and the *brath-thitho* is to have established large diasporas in the UK. They have done so by providing new migrants with financial assistance, practical advice and displays of solidarity. Personal opinions of the rapidity and magnitude of this social change are largely irrelevant: British Pakistanis and Bangladeshis are here to stay and contribute to British society. For all that, the clan system must be dismantled, just as differentiated institutions – banks, charities, schools, political parties, monogamous marriage – are made more accessible and better regulated than they are already. Indeed, dissolving the clan will reduce corruption across these legitimate institutions and enable British Muslims to thrive more safely, more freely and more extensively than they already do. The cumulative weight of evidence presented throughout the second half of this book suggests that clannism cannot simply be lived with and its symptoms mitigated piecemeal. It is a clear, present, growing danger at every level: to individuals inside and out, to other minority and civil society groups, to the general public, to the integrity of democracy and the state, and to the very concept of nationhood itself. Dissolving clans by banning cousin marriage is a matter for the whole nation and not simply an expedition into minority internal affairs. In such cases, as Gierke put it,

> the whole community and every group of the people which is concerned should consider, choose, act. Even here, the methods that legal science has at its disposal are not enough: it is not just knowledge that is required, but wisdom, practical skill, a predictive perspective . . . Out of understanding grows love, out of insight into context a feeling for the whole, out of immersion in history a sense of the future.[274]

Put differently, if there is a road to social harmony, it will be paved by the resolute, the ruthless and the shrewd. The point of law reform is not to keep a lid on social tensions but to resolve them. Difficult questions cannot be

272 Ibid.; Law Commission, 'Getting Married: A Scoping Paper' (Law Commission, December 2015).

273 See Patrick Nash, '"Regrettably It Is Not That Simple": The Case for Minimalistic Marriage Laws' in Akhtar et al. (eds.), *Cohabitation and Religious Marriage: Status, Similarities and Solutions*, ch. 11, pp. 143–54 and Nash, 'Sharia in England'.

274 Otto von Gierke, 'The Social Role of Private Law', Ewan McGaughey (transl.), (2018) 19(4) *German Law Journal* 1017–16, p. 1032.

dodged, group-specific patterns of bad behaviour cannot be excused, emotions cannot replace policy, clannish agitation cannot be met with obsequiousness, necessary measures cannot be fudged. If they are, it takes little imagination to see what the future has in store. One need look no further than Pakistan, a nation left perpetually 'on the brink' by its gruelling, violent and probably unwinnable struggle against its own clans.[275] The hallmarks of clannism pervade state institutions which, once renowned for their professionalism, have decayed to the point of ineffectiveness and 'seriously undermined the welfare of [Pakistani] citizens'.[276] Some of the starkest examples range from the Army and ISI sheltering Osama bin Laden under the *Pashtunwali* hospitality code to Pakistan International Airlines (PIA) grounding a third of its pilots suspected of holding fraudulent licences and obtaining their jobs through patronage.[277] Honour violence 'is, for the most part, socially sanctioned' and confidence in the authorities is justifiably low.[278] The first reaction to any major scandal is denial, then an attempt at suppression, followed by a backlash against the accusers 'to protect Pakistan's honour'.[279] The country and its people suffer as they do, not because they are somehow inferior or evil, but because they must live with the consequences of clannism every day.[280] If the UK is to avoid the same fate, it must act decisively to arrest the importation of clans. Long-term joined-up thinking about groups – sometimes called 'cathedral thinking' – is difficult and rare at the best of times, more so when it is likely to be met with noisy protestations and even violent disorder.[281] It is essential nevertheless, as Gierke well knew. If we rise to the occasion, there is every reason for confidence in the future for British Muslims and Great Britain itself.

[275] Ahmed, *The Thistle and the Drone*; Ahmed Rashid, *Pakistan on the Brink* (London: Penguin, 2013).

[276] Natasha M. Ezrow and Erica Frantz, *Failed States and Institutional Decay* (London: Bloomsbury, 2013), pp. 118–19.

[277] Weiner, *The Rule of the Clan*, pp. 106–8; BBC News, 'Pakistani Pilots Grounded Over "Fake Licences"' (*BBC News*, 25 June 2020).

[278] Shaw, *Kinship and Continuity*, pp. 260–2, 296. [279] Rashid, *Pakistan on the Brink*, p. 9.

[280] Anatol Lieven, *Pakistan: A Hard Country* (London: Penguin, 2012), pp. 1–40.

[281] Roman Krznaric, *The Good Ancestor: How to Think Long-Term in a Short-Term World* (London: W.H. Allen, 2020).

Conclusion

Woe to the nation which foolishly gives itself such injuries![1]

Thomas Cole's *The Voyage of Life: Youth* (1842) could well serve as an oil-on-canvas meditation on classical pluralist themes. It is a self-contained work that cannot be understood in isolation from the rest of the cycle. It is as personal as it is universal. The individual is central but dwarfed by his surroundings. He is constrained by these, yet takes control of his own destiny within them. His journey and life depend on his vessel's sturdiness as much as his own helmsmanship. Oblivious to the real beauty around him, he strains for a perfect world hovering just out of reach. The ephemeral is in pursuit of the ethereal. Lacking experience or detachment, he does not foresee the rapids lurking just around the river bend. Only the perspicacious observer can absorb the peripheral detail and imagine where naïve obsession leads. Cole's art was as much a call to history as a part of it, his paintings an appeal to take ideas and history seriously.[2] For Otto von Gierke, this meant studying groups. There are more insights into the nature, functioning and regulation of groups to be gleaned from the most partial translations of his works than from a century of subsequent political theorising. First and foremost, he supplies the versatile vocabulary necessary to differentiate among healthy groups possessed of rights, dangerous groups in need of containment or dismantling, and general classes of people which have no meaningful cohesion. This in turn facilitates a much clearer diagnosis of social problems with a collective dimension, the best and most pressing example of which is clannism. The language of individualism and personal responsibility cannot capture what is going on, just as the language of class and race precludes serious discussion of the underlying issues. It is only by recognising the distinctive nature of the entity in question, and dissecting its internal mechanics, that workable solutions begin to present themselves. Gierke is thus especially useful in the fraught context of law and

[1] Otto von Gierke, 'Natural Law and German Law: A Speech on Taking Up Office as Rector of the University of Breslau' (15 October 1882), Julian Rivers (transl.) (unpublished, 2020).

[2] See Earl C. Powell III, 'Thomas Cole's Voyage of Life in the National Gallery of Art' (January 1997) *Magazine Antiques* and Joy S. Kasson, 'The Voyage of Life: Thomas Cole and Romantic Disillusionment' (1975) 27(1) *American Quarterly* 42–56.

religion, but his ideas have enormous potential for application to other fields from capitalism through political corruption to geopolitics. That all of this should come from a mere fraction of his *oeuvre* is even more remarkable.

Conventional jurisprudence has proved itself inadequate to the task of conceptualising the relationship between Islam and English law. Liberal individualism, as championed by Ronald Dworkin, has all the benefits of moral consistency and systematic rigour with all the drawbacks of abstract dogma. Individual rights are insulated from collective aggression by statism and a legalistic public ethos; the cost is a thoroughgoing disregard for groups and their societal importance. As regards Islam, this makes it difficult to diagnose even the most pressing problems, let alone solve them with any kind of imagination. It is hard to see how Islamic banking could have prospered under a purely liberal individualistic system, for example, and many other vital institutions – marriage foremost among them – remain in a dangerous state of disrepair. Malign groups are discounted as actors in their own right and the threat they pose reworked as an aggregate of individuals' poor personal choices. The ultimate result is stasis and stalemate, a society preoccupied with rights and offering little more than the preservation of a fraying status quo. To their credit, Parekh and Modood consistently grasp these deficiencies and attempt to refocus the discussion around groups. That, however, is the extent of their achievement. The subplot of this book has been a kind of intellectual and institutional failure brought about by multiculturalism. Its hallmarks are unmistakable: incoherent emotivism, class agency, nebulous definitions of racism, the avoidance of scandal. As scholarship, it is lamentable, tending towards conspiratorial activism, culture warring, and taking the claims of research participants uncritically and at face value. On the important practical problems affecting British Muslims, from Islamic banking to marriage regulations to dangerous religious organisations, its leading exponents have contributed nothing but 'magic slogans … frittering energy and social decay'.[3]As a school of thought, it is constitutionally incapable of generating a viable response to increasing diversity. For the most part, the English law of religion is a mouldering hash of these two unsatisfactory traditions: a baseline of individual rights grafted with concessions to group sensibilities. This has left many legal problems unsolved and created many others as slippery abstract nouns are pursued over sound legal policy. That this has inflamed fruitless culture wars and was avoidable is most regrettable. The relationship between organised religion and English law can be seen at its best when relevant institutions are taken seriously, in historical perspective, and for their own sake. This is where Gierke's legacy, classical pluralism, is more relevant and vital than ever.

[3] Harold Laski and Hubert Nicholson quoted in Richard Overy, *The Morbid Age: Britain and the Crisis of Civilization, 1919–1939* (London: Penguin, 2010), p. 383.

The sector-specific prescriptions inspired by pluralism can be restated concisely enough. First, the rapid success of Islamic banks is perhaps the greatest argument for pluralism. This is because the government acted early in the national interest to create a prosperous new industry of competitive institutions via limited regulatory reform from which Muslims and non-Muslims alike are benefiting. Under a general regulatory framework, with occasional corrections from the courts and innovations like the anticipated non-interest-based alternative liquidity facility, this sector is rightly being left to mature organically. As regards *hawala*, either an outright ban or a light-touch regulatory regime may improve security against terrorist financing and money laundering. Neither option is likely to be decisive against the untraceable transactions conducted through these informal kinship networks, however. The risks will remain for as long as these clan structures remain operational. Second, while Muslim or Muslim-led charities are generally doing well, the wider charitable sector is in need of some fairly basic legal renovations. Aside from the political issue of greater funding for the Charity Commission, administrative abuse would be curtailed by making licences for direct debit agreements compulsory during face-to-face collections and by ensuring that online fundraising platforms are adequately incorporated into the regulatory framework. Greater powers for the Commission to close down rogue charities as such and tougher penalties for breaches would also encourage compliance, as would making libel law more hospitable to investigative journalism as it performs its vital function of uncovering wrongdoing. Foreign state funding of educational and religious charities should be prohibited to end the dependency of universities and mosques on dangerous actors such as China, Iran and Saudi Arabia. At the same time, sedition and subversion must be substituted for the confusing and ineffectual concept of extremism, while political propaganda masquerading as religion should be fatal to any application for charitable status. Together, these measures would enable the state to target malign non-state entities undeserving of charitable status. This would include groups such as the Muslim Brotherhood which exploit the existing system with a view to overthrowing the nation itself. A Bar Standards Board (BSB)-style professional code for charity trustees would also serve to clarify expectations, improve certainty and depoliticise actions taken by the Commission against unacceptable but mundane behaviour. Finally, providing greater powers to the Commission to discipline charities as distinct from their trustees would better reflect the collective dimension to institutional abuses of charitable status.

Third, while there is no strong evidence to suggest that Muslim or Muslim-majority schools are inherently problematic, the Trojan Horse Affair exposed important weaknesses in the schools regulatory system. There were failures on the part of local government, namely an unwillingness to confront minority-perpetrated misconduct; there were failures in the academies regulations which enabled rogue governors and teachers to turn academy trusts into corrupt petty fiefdoms; there were failures in the government response and disciplinary processes; there were failures in academia to acknowledge that anything untoward had taken place. Some of these issues have been addressed through the Prevent duty and new regulations applicable to governors, but there is a lot more to do. As regards schools, and academy schools in particular, the introduction of a BSB-style code for governors, coupled with a general programme of legal simplification and consolidation, would clarify the expectations of all parties and ensure that any future disciplinary action is conducted competently and efficiently. As regards unregulated schools and madrassas, these must be swiftly brought within the scope of Ofsted's oversight or else closed down altogether and their leaders sanctioned. There is only so much that all of this can achieve, however, as long as seditious and subversive groups and clans can exert influence over schools. The former must be dealt with as recommended in the charities discussion just now, and the latter dissolved via the means recommended in the clans paragraphs later in this Conclusion. Fourth, British Muslims have a lengthy, demonstrable record of contributions to British democracy and there looks to be no lack of willingness to engage in politics through legitimate means today. However, the uncomfortable truth is that South Asian kinship networks, typically intertwined with the Islamic faith, are facilitating large-scale election fraud with alarming regularity. Election law is in poor shape to begin with and is concealing the real extent of the problem while making it harder to address. It needs a drastic overhaul: replacement of private law petitions with a party- and police-led public law complaints system; simplification of offences and toughening up of criminal penalties for corruption and a specific prohibition against courting clans for bloc votes; introduction of voter ID requirements and an end to postal voting on demand; consolidation and simplification of statutory election law; and greater regulatory coverage of non-party groups. Again, however, there is only so much that all of this can achieve while the clans remain intact. As in the other sectors studied, this group unit lies at the root of the major problems and must be addressed directly.

The pluralist reform programme outlined in this book has two dimensions. The first is constructive: improving the law and regulation of institutions to enable them to function optimally as such, inside their appropriate jurisdictional sphere within the nation, according to their *raison d'être*. It is encouraging to note that, in relation to banks, charities, schools and elections, the main issues are not exclusion or self-segregation: British Muslims are enthusiastic participants and institution-builders making significant contributions to the common good. If British Muslims ever found it difficult to adapt to what are essentially 'the institutional forms of a secularised Christianity', there is little sign of it today. In all of these areas, they have risen to the occasion and are thriving in this regard.[4] The second aspect of the agenda requires creative

[4] Julian Rivers, 'Islamic Courts in the English Legal System' in Steve Bell and Colin Chapman (eds.), *Between Naivety & Hostility: Uncovering the Best Christian Reponses to Islam in Britain* (Milton Keynes: Authentic Media, 2011), pp. 183–4.

destruction: types of group that endanger the nation, state, civil society and individual rights must be identified (if not necessarily defined) and dissolved using the most proportionate legal means available. Two such species have been classified in the preceding chapters. The first kind are those revolutionary religious groups that threaten to overthrow the nation itself by sedition or the subversion of key domestic institutions. Framing this issue around abstract nouns like 'extremism', 'hate' or 'Islam' has proved ineffectual or counterproductive. The correct legal response is altogether simpler: creating a civil blacklist to degrade and destroy the financial and organisational capacity of these networks and their members.

More widespread and cumulatively destructive by far, however, are the deleterious effects of transnational clans. These kinship networks facilitate all manner of criminality and corruption: terrorist financing, money laundering, school misgovernance, election fraud, the toxification of politics, the disenfranchisement of young British Muslims, child sexual exploitation, drug trafficking, racial and religious hatred, misogyny and honour violence, forced marriage, cold-blooded murder, the obstruction of justice, and so forth. It is astounding that so many of the sociologists studying this phenomenon for so long have compiled such an enormous damning body of evidence without drawing the obvious conclusion: that clans are so detrimental to the lives of members and non-members, to public health and to the integrity of the nation as a whole that they cannot be allowed to persist. Their legitimate functions to do with family and finance can be differentiated and transferred to legitimate formal institutions such as banks, charities, schools and political parties. That process is the main constructive task of pluralism, which must include making monogamous marriage more accessible to British Muslims (and indeed everyone else). As to the deconstruction of clans, that requires little more than a halt to the inflow of consanguineous relationships via an adequately enforced ban on cousin marriage up to and including the second degree. A comprehensive new Marriage Act – raising the age of marriage to eighteen and incorporating safeguards against the other emergent threat of de facto polygamy – and minor changes to the immigration rules will accomplish all of these objectives, although the government would need to find the patience and resolve to withstand baseless litigation and accusations of racism, Islamophobia, etc. It should stand its ground regardless and stress repeatedly that the target of the ban is not 'Muslims' or 'brown people' or 'immigrants' – it is the clan. In the generation or so it will take for clan structures to dissolve, one is likely to see many of the problems associated with, or attributed to, British Muslims dissipate.

While there will always be scope for reasonable disagreement over sector-specific recommendations, this book has sought to persuade the reader of something more fundamental: that English jurisprudence has taken too narrow and unserious a view of group phenomena in general and civil society institutions in particular. Setting that right is the great philosophical promise of pluralism. Its more worldly hope is simply this: to maintain a healthy body politic composed of a thriving population of individuals and Gierkean fellowships, all bound together under a coherent system of rules directed towards the common good. Historically speaking, the best thing that successive governments can do is to keep a tight focus on the purposes of institutions. This includes their own, which is to govern the whole of a nation rather than distinct categories of people each with special or competing interests. Institutions stand the best chance of success if they remain differentiated *and* integrated into the system of society. Law and policy stand the best chance of being effective and popular if they are generally applicable and straightforward to the everyman/woman. Getting this right matters greatly and for one simple reason: overcomplicating things leads to social collapse.[5] Adrian Goldsworthy concludes his autopsy of the Roman Empire with a sobering moral:

> All human institutions, from countries to businesses, risk creating a . . . short-sighted and selfish culture once their success reaches a point where they become cushioned from mistakes and inefficiency . . . [because] it takes a long time for serious problems or errors to be exposed . . . [I]t is only human nature to lose sight of the wider issues and focus on immediate concerns . . . [and] if governments or agencies forget what they are really for, then decline will occur, however slowly. It is no easy thing to keep or to recapture this sense of perspective and purpose.[6]

It should never be taken for granted, therefore, that the UK and the English legal system are too robust and well-entrenched for something similar to happen to us. The tendency for Western institutions to forget their own history is well-attested in these pages and elsewhere.[7] That said, it is both our good fortune and to our credit that the English imagination is more ancient, more coherent and more absorptive than any other on earth; from the early Middle Ages, it has been spinning language, literature and law into a truly exceptional national fabric.[8] With such a dependable resource, there is every reason to be optimistic about the future of British Islam and much else besides.

As Cole and Gierke illustrate in their respective media, even 'when we think we are happy and at peace, as individuals and as communities, awful things may be waiting just around the corner'.[9] Pluralism is not a panacea for all social ills – no such cure exists. It is not a roadmap to utopia – there is no such place.

5 Joseph A. Tainter, *The Collapse of Complex Societies* (Cambridge: Cambridge University Press, 1988).

6 Adrian Goldsworthy, *The Fall of the West: The Death of the Roman Superpower* (London: Phoenix, 2010), pp. 418–19, 423.

7 Christopher Andrew, *The Secret World: A History of Intelligence* (London: Allen Lane, 2018), p.1 and Francis O'Gorman, *Forgetfulness: Making the Modern Culture of Amnesia* (London: Bloomsbury, 2017).

8 Peter Ackroyd, *Albion: The Origins of the English Imagination* (London: Vintage, 2004), pp. xix–xxii, 448–9.

9 Teofilo Ruiz, *The Terror of History: On the Uncertainties of Life in Western Civilization* (Princeton, NJ: Princeton University Press, 2011), p. 22.

Rather, it is an understated form of jurisprudence attuned to history, principle and pragmatism. What it offers is altogether more modest and the better for it: a means for putting law into context, to 'do things' with rules and live well in the world, together.[10] What it shows is that getting the most out of English law requires a concomitant commitment to the practice of history.[11] What it requires is a certain loathing for 'theory' and a certain love for humanity's infinite capacity to frustrate it.[12] This book began by stating what it was not about. To close, it is simply worth restating that it was really about what we are about: as individuals, as group members, as citizens, as heirs to the common law tradition, and as social creatures. The plea throughout has been to ask better questions of ourselves in each of these capacities. While there is no single direct answer to the question 'How should English law relate to British Islam?', there are many discrete, surmountable problems in the regulation of institutions. Taken cumulatively, the answers to these amount to something like a pluralist vision for law, religion and society.

[10] On this movement, see generally William Twining, *Jurist in Context: A Memoir* (Cambridge: Cambridge University Press, 2019) and William Twining and David Miers, *How to Do Things with Rules: A Primer of Interpretation* (5th ed., Cambridge: Cambridge University Press, 2010).

[11] Richard Mullender, 'Law as a Practice: Inaugural Professorial Lecture at Newcastle Law School' (Newcastle, 16 October 2014).

[12] See David Abulafia, 'University Challenge: Conservatives Are Now the Radicals on Campus' (*The Spectator*, 3 April 2021) and Barbara Tuchman, *Practicing History: Selected Essays* (New York: Random House, 2014).

Index

For EU product safety concerns, contact us at Calle de José Abascal, 56–1°, 28003 Madrid, Spain or eugpsr@cambridge.org.

www.ingramcontent.com/pod-product-compliance
Lightning Source LLC
LaVergne TN
LVHW062207200926
848484LV00006B/1342
* 9 7 8 1 1 0 8 4 9 3 9 1 8 *